LORD DEVLIN

Lord Devlin was a leading lawyer of his generation. Moreover, he was one of the most recognised figures in the judiciary, thanks to his role in the John Bodkin Adams trial and the Nyasaland Commission of Inquiry. It is hard then to believe that he retired as a Law Lord at a mere 58 years of age. This important book looks at the life, influences and impact of this most important judicial figure. Starting with his earliest days as a schoolboy before moving on to his later years, the author draws a compelling picture of a complex, brilliant man who would shape not just the law but society more generally in post-war Britain.

T0034709

Lord Devlin

Justice John Sackar

·HART·

OXFORD · LONDON · NEW YORK · NEW DELHI · SYDNEY

HART PUBLISHING

Bloomsbury Publishing Plc

Kemp House, Chawley Park, Cumnor Hill, Oxford, OX2 9PH, UK

1385 Broadway, New York, NY 10018, USA

HART PUBLISHING, the Hart/Stag logo, BLOOMSBURY and the Diana logo are
trademarks of Bloomsbury Publishing Plc

First published in Great Britain 2020

First published in hardback, 2020

Paperback edition, 2022

A catalogue record for this book is available from the British Library.

Library of Congress Cataloging-in-Publication data

Names: Sackar, John, author.

Title: Lord Devlin / Justice John Sackar.

Description: Oxford, UK ; New York, NY : Hart Publishing, Bloomsbury Publishing Plc, 2020. |
Includes bibliographical references and index.

Identifiers: LCCN 2020023060 (print) | LCCN 2020023061 (ebook) |
ISBN 9781509923700 (hardback) | ISBN 9781509923724 (ePDF) |
ISBN 9781509923717 (Epub)

Subjects: LCSH: Devlin, Patrick, Baron, 1905-1992. |
Judges—Great Britain—Biography. | Lawyers—Great Britain—Biography.

Classification: LCC KD632.D48 S23 2020 (print) | LCC KD632.D48 (ebook) |
DDC 347.42/02534 [B]—dc23

LC record available at https://lccn.loc.gov/2020023060

LC ebook record available at https://lccn.loc.gov/2020023061

ISBN: PB: 978-1-50994-469-9
         ePDF: 978-1-50992-372-4
         ePub: 978-1-50992-371-7

Typeset by Compuscript Ltd, Shannon

To find out more about our authors and books visit www.hartpublishing.co.uk.
Here you will find extracts, author information, details of forthcoming events
and the option to sign up for our newsletters.

Foreword

I AM ONE of those who had the privilege some 50 years ago to belong to a small set of Chambers at 1 Brick Court in the Temple. There we served under the legendary clerk, known to all by his surname, Burley. When, not infrequently, we did not measure up to the standard that he expected of us, he would compare us adversely to a former member of Chambers, Patrick Devlin. He had left Chambers in 1948 when appointed to the High Court Bench at the age of only 42. Fifteen years later he retired from the Bench, having been made a Law Lord only three years before. His early retirement robbed me of the chance to appear before him and I never chanced to meet him. John Sackar's invitation to write a foreword to this biography has given me the belated chance to do so, and I have enjoyed the experience.

The man we are introduced to is an enigmatic figure. Although he wrote extensively about morality and the law, he did not bare his soul. He was born into an Irish Catholic family – one of six children. Three siblings went into the church – two sisters who were to lead cloistered lives and a much-loved brother, Christopher, who became a priest. Patrick was destined for the same calling, but at the age of 18, Brother Ignatius Devlin abandoned the church and went up to Christ's College, Cambridge to read History and Law. The reason for this change of course he never explained, though at Cambridge he lost his faith altogether, only to recover it shortly before his death. He made no secret, however, of the reason for his choice of the law as a profession. As he explained in his memoir *Taken at the Flood* he had a lifetime conclusion that one's aim should be to obtain the greatest enjoyment out of life.

As we follow his life it becomes plain that, to a large extent, Devlin was successful in this aim. At Cambridge he took no joy in academic study and achieved only a lower second class degree in both parts of the History and Law Tripos, and later he managed to fail the Constitutional Law paper in the Bar Finals exam. He did not attribute this mediocrity of performance to the fact that his handwriting was so execrable that the examiners were unable to read what he had written. He candidly admitted that he was simply bad at exams. Study, without a practical goal had no appeal.

What he did delight in was debate. He rose in the ranks at the Cambridge Union, forming a lifelong friendship with 'Rab' Butler, who preceded him as President. If he did not excel academically his qualities were, nonetheless, appreciated by his supervisor, Arthur Goodhart, who, when Patrick went down, provided him with sustenance of £200 a year in consideration for proof-reading articles for the *Law Quarterly Review*, which Goodhart edited. Later he was taken on as a 'devil' by Sir William Jowitt, who, in 1929, had been appointed

Attorney-General by Ramsay MacDonald, leader of the minority Labour Government. Jowitt it was who founded chambers at 1 Brick Court, and invited Devlin to join them. It was to be Jowitt, as Lord Chancellor, who would cut short Devlin's career at the Bar by appointing him to the High Court Bench.

In 1932 Devlin married Madeleine Oppenheimer, who later adopted the Catholic faith that he had abandoned. They were to have six children and their family life, based on a farm that they bought in Wiltshire, provided until his death the foundation of that enjoyment of life that was his goal.

When I joined 1 Brick Court this was a small set doing a variety of work, with a head who practised criminal law on the Welsh circuit. As I read of the practice that Devlin built up before and through the war – he had rickets, a condition that rendered him unfit for military service – I recognised the range of high-class commercial work that Burley was to recover by a skilful campaign of recruitment that began with Bob Alexander, later Lord Alexander of Weedon. I now appreciate that the leading commercial solicitors that he succeeded in attracting were renewing acquaintance with the path that had brought them to the door of Patrick Devlin. He rapidly built up a Commercial and Admiralty practice of the highest quality that brought him a retainer from Shell and was to see him briefed as a junior to appear against Tom Denning QC. Devlin took silk at the age of 40 in 1945, together with two other future Law Lords, Donovan and Holroyd Pearce. Then in 1948 he was appointed to the High Court Bench.

I am grateful to John Sackar for introducing me to Devlin's early days, because, hitherto, I have only been acquainted with Devlin the judge and the author. In the latter part of his life Devlin formed two close trans-Atlantic friendships, one with Felix Frankfurter, a Justice of the United States Supreme Court and the other with Dean Acheson, Secretary of State under President Truman. Devlin corresponded with these friends at length and perhaps with greater frankness than he did with friends in this country. Recourse to archive material in the United States has enabled John to throw new light on what was contributing to and what was detracting from Devlin's enjoyment of life.

This biography demonstrates three recurring preoccupations on the part of Devlin: the merits of trial by jury; the relationship of morality and the law; and the perceived shortcomings of Reginald Manningham-Buller, later Lord Dilhorne. All three preoccupations have their origin in Devlin's experiences as a puisne judge. He served in the Queen's Bench Division for about 12 years, which involved a mix of civil and criminal work. The latter will have been new to him but, like other judges with a commercial background, he made criminal law and procedure his own.

In Devlin's day the 'right of silence' was a sacrosanct principle that protected the citizen accused of a crime against being put under what might be considered to be unfair pressure. The accused, when arrested, had no obligation to answer questions put to him by the police; and at trial the accused had no obligation to go into the witness-box to give his explanation in respect of the case advanced against him. It was part of the judge's task to direct the jury that they should draw no adverse inference from the fact that a defendant had declined to submit to cross-examination, no easy task, as common sense might suggest that a defendant who chose not to give evidence had something to hide. The direction that Devlin gave in the Bodkin Adams case – as to which see more below – was considered a model of its kind. The law in the UK has now changed and the modern judge can, in defined circumstances, permit the jury to draw an adverse inference from the exercise of the right to silence.

Devlin's enthusiasm for jury trial was made clear in the Hamlyn Lectures on the Jury that he gave in 1956, and his subsequent book on *The Jury* based on these. His thesis was not that the jury was always right, but that the need to persuade a jury to convict provided a vital safeguard against abuse of the legal system by the state. A jury would not convict if persuaded that to do so would perpetrate a serious injustice. As he was later to put it in an article in the *Law Quarterly Review* the jury 'respects the law but will not put it above the justice of the case'. In a phrase that has resounded around the common law world, jury trial 'is the lamp that shows that freedom lives.'

In 1957 the Wolfenden Report was published recommending that homosexual acts committed in private should no longer constitute a criminal offence. Devlin had given evidence to the Committee and was in favour of its recommendation. But this was not because he believed that the criminal law should have no concern with private morality. He made plain his view to the contrary in his 1959 Maccabaean Lecture at the British Academy, subsequently expanded in his book *The Enforcement of Morals*, published in 1965. His thesis was that the law had a duty to proscribe conduct that reasonable members of society considered to be morally unacceptable. This proposition brought him into a prolonged public debate with Professor HLA Hart. Three decades later the debate was revived by the case of *R v Brown* (1993). Devlin would not have approved Lord Mustill's dissent.

In 1957 the Lord Chief Justice, Lord Goddard, selected Devlin to preside over what was probably the most sensational murder trial of the century, which this book explores in some detail. Dr John Bodkin Adams was widely suspected of having hastened the passing of large numbers of his elderly patients in anticipation of being remembered in their wills. He was indicted for murdering two of them – Edith Morrell and Gertrude Hullett. At his trial for murdering the former, the prosecution was led by the Tory Attorney-General, Sir Reginald Manningham-Buller, later to become Lord Dilhorne, Lord Chancellor. Devlin gave a summing up that favoured the defence, and Bodkin Adams was acquitted. Manningham-Buller then declined to proceed with the trial in respect of Gertrude Hallett. He considered that Devlin had wrongly downplayed a damning admission made by the accused, and said as much in Parliament. Devlin, for his part, did not disguise his view that the prosecution had been mishandled by Manningham-Buller.

The trial was the start of a life-long antagonism between the two, augmented when, in 1959, Sir Reginald, speaking in Parliament on behalf of the

Government, rejected a number of important findings made by the Commission of Inquiry, chaired by Devlin, into a state of emergency that had been declared by the Governor of Nyasaland. After Manningham-Buller had been made Lord Chancellor, Devlin wrote of him to Acheson:

> 'The Lord Chancellor is an industrious and competent man but I should not trust his judgment on any point at all. It is not merely that I should not accept it. I should regard it as a pointer in the opposite direction'.

It was not only in personal letters that Devlin expressed his low regard for Manningham-Buller. After his death and two years after Bodkin Adams died, Devlin published a book about the trial. It was a quite extraordinary thing to do, and was widely criticized for that reason, though not for its readability. It pulled no punches. Sackar summarises its effect:

> 'the treatment of Manningham-Buller was consistent with the view that a possibly guilty man went free due to the incompetence and stupidity of prosecuting counsel'.

For Sackar, Devlin's treatment of Manningham-Buller was his Achilles heel. He appeared before him, then Lord Dilhorne, in the Privy Council. He comments:

> 'He was not as stupid as Patrick thought he was and not as vain as Patrick certainly was. His rudeness was part of his personality, but he was not particularly mean'.

I too appeared before Dilhorne and I endorse Sackar's appraisal. It seemed to me that Dilhorne had read the papers with more industry than some of his colleagues and his interventions were not merely pertinent but polite.

Devlin entered the law seeking enjoyment; as counsel and as a puisne judge he found it. The appellate role brought his enjoyment to an end. It is hard for those without experience of the pre-electronic world, or even the photocopier, to envisage the languor of the appellate process half a century ago. It was considered desirable in principle that the judge should approach the case with a completely open mind, so there was no question of a judge so much as opening the papers before the appellant's counsel opened his case. Where a case was cited, the ushers would remove copies of the relevant report from the shelves and counsel would then read the passages relied upon *in extenso*. Progress was so slow that towards the end of the hearing it would become apparent that the judges were concentrating more on sketching out '*ex tempore*' judgments than on counsel's submissions in reply.

Devlin wrote to Frankfurter:

> '... our methods are deadening.
>
> I find our practice of going into the court with a blank mind and listening to days and days of argument quite intolerable ...
>
> In the important cases on which I have sat I have found at the end of two or three weeks' argument the point that I think, rightly or wrongly, is decisive has hardly been mentioned ...'

And to Acheson:

> 'The thought of writing no more judgments on piffling technicalities fills me with joy … the great thing is to be quit of London'

He hoped that the regime in the House of Lords would be better than that in the Court of Appeal, but was disappointed. He retired as soon as he had served the fifteen years needed to qualify for a full pension. He was active in retirement, chairing the new Press Council, arbitrating at home and abroad, writing and lecturing. He advocated the creation of a Supreme Court and the enactment of a bill of rights. The former has come to pass and many believe that the latter is only a question of time. As Lord Reid remarked, had he served his time as a Law Lord, he might have been the greatest jurist of them all. As this biography demonstrates he was, however, 'a cult figure whose life remained of constant and intense interest'.

Lord Phillips of Worth Matravers

Acknowledgements

BEFORE COMING TO some long overdue and necessary acknowledgements I should say something about the writing of this book. I had long been intrigued by Lord Devlin. He was to me both a luminary and a mystery. His judgments could hardly go unnoticed from the very start of his judicial career. His meteoric rise, especially through the appellate ranks, and his very short sojourn in the House of Lords, which he left while in such rude health, added to the intrigue. His books, always informative and engaging, set him way apart from his judicial contemporaries. But what finally impelled me to put pen to paper was the realisation that no-one had at the very least collected in one place his immense output. This work, I trust, is an appropriate recognition of his energy and imagination.

In addition, in an interview with Joshua Rozenberg in 1985 Lord Devlin said:[1]

> You have to give an accurate account of what you think. You can't say, 'well this is being unkind to ...' and no doubt they'll be equally unkind to me and one must accept that, in the interests of getting an accurate account of what somebody thinks.

The work is also intended to pass the accuracy test as well.

In writing a judicial biography and with some trepidation I could not ignore the comment of Professor Phillip Girard that judicial biography had, in his view, been a 'halting and sporadic enterprise' in which only a 'few pearls glitter in the mud' and further that the genre in England had run out of steam.[2] I was, however, on the other hand, buoyed by Professor David Sugarman's view (writing in 2015, the year I started the book) that it not only appealed to a 'universal human interest in gossip', but that it also answered a need within us to 'understand each other better'. He happily expressed the view that judicial biography was enjoying a 'recent renaissance'.[3] Lastly Professor Robert Heuston, judicial biographer and gossip par excellence, gave a fascinating lecture in 1967 in which he helpfully set out a template of the 'do's' and 'don'ts' in writing such a work.[4] I have done my best to follow that template.

---

[1] 'Interview Joshua Rozenberg and Lord Devlin', *BBC Radio 4* FM, 25 November 1985.

[2] Professor Philip Girard, 'Judging Lives: Judicial Biography from Hale to Holmes' (2003) 7(1) *Australian Journal of Legal History* 87–106, 87.

[3] Professor David Sugarman, 'From Legal Biography to Legal Life Writing: Broadening Conceptions of Legal History and Socio-Legal Scholarship' (2015) 42(1) *Journal of Law and Society* 7–33.

[4] Professor RFV Heuston, 'Judges and Biographers', an inaugural lecture, delivered at the University of Southhampton, 24 January 1967.

In writing this book I have encountered a generosity of spirit I never expected. I was provided with the most extraordinary assistance at every turn.

First and foremost, I must profoundly thank the Devlin family, especially their spokesperson Tim Devlin, for their candid and timely replies to requests for information. Without their willingness to impart information about their father this book would likely never have eventuated. I should hasten to add this is not an authorised biography. The Devlin family received only a glimpse of the work prior to its publication.

I was fortunate also to have interviewed Professor Tony Honoré and Sir Louis Blom-Cooper QC. Each had his own interesting tales, told often with a mischievous sense of humour. Both have sadly since died. It was also a privilege to interview Marcel Berlins, lawyer, journalist and broadcaster, who had himself interviewed Lord Devlin. He has since also sadly died.

I was happily able to interview Sir Sydney Kentridge QC, Professor Robert Stevens, Professor Nicola Lacey, and Professor John Finnis. Professors David Sugarman, Alan Paterson and Francis Reynolds generously answered a number of queries I posed for each.

Joshua Rozenberg QC was willing, it seems, at almost all hours of the day, promptly to answer my sometimes trivial questions. He had also interviewed Lord Devlin. He has my warmest thanks for his generous assistance.

There was a category of persons who as a class displayed generosity well beyond that which was expected. That group comprised persons at the National Archives at Kew, Christ's College Cambridge, Churchill College Cambridge, Rhodes House Oxford, Yale University Law School Library, Howard Gotlieb Archival Research Center at the University of Boston, the Bodleian Library University of Oxford, Bedford College at the University of London, the Society of the Sacred Heart, the Jesuits in Britain Archives, and the archivist at Douai Abbey. My special thanks to Ms Tracey Horrell of Gene Tracers whose keen forensic instincts uncovered the records dealing with Lord Devlin's time as a Dominican novice.

The archivist at Stonyhurst College, Mr David Knight, and his staff were of great assistance, as was Mr Thomas Muir, author and former head of history and politics at Stonyhurst College.

I must also thank Mr Andrew Mussell, archivist at Gray's Inn, and Dr David Trippett, head of University Archives at Cambridge University Library.

The Law Courts Library in Sydney has some of the most thoughtful and talented librarians in the Southern Hemisphere. I have had the good fortune to work with many. In particular I wish to thank Fang Zhao, Michael Unwin, Niall Clugston and Stacey Wilson for their courtesy and professionalism. I must also thank Tom Kavanagh, Daniel Habashy, Rebecca McKewan, Nick Saady, Anthea Burton, Hugh Montgomery and Hannah Cameron for their sheer enthusiasm.

I also wish to thank Ms Kasia Czarnota who not only typed parts of the manuscript but whose ever-helpful suggestions and reading assisted me very substantially. I must also thank Ms Madeline Muddle for putting some finishing touches on the manuscript including the preparation of the biographical details.

My very special thanks must go to Ms Catherine Young, my professional assistant of more than 20 years, who for as long as I can remember, whether as barrister or judge, has with extraordinary commitment and focus managed to keep my professional life on course.

I also owe a debt of gratitude to the Honourable J D Heydon AC QC, former Justice of the High Court of Australia, who provided insightful and invaluable suggestions and contributions.

Lastly, I would like to thank my wife, Alison Renwick and family for their unquestioning and endless support and encouragement at times when the end just seemed too far away.

Contents

1

Ab Ovo

THE LUCKIEST DAY of William John Devlin's life would appear to have been a chance meeting with Frances (Fanny) Crombie on a sea voyage back from South Africa in 1898. Patrick's parents, William and Frances, were married in 1900 and for a time went to live in Chiselhurst on the outskirts of London. William was a devout Irish Catholic and Frances, though of Scottish Protestant blood, would embrace Catholicism with some vigour. As in many Catholic families of that time, numerous children followed – five in all. Patrick was the second eldest and was born there on 25 November 1905.

Patrick's father was an architect. But he had no practice of any substance and was never to have one. Equally he had no business sense. He was slow, earnest and trusting but more importantly trusted.[1] A move to Aberdeen in the hope of work from the Catholic Church, which never materialised, did little to enhance the family's wellbeing. By some means his family was eventually able to purchase a house in Aberdeen. Patrick did not know his father particularly well, but was provoked to describe his father's career as a manifest and total failure.[2]

His mother was a member of a wealthy Aberdeen family of cloth manu-facturers whose support was not infrequently resorted to for financial back-up. After Patrick's maternal grandfather died, his mother's income from the estate kept the family going. The famous Crombie overcoat was an item of clothing of which Patrick was always proud. It was the flagship item of apparel for the busi-ness. Readers of Patrick's memoir, *Taken at the Flood*, will readily appreciate he was far better informed about his mother's family lineage than that of his father. Part of the reason is that, as Patrick explains, his father never spoke to him or his siblings about his family in Ireland. He knew his paternal grandmother had died prematurely and, as Patrick describes it, the family then disintegrated. On the other hand, almost all of the Crombies are mentioned in the memoir. Although his maternal grandfather was affectionately referred to as Papa, he seems clearly to have been a most unlikeable and immensely selfish widower.[3]

According to Patrick, his father was, as it seems, not only an unsuccess-ful but also an uncommunicative man. He was fortunate to have a wife with some means, as his practice could not have at any time comfortably supported

---

[1] Patrick Devlin, *Taken at the Flood* (Taverner Publications, 1996) (TATF), p 24.
[2] Ibid, p 37.
[3] Ibid, p 18.

his wife and their three sons at Stonyhurst, a Jesuit school in Lancashire that all three boys attended. It must be said that at the time the difference between fees at Stonyhurst as compared to one of the equivalent Protestant schools such as Winchester or Westminster was stark indeed. The latter were almost double. Somehow, his parents found the money to secure their children's education, supplemented from time to time when the boys in particular won prizes. Eventually his two sisters became nuns. One brother became a priest, the other an actor. Arthur Conan Doyle, however, may well have the explanation for how Patrick's parents managed to pay the fees. The Jesuits at Stonyhurst were very happy to do deals with parents. If the child was dedicated to the church the fees would be remitted. Conan Doyle's mother did not agree,[4] but Patrick's parents especially may well have done so. After all, out of the three boys, the church secured one out of three, and almost two.[5]

Patrick's mentor, benefactor and de facto father was, for all relevant purposes, his Uncle George, one of his mother's brothers. A bachelor of clear and abiding Protestant views and prejudices, Uncle George clearly favoured two of his sister's sons, for when he died in 1946, Patrick (by then a successful barrister) and his brother William were two of the principal beneficiaries. Each inherited £15,000. While he refused to make any contribution to the fees at Stonyhurst, he gave Patrick's mother about £200 a year. He did, however, provide the means by which Patrick could go to Cambridge.[6]

Uncle George taught Patrick about business and political philosophy. He persuaded him that, as Aesop had advocated, the ant was perfectly correct to shut the door in the face of the grasshopper. As Patrick puts it, he also taught him about the facts of life. Patrick and Uncle George became very close over the years. So much so that he appointed Patrick his co-executor (along with his solicitor) and entrusted him with his funeral arrangements.

Patrick attended Stonyhurst, 'a school for Catholic gentlemen',[7] in the years 1914 to 1922. The school was situated in an area which had historically been very much a Catholic part of England, notwithstanding the persecutions in Elizabethan times. The recusants had never been fully rooted out. As far as can be seen, Patrick's family had no connections with Stonyhurst, whereas some families had sent their children there for generations. No entrance examinations were necessary, not that that would have been an obstacle for Patrick or his brothers. Each of them was obviously intelligent, charming, if not bordering on cheeky. The Jesuits can and did do wonders with mediocre intellects but with Patrick and his brothers they were presented with an embarrassment of riches.

---

[4] Arthur Conan Doyle, *A Life in Letters* (New York, The Penguin Press, 2007), p 39.
[5] TATF, p 35.
[6] See, for example, TATF, p 49.
[7] Macdonald Hastings, *Jesuit Child* (Newton Abbott, Readers Union Book Club, 1972), p 18; TE Muir, *Stonyhurst College 1593–1993* (London, James & James Ltd, 1992), p 54.

Patrick was eight years old when he was taken by train from Aberdeen to Stonyhurst in Lancashire.[8] It was a very long way by any standards. It was somewhat reminiscent of the great journey on horseback from Scotland undertaken in 1718 by the other Jacobite, William Murray (later Lord Mansfield), then only 13 years old.[9] Mansfield travelled alone. Almost certainly Patrick did not. This was no doubt an adventure habitually made by young men at this time.

Stonyhurst's history is nothing short of dramatic. Originally founded in northern France at St Omer in 1592 to provide education for English Catholics, it was forced by the French Government to seek asylum at Bruges in 1762, later in Liège in 1773, and finally at its current location in 1794 as a result of a benefaction of Thomas Weld. In an advertisement for the school published in *The Dublin Review* in September 1922, it was described as being '360 feet above sea level, and with a bracing and healthy climate' providing the usual 'English public school education'.[10]

In the early twentieth century, the train to Stonyhurst stopped at Whalley, from which transport to the school was available by a two-horse-drawn carriage. On a clear night from the railway line between Clitheroe and Blackburn a line of lights could be noticed blinking in the West, against the dark shape of Longridge Fell. Stonyhurst College stood alone on that hillside a little way from the village of Hurst Green, above the Hodder, a tributary of the Ribble. Its Catholic owner, Thomas Weld, gave the then sandstone Tudor manor house to the Jesuits after they fled the French Revolutionary Army in 1794.

Over the years, Stonyhurst College has been extended. It is now an architectural melange, some have said a monstrosity. In parts it echoes the Bodleian library, and in parts King's College Chapel, Cambridge. Beauty is truly in the eye of the beholder and it was not sufficiently ugly or ungrand to deter *Country Life* in October 1910 (just a few years before Patrick started) from devoting large slabs of two of its issues to the College. In typical *Country Life* style, big lavish photographs in sepia-like tones were spread over eight pages in the first issue and nine pages the following week. Appropriately, perhaps, in neither article is there a photograph of a student. Instead we have a priest either wandering in the garden reading or peering up at some ornamentation on a garden house. The College, now co-educational, appears regularly today in the same magazine in blazing colour as part of its annual marketing and recruitment campaign.

Notwithstanding the *Dublin Review* advertisement, Stonyhurst was described by others as a secluded, spartan place in an unwelcoming climate.[11] It should be acknowledged, however, that it was the first private institution with its own

---

[8] TATF, p 12.

[9] Norman S Poser, *Lord Mansfield, Justice in the Age of Reason* (Canada, McGill-Queens University Press, 2013), the Chronology, pp 18–21.

[10] (September 1922) 171 *The Dublin Review* 176.

[11] Macdonald Hastings, *Jesuit Child* (Readers Union Book Club, 1972), pp 16–17.

gas works and the first also to have a macadamised road into its grounds,[12] all through the resourcefulness and genius of the Jesuits. The praise should not stop there. It is lovingly and lavishly captured in great detail along with much more of its history by Father John Gerard SJ in his 'Centenary Record', published in 1894, by which time the school had reached its peak and was the leading Catholic school in the country.[13]

Patrick started at Hodder, the preparatory school, a few miles from Stonyhurst. Until 1855, when it became a preparatory school, it had been run as a Jesuit novitiate. Patrick was starting his education at the beginning of the Great War. Compelling children to leave home at such an age and sensitive moment and to board a long way from home is something peculiarly English, and the perceived benefits of which many have found to be more than debatable.

In his memoir Patrick only allows the reader a brief and somewhat narrow window into Stonyhurst and his activities there. There is no mention at all of the preparatory school Hodder. No teachers, in those days almost all priests, are mentioned either. Privacy or circumspection might explain some of this, but it certainly cannot be put down to memory lapse. There is a brief reference to the regime of assigning a boy to read to the others at mealtimes. One of the students mentioned, 'Bolshie Curran', is singled out seemingly for two reasons. The first is that he supplied Patrick, at a cost, with a speech for Patrick's debating audition; secondly, because Patrick found him a 'quiet and ugly' boy. What of all things would possess Patrick to waste one of his preciously crafted sentences to share that particular observation is a little hard to fathom, apart from a streak of cruelty not unknown amongst certain other members of his own family.[14]

At Hodder the prefects were in a powerful position. One eccentric old boy Charles Waterton, writing in his autobiography in 1837, called them 'lynx-eyed' guardians.[15] Some of them meted out appalling corporal punishment to some of the junior boys.

The routine at Hodder was strict, often severe, and, Father Turner thought, far too narrow.[16] Mass in the morning and evening was customary. Holy Communion to one side, confession, which was encouraged, was a little lacking in utility one might think for a seven year old. However, the Jesuits also encouraged and had a capacity to cultivate a student's interest and love for cultural things, theatre, elocution, argument and the joys of conversation. The Jesuits

[12] *Country Life* Magazine, vol XXVIII (719), Saturday 15 October 1910, p 534; *Country Life*, vol XXVIII (720), 22 October 1910, p 574.

[13] Reverend John Gerard SJ, *Centenary Record, Stonyhurst College* (Belfast, Marcus Ward and Co, 1894), p 25 and following. See also Rev George Gruggen, SJ and Rev Joseph Keating, SJ, *Stonyhurst College* (London, Kegan Paul, Trench, Trubner & Co Ltd, 1901).

[14] TATF, p 13.

[15] Charles Waterton, *Essays on Natural History* (London, Longman, Brown, Green, and Longmans, 1837, New Edition, 1854), p xxiv.

[16] 'Father Turner', *The Stonyhurst Magazine*, Autumn 1987.

were especially good at tolerating the awkwardness of individuality. They were strict disciplinarians who kept a 'hawkish watchfulness' over the boys at all times, including their daily ablutions.[17] There was compulsory exercise and ball games. Classics and humanities were heavily emphasised. The Jesuits excelled in encouraging enquiring minds and reflection in an atmosphere of discipline and intellectual stimulus.

As Thomas Muir, in his masterful and scholarly history of Stonyhurst explains, a Jesuit education was so distinctive in part because of its Catholic emphasis.[18] There was an emphasis on Latin grammar, on learning Greek and even Hebrew, and an insistence that Latin be spoken on virtually every occasion. Again, as Muir points out, this resulted in a very curious compound. As St Ignatius of Loyola himself explained:[19]

> The order to be observed in the subjects is that a solid foundation should be laid in the Latin language before the Liberal Arts, in the Liberal Arts before Scholastic Theology, and in the Scholastic Theology before Positive Theology, the Sacred Scriptures can be studied at the same time or later.

Although structure was all-important, the Jesuits loved disputation,[20] soothed perhaps by the monastic habit of having readings at mealtimes: 'Theirs was a more systematic method of study designed to bring the average and not the best pupil forward'.[21]

As MacDonald Hastings, author and journalist, explains, when Patrick was at Stonyhurst, the Jesuits eyed all women in the context of the 'Biblical Eve'.[22] According to him, they also devoted an unconscionable amount of time getting boys ready for the next world. The only women the boys were exposed to during school term would have been the Matron and the servants. Visits by parents were infrequent and were indeed discouraged. The Jesuits, according to Thomas Muir, were afraid of parents, especially women. Perhaps they were afraid that a maternal touch would weaken the rigour and discipline they sought to inculcate in the boys. As a matter of practical reality, the remote location of the school aided the Jesuits' aim. Most boys did not see their parents during the term. Some boys, especially those whose parents were in India or other parts of the Empire, might not see them for years. Patrick would have had four weeks holiday at Christmas, three at Easter and about seven weeks in the summer.

In addition, Jesuit schools at the time had a high teacher–pupil ratio. The Jesuits also had a peculiar practice by which the master stayed with his class as

[17] Macdonald Hastings, *Jesuit Child* (Newton Abbott, Readers Union Book Club, 1972), 18; Charles Waterton, *Essays on Natural History, chiefly Ornithology*, with an autobiography of the author, (London, Longman, Brown, Green & Longmans, New Edition 1854), p xxiii.
[18] TE Muir, *Stonyhurst College 1593–1993* (London, James & James Ltd, 1992), pp 22–23.
[19] Ibid, p 31.
[20] Ibid, p 27.
[21] Ibid, p 27.
[22] Macdonald Hastings, *Jesuit Child* (London, Readers Union Book Club, 1972), p 47.

it moved up the school. This allowed him to build up close relationships with pupils. All this, flavoured with constant watchfulness, helped to counter bullying or fagging, and also enhanced religious habits with a keen eye being kept out for possible recruits, of whom there were on average about four a year. In due course, Patrick was to become one himself.

Father Turner thought that after the school's centenary in 1894, 'it gave itself over to hubris, failed to adapt and lived on its reputation'. In addition, the Jesuit Society at about this time had started to found day schools to which it sent many of 'its best men'.[23] Hence, prior to the 1920s the quality of the almost entirely clerical staff was thought by Father Turner to be mediocre. This engendered a rather club-like atmosphere instead of that of a first-class secondary institution. In turn it has been said that this allowed students to lead a 'gentleman's existence in the good, bad and indifferent senses of the phrase'.[24]

The quality of debating was said to be especially high on occasions. This was of course fertile territory for Patrick. In his memoir, borrowing from Milton, Patrick said of himself:[25] 'I had no talent which it would be death to hide. I had not at my school, Stonyhurst, excelled at anything. Nevertheless I fancied myself as a performer of some sort.' This is somewhat of an understatement. Patrick was a young man of some acuity who, in the end, excelled because of his Jesuit education. It is true, examinations were something Patrick could never master, but skill at public speaking was for him innate.

At Stonyhurst, certainly during the Great War, the heating was erratic, and the food was said to be 'execrable'.[26] Wealthy parents could pay for extras in which case a student would get bacon and eggs. Patrick was not amongst that group. Father Turner remembers that when in season, the boys had a glut of vegetables often badly cooked and prepared with 'little imagination'.[27] On some occasions the boys were treated to what was colloquially known as a 'shouting cake' because the raisins were so far apart they had to shout to make the next one hear.[28] It is perhaps little wonder, when one adds the weather, that Patrick contracted rickets. This was to have lifelong effects: first, a period of treatment and rehabilitation; and second, a lifelong stoop. However, his handsome angular features and shock of thick red hair preserved an appearance of vitality.

Patrick's first year at Hodder would have been traumatic enough as a small boy leaving home, but the Great War was to impose an even greater trauma on him, along with the whole nation.

---

[23] 'Father Turner', *The Stonyhurst Magazine*, Autumn 1987.
[24] Ibid.
[25] Taken from one of the best known sonnets of John Milton (1608–74), 'When I Consider How My Light is Spent'.
[26] Macdonald Hastings, *Jesuit Child* (Newton Abbott, Readers Union Book Club, 1972), p 18.
[27] 'Father Turner', *The Stonyhurst Magazine*, Autumn 1987.
[28] Macdonald Hastings, *Jesuit Child* (Newton Abbott, Readers Union Book Club, 1972, pp 23–24).

In the early part of 1914 school business was conducted as usual. The magazine had the usual obituaries, announcements concerning various school societies and activities, including a lavish description of a visit by a Mr O'Mara, a then quite famous Irish tenor.[29] The magazine would frequently contain Chinese proverbs and quotations from the redoubtable Francis Bacon – his essay 'Of Cunning' was a particular favourite of one of the priests.

Unsurprisingly during the Great War, the regular attempts at levity of the school magazine would become interspersed with somewhat dramatic and mournful obituaries of old boys. However, it could not be said that the Jesuits of Patrick's day were sentimentalists. In the June 1914 edition of the magazine there appeared an obituary of an old boy and teacher at the school, a Father John Clayton SJ. He had attended the school in 1857 and later taught there. In what is in many ways an endearing account of Father Clayton, the eulogist, however, found time for the following observation:[30]

> When he asserted that the anxieties of his office as Provincial never cost him an hour's sleep we can accept his words as quite in keeping with his impassive, imperturbable disposition, destitute of nerves and unhampered by imagination.

This put down was what might be identified in some respects as the house style, but in any event, the nurturing by wordsmiths like this of Patrick's natural wit and charm goes a long way to explaining the writing style he ultimately evolved.

The school for a time kept an aviary to which were added exotic species, a serious observatory and a rather eclectic collection of taxidermy and curiosities left to the school by an eccentric old boy, Charles Waterton. Waterton had written a book of essays on natural history which the boys were understandably encouraged to read. He was truly of Roman Catholic aristocracy, for his ancestry allegedly included eight saints, and he asserted he was a direct descendant of Sir Thomas More. In his autobiography, originally published in 1837, Waterton describes the discipline at Stonyhurst as follows:[31]

> The watchfulness over the morals of their pupils was so intense, that I am ready to declare, were I on my death-bed, I never once had it in my power to open a book in which there was to be found a single paragraph of an immoral tendency.

However, much more importantly for a wild adventurous and imaginative boy like Waterton, the Jesuits were able to bring out the best in him. As he recognised:[32]

> I owe everything to the fathers of the order of St Ignatius. Their attention to my welfare was unceasing; whilst their solicitude for my advancement in virtue and in

---

[29] *The Stonyhurst Magazine*, February 1914, p 829.

[30] *The Stonyhurst Magazine*, June 1914, p 895.

[31] Charles Waterton, *Essays on Natural History* (London, Longman, Brown, Green, and Longmans, 1837, New Edition, 1854), p xxiii.

[32] Ibid, p xxvii.

literature seemed to know no bounds. The permission they granted me to work in my favourite vocation, when it did not interfere with the important duties of education enabled me to commence a career, which afforded me a world of pleasure ...

A similar sentiment comes out of the pages of Patrick's memoirs. This ethos at Stonyhurst was one of intellectual vibrancy.

By the middle of 1914 Father Bede Jarrett OP, a man who was to play a significant role in Patrick's life, had emerged as a prominent Dominican. In that year he was appointed Prior of the famous St Dominic's in London's Haverstock Hill. For him, and unlike Patrick, Stonyhurst was the family school and he followed his five brothers there. He was one of Stonyhurst's brighter students, matriculating as a member of the University of Oxford in October 1904. Father Bede Jarrett had, by the time Patrick went to Stonyhurst, become a famous preacher: 'In his sermons his silver voice, his utter conviction, the spontaneity of his phrasing all became a single living thing'.[33]

Whilst at Haverstock Hill, because of the poverty of the parish then, Father Bede Jarrett became passionately interested in Socialism.[34] But he did not believe it was the remedy. It was said of him that 'All his life he was so non-political that it is hard to diagnose his standpoint, but it seems truest to say that he was a natural Tory with instinctive liberal sympathies'.[35] Again, this bears a remarkable similarity with the way Patrick could also be described. It is easy to understand why they had such an affinity for each other.

The English Dominican tradition had survived for nearly 680 years but Father Bede Jarrett had played a significant part in its twentieth-century revival. Jarrett was 'clothed' at Woodchester,[36] when the province still retained much of the atmosphere of late Georgian England, with its emphasis on good manners, easy personal relationships and antiquarian and classical interests. From the middle of the nineteenth century this was being increasingly combined with an emphasis on preaching and with the maintenance of a high standard of strict observance and personal austerity. In due course Patrick was to find all these things mesmerising.

By the October 1914 edition of the school magazine, the war was well under way. The boys were encouraged to sing patriotic songs. The war was already changing the school and the whole country. For most, life would never be the same ever again.[37] This was the edition of the magazine that announced the first casualty. Lieutenant Maurice Dease of the 4th Battalion

---

[33] Kenneth Wykeham-George, OP and Gervase Mathew, OP, *Bede Jarrett of the Order of Preachers*, (London, Blackfriars Publications, 1952), p 35.

[34] Ibid, p 35. Although Jarrett wrote numerous works, he wrote an important work entitled *Medieval Socialism* (Edinburgh & London, Ballantyne, Hanson & Co, originally published in 1914).

[35] Kenneth Wykeham-George, OP and Gervase Mathew, OP, *Bede Jarrett of the Order of Preachers* (London, Blackfriars Publications, 1952), p 34.

[36] Ibid, p 3.

[37] *The Stonyhurst Magazine*, October 1914, pp 975–76.

Royal Fusiliers, whose family came from County Meath, was killed in action on 23 August 1914. He was 24 and had left Stonyhurst in 1903. He was an only son. His parents consented to the letter they had received about his death being published in the magazine. Two other old boys were reported as wounded and many more as serving, with quite a number identified as being at the front. For the next four years, the war was to become part of the daily life of England, even in this remote school community. The school magazine would be virtually nothing else.

The December magazine announced with understandable pride that Dease had been awarded the Victoria Cross, posthumously.[38] His death had been added to by another nine young alumni who had been killed since the October edition. The wounded, the missing and those at the front were vastly increasing in numbers. With the death toll rising and the full-page photographs of the dead occupying much greater space in the magazine, the obituaries of priests were squeezed to the back pages, along with truncated reports of other activities and societies. Even the famous Christmas truce was relegated to only a small column to make way for all-important obituaries. With many letters from combatants and families alike, the magazine provided a significant mechanism for the Stonyhurst community to share its grief.

On 15 December 1914, the then Prime Minister, Herbert Henry Asquith, appointed a committee to investigate alleged German outrages during what was to be just the first six months of the much longer war. It included Lord Bryce, who had been ambassador to the United States until 1913, Sir Frederick Pollock Bt KC and Sir Edward Clarke KC. They were specifically to look at the outrages allegedly committed by German troops and in particular the maltreatment of civilians.[39]

The Committee's report was published on 12 May 1915. It would have been of particular interest to the school community at Stonyhurst because many of the atrocities had been committed in the Liège and Louvain districts, with which the school had close historical connections. The Committee chronicled in chilling detail the massacre of soldiers and civilians alike. Unashamedly it was intended as propaganda for those at home and, more importantly, in the United States where it was hoped it would influence public opinion regarding America joining the war. It was solely directed to investigating and reporting on alleged German atrocities in Belgium. Whilst allowing for the so-called exigencies of war, the Committee commented:[40]

> In the present war, however – and this is the gravest charge against the German army – the evidence shows that the killing of non-combatants was carried out to an extent for which no previous war between nations claiming to be civilised furnishes any precedent.

[38] *The Stonyhurst Magazine*, December 1914, p 1005.
[39] Report of the British Committee on Alleged German Outrages: Presented to both Houses of Parliament by the Chairman Right Hon, Viscount Bryce, OM, Critchley Parker, 1915.
[40] Ibid, p 10.

The Committee reported its findings in anger and disgust, no doubt shared by the whole country and the Stonyhurst population *en masse*. It specifically found the systematic massacres of men, women and children were deliberate. It also found that the German attempt to attack priests on the basis that they were stationed on church towers expressly for the purpose of targeting German soldiers was highly improbable.

The year 1915 brought increased suffering with battlefield losses. On 27 April, Father Bede Jarrett's brother Charles was killed at Gallipoli. In June, another brother Aylmer died of wounds in Flanders. By the middle of 1916, 32 old boys had died in the conflict with scores more wounded and large numbers missing. Yet another old boy, Captain Aidan Liddell, 3rd Battalion, Argyll and Sutherland Highlanders, was awarded a Victoria Cross. By the end of 1916 there were 57 old boys who had lost their lives, and their photographs and tributes continued to fill the pages of the magazine. In due course Britain alone was to lose nearly a million soldiers, with hundreds of thousands more from the Empire.

Amidst the controversy, in the latter part of 1916, Patrick was starting to emerge as a personality at Hodder. In the election of the Apostleship, Patrick was elected an Acolyte.[41] He was then 11 years old. It is not exactly known what he was required to do to be elected or how the election was conducted.

By Easter of 1916, Holy Week services were held for the first time at Hodder. Patrick was one of two acolytes.[42] During the same period he came second in a religious examination to Herman David, who was to become a lifelong friend. The first prize in the examination was for an amount of £20 a year for two years. At this time school fees were approximately £65 a year. There is no indication of how much the second prize was worth, although whatever it was it certainly would have to a significant extent eased the financial burden on Patrick's family.[43]

October 1916 brought the announcement of the award of the third Victoria Cross for Stonyhurst to Lieut. Gabriel Coury. He had mercifully survived his ordeal, which was set out, as was the custom, in considerable detail.[44] By 1917 the school needed to plan for a war memorial with so many dead and wounded. The response from the school community was unsurprisingly swift and generous.

On 26 March 1918, Patrick and his family were personally devastated by the death of his cousin John Duncan Abel, aged 20. Patrick was then 13 and was very much affected by his cousin's death. He would not forget the tragedy or its futility. His rather lengthy work on Woodrow Wilson published in 1974 and

[41] *The Stonyhurst Magazine*, June 1916, p 1583.
[42] Ibid, p 1583.
[43] Ibid, p 1584.
[44] *The Stonyhurst Magazine*, October 1916, p 1692.

upon which he worked for much of his life was dedicated to his cousin. In the dedication he says:[45]

> I was young enough to miss the Great War of 1914 and so to speed to early attainment through the gaps it blasted out of the classes above me. The chance was bought for me by the dead: my gain is what they lost. I write about life in the office and not on the battlefield, but beneath the text there is the insistent drumming of the fight, of wounds and death. The death of the unripe. All through the writing I have been pricked by that.

His cousin had been the Captain of Uppingham School, a scholar of Corpus Christi College, Oxford and a second lieutenant in the Seaforth Highlanders. He was killed in action at Dernancourt.

Many years later, when he was 80 years old, Patrick confided to Marcel Berlins in an interview for *The Times* in June 1985 about the impact of the Great War, and in particular the impact that Wilson had upon him. He said:[46]

> It was 1918 about the time I was becoming politically conscious. I was 13 and found it totally incomprehensible that there should ever have been a war. And there was this great evangelist coming from the other side of the Atlantic saying that there would be no more war and the world would be safe for democracy. I did not know anything about the man but the idea was immensely attractive.

By November of that year the Great War was officially over. One hundred and sixty seven old boys had died and scores were wounded.[47] The Great War had had a profound impact on Britain, its Dominions and its colonies, with over a million dead soldiers. In relative terms Stonyhurst was likewise affected.

In late March 1918, Patrick and his younger brother Christopher sat exams for scholarships. Again Patrick came in second in the Junior Association scholarship.[48] Christopher, who had been at preparatory school in Aberdeen prior to Hodder, won the prestigious Shireburn scholarship.

At the end of 1919 Patrick won a third prize in religious doctrine in the category 'First Class, Second Division'.[49] Francis Sullivan, a friend of Patrick's, won first prize, with Herman David this time coming second. Sullivan, a rather heavily built boy, was to become a well-known stage and screen actor. In physical appearance he bore an uncanny resemblance to the actor Charles Laughton. Sadly, this slightly held his career back because he was always being compared to him. The comparison did not stop there. Laughton had also attended Stonyhurst some years before. Both later became US citizens and by total coincidence

[45] Patrick Devlin, *Too Proud to Fight: Woodrow Wilson's Neutrality* (New York/London, Oxford University Press, 1975), dedication.

[46] 'Interview with Marcel Berlins', *The Times*, 11 June 1985, p 10.

[47] Authorities of Stonyhurst College, *Stonyhurst War Record, A Memorial of the Part Taken by Stonyhurst Men in the Great War* (London/Derby, Bemrose & Sons Ltd, 1927), p xiii.

[48] *The Stonyhurst Magazine*, June 1918, p 299.

[49] *The Stonyhurst Magazine*, December 1919, p 46.

Sullivan won a Tony award in 1955 for his performance in the play *Witness for the Prosecution*, whereas Laughton was nominated in 1957 for his role in the film.

Herman David, on the other hand, who was the same age as Patrick, would go on to play Davis Cup tennis for Britain in 1932. As an entrepreneur he was the father of modern Wimbledon.[50]

Even prior to Patrick moving from Hodder to Stonyhurst, he was attracted to debating. In addition, he was addicted to reading. In July 1918 a new Club was formed which suited Patrick's interests completely. It was called the Popinjay Club.[51] A popinjay is a person who is both talkative and cocky and who struts around chattering like a parrot. The first part of the definition was particularly apt in Patrick's case.

The Debating Society or Club at Stonyhurst had first got under way in about 1850. After sizeable interruptions it was again in full swing by late 1919. Patrick wanted to ensure that he was very much at the centre of it. He no doubt thought it would give full vent to his desire to perform. In the debate for 16 November 1919, for example, the boys were given the rather provocative subject: 'That in the opinion of this House, a total embargo on German goods would be detrimental to the interests of this country'. So popular was the topic that 13 boys were prevented from speaking due to time constraints. Some notable priests even joined in. One visitor, Sir William Heathcote SJ, described as a 'furious Tory' spoke against the embargo but added his dismay at having to pay more for his suits under the current regime. Patrick did not speak but was present.[52]

The next debate concerned a motion 'That this House would regard the total disappearance of Great Empires as a misfortune'. In his memoir Patrick recounts this as his first outing as a putative debater. So concerned was he at making a good impression that he purchased a prepared speech from the 'ugly' boy Charles Curran.[53]

As was customary, each boy was assigned a constituency. Patrick's was for good reason Belfast and he was to speak in favour of the motion. As was also customary there was to be a second session. Charles Curran, the author of Patrick's speech, was to speak in the second session but against the motion. His constituency was Sligo. Apart from his performance it seems never to have occurred to Patrick that Curran had set him up having taken his money. The extracts from the magazine are telling:[54]

> P Devlin (Belfast), recited his speech so glibly that it did not need the testimony of a member the Board of Six who lives next door to prove that he had practised

[50] Rob Steen, *Floodlights and Touchlines: A History of Spectator Sport* (London, Bloomsbury Sport, 2015), p 311.

[51] *The Stonyhurst Magazine*, July 1918, p 420.

[52] *The Stonyhurst Magazine*, February 1920, p 129.

[53] TATF, p 13.

[54] *The Stonyhurst Magazine*, December 1919, p 83.

assiduously. The state is necessary to civilisation; the Empire is a super-State a fortiori. His statement that without the Roman Empire England would be to-day a wilderness provoked expressions of dissent from the House.

The following is then recorded:[55]

Curran (Sligo) swelled the ranks of Indian arguers again denouncing the militaristic government of India, and followed by an appeal to and from Ireland.

There was some discussion in the Committee as to whether Patrick had learnt the speech by heart and whether in that event he should be refused admission to the Debating Society. His own recollection as recorded in his memoir is perhaps unsurprisingly a little more generous than the entry in the school magazine.[56]

The motion was rejected 13 to 12. Notwithstanding Patrick's investment, his point of view had not won favour, perhaps because of its poor execution. Notwithstanding this, Patrick along with five others were admitted to the 'Club.'

What followed at the 16 November meeting of the Club perhaps explains why Curran, whose nickname was 'Bolshie', became a successful barrister and Conservative MP for Uxbridge. No one, perhaps not even Patrick, could have predicted that Curran was about to execute a coup d'état on the committee of six. No doubt with Patrick in tow, Bolshie, living up to every ounce of his sobriquet, unleashed his venom by proposing a motion: 'That this House has no confidence in the "Board of Six".' His criticism was that the motions proposed for debate were 'poor, as being over the heads of the speakers for admission and as having produced poor debates'. A boy named Kane, who seconded Bolshie's motion, added that the committee had meant well. This was regarded as the 'cruellest of criticisms'.[57]

The Hon. Secretary congratulated Bolshie on having realised so early that his only road to notoriety lay in making himself conspicuous in various 'undesirable roles'.[58] The motion of no confidence was carried 12 votes to 6 and the Committee was forced to resign. The coup was accomplished and Bolshie and his supporters were vindicated. A deadlock then arose as to when and how a new committee was to be elected. A compromise was found and the evening debate proceeded with Bolshie filling the role as Prime Minister to enthusiastic applause.

By the end of 1919 and notwithstanding the daily devotional regimen, Patrick was clearly heavily involved in all manner of school political activities. Religious ideology for the time at least was to take a back seat.

After his first and almost disastrous start to debating Patrick decided it would be better in future debates that he should determine his own style and

[55] *The Stonyhurst Magazine*, December 1919, p 84.
[56] TATF, p 13.
[57] *The Stonyhurst Magazine*, February 1920, p 130.
[58] TATF, p 13.

content, in what he described as a DIY approach. Other factors aside, Bolshie's prices were steep at a penny a minute.[59] Patrick's next chance to debate came on 7 December 1919. It was the second session on the motion 'That in the opinion of the House, the treatment of the Sinn Fein movement by the English Government was totally unjustifiable.' This time Patrick (Belfast) and Bolshie (Sligo) were on the same side. In the meantime Bolshie (unsurprising given the coup) and Sullivan had co-opted the Board of Six. Patrick is recorded as having delivered a 'very good speech', although at times 'sarcastic', which would not have been appreciated by all:[60]

> Of course, England has given Ireland many benefits; for instance, Cromwell, after killing off a third of the population, actually gave Ireland thirty members of Parliament, and as Catholics were not allowed to vote, this merely benefited the English colonists.

Curran gave 'another history of Sinn Fein' – that there were people kept in prison, some dying, on the basis of cases that could not be proved. These sentiments came to resonate deeply and lastingly with Patrick. Miscarriages of justice, including those imposed upon suspected members of the IRA, were to occupy much of his later life.

Those who especially excelled during the regular Sunday night meetings were given an opportunity to participate in 'The Prize Debate' which was held separately. Only a select few were invited to participate and Patrick was one. The motion was 'That in the opinion of this House, England is the enemy of weaker peoples'.

It is clear from the record of the proceedings that as always the boys were encouraged to engage in and did engage in a most robust debate on a no holds barred basis. Accordingly as an example, one boy Carrigan (the member for Tipperary) in introducing the motion referred to 'our Imperial bunglers', identifying Curzon and Milner. He also referred to Rudyard Kipling as a 'third-rate Jingoist'.[61] The commentary on Patrick's speech was as follows:[62]

> P Devlin (Belfast) supported the motion and told the House in cutting tones that it 'perfectly obvious' that our motives were self-interest in 1914. As for Belgium it would have been better if she had been completely overrun than made the battleground of so many engagements. An Empire was bound to be the enemy of smaller peoples since it comprised them or annexed them. It was 'no use reciting History.' Ireland was witness to the truth of the motion.

The magazine's editor was provoked to describe Patrick's speech as 'very fair,' but added 'assertion is not proof'. Patrick did not win a place but his friends Bolshie and Sullivan came in second and third respectively. Nonetheless this was

---

[59] Ibid, pp 12–13.
[60] *The Stonyhurst Magazine*, February 1920, p 132.
[61] *The Stonyhurst Magazine*, April 1920, p 173.
[62] Ibid, p 173.

a step up for Patrick. To be included in this select group in the first place was a huge compliment. It was also a recognition of his talents among a select and talented group of boys and masters who were unflinching in the exercise of their right to say precisely what they thought and were marked down for the slightest imperfection in tone or content. This training ground would obviously prove invaluable for anyone contemplating a career as a 'performer'.

By early 1920, Patrick was debating regularly. He developed a reputation for colourful phrases. On 28 February, in a debate as to whether the 'Liquor Traffic' should be nationalised, he coined such phrases as 'the apologetic herd of the beerage' and 'Pussyfoot and his satellites'. The latter is probably a reference to David Lloyd-George. Coincidentally there had been a temperance movement started in nearby Preston in the nineteenth century which had gathered national attention. In addition, regulations were made under the Defence of the Realm Act in 1914 which severely restricted the hours pubs could open, provided for the sale of watered-down beer and otherwise limited the sale of alcohol to keep the population sober.[63]

On a further occasion, when the question debated was whether the OTC (the Officer Training Corps) should be compulsory, Patrick asserted that to say it was necessary for discipline was 'absurd', as there was plenty of that without 'militarism'. Further, he added, he had come to the college to be educated, not to join the OTC. Patrick was never afraid to offer an opinion; nor were the other boys.[64]

The Syntax Academy comprised a group of boys chosen to be prepared for entrance to Oxford or Cambridge. Patrick also became a member of that group. He had performed well in a play on 25 May that year with C Oddie, prompting the master to comment:[65]

> Swinburne, Longfellow and Kingsley were all parodied to some effect ... The delivery of both speakers was good and clear ... This was followed by an excerpt from the Westminster Play, an amusing burlesque. Devlin's staccato tones as the distressed victim of prices contrasting well with the ex-soldier (W. Drake-Lee), and the superstatesman, admirably acted by P. Rooney.

A little later, in June of that year, Patrick entered the Elocution competition. The judges were three priests. Anyone over 16 might enter for what was called the 'First Division.' Patrick would not turn 16 until the November of the following year but the priests allowed him to enter. However, Francis Sullivan won. Praise was, more or less, heaped upon him. He performed an extract from Richard II. Although successful it was said:[66]

> Sullivan's piece was well chosen and evidently been carefully prepared. He was, however, sometimes inaudible and he had a tendency to hurry over his gestures.

---

[63] Ibid, pp 186–87.
[64] *The Stonyhurst Magazine*, April 1920, p 188.
[65] *The Stonyhurst Magazine*, July 1920, pp 214–16.
[66] Ibid, p 213.

Also at the climax, he seemed to the writer hardly to let himself go sufficiently. Still he well deserved the judges' decision.

On the other hand Patrick was marked down with the following comments:[67]

P Devlin, the next competitor, was badly handicapped by the behaviour of a section of the audience, but he had numerous faults. He was quite inaudible at times, and he spoke much too slowly, giving a disconnected effect. His voice was unvaried through-out and his single gesture became wearisome.

Undaunted, Patrick spoke again at the second session of the competition:[68]

P Devlin having unsuccessfully competed in the First Division, but being by no means disheartened, returned again to the assault with 'Domine Quo Vadis' by William Watson. He was certainly better than before, but his voice is absolutely unsuited for elocution, although he might possibly become a good political speaker. His gestures were ungainly.

On Sunday 13 February 1921 Patrick led for the Ministry on the motion 'this House would welcome the downfall of the Coalition.' Patrick spoke confidently. He told the House that 'All prominent men in England had common sense with-out being brilliant. Lord Robert Cecil was the only man who could possibly steer the country through the next few years. Labour was however sure to get into power some time.' The motion was narrowly defeated, 12 to 11.[69]

Two weeks later on Sunday 27 February, again leading the debate for the Ministry, he argued in support of the motion that 'that classics must form the base for all education' by announcing in a somewhat dissenting tone that he was of the opinion that although classics enlarge and train the intellect, it was useless to go out into the world to 'spout Latin and Greek'.[70]

On Saturday 12 March, the Prize Debate was held. The motion was: 'That in the opinion of this House the Coalition Government is responsible for the present Industrial Unrest'. As usual Patrick represented his constituency of Belfast and went first in support of the motion:[71]

P Devlin opened the debate. He contended that the Government's promises had not been fulfilled, and that unrest was due to this. Constituents had been deceived over and over again. Therefore in this way directly, and indirectly inasmuch as it had failed to do its duty when problems arose the Coalition Government was respon-sible for the present state of affairs. A Liberal Government, he said, would have done better. The Coalition was opportunist, lacked foresight and merely staved off trouble – it failed to grapple with its problems. He instanced faulty housing measures, unemployment doles etc. The Government was reaping the fruit of its insincere policy.

---

[67] Ibid, p 213.
[68] Ibid, p 214.
[69] *The Stonyhurst Magazine*, April 1921, p 453.
[70] Ibid, pp 454–455.
[71] Ibid, pp 425–426.

As always the criticisms were somewhat trenchant and caustic:[72]

> The standard of the debate was lower than we had expected. The speakers were distinct and fluent, but there was little attempt at debating. The spirit of a debate was absent, in fact the spirit aboard that afternoon was dreadful. There was present an air of restraint and even depression that would have paralysed the proceedings at a bankruptcy court.

The criticism did not stop there:[73]

> We can only suppose the speakers, and indeed the whole company for that matter, were overcome by the solemnity of the occasion, for it is incredible this affair represented what usually occurs at Stonyhurst debates. The Club would have died of boredom long ago.

Some of the speakers were castigated for being distressed and embarrassed at the presence of listeners. Hence it was suggested that the Debating Society was not doing its job properly. It was precisely to overcome this sense of nerves and shyness that was one of the ends of the Society.

In May 1921 Patrick performed a prologue he had written together with his brother, Christopher. He was a hit. He 'dealt in a fresh and pleasant style with the external domesticities':[74] 'Devlin gave it forth with plenty of vigour and excellent elocution.' He so impressed some individuals that 'B' wrote a rather long poem, under the pseudonym 'wrong fellow', metrically based on Longfellow's *Hiwatha*:[75]

> First came Devlin (P.) the dauntless,
> Giving forth a noble prologue,
> Full of very ancient History,
> Full of very future History.
> How the galleries were painted,
> How the boiler boils our heads off,
> How electric light is coming.

Patrick had also secured himself the role of Celimene in the school's production of Molière's *Le Misanthrope*.[76] Celimene was of course a young woman who was the object of attention of several men. She was indeed the centre of attention for much of the play. However, his portrayal was not convincing. As the vocal 'B', wrote:[77]

> Next old Molière the comic,
> Should have made us laugh, but didn't
> For they did him how they shouldn't,

[72] Ibid, p 427.
[73] Ibid, p 427.
[74] *The Stonyhurst Magazine*, June 1921, pp 486–87.
[75] Ibid, p 488.
[76] Ibid, p 488.
[77] Ibid, p 488.

With such mournful tones of anguish
With such long pensive faces,
With such drooping sad moustaches,
Like the big clock at 8–20,
All so cui-earthly-bono.
And they spake so soft and lowly,
In such still-small-zephyr voices,
That we really couldn't hear them,
Couldn't hear except their accent,
Which we thought was quite distingué.

Notwithstanding his rather lacklustre attempt at Molière, Patrick won the Dobson prize at the end of the year. It provided for £30 a year for two years.[78]

In the middle of the year Patrick sat for some public examinations, which, if passed, secured entrance to Oxford and Cambridge. In October, he obtained his school certificate with credits in History, Latin and French. He was now also the secretary of the Popinjay Club.[79] During the latter part of 1921 and into 1922, Patrick played far less of a role in debating, although he did enter the Prize Debate on 26 March 1922. The topic was 'That this House would regard the total disappearance of great empires a misfortune'. He shared first prize in the debate, which he delivered in a lighter vein, but with the admonition: 'Devlin's fault in an otherwise first rate effort was the tendency to scold his opponents. He lost a little sympathy and would have done better to have to have retained a more dignified manner.'[80] Further, in his last school year in 1922, Patrick won numerous prizes for religious doctrine, the 'Harry Keating' memorial prize, several essay prizes, the silver prize in Modern Group honours and equal first prize in debating.[81] However what was to eclipse all of this and more was a retreat Patrick went on in October 1921, led by Father Bede Jarrett OP. He was then the Provincial of the Dominican order and had been since 1916. Father Bede Jarrett wrote to a friend in London from Stonyhurst in that autumn:[82]

> You will see that I am pretty nearly 200 miles from London … I am giving a retreat to the boys and you can imagine what this means to my sentimental nature: a boy here as late as 1898 and now back to preach 'em …

Jarrett had joined the order direct from Stonyhurst in 1898 and was 'clothed' at Woodchester priory in the Cotswolds in September that year, when Cyril Jarrett became Brother Bede Jarrett. He would spend the next two years at Woodchester, followed by Hawkesyard Priory, Staffordshire and then Oxford (the first Dominican to study there since Giordano Bruno in the reign of Elizabeth).[83]

---

[78] *The Stonyhurst Magazine*, July 1921, p 575.
[79] *The Stonyhurst Magazine*, October 1921, p 89.
[80] *The Stonyhurst Magazine*, April 1922, p 210.
[81] *The Stonyhurst Magazine*, July 1922, pp 298–99.
[82] Dominican Archives Douai Abbey, Typescript biography of Bede Jarrett, p 30.
[83] Kenneth Wykeham-George, OP and Gervase Mathew, OP, *Bede Jarrett of the Order of Preachers* (London, Blackfriars Publications, 1952, p 21.

In one of his earliest recorded sermons Jarrett is quoted as saying:[84]

> The priest and his divine friend are together surely throughout the day … [W]hen
> alone in his cell, when working among his people, at home and abroad, in the silent
> Church as well as crowded rooms, he has his Friend with him …

Father Jarrett was a perfectionist. He insisted Aristotle should be studied in the original Greek, 'since no man can be an expert on texts he knows only from translations.'

A year before Patrick was born Jarrett went to Oxford. Unlike Patrick, Jarrett excelled at exams. However, like Patrick, he hated them and described them as 'cramping, narrowing and inhuman'.[85] He and Patrick had many other things in common which explains why they bonded so warmly. As seen above, Jarrett was described as a natural Tory with instinctive liberal sympathies. The same could be said of Patrick. Like many of their compatriots, both had also lost relatives in the Great War.

Jarrett was wide-visioned and sophisticated. His skill and charisma were singlehandedly responsible for the expansion of the Dominican order in the United Kingdom. He was as adept at raising benefactions as he was in persuading young men of the benefit of monastic life. He was a man of intense energy who had so much to say that at one point he wrote entirely in abbreviations.[86] He was during his lifetime regarded as the greatest preacher in Catholic England. He was also responsible for founding Blackfriars Priory at Oxford in 1921, formally reinstating the Dominican order at the University for the first time since the Dissolution of the Monasteries under King Henry VIII.

It was then unsurprising that Jarrett had such a profound effect on Patrick and it is equally clear that Jarrett facilitated Patrick being accepted as a novice at Woodchester in September 1922, just prior to Patrick's seventeenth birthday. Patrick started at Woodchester on 14 September of that year. On 19, 20 and 21 September Patrick and six others, including a young man who would come to be known as Brother Ninian, were examined by the Prior 'for clothing and profession'. Each passed. From that moment Patrick became Brother Ignatius Devlin.

Soon after his arrival in October 1922, Brother Ignatius became the chronicler. The function of the monastic chronicler was an important one. His first entry which he made on Sunday 29 October reads:[87]

> We might very properly begin, – indeed we shall do so, – by commenting appropri-
> ately upon the harshness of the times, emphasised by the fact that whereas the large
> tome filled with the labours of our predecessors in office (compared to which this is
> but a scrap of paper purchased in 1915, cost 2 /– this miserable booklet has deprived
> the Consolidated Novitiate Fund of 2/6d.

---

[84] Ibid, p 35.
[85] Ibid, p 23.
[86] Ibid, pp 122–23.
[87] Dominican Archives at Duoai Abbey, Log-book of the Conventual Council Woodchester, beginning 9 October 1909, ending 16 May 1946, entry 29 October 1922 ('Log-book').

Having got this off our mind, we may proceed to inform our gentle readers that on the day above denoted, after an excellent dinner, the brethren repaired to the Brothers common room, there to enjoy the warmth of the fire. Bro. Denis skilfully alleging that he could perform a trick with a cigarette was presented with one. After vespers the novitiate fire was started – badly needed it is becoming bitterly cold. The gases were very bad at matins and the candles on the lectern had to be lighted.

This was a busy time of year for Brother Ignatius. The next day (30 October) was the Feast of the Holy Relics, a now abandoned feast in commemoration 'of holy martyrs and of the other saints whose bodies or relics are preserved in the order's churches'.[88] However Brother Ignatius found time to join two of his brethren in visiting nearby Stroud. He describes having encountered a Captain Clarke 'with his hat rakishly set on one side, and a large expanse of red waistcoat, canvassing for the Conservative candidate in the General Election.' Happily for Captain Clarke, his candidate, a Mr Stanley Tubbs (later Sir Stanley Tubbs, High Sheriff of Gloucestershire) won handsomely.

The very next day was All Hallows' Eve. Brothers Ignatius and Ninian were 'with joy' relieved of manual labour so that they could go to the station to meet a new postulant. Brother Ignatius describes watching 'the postulant making his last meal in the wicked world and toying delicately with his food whilst they were constrained to hold in their empty bellies'. He concluded his entry for the day with the following:[89] 'There was absolution after Vespers, at which the brethren greatly rejoiced, as their lists were three weeks long, and rather formidable.'

The brethren had expected the next day (All Saints' Day) would be one of recreation for the whole of the day, 'from the beginning even unto the end'.[90] With some indignation Brother Ignatius records that this was not a valid assumption to make. The brethren were sent to their rooms for the whole day. What was worse it began to pour with rain. These two events 'caused the brethren to feel somewhat depressed'. The day ended, however, with a good dinner which was served to 'lighten their spirits and weighten their bellies'.[91]

All Souls' Day (2 November 1922) was spent by attending a requiem mass at 10.30am 'followed by procession to the graveyard'. One of his brethren, Brother Quentin, could not complete his 'simple novitiate'; because as he had fought in the war, he needed dispensation.[92]

These chronicles show eagerness to debate and question. The entry for 3 November records Brother Ignatius being late for 'Prime' (a fixed time of prayer at the first hour of daylight).[93] He however records for all to see that he and his colleague had not been called properly, a somewhat audacious move one might think for a budding novice.

---

[88] Log-book, entry 30 October 1922.
[89] Log-book, entry 31 October 1922.
[90] Log-book, entry 1 November 1922.
[91] Ibid.
[92] Log-book, entry 2 November 1922.
[93] Log-book, entry 3 November 1922.

A sense of humour was something Brother Ignatius enjoyed his whole life. His superiors at Woodchester may not have. His entry for Saturday 4 November is representative:[94]

> Bro. Ignatius to-day changed his room to the one next to the bath-room. The water for baths to-day was not hot. Lest we run the risk boring the reader by the oft-repeated tale, in future we shall mention the subject only when it is hot.

It is clear that this life Brother Ignatius had chosen was a course that did and was meant to test his resolve. This was not a career for the faint hearted. Early in his time at Woodchester, Brother Ignatius somewhat poignantly recorded:[95]

> At matins this evening after the versicle, before the lessons of the 2nd nocturn Bro. Ninian caused consternation by suddenly coming out with a loud 'Alleluia', all by himself!! These are the little things which help make life worth living.

The monastic life was not for all. Each candidate was very carefully scrutinised for fitness. Prospective postulants were examined to ensure it could not be said they were, for example, a 'serious minded individual with obliquity of vision', in which case they might return to the 'flesh-pots of Egypt'.[96] But whatever the issue, Brother Ignatius, with his innate love of fun, was concerned a little more with levity than the divine. A further entry for 18 November makes this clear:[97]

> Tonsures were given in the afternoon. Bro. Ninian experimented in hair cutting on Bro. Ignatius' head. It was not a great success as may now be seen by certain peculiarities in the remnants of capillary substance still adhering to the latter brother's cranium.

Reading at mealtimes, an ancient monastic tradition, was very much a part of Woodchester life. The Dominicans, like the Jesuits, were always interested in more than the divine. There would be just as much read about the life of, say, Christopher Columbus as there would be about the lives of the saints. That tradition was one Brother Ignatius was already familiar with from his Stonyhurst days. At Woodchester on special occasions dinner might be followed by cigarettes and coffee in the fathers' common room. These were aspects of monastic life Ignatius found most pleasing. He was gregarious, witty and loved a good argument and the company of like-minded people.

Like the Jesuits, the Dominicans questioned. They, too, were political realists who involved themselves deeply in world affairs. It would not have been uncommon for one of the fathers to have given a morning lecture on Catholic aspects of the General Election. Members of the Order of Preachers were intended to be informed conveyers of the gospel. The views of political candidates were important to the brethren. Mr Stanley Tubbs, the local Conservative candidate,

---

[94] Log-book, entry 4 November 1922.
[95] Log-book, entry 5 November 1922.
[96] Log-book, entry 9 November 1922.
[97] Log-book, entry 18 November 1922.

favoured the Catholic view with respect to compulsory education. Clearly his candidature was sponsored within Woodchester. Some were permitted to go into Stroud to pick up some news of the election. Brother Ignatius announced in his entry for 16 November: 'Mr Tubbs has secured his seat amid jubilation.'[98]

The result of the Provincial visit to Woodchester towards the end of November was regarded by all, but especially Brother Ignatius, as an exciting event. He arrived somewhat late in the evening of 24 November but stayed talking to the brethren for some time.[99]

The very next day, St Catherine's Day, as Brother Ignatius recorded, was also his own birthday. Unashamedly he was provoked to say:[100]

> We take great pleasure in recording the 17th recurrence of the natal day of Brother Ignatius. This was signalised by the victim's providing sundry cakes, fruits, biscuits and divers chocolates & other sorts of sweets which were consumed during recreation.
>
> The Provincial left today for Cambridge. He had just spent the night here on his way from Cardiff.

Brother Ignatius was a natural leader. He had been prominent at Stonyhurst for good reason. It is likely he was better educated, although younger, than most of his brethren. He was also eager to expand his horizons. A sound knowledge of Latin was necessary for a novice to move on to Hawkesyard Priory in Staffordshire to continue his education. He quipped on 28 November:[101]

> Be it known unto all here present that a Latin class consisting of Bros. Ninian, Romuald & Denis, & conducted by Bro. Ignatius has been instituted on the most autocratic lines, & holds its seances four times in the week.

The community, being made up of so many young boys, was often cheered up by the arrival of one of their birthdays, as it frequently coincided with the delivery of some extravagant food parcel, often quantities of chocolates or cakes, which pleased them greatly.

Female company was virtually unknown except if a woman was encountered on a trip into Stroud or, for example, if a holy day led to a visit to a neighbouring convent to celebrate the Feast of the Immaculate Conception.[102]

Preparation for Christmas was a treat. Brother Ignatius and three others were allowed to travel into Stroud for that purpose, although several days were spent on the endeavour. Brother Ignatius characteristically records that:[103] 'Today (December 22) was spent on the congenial task of decorating the Church with the object of making it look as hideous as possible.'

---

[98] Log-book, entry 15 November 1922.
[99] Log-book, entry 24 November 1922.
[100] Log-book, entry 25 November 1922.
[101] Log-book, entry 28 November 1922.
[102] Log-book, entry 8 December 1922.
[103] Log-book, entry 22 December 1922.

Christmas Eve was spent with full rigour concluding in midnight mass.[104] Christmas day commenced with Prime at 7.45am, breakfast at 9am, followed by high mass sung by the Prior at 10.30am. Brother Ignatius and his brethren sat down at 12.30pm to turkey, plum pudding and mince pies in the fathers' common room 'provided by a generous benefaction'. The afternoon was spent at rest with most members 'reclining on their beds with plenty of food & light literature'.[105]

Towards the end of 1922 Brother Ignatius became somewhat sporadic in his chronicling. This trend continued into 1923. Indeed, his entries had started to become decidedly perfunctory and distinctly lacking in humour. A more serious tone descended. January passed somewhat uneventfully. February commenced with Brother Celestine, one of the original six, being 'advised ... that he had not a Dominican vocation'.[106] He was to depart the next day.[107]

On 9 February 1923, Brother Ignatius announced:[108]

And now for the most joyful event of the day to record.

The reader has seen no doubt that the account of the last month or so has been more conspicuous for its gaps than its entries. In view of the present chronicler's manifold activities he is succeeded in this office by Bro. Ninian.

Brother Ignatius thereafter became the librarian as his sole function.[109] Brother Ninian made his concluding remarks for the month with the following quotation from Macbeth:[110] 'Nothing in his life became him like the leaving of it.' He ended that volume of the chronicles with 'Close our unworthy contribution to this monumental record.' This was a sign of things to come, perhaps. Brother Ninian also recorded that his predecessor (Brother Ignatius) had spoilt the last page for February 1923 and that it had to be torn out and recopied.[111]

The records that do exist after this do not mention Brother Ignatius until Monday, 7 May 1923. Brother Ninian simply records:[112]

Though the weather this morning makes one as happy as can be, there is a little note of sadness in the rather sudden termination of the career as a novice of Brother Ignatius Devlin, who left early this morning to seek the vocation predestined for him, having decided, though not till after a long and brave trial of almost eight months, that he is not called to follow our holy Father St. Dominic. We all wish him Godspeed & every blessing although – possibly through his train being unfortunately early – he disappeared without a farewell to any of us. We are now only

---

[104] Log-book, entry 24 December 1922.
[105] Log-book, entry 25 December 1922.
[106] Log-book, entry 2 February 1923.
[107] Log-book, entry 3 February 1923.
[108] Log-book, entry 9 February 1923.
[109] Ibid.
[110] Ibid.
[111] Log-book, postscript.
[112] Log-book, entry 7 May 1923.

five – the remainder of nine and since the lay-brothers have also had considerable changes in strength recently perhaps it would be as well – for the benefit of any future-comer who may be interested to give the present state of the novitiate as a whole.

Brother Ninian's record shows four had left the order between December 1922 and May 1923.[113] Precisely what happened to cause Patrick to leave is a mystery. It seems he never told his children, although he may of course have told Madeleine.

Patrick formally enrolled in the University of Cambridge on 23 October 1923.[114] Undoubtedly in the meantime he would have gone home and discussed his future with his family and of course his benefactor, Uncle George. Patrick gives no insight in his memoir as to this aspect of his life but it is safe to conclude he needed to organise much within a short space of time. Although Uncle George made, it seems, no contribution to school fees, university fell into a very different category. Uncle George was prepared to pay for his entire tuition at Cambridge. However, why Cambridge or, for that matter, Christ's College is not entirely explained. Patrick's other uncle (Theodore, George's brother) had gone to Oxford but there was simply no obvious connection otherwise.

[113] Log-book, entry 7 May 1923.
[114] Student Record Card, Patrick Devlin, University of Cambridge Archives.

2

God's House

A H LLOYD, WRITING in 1934, remarked that most colleges had to be content with one founder, and while some like Gonville and Caius had two, Christ's College had three.[1] Founded originally by a 'plain parochial rector' and priest of St John Zachary in London, William Byngham in 1442, Christ College was re-founded by Henry VI in 1448 and re-founded again by Lady Margaret Beaufort (mother of Henry VII and paternal grandmother of Henry VIII) in 1505. In its first two incarnations it was known as God's House. However, Lady Margaret renamed it Christ's College.

Until the last quarter of the nineteenth century the University of Oxford – described by Catholics of the period as 'one of the two national Protestant universities' – was an Anglican preserve from which preserved Catholics were barred. When the University lifted its ban, excusing religious Tests in 1854 (Cambridge in 1856), the English Catholic hierarchy retained its own ban so that as a general rule (broken only by a dozen or so students at any time) Catholics were still not formally permitted to become members of the University. The Church relented in 1896 after the death of Cardinal Manning, who had been implacably opposed to both centres for Catholics. Immediately the religious orders founded Private Halls in the University, and a chaplaincy was opened for secular students.[2]

In 1899 the Cambridge University Catholic Association was formed and rented rooms for the use of a chaplain and undergraduates. With substantial benefaction from the Duke of Norfolk, premises were permanently acquired in 1924 and a suite of sixteenth century buildings was renamed Fisher House after martyr and chancellor Saint John Fisher (Bishop of Rochester in 1504 executed by order of Henry VIII in 1535).

---

[1] AH Lloyd, *The Early History of Christ's College, Cambridge: Derived from Contemporary Documents* (Cambridge, Cambridge University Press, 2010 [1934]), preface July 1934, chapter 1, p 1. See also John Peile, *University of Cambridge College Histories: Christ's College* (London, FE Robinson & Co, 1900), pp 1, 111, 145 and 294; Nicholas Rogers (ed), *Catholics in Cambridge* (Cambridge, Gracewing, 2003) pp 29–30.

[2] Alberic Stacpoole OSB, 'The Return of the Roman Catholics to Oxford' (May 1986) 67 *New Blackfriars* 221–32, p 222.

Patrick's father had a hand not only in choosing Cambridge, but also in choosing Christ's College. As Patrick puts it somewhat enigmatically:[3]

> It might have been difficult to get at short notice into one of the more fashionable colleges. But I was very content to go to Christ's College which my father had been told would have vacancies for the likes of me.

When first at university, Patrick lived in as he describes it 'small and doleful rooms in Earl Street in the purlieus of Parker's Piece', involving isolated evenings, hot water in a jug for a wash, and a communal bathhouse. That was all to change in his third year with rooms in college, which were relatively palatial.[4]

Cambridge was one of the most significant periods in Patrick's life. Indeed, he unsurprisingly devotes a goodly proportion to it in his memoirs. Most notably it was during his time there that he turned his back on the Catholic faith, but there is not a mention of what passed through his head about the church or religion for that matter.

As Professor Tony Honoré puts it:[5] 'All his life he needed time for reflection. He ceased at Cambridge to be a practising Catholic, though his cast of mind continued in the Jesuit mould.' In his obituary in *The Times*, written by his friend Sir Charles Fletcher-Cook, it is tersely and simply stated that Patrick renounced his Catholic faith at this time.[6]

In some records kept in his old school, Stonyhurst College, the archivist simply records 'Devlin, publicly lapsed.'[7] This was challenged by his wife, Madeleine, who when writing some years after Patrick's death said that his faith returned in the very last days of his life: 'in the interval there was a time of pause'.[8]

Whatever it was that caused the disaffection, Patrick chose not to share it with the reader of his memoirs. If he shared it with Madeleine, she never betrayed his confidence. He did not, it seems, share his reasons with his children. None of them were brought up in the Catholic faith, although a number of the children, along with Madeleine, later converted.

Patrick thrived at Cambridge. His examination results would never match his success in the Union. From the very outset he actively sought out debating opportunities. His studies were never graced with the enthusiasm and vigour he applied to his opportunities to perform.

Unsurprisingly, he was instantly attracted to the Union debates. His father had paid 7 ½ guineas for life membership of the Union, which entitled him to use its premises and of course to attend the debates.[9]

---

[3] TATF, p 42.

[4] Ibid, p 53.

[5] Tony Honoré, 'Devlin, Patrick Arthur, Baron Devlin 1905–1992' in HCG Matthew and B Harrison (eds), *Oxford Dictionary of Biography*, revised edn (Oxford, Oxford University Press, 2004) p X.

[6] *The Times*, 11 August 1992, p 13.

[7] Handwritten notes kept within the Patrick Devlin file, *Stonyhurst Archives*.

[8] Portion of a letter from Madeleine Devlin to the Stonyhurst archivist at or after Patrick's death, Patrick Devlin file, *Stonyhurst Archives*.

[9] TATF, p 42.

In his first term he made several attempts to speak but did not succeed. When visiting Aberdeen for Christmas vacation in 1923, at a party he met a young woman who told him she had a cousin at Cambridge, by the name of RA Butler (otherwise known as 'Rab') who had become the Secretary of the Union in the Michaelmas term of 1923. Rab was at Pembroke College and was an outstanding scholar.[10]

After Christmas in early 1924, Patrick managed to meet Rab for tea. As he describes it in his memoirs, the meeting was the beginning of a friendship which lasted until Rab's death in 1982. Through Rab came an introduction to his uncle Sir Geoffrey Butler, a fellow of Corpus Christi College and junior burgess for the University in the House of Commons. These connections opened doors for Patrick which, once opened at Cambridge, remained so through much of his life.

While at Cambridge Patrick became very firm friends with the Butlers, who were as close as one could get to Cambridge aristocracy. The family had attended the University for generations. Sir Geoffrey would remain Patrick's mentor until his untimely death at the age 42 in 1929. Rab became a close friend of Patrick's while at Cambridge. He preceded Patrick as President of the Union, holding office in 1924 (Sir Geoffrey had also been President in 1914) and they worked together in the University Conservative Association.[11] He was also the first of Patrick's friends to marry. He and his wife, Sydney, an heiress to the Courtauld textile fortune, married on 20 April 1926 at St Mary Abchurch, a charming Wren church off Cannon Street. His uncle Geoffrey was his best man. Rab's father-in-law made Rab's future security a certainty by awarding him a private income of £5,000 a year after tax for life.[12]

Although Rab would enter into Parliament in 1929 and enjoy a successful political career, he had a somewhat fragile period just prior to his marriage. Perhaps because he had so much on his plate – lecturing at Cambridge, political life and marriage – he had a breakdown. Patrick was one person he could rely upon and the two would often spend time together walking, for example, on Dartmoor.[13]

Amongst other things, Rab's uncle Sir Geoffrey was a talent scout for the Conservative Party. Patrick fitted the bill admirably. Thoughtfully pragmatic, Sir Geoffrey was part of a family line of Cambridge dons dating from 1794 until the end of Rab's time as Master of Trinity in 1978. Like his nephew Rab, Sir Geoffrey had a glittering undergraduate career.[14] A series of lectures given by him in 1914 at the University of Pennsylvania were collected in his book entitled

[10] Ibid, p 43.
[11] Percy Cradock, *Recollections of the Cambridge Union 1815–1939* (Cambridge, Bowes & Bowes, 1953), pp 184–87.
[12] TATF, p 58.
[13] Ibid, p 58.
[14] Stephen Parkinson (Director of the History Conservative Group), 'Sir Geoffrey Butler and the Tory Tradition' (Autumn 2014) II(2) *Conservative History Journal* 18–26.

The Tory Tradition.[15] Sir Geoffrey died prematurely from cancer in 1929 but not before he had given Patrick (amongst others) considerable assistance.

Patrick described Sir Geoffrey as the 'godfather of all our careers' and remembers him as a man of great kindness and geniality. Each shared a singular destiny. Each was a Conservative and each had, or would, become in turn President of the Union. However one of the most significant consequences of Sir Geoffrey's benefaction arose from the lack of law fellows at Christ's College. Sir Geoffrey promptly arranged for Patrick to be supervised by Arthur Goodhart.[16] This was to provide Patrick with yet another powerful connection and lifelong friend.

In the first half of 1924, Patrick was making considerable progress at the College debating society. Somewhat quaintly he confesses in his memoir that some of the people he met during the debates were 'Socialists'.[17] Indeed, he says it was the first time he had met anyone of that persuasion. Notwithstanding that their respective politics were diametrically opposed, he seems to have enjoyed their company.

By now Patrick had made a sufficiently good impression to be, as he describes it, 'put on the paper at the Union';[18] that is, he was finally given an opportunity to speak. He would often be joined by Michael Ramsey, later to become Bishop of Durham and Archbishop of Canterbury. Even at this early stage, he regarded himself as a card-carrying Conservative.[19] *The Cambridge Review* records his first debate as having occurred on Tuesday 12 February 1924. It said 'Mr Devlin made a maiden speech which gave promise of debating brilliance'.[20]

A few weeks later on 26 February, Patrick spoke again.[21] On this occasion *The Cambridge Review* spoke of Patrick's 'remarkable appearance' during which he spoke entirely without notes, and concluded that he was a 'great discovery'. Further plaudits followed him during 1924. By the middle of the year he was being described as one of the best debaters in the House, and from time to time as being in 'superb vein'.[22]

Michael Ramsey, writing in 1953, remarked:[23]

A politically minded freshman arriving in Cambridge in October 1923 found himself in the early stages of a period of vigorous party polemics. The fall of the Lloyd George Coalition in 1922 had opened the way for a triangular party warfare, and

---

[15] Geoffrey Butler, *The Tory Tradition. Bolingbrohe, Burke, Disraeli, Salisbury* (London, Conservative Political Centre, 1957 [1914 John Murray Press]).

[16] TATF, p 56.

[17] Ibid, p 43.

[18] Ibid, p 43.

[19] Ibid, p 44.

[20] 'The Union Society', (1923–27) XLV–XLVIII *The Cambridge Review*, 12 February 1924.

[21] 'The Union Society', (1923–27) XLV–XLVIII *The Cambridge Review*, 26 February 1924.

[22] 'The Union Society', (1923–27) XLV–XLVIII *The Cambridge Review*, 3 June 1923.

[23] Percy Cradock, *Recollections of the Cambridge Union, 1815–1939* (Cambridge, Bowes & Bowes, 1953), p 122.

the unusual circumstance of general elections in three successive years kept interest at a high pitch. At the Union the domination of men who had served in the Great War had recently ended and the first 'post war' generation was coming into its own. Within it were debaters destined to hold high office in public life. The freshman felt that he found in the Union a microcosm of national politics and not a little of its heat and fervour ... Conservatism was numerically the strongest force and in the middle nineteen twenties it had perhaps the ablest speakers.

In the same reminiscence, he spoke of Patrick in comparison to Rab Butler and GW Lloyd (Union President, Lent term 1925):[24]

Neither Butler nor Lloyd however had his rapier-like agility in meeting, destroying and ridiculing a preceding speaker which Patrick Devlin, now Mr Justice Devlin, possessed. Devlin of Christ's outstripped all rivals in the oratory of the advocate: he was the F.E. Smith of the Union in the 1920's.

In his autobiography published much later in 1971, Rab heaped similar praise upon Patrick:[25] 'Conservatism at the Union was strong, and the debates were lively. Patrick Devlin, then as now, was the wittiest extempore speaker.'

The debates at the Union not only provided ample opportunity for Patrick's performances but brought him in contact with important and influential people. The debates gave him opportunities to pitch his abilities not only against the best at Cambridge but also those from Oxford. On occasions politicians attended the debates and participated in them. Memorably, on 27 April 1925, Patrick led the debate against, amongst others, Sir Patrick Hastings KC MP. A Boer War veteran, Hastings was a prominent barrister. Regarded as one of the best cross-examiners of his day, he was appointed briefly Attorney-General in 1924 by newly-elected Labour Prime Minister, Ramsay Macdonald.

At the time of the debate Hastings was the Attorney-General and aged 45. He was a seasoned and experienced advocate. Patrick was 20 years old. He was untroubled and gave no quarter. This was the opening debate of the term and it was described in *The Cambridge Review* as 'enthralling'. The two Patricks' speeches were delivered to a packed House and were described as 'arresting, able, witty and wise'.[26]

Sir Patrick complimented the young Patrick by saying that if the motion being debated was to take place in the House of Commons there would not be nearly so many people in the smoking rooms as there were. *The Cambridge Review* recorded that Patrick's speech was 'clever' and that Sir Patrick's speech was delivered 'practically devoid of bitterness and spleen'.[27]

---

[24] Ibid, p 123.
[25] Lord Butler, *The Art of the Possible, the Memoirs of Lord Butler* (London, Hamish Hamilton, 1971), p 16.
[26] 'The Union Society', (1923–1927) XLV–XLVIII *The Cambridge Review*, 27 April 1925, p 365.
[27] Ibid, p 365.

All of these events did Patrick's political ambition, such as it was, no harm at all. However, in June 1925 when Patrick stood for Secretary of the Union, he was narrowly defeated by HGG Herklots of Trinity Hall.[28]

It was in 1925 that Patrick was first exposed to debaters from the United States. In mid-September of that year, Patrick joined a team of students who visited the United States to represent Cambridge in a number of debating events against universities there. Prior to him leaving, and as a sign of increasing friendship between the two, Rab Butler invited Patrick to stay with him at the Ben Wyvis Hotel at Strathpeffer Spa for some light-hearted trawling on the loch, some tennis and long walks.

Patrick sailed to New York on the RMS *Laconia*, a one class boat on a voyage which took seven days.[29] Oxford made the journey around the same time as Cambridge. Each time, the respective universities would alternate between the East Coast and the Mid-West. In 1925 it was Cambridge's turn to take the Mid-West. From New York, Patrick and the delegation headed for Detroit. Patrick did not find the Americans he met to his liking. Indeed he found them quite rough, unmannered, surly and uncongenial.[30]

Debating was taken very seriously in the United States.[31] As Patrick explains in his memoirs, the debate was a contest which had to be trained for and won. The coaches of the team had a working card index system and whenever a point was raised outside the prepared speeches the coach would pull out a card which contained the answer. As the tour progressed Patrick's somewhat flippant and light-hearted style became well-known. He detected that the Americans relaxed somewhat.

During the time Patrick was away, he discovered two things. First, Michael Ramsey was entirely eccentric. On one occasion he had to be saved by one of his fellow debaters because in somewhat absent-minded fashion he was seen to be wandering out into the midst of heavy traffic without any sense of danger. He would frequently speak to himself and was a positive danger when driving a car. Patrick was later to describe Ramsey in the following terms:[32]

> He was not clever or epigrammatic in the Union manner and only occasionally witty, but always spoke as though he had something to contribute to the debate. He projected himself as a man it would be worth listening to. He spoke weightily – the words deliberately pronounced and, as it were, lay on the table. He left behind the impression – but not as if he had ever meant to say it – that anyone who disagreed with him must really be rather stupid.

---

[28] Percy Cradock, *Recollections of the Cambridge Union, 1815–1939* (Cambridge, Bowes & Bowes, 1953), p 186.

[29] TATF, 50.

[30] Ibid, p 51.

[31] Ibid, p 51.

[32] Owen Chadwick, *Michael Ramsey, a Life* (Oxford, Clarendon Press, 1990), p 18.

However, the visit to the United States in 1925 had a much more profound effect upon Patrick. It may have provoked his lifelong interest in President Woodrow Wilson. Indeed he was later to publish in 1974 a large study on Wilson entitled *Too Proud to Fight*. Patrick ruminated over the work for almost 20 years.

Prior to his going to the United States at Easter 1925, Patrick told his father that he wanted to go to the Bar. To achieve this Patrick had to spend a fourth year at Cambridge.[33] When considering Patrick's lacklustre examination results, his prominence in the Union and his representing Cambridge in the United States, the question was whether Uncle George would fund it.

In *The Cambridge Review* of 17 November 1925,[34] there was an announcement that on 1 December, the Union Society would be giving itself over 'either to pessimism or flippancy'. The motion was 'That this House, believing the prosperity of England to be on the wane, has grave fears for the happiness of its grandchildren'. It forecast a debate between two sides, one represented by Michael Ramsey and the opposition by Patrick. Readers were informed that both were presently on the high seas on the way back from the United States and were both eager for the fray. Rab Butler would also speak, along with Viscount Younger of Leckie. The motion concerned the waning prosperity of England. Ramsey spoke of sterile architecture and the loss of creative ability. Notwithstanding its tone, Ramsey's speech was described as 'delightful'. Patrick commenced his speech by attacking Ramsey. *The Cambridge Review* commented that it was 'refreshing to hear his effective terms again' and that 'Mr Devlin was at his very best, which is saying a great deal'.[35]

Early in 1926, Michael Ramsey was elected President of the Union unopposed. Patrick was elected Secretary by a healthy margin of 330 to 234. A number of 'very clever speeches later', Patrick was elected unopposed to the position of Vice President of the Union.[36]

Patrick never fared well in examinations at Cambridge, although he did spend much of the long vacation in mid-1925 reading through a 'load of law books' which he had acquired at half price from a friend David Hardman (the first Socialist President of the Union, who entered Parliament in 1945). Patrick began his reading with *Salmond on Jurisprudence* and 'enjoyed it enormously'.[37] Patrick posed the question:[38]

> But how does one set about preparing for an examination? I have no idea now and I had none then. What I lacked was an object. At the bar when I knew that I had on the next day or the following week to make an opening speech or cross-examine a

---

[33] TATF, p 49.

[34] *The Cambridge Review*, 17 November 1925, p 36.

[35] *The Cambridge Review*, 1 December 1925.

[36] Percy Cradock *Recollections of the Cambridge Union, 1815–1939* (Cambridge, Bowes & Bowes, 1953), p 186.

[37] TATF, p 50.

[38] Ibid, p 69.

witness, I never had any difficulty in absorbing the necessary material, whether it was fact or law. Likewise on the bench if I had to deliver an unreserved judgment or a summing up. What makes that sort of work easy and interesting is that every bit of material as it comes in is either given an immediate place on the structure or else asked to take a back seat in the waiting room as there may be a short delay until a vacancy is found. If it is not wanted, it goes into limbo where its existence may or may not be forgotten.

Patrick wrote beautifully all of his life. His subtle and luminous intellect was ever present. On his feet in the middle of a debate he could produce exceptional repartee and witticisms. On occasions, however, without any malice intended, he could be extraordinarily cruel and insensitive. Perhaps no one could have been more supportive and generous toward Patrick than Arthur Goodhart, and yet in his memoirs he says of him that 'He was as ugly as he was good and as generous and as witty as he was learned.'[39] This type of unfiltered remark is not uncommon on Patrick's part and this patron and lifelong supporter was not the only person to come in for such treatment. Patrick had no need, given his privileged life, to resort to such scarifying descriptions. His cleverness in this regard could perhaps best be described as a legacy of the many cutting remarks made about the efforts of small boys, delivered by the odd scornful and tormented Jesuit.

Patrick described his political philosophy as follows:[40] 'While I should always have recoiled as far from the right wing of the right party as from the left wing of the left, fundamentally I believed, then and now, in individualism rather than collectivism.'

Patrick became secretary of the University Conservative Association whilst at Cambridge.[41] In May 1926, during a debate on compulsory free education, Patrick allowed his personal views to intrude. He spoke of the 'absurd idealisation of the working man'. Stridently he asserted that free education stifled individual enterprise 'at its very roots'. People, he opined 'should be taught to read and write but no further unless they show a marked attitude to learning'. This prompted *The Cambridge Review* to remark the Vice-President was as effective and provocative as ever, 'But he is suffering from a disease of personal explanation'.[42]

In July 1926 Patrick published an article in *The English Review* entitled 'The Outlook of a Young Conservative'.[43] He pronounced somewhat pompously that 'Conservatism is not a creed instantaneously attractive to young men.' He went on:[44]

For youth will not tolerate the conservatism that is the conservation of decay, the prejudiced obstruction of all progress, or the preservation upon a care-and-maintenance

[39] Ibid, p 56.
[40] Ibid, p 54.
[41] Ibid, p 57.
[42] 'The Union Society', (1923–1927) XLV–XLVIII *The Cambridge Review*, 25 May 1926.
[43] Patrick Devlin, 'The Outlook of a Young Conservative', *The English Review*, July 1926, p 119.
[44] Ibid, p 120.

basis of institutions that have long since served their time. Rather it demands the conservatism that does not blind itself to changing needs, that offers to the onrushing forces of reform, not an unyielding resistance, but a slow and discriminating check, and that selects from those forces the sounder elements, formulates them, and harmonizes them with the traditions of the past.

The article went on to announce the collapse of the League of Nations and to state that England's continued participation in it was 'prejudicial to the interests of the British Empire'. As a Brexiteer way ahead of his time, Patrick announced:[45]

The collapse of the League of Nations releases us from the only obligation to untangle ourselves with European affairs. Our interests are bound up primarily with those of our Dominions and their markets are more valuable to us than those of Europe.

He then moved seamlessly as part of his sermon to a restatement of more traditional Conservative dogma. He declared:[46]

The connection of the Tory party with an active policy of social reform began in the middle of the last century in opposition to the laissez faire school, in whose grip the Liberal party was held. This connection fulfilled a useful purpose because the conditions of the time were not such as could well be let alone. But the kernel of the Benthamite creed, which is individualism, is good, and to the end of time remains good. It is the duty of a government then not on the one hand to leave existing evils to right themselves, nor on the other to arrange every detail according to its own ideas of perfection, but so to order the conditions of its time as to give the fullest and fairest scope to individualism. The time is opportune for the Conservative party to stand firmly by this principle for its opponent during the century will not be the old-time Liberalism but the new Socialism which must be fought with the weapon of individual enterprise.

He ended, 'Imperialism and Individualism should be the two essentials of the Conservative theory.'[47]

At the age of 21, with Stanley Baldwin and the Conservatives well and truly in power, and with Sir Geoffrey Butler cheering from the sidelines, this was as good a time as any to emphasise the Tories' virtues. Patrick would not have been the only young man inspired to think and write about politics.

Patrick was fortunate in that the affairs of the Union provided him with ample opportunity to meet important, interesting, and hugely stimulating people, including Stanley Baldwin himself, FE Smith, Winston Churchill and other prominent politicians. At the dinner at which Churchill attended as guest of honour Patrick proposed a toast to his health. Patrick records in his memoir that his speech was of 'Churchillian magnificence' which was recorded in great length in the *Cambridge Daily News*. Patrick noted that the other speeches went

---

[45] Ibid, p 121.
[46] Ibid, p 122.
[47] Ibid, p 123.

well and 'Mr Churchill noted on the back of his menu card one or two phrases from mine'.[48] He observed that of all the great men he met Mr Baldwin was, with one exception, the most impressive 'because he made no effort to impress'. However, Lloyd George was the true exception because, as Patrick explains, 'he was more than a great man, he was a magnetic force who, with the look, a handshake or a word, could lift you off the ground and you could think of nothing else until you can do it again'.[49]

In the meantime, Patrick began submitting racy contributions to *The Sunday Times*.[50] In one article he pithily commented on the General Strike of 1926 which lasted 10 days. The strike was called by the General Council of the Trades Union Congress. Patrick describes it as having devastated Trinity Term. Many people volunteered to perform various tasks to keep the country going. As Vice President of the Union, Patrick was given what he describes as a 'lowly position' which called upon him to dispense encouragement by telephone to the 'mayors of the province'.[51]

A news service was set up in the debating hall in order to meet the crisis. To Patrick's observation Michael Ramsey detached himself from the national effort.[52] The Liberals, of which Ramsey was one, were divided on the issue. Patrick thought Ramsey put social issues ahead of political ones. It came as no surprise later in the year for Patrick to hear that Ramsey was going into the Church.

In his *Sunday Times* article Patrick describes how 2,200 undergraduates left Cambridge during the strike to volunteer in the community. With a heavy odour of sarcasm he describes how 'Lecture rooms were almost deserted. Indignant professors who had secretly hoped to escape their duties, found themselves forced to communicate their words of wisdom to a listless attendance of two or three.'[53]

He describes 'earnest members' of the University:

> whose patriotism outran their knowledge of undergraduate psychology and made powerful speeches about British grit and the determination of the bulldog breed and applauded the gallant action of these youths in sacrificing their studies for the cause of King and country.

After the dramatic termination of the Great Strike, normal life resumed at the University and the undergraduates began to realise that examinations were still

---

[48] TATF, p 59.
[49] Ibid, p 45.
[50] Patrick Devlin, 'The "Varsities" and the Strike – Cambridge Contributes 2,200 workers', *Sunday Times*, 23 May 1926.
[51] TATF, p 59.
[52] Ibid, p 59.
[53] Patrick Devlin, 'The "Varsities" and the Strike – Cambridge Contributes 2,200 workers', *Sunday Times*, 23 May 1926.

in prospect, however the 'noble two thousand two hundred' found themselves 'once more at a University fit for heroes to live in'.[54]

It is not suggested Patrick delighted in the defeat of the miners in the General Strike. He was fascinated in the political dynamics and had sought, in anticipation of becoming President of the Union, to organise a topical debate among prominent participants on the very issue. Indeed he had invited a number of people, including AJ Cook, the secretary of the Miners' Association, who had been regarded as the 'Moscow disciple' and the director of the strike.[55] A number of persons in Cambridge were very concerned a visit by Cook could lead to rioting.

The Senior Proctor required Patrick to attend upon him in his rooms at Emmanuel College. When being quizzed by the Proctor about arrangements, Patrick decided that 'silence that stops short of "mute of malice" is in this situation always the golden rule.' The Proctor placed pressure on Patrick to reconsider the invitation. Luckily Cook, quite by coincidence, wrote to say that it had become impossible for him to fulfil his engagement.[56] Crisis averted.

Walter Citrine, the Secretary of the Trades Union Congress, accepted the invitation to fill Cook's place. As Patrick puts it, 'his magnificent speech was possibly responsible for the size of the minority vote'. The motion which Patrick devised was 'that the power of Trade Unionism in England is increasing and should be diminished'. It was defeated 378 votes to 237.[57]

In Michaelmas term 1926, Patrick was elected President of the Union. This brought more debates and more important and influential people into Patrick's life. He says Churchill had told him 'You should go into politics. Fight an East End constituency and learn to fight with your fists as well as your mouth'.[58] To the Law's eternal good fortune, Patrick rejected that idea. In October, *The Granta* published a full-page article on him with a rather stern photo. Notwithstanding the typical undergraduate hyperbole and pretentiousness it makes for insightful and humorous reading. He is described as a gifted public speaker and consummate organiser, who still 'devotes long hours to tennis, golf, badminton and squash, where his vigour is more noticeable than his skill.' The writer concludes with a gush:[59]

> Despite the fact that his name betrays him as obviously Irish there is very little of the Celt in him except perhaps that he has a passion for music. His political creed is ultra-Conservative, though defended by reason and not by prejudice. His speeches are never emotional (other authorities say his emotions are never speechless), though they suggest the possibility that on occasion he might be roused from his even tones. His manner is courteously distant to the public, charming and unaffected to his

[54] Ibid.
[55] TATF, pp 60–61.
[56] Ibid, p 66.
[57] Ibid, p 64.
[58] Ibid, p 67.
[59] 'Those in Authority', *The Granta*, 15 October 1926, p 17.

friends, and almost serious to his intimates. He has a wealth of amusing conversation. Academically he is not brilliant – he steers his course between the ostentatious first and the vulgar third – but a sanity of outlook, an attractive personality and a force of character ensure that Clotho will spin his thread in the better class of web.

By early November 1926, his contacts secured him entry to a number of interesting events. For example an invitation to the Marquess of Londonderry, a very rich coalmine owner, to speak at the Union led to an invitation to a cocktail party for a couple of hundred held at Londonderry House as guest of his Lordship, together with an intimate luncheon the next day for a dozen or so.[60]

On 25 November, Patrick turned 21. He was busy organising debates. Mr Brown, the Chief Clerk of the Union, thought it appropriate that the committee room should be made available for dinner in celebration. This was the first in his life of many enjoyable discussions about what to eat and drink. The steward from Peterhouse, AT Bartholomew, made recommendations on the wine. The champagne Duc de Montebello, 1911, favoured by King Edward VII, was recommended. Fourteen of his best friends (not named in his memoir) attended. The dinner was hosted by his uncle Theodore (Uncle George's brother) who had attended Oxford. Uncle Theodore tipped in £15 which 'just about paid for the dinner'.[61]

Whilst not neglecting his studies, Patrick had put off any serious study for his exams until he ended his term as President. That may have been a mistake. Patrick was clearly at his best when he was in control. In exams, he was not, which may explain why he never was very successful academically. Another explanation, which did not occur to him, was that his handwriting was illegible in part.[62] He was awarded a lower second class pass for Part I of his tripos in History, and the same in Law.

However, Patrick acknowledges he owed a great deal to Arthur Goodhart, then a fellow of Corpus Christi College. Goodhart was a graduate of Yale and Cambridge and an enthusiastic anglophile. Patrick quipped that Goodhart 'made learning a pleasure, although his presentation in lectures and tutorials was unexciting, unlike his private conversations and/or after dinner speeches, which were witty and nimble'.[63]

In the end, Patrick's fourth year at Cambridge was made possible through the loyalty and generosity of his Uncle George. Although he was unable to brag about his examination results, his attainment of the Presidency of the Union was something of which his uncle was rightly very proud. As to his results, although Patrick was bitterly disappointed, Uncle George neither 'commiserated nor reproached'. He did demand that Patrick explain what his future plans were. He was concerned to know whether Patrick had any debts. Patrick told

---

[60] TATF, p 67.
[61] Ibid, p 68.
[62] Ibid, p 64.
[63] Ibid, p 70.

his uncle that he planned to spend a year or so in a solicitor's office in London; he was unsure what he would earn but he did plan eventually to go to the bar. Uncle George agreed to give him an allowance of £200 per year. If Patrick made any earnings, he could keep them.[64]

Patrick had no family members in the law, but he had been greatly stimulated and inspired by Arthur Goodhart. What he enjoyed most was debating. In that context the law was a logical choice. As he says in his memoir: 'Between me and the service of the law there was no pledge.' He felt no particular calling for the legal profession. He chose it in the end because he thought it would be rewarding intellectually and hopefully financially, as 'there is no pleasure except in a life of occupation'. And so 1927 was spent completing his studies at Cambridge. Patrick was crystal clear about one thing, and that was whatever his occupation, it had to be something from which one obtained the greatest enjoyment in life.[65]

In one sense Patrick was happy to be leaving Cambridge. He told Rab Butler in a letter on 15 July 1927:[66]

> You are right as usual about my exam: I have realised that here to my cost. The theories and excuses that you will have read in my last letter were written in the first moment of pique, the truth of the matter is that I cannot do exams. The first rush of indignation after I had arrived here I did 10 hours work per diem for five days and since then have not looked at a book. I've employed my time since then instead, – pride and an empty purse combined to keep me here! – am starting to write a novel in case I'm someday of need. I might be able to part with it for a mess of pottage. The exam is on Tuesday and I shall slink through it ingloriously and blame the heat! But I liked your metaphors of seising viewpoints and sparring light-armoured into the fray: they are very consoling.

Patrick graduated in late 1927. At that time Arthur Ponsonby, who had joined the Labour party prior to its election win in 1922, was member for the Brightside division of Sheffield. In 1927 he ran a significant Peace Letter campaign against British preparations for a new war. Patrick wrote an article for *The English Review* entitled 'Pacifist Propaganda', published in September 1927.[67] Prior to its publication Patrick had obviously had words with Rab about the topic. In the same July letter he told Rab:[68]

> About my 'unreal and childlike' views on war (!). I do not agree with you. I belong to the type of person who is <u>most</u> entitled to have views on war, and whose views on war are really important. Old men of 60 maybe more experienced but if the war were declared to-morrow, it is I who would be expected to fight and not they. To expect that of me and yet to deny me a hearing for my views on the grounds that they are unreal

---

[64] Ibid, p 70.
[65] Ibid, p 73.
[66] Letter from Devlin to Butler, 15 July 1927, CPP/RAB/1/1 Bodleian Library Archives.
[67] Patrick Devlin, 'Pacifist Propaganda', *The English Review*, September 1927, p 292.
[68] Letter from Devlin to Butler, 15 July 1927, CPP/RAB/1/1 Bodleian Library Archives.

and childish, is unfair. Anyway, I've written a very profound article on the matter which is being published in the 'English Review' and when you come back, I shall get Sydney to read it to you – a paragraph per night before you go to bed.

Patrick's article was an outright assault on Ponsonby. It spoke of the boast by Ponsonby that he had collected 150,000 pledges from men pledging that in the event of war they would not fight. Patrick's powerful argument was that it is easy for the pacifist to say war was bad, but the pacifist must say that it is always so. This, said Patrick, does not allow for self-defence. He explained:[69]

> To go to war is bad, but an act in itself bad may be justified by circumstances. To kill a man is bad; more often than not it is murder; but on the field of battle it is sometimes known as heroism, and on the scaffold it is called justice. The pacifist must therefore, prove, not merely that war is generally unjustifiable, but that it is always so.

Patrick went on to point out that it was impossible logically to deny the right of a country to defend itself:[70]

> An evil, no matter what its magnitude, when it is inevitable, must be faced. Confronted by a determined aggressor, a country has no alternative but to fight: no permanent peace and security are achieved by submitting to aggression, even were it right that they should be achieved at the cost of liberty.

Patrick concluded by announcing 'pacifism bears no relation to any intelligent conception of international peace.'[71]

Of course, Ponsonby was forced to reply. After all, that was the point of Patrick's provocation. He accused Patrick of retaining and deploying 'some of the fallacies and delusions which the war tradition has created.' He effectively accused Patrick of being simplistic in espousing the notion that there could ever be an unexpected attack from an aggressor and further, Patrick had presented a 'clumsy representation of the case, this crude vilification of the enemy, is palpably absurd, and quite irrational'.[72] In addition, Ponsonby rightly pointed out that the so-called defensive warfare was the only form of warfare which 'Mr Devlin justifies'. He continued:[73]

> ... and as I am convinced that he is basing his case upon a fallacy, I am quite prepared to accept the challenge and declare that warfare in these days can never be justifiable and refuse to admit the validity of any war.

Ponsonby had taken the bait as would, many years later, Herbert Hart.

---

[69] Patrick Devlin, 'Pacifist Propaganda', *The English Review*, September 1927, p 293.
[70] Ibid, p 295.
[71] Ibid, p 295.
[72] Arthur Ponsonby, 'Pacifist Propaganda – A Reply', *The English Review*, November 1927, pp 552–53.
[73] Ibid, p 554.

Patrick of course had the right of reply. In a further article he exercised it lavishly in December 1927. In a manner reminiscent of the Union, Patrick sarcastically purred:[74]

> Personally I must express my gratitude to Mr Ponsonby for the kindly and considered way in which he dealt with arguments I raised; but his readers, I think must have cherished a regret that, in his anxiety to inform his tone with the practice of his pacifist principles, he did not come to grips with the subject quite as adequately as otherwise he would have done.

Fresh from his recent in depth study of the subject he quoted from *Salmond on Jurisprudence*.[75] He systematically demolished Ponsonby's arguments one by one, so at the end of which the reader would inevitably come to the clear view Ponsonby was not a patriot, and further he was downright paranoid as much as he was naive. Ponsonby did not, as far as one can tell, come back for more. Perhaps he had realised he had been outclassed by a bumptious 22 year old. Here he was a member of the House of Commons sucked into a debate with someone barely out of university. On the other hand, if Patrick was making a job application for the Conservative party, he could not have done a better job. Either way, Patrick was ready to go to the Bar.

---

[74] Patrick Devlin, 'Pacifist Propaganda II', *The English Review*, December 1927, p 667.
[75] Ibid, p 688.

3

The Early Years in the Law

ATRICK LEFT CAMBRIDGE with possibly as many advantages as one could enjoy except for a first class degree. However he had made good and powerful friends, he had achieved the Presidency of the Union, he had been published in some important quarters and he still had Uncle George as his patron. Next step, the Bar.

In 1927 when Patrick went to London he assessed quite correctly that he was in financial difficulty. Uncle George had provided him with a fixed sum of £200 a year but that was not really enough. Sir Geoffrey Butler suggested he speak to Arthur Goodhart about his financial predicament. Goodhart was a graduate of Yale and Cambridge and an enthusiastic anglophile. Clearly Sir Geoffrey knew not only that Goodhart was generous but also that he held Patrick in high regard. Fortunately as it turned out, Goodhart was not the least concerned about Patrick's examination results. He was confident Patrick had a future so much so that he was one of the people who are urged Patrick to go to the Bar. Nonetheless, Patrick approached Goodhart with his dilemma. Goodhart had no hesitation in offering Patrick £200 a year for two years to assist Goodhart with proofing articles for the *Law Quarterly Review*, of which Goodhart was editor.[1] It did not take Patrick long to accept.

He wrote to Goodhart on 28 April 1927 in an understandably deferential fashion:[2]

> Dear Mr Goodhart,
>
> This is just a line to express more adequately than I was able to do yesterday my great gratitude for your exceedingly kind offer. It completely transforms my outlook on the future and quite apart from anything else, I am most encouraged by what you think about my prospects. I hope to see you again soon after your return from America in July and in the interval shall talk everything over with Sir Geoffrey.

Living in London would be expensive but it had to be addressed. For a time he lived in unfurnished rooms in Half Moon Street. Up several flights of stairs was a tiny flat, comprising a small sitting room, bedroom and bathroom, all for £4 a week. Having visited a few of the antique shops in nearby Praed Street, he was

---

[1] TATF, p 75.
[2] Letter from Devlin to Goodhart, 28 April 1927, papers of Arthur Lehman Goodhart, Bodleian Library Archives, University of Oxford, folio 62.

able to buy quite cheaply some period reproduction furniture. For a few months Patrick was happy there. The couple who owned the house were supposed to supply meals at a reasonable charge, but the man found climbing four flights of stairs to deliver meals an unattractive proposition and the woman of the household was an appalling cook.[3]

Notwithstanding the support of Uncle George and Arthur Goodhart, Patrick was still having trouble making ends meet. Indeed he resorted to borrowing from Rab Butler. On Boxing Day 1927 he wrote to Rab from Half Moon Street:[4]

> Thank you very much indeed for the £10. I seem to have been financially a little reckless! At least, in an examination of my assets and liabilities, the latter have loomed rather more conspicuously than the former. I have also made the discovery which had not occurred to me very forcibly before that the rent of my flat absorbs nearly all my available income!
>
> However I am taking the matter very seriously in hand and hope to sublet my flat early next year. I think I have now definitely passed through the phase of youth in which one spends money without the least relation to income. I anticipate a period of some difficulty in the near future but hope eventually to regain solvency as a permanent acquisition. I tell you all this partly as an excuse of my borrowing from you, – of which I know you most rightly disapprove! And which I assure you only extreme urgency dictated – and partly because I'm sure you'll be relieved to hear of my good resolutions.
>
> Do you and Sydney come to tea on Sunday afternoon if you're back in town and not doing anything, and meanwhile all wishes for Christmas.

Through two acquaintances from Cambridge, Patrick became a member of the Savile Club. He had in the past dined there quite regularly. The Club had recently moved to a new address at 69 Brook Street. It consisted of two large houses which previously had been the London residence of Lord and Lady Harcourt. The Club had many more bedrooms than it needed or wanted to furnish at that time. When Patrick approached the Secretary he was delighted about the possibility of Patrick becoming the long-term resident. Not far from Connaught Grill in Berkeley Square, where one could dine on special occasions, the Club was perfectly located. The Club was quite content for Patrick to furnish his room as he pleased. He paid somewhere between £2 and £3 a week and this included all the amenities of club service. Patrick lived there for four years until his marriage in 1932.[5]

Whilst there he met and became friendly with Evelyn Waugh. Patrick found 'his talk was a point or two lower than his writing'.[6] The irony of course, which Patrick perhaps did not pick up, was that as determinedly as Patrick had moved

---

[3] TATF, p 76.
[4] Letter from Devlin to Butler, 26 December 1927, papers of RA Butler, Trinity College Cambridge Archives, A1212(1).
[5] TATF, pp 78–79.
[6] Ibid, p 80.

away from his Catholicism, Waugh was just as determinedly embracing his. However, Waugh was the source of Patrick's introduction to the odd eccentric bohemian woman at the occasional party they attended.

At the time when Patrick was entering the profession in the late 1920s, to be called to the Bar it was necessary to join one of the Inns of Court and to pass some more examinations. The good news was, however, that with the Cambridge degree he would be exempted from most of the Bar exams. Although he had not finished Cambridge with a first class degree, he was perhaps overly confident that the remaining examinations would be a breeze. To his horror he failed Constitutional Law on his first attempt, but in 1928 and 1929 he managed to pass the balance of his exams (Roman Law, Real Property and Conveyancing).[7]

For much of 1928, at the suggestion of Sir Geoffrey, Patrick obtained employment in a law firm headed up by a successful London solicitor called Sir John Withers.[8] He had been appointed a CBE in the 1918 New Year Honours for his efforts during the Great War. He was also a Conservative Member of Parliament for Cambridge University. Withers, at Sir Geoffrey's intercession, agreed to take on Patrick and waive the customary pupillage fee Patrick would otherwise have paid.[9] Withers' firm was one of the biggest in the West End. The firm still exists and is now global in its reach, modestly known as Withersworldwide. He was, it has been said, a man with something of a genius for human relationships; a man of great natural generosity with a passion for mountaineering.

Withers, with his Eton and King's College Cambridge background, had established a stable of rich, society and aristocratic clients. That to one side, Patrick learned some valuable lessons – the value of teamwork, the heavy cost of litigation but also the need of a forensic strategy, firmly directed throughout, preferably by one person. During his stint with Withers he was lucky enough to get a trip to Paris. Patrick had never been to Paris before and had not travelled by plane either. He flew on the then Imperial Airways – another first. The time with Withers went quickly but obviously very enjoyably and productively. Life after Withers needed to be addressed. Pupillage was the next logical step. The work Withers had done involved mostly divorce, which held no interest for Patrick. One anxiety Patrick rightly had about any pupillage was the need for him to write for his pupil-master. He worried that his illegible handwriting, a potential reason why he fared badly in exams, would come up against him again.[10]

1928 was an important and busy year professionally. But it was also the year his personal life would change profoundly forever. Sometime during the year he

---

[7] Ibid, p 75.

[8] Simon Cretney, 'Sir John Withers MP – the Solicitor, in the Private Practice and Public Life in England between the Wars' (2007) 66(1) *Cambridge Law Journal* 200, p 214.

[9] TATF, p 80.

[10] Ibid, p 87.

met Madeleine Oppenheimer. Madeleine's sister Elsie was married to a solicitor whom Patrick knew called Leonard Rossiter. He had invited Patrick to a dinner party at their home in London. One of the female guests dropped out at the last minute so Madeleine was asked by her sister to fill in.[11] The Oppenheimers were part of the diamond dynasty. However, her father, Sir Bernard, who was South African born, had died suddenly in 1921. He was a man who enjoyed mixed fortunes. He was an extraordinarily generous man who from his own funds set up a business specifically designed to employ disabled soldiers after the Great War. Sadly, the business failed. Nonetheless, he had managed to leave his family comfortable to a limited extent, and with an ever-generous patron in her father's brother Sir Ernest Oppenheimer, they survived. Madeleine was at Somerville College, Oxford, in 1928 studying Philosophy Politics and Economics. She graduated in 1931.

The moment they met, Patrick was instantly and unsurprisingly attracted to the dark, diminutive, intelligent and beautiful young woman. At 19 years of age she was also clearly attracted to Patrick, who was now 23. The arrangement at the dinner party was that at certain designated points the guests were expected to circulate but Patrick and Madeleine stayed glued to each other all evening, refusing to comply with her sister's invitations. This was the beginning of a four-year courtship. The fact that Madeleine was Jewish was of no moment for Patrick, who had by now in any event become firmly disengaged from his Roman Catholicism.[12]

By late 1928 or early 1929 Patrick thought he had turned the corner financially and bought himself a small car. A Baby Austin decked out in red and black 'like a ladybird'.[13]

On 14 January 1929 Patrick participated in a moot in the Gray's Inn. The moot was conducted before Mr WA Jowitt KC, as President, and a number of other 'Masters'.[14] Patrick did not then have any appreciation of the role Jowitt would ultimately play in his career, both in the short and longer term. Having taken silk in 1922, Jowitt was a leading barrister by early 1929. Since that time, he had been a Liberal politician, having initially entered the House in the general election in the same year. At the beginning of 1929 he was out of the Parliament, but he would be re-elected in May of that year.

At all events Patrick, as a well-informed young man, would have appreciated Jowitt's then position. The moot on the other hand, was on a somewhat dreary topic. It involved adjoining land owners and the somewhat improbable escape of some tiger cubs from a travelling circus. The 'gripping' principles of *Rylands v Fletcher* were engaged. The President gave judgment, finding for Patrick's team. A second moot with other participants was held some little time later.

[11] Ibid, p 79.
[12] Email, Tim Devlin to the Author, 26 April 2016.
[13] TATF, p 95.
[14] Account of moot on 14 January 1929, *Graya*, pp 43–45.

On 16 January 1929 Patrick, bursting with pride, wrote to Arthur Goodhart. By now he felt relaxed enough to commence with a 'Dear Arthur'. He wished Arthur and Cecily a belated happy Christmas and New Year. He then went on to explain in excruciating detail the twists and turns of his recent and first forensic triumph. Notwithstanding his success, he rebuked Jowitt for not giving reasons. He demurely concluded:[15]

> Well, well, – all this is very elaborate. However, I was greatly pleased because Sir Plunkett Bastion, the Master of the Moots, told me afterwards it was the best speech he had heard in a Grays' Inn moot for many years. The oratorical standard, I may mention, is not high!! All the people have their speeches carefully written out and when they're interrupted by the judge they say: – May it please your lordship, I am much obliged to your lordship, I am entirely in your lordship's hands? – and go on where they left off. I rejoice to tell you that the Benchers have awarded me a prize of 100 guineas to pay my fees for reading in Chambers. I am very relieved as I did not know where it was going to come from. I was very lucky to get it, as a First is considered a sine qua non. But Withers and Henry Holland played up nobly and gave me superb recommendations and I was able to secure one from Birkenhead, which in Grays' Inn almost amounts to a unit of congé d'élire.
>
> Also I have met Mr Justice Charles one of the new judges at the Savile and he has promised to take me 'marshalling' in the summer which besides bringing in a few guineas will be very valuable experience in the conduct of nisi prius cases. After that life is not so rosy. The serious problem at first is not how to do work but how to get it, and I am concentrating all my efforts on that. It depends almost, entirely, of course, on what Withers intends to do for me; he has practically no small work and I cannot expect to jump into small cases at once. The atmosphere of the Temple with the hordes of men in their early thirties who are still more or less briefless is very discouraging.
>
> Talking of the Savile, Romney Sedgwick has gone off to the West Indies and has left to me the conduct of your election which takes place at the end of the month. The duty is however a completely fictitious one as you have masses of supporters and are sure to be elected. I must now do some work.
>
> Ever and anon
>
> Patrick
>
> P.S. Rab and Sydney Butler have just had a son amid much gratification.

One of the first judges Patrick ever met or at least was on speaking terms with at that stage was a fellow member of the Savile called Sir Ernest Charles. Justice Charles had been appointed after a long, patient wait to the King's Bench in 1928. He was an unprepossessing and solitary man by nature who did not read much at all, rarely if ever worried about his cases, enjoyed a whisky and soda or two at the end of the day and was quite content to dine when in London at one or other or of his three clubs. On one of their chance meetings at the Savile he invited Patrick to join him on circuit as his marshall. Patrick thought this

[15] Letter from Devlin to Goodhart, 16 January 1929, papers of Arthur Lehman Goodhart, Bodleian Library Archives, University of Oxford, folios 64–67 inclusive.

was 'a great piece of good fortune' and he readily accepted. It would only last a few months, but would pay reasonably well, apart from which Patrick was introduced to the pomp and ceremony of a judge on circuit with visits to the judge from the local Mayor, Chief Constable, Sheriff and church dignitaries. This would in due course become all too familiar to Patrick. He would many years after these events enjoy the same rites when as a judge, he attended the relevant Assizes.[16]

Whilst Patrick was on circuit, nothing of note occurred or was necessarily learned. But the experience was itself a worthy addition to the CV.

The summer of 1929 Patrick describes as the 'best I have ever known'.[17] Patrick joined his father and youngest sister, Frances, on a road trip around Ireland. What possessed his father to organise the trip is not a matter of record, but it struck a chord. It imprinted itself indelibly on Patrick, as some family experiences do on everyone.

Both of Patrick's sisters, Frances his youngest and Joan his eldest, had become nuns. Both joined the Society of the Sacred Heart. Both women, along with the other members of the family, had gone to the primary school at the Convent of the Sacred Heart in Aberdeen. Both women would excel academically against the odds and the times. Joan got a BA in English literature from Oxford and Frances would excel in languages, graduating from University College Dublin with the gold medal for French. Frances would die prematurely at the age of 32 in 1941 in Ireland.[18]

Although by the end of 1929 he had been called to the Bar, Patrick thought he had few options professionally and he was accurate in his assessment. Patrick had some options for work, none of which were terribly exciting; he also had some offers for chambers, but none of which were all that enticing. He had previously commenced his pupillage in a set which specialised in common law work and whose occupants were, according to Patrick, irritatingly cheerful.[19] He found the work spectacularly unstimulating and although he had the option of returning there, the idea did not excite him. So he moved into a new set, the Cloisters, which was later destroyed in the war. He managed to obtain the position through an influential friend and barrister Stuart Bevan. Bevan was also a Cambridge man and commercial silk who had won the seat of Holborn for the Conservatives in 1929.[20] This was quite a prestigious set and, notwithstanding his shoebox-size room, he did not have to share. Patrick was formally admitted to the Bar at the end of 1929. He celebrated by getting a dock brief which Mr Justice Charles, true to his word, organised. His client was rightly convicted but it was his foray into the real world.

---

[16] TATF, pp 83, 93–95.
[17] Ibid, p 95.
[18] Extract from the Archives of the Society of Sacred Heart, University of Roehampton in London.
[19] TATF, p 105.
[20] Ibid, p 106.

After the initial elation, Patrick returned to chambers without one jot of work to do, paid or unpaid. Of course, luck and connections came into their own. Another friend, this time a journalist, suggested lunch in Lincoln's Inn with a group of people including Colin Pearson (later Lord Pearson). Pearson was Canadian-born and a devout Socialist. He had secured a position in Walter Monckton's chambers but was also doing great deal of work with the new Socialist Attorney-General, none other than William Jowitt. Jowitt had 'good looks, magnificent voice, charm and commanding presence, wit, intellect, a penetrating feel for the law, and a flair for politics'.[21] Although elected in 1929 as a Liberal, he had chameleon-like tendencies. He resigned his seat to contest a seat for the Labour party in a by-election in July 1929 so as to able to accept the position as Attorney-General in Ramsay MacDonald's minority Labour government. That said he was an excellent and skilled barrister and a great asset to his new party which was devoid of experienced lawyers.[22] Jowitt had taken silk in 1925 and had developed a large and successful practice. As a result he was enormously prosperous. According to Pearson, he was looking for another junior counsel or 'devil' as these assistants were more affectionately known. As luck would have it, Pearson was asked to put a name forward and nominated Patrick.

Patrick obviously recalled his experience before Jowitt and others at the moot in Gray's Inn in January and he should have felt confident, but was strangely very nervous about his impending interview. Jowitt would probably have recalled him because he was likely party to awarding Patrick the moot prize. However the absolute horror when Jowitt asked for a specimen of Patrick's handwriting must have been palpable. Upon inspection Jowitt's reaction said it all. More importantly, however, Jowitt was more concerned to know how close to Jowitt's chambers Patrick lived. That received a much more positive response. Proximity was important, given the late night demands. Jowitt had a house in Upper Brook Street, only a few minutes' walk from the Savile.[23]

Jowitt had been enormously successful at the private Bar. He had been the leader of the commercial Bar but also had more than a thriving practice in admiralty and libel and slander. Although he had on nine separate occasions tried to enlist for the Great War, he had been rejected on health grounds.[24] He certainly never advertised his many but failed attempts. As a result, there were people in the profession who despised him on the basis he had never heard the sound of the bugle. He was loathed by others for his politically ambiguous relations with his own party, which were clearly seen by some as naked opportunism. Envy undoubtedly also played a part. But the attitudes of others had little impact on his practice or the high offices he acquired and the lifestyle he led. Apart from

---

[21] Ibid, p 103.
[22] Ibid, p 106.
[23] Ibid, p 104.
[24] RFV Heuston, *Lives of the Lord Chancellors, 1940–1970* (Oxford, Clarendon Press, 1987), p 68.

his London house, he had a 250 acre farm in the country behind Rye, East Sussex, which at one point had 10 gardeners. He owned an art collection which included the odd Matisse and Sickert and many others of similar note. The fact of the matter is that he was a highly intelligent and skilled practitioner who had many admirers. Among them was Lord Radcliffe, who thought him one of the greats.[25]

However, some never forgave Jowitt. For example, Lord Simon of Glaisdale told Robert Heuston in an interview for Heuston's book on the *Lives of the Lord Chancellors*:[26]

> When I myself was struggling to get back my practice after the 1939–1945 war, I felt considerable resentment at those who had built up substantial practices during those war years even though they hastened to assure me that they had volunteered for and been refused service in the armed forces on the grounds of health. I knew that many whose health was far more fragile had spent arduous years in the various Ministries concerned with prosecuting the war effort. I sympathise with those who held it against Jowitt that the foundation of his practice was laid at a time when so many of contemporaries were being slaughtered in Flanders.

In 1929 Patrick was far too young to have been privy to such sentiments. It obviously never came to his attention. All he wanted was work, and he got it.[27] Pearson's recommendation would have played a part but Jowitt clearly had already determined that Patrick had a big future. So Patrick's anxiety was probably unnecessary.

The work of the devil was unpaid but at least three substantial benefits flowed. Firstly, the experience would be invaluable. Secondly, the public association with the likes of Jowitt would boost Patrick's reputation. Thirdly, the real possibility of a paid Government brief was enhanced.

The rather extraordinary coincidence was that Patrick and his fellow devil would move professionally almost in parallel. Patrick, however, was always a little ahead even though Pearson was six years older. Both would take silk (Patrick in 1945, Pearson in 1949). Both would become judges (Patrick in 1948 and Pearson in 1951). Both would be President of the Restrictive Practices Court (Patrick in 1958 was its first President; Pearson assumed that role in 1960). Patrick was appointed to the Court of Appeal in 1960, Pearson in 1961. Patrick was then appointed to the House of Lords in 1961, Pearson in 1965.

As luck would have it, Patrick started to get some work in his own right. It was just a trickle but enough to have him believe that he had not made an entirely bad choice of a career. His work with Jowitt made him a regular visitor at the House of Commons where he would often consult him. Otherwise, after dinner he might go to Jowitt's house in Upper Brook Street, where he

---

[25] Ibid, p 69.
[26] Ibid, p 68.
[27] TATF, p 104.

would regularly be offered a drink to start. Jowitt's wife, Lesley, was charming and welcoming. Most weekends Patrick went down to Budd's farm, Jowitt's country retreat, which was itself like a holiday. Having decided the train journey was tedious, Patrick took to driving his small Austin down, which was much more convenient because of the need to take a load of law books.[28] Patrick and Jowitt formed a lasting bond. In the law it is often the case that a senior practitioner will form a bond with a junior one which is both enduring and extremely rewarding in every respect. The senior practitioner at first will provide opportunity, which in many cases is reciprocated down the track. It is always built on trust and respect.

As expected and as a result of Patrick's work with Jowitt, he was involved in some fascinating and high-profile cases. In a number of these Patrick did not actually appear in court, despite being very involved in the preparation.

One of the first was a criminal case which had all the hallmarks of a Victorian melodrama.[29] The death of a mother, a son who had a penchant for passing valueless cheques, a hotel in Margate, and an insurance policy on the mother's life, extended by the son shortly before his mother's death. A fire had broken out in the hotel late in the evening. The mother and son had apparently happily dined together earlier in the evening. The mother was found dead in her bed in a smoked-filled room. The son was tearful upon being told of the mother's demise. But did she die of smoke inhalation or strangulation?

The coroner had initially found death by misadventure caused by some faulty gas heater. The mother was buried, but as a result of further enquiries by Scotland Yard and additional information (in particular the insurance policies), the mother was exhumed and the son was charged with murder. The Crown case of murder by strangulation – led by Jowitt and a team of luminaries which included Patrick on the sidelines – was based upon the expert opinion of Sir Bernard Spilsbury, the then accepted doyen of forensic pathology.[30] The defence case – led by James Cassels, later Mr Justice Cassels, and funded by the *News of the World* in return for an 'exclusive' – was death by accident and or from natural causes. Spilsbury asserted he had found evidence the mother was murdered by strangulation before the fire, by reason of a bruise he said he had observed on her epiglottis upon autopsy.

The tussle which ensued between lawyers and experts alike was monumental. Spilsbury said he had seen a bruise but the defence expert testified that no such bruise could be seen. The expert for the defence was Dr Sydney Smith. He challenged Spilsbury to produce for microscopic examination some tissues from the larynx in his laboratory. Spilsbury refused. It was also not an easy task for Spilsbury to prove the precise mechanism by which the bruise could have been

---

[28] Ibid, p 106.

[29] Ibid, *The Fox Case*, pp 107–108.

[30] Andrew Rose, *Lethal Witness, Sir Bernard Spilsbury, Honorary Pathologist* (Stroud, Sutton Publishing, 2007).

caused. This had Jowitt in his hotel room bizarrely attempting to replicate by practising on his own wife, with Patrick present, the possible position the son had to have been in to inflict the requisite force which caused the bruise. Spilsbury, who was known in some quarters even at the time as autocratic, obstinate and secretive, agreed with Jowitt's amateur hypothesis. Jowitt thought Spilsbury a most eminent expert and produced a glowing portrait of Spilsbury in his own memoirs some 25 years later.[31]

The son gave evidence and Jowitt ruthlessly and effectively cross-examined him.[32] Cassels was later to describe it as one of the most gruelling ever conducted in a murder trial.[33] Because of Cabinet business Jowitt did not give the closing address for the Crown. His junior, Sir Henry Curtis-Bennett KC, the best known silk at the criminal Bar, did that brilliantly. The jury, after a low-key summing up from Mr Justice Rowlatt, took 90 minutes to find the defendant guilty. The son surprisingly lodged no appeal from the verdict. He was hanged at 8.15 am on Tuesday 8 April 1930. Spilsbury's evidence was problematic to say the least but for Patrick he was witness to the then harsh reality of criminal cases.[34] A guilty verdict for murder would inevitably mean a death sentence, subject only to the Home Secretary advising the monarch to exercise the prerogative of mercy. Patrick would experience that reality often enough as a trial judge.

Early in 1930, Jowitt appointed Patrick counsel to the Mint at the Old Bailey.[35] This involved prosecutions for counterfeiting, defacing or impairing gold or silver coinage manufactured by the Mint. The work was not riveting but it paid. Patrick also had the right to private practice which at the time in his case involved the odd dock brief. Again, it was invaluable experience.

On 5 October 1930 a British-constructed, experimental hydrogen-filled airship, the R101, had barely crossed the Channel before it crashed at Beauvais, killing all but eight of its 54 passengers. The Government appointed an inquiry to be headed by Sir John Simon (the politician and former Attorney- and Solicitor-General who would later become Home Secretary, Foreign Secretary, Chancellor of the Exchequer and then Lord Chancellor under Churchill). He would be assisted by two expert assessors, Lieutenant-Colonel John Moore-Brabazon (an aviation pioneer) and Professor Charles Inglis (an engineer and academic).[36]

The Government would be represented by Jowitt the Attorney-General, with the new Solicitor-General (Sir Stafford Cripps) and a senior junior Wilfred Lewis (one of the most senior government lawyers of the day, later to be made a High Court judge). Patrick described the combination of Jowitt and Cripps

---

[31] The Earl Jowitt, *Some were Spies* (London, Hodder and Staughton, 1954), p 196.
[32] TATF, p 111.
[33] Ibid, p 109.
[34] Ibid, p 113.
[35] Ibid, p 114.
[36] Ibid, p 121.

as formidable and said that 'they were both men of high intellectual power and they both lacked any understanding of pedestrian thought'.[37] Both Jowitt and Cripps would also share the same political fate in being later expelled by the Labour Party.

Jowitt relied on Patrick to prepare a detailed chronology of events.[38] By now, Jowitt trusted Patrick sufficiently to take the normally risky course of slavishly relying upon the document without checking it, such that Jowitt was able to open the enquiry by simply reading it.[39] This experience for a junior like Patrick was spellbinding and unique. It also cemented his relationship with Jowitt.

The Court of Enquiry reported efficiently on 1 April 1931 and found that apart from exceedingly bad weather, there was a sudden loss of gas which caused the ship to dive uncontrollably and crash. The enquiry attracted immense publicity and Patrick was photographed along with Jowitt and others for the *Illustrated London News*.[40]

The *Hearn* case was the first where Patrick got to work with another leader of the Bar, Herbert du Parcq QC.[41] He had taken silk in 1926 and was one of the leaders of the commercial Bar, who also dabbled in crime. In 1946 he would be appointed to the House of Lords. The case involved an alleged poisoning, this time of the accused's sister and of a neighbour's wife. Jowitt was responsible for getting Patrick briefed. The trial would receive national attention. Patrick did the committal proceedings (before eight magistrates) on his own, having first consulted with Du Parcq. It took place at Launceston, Cornwall. Patrick's photograph appeared in the local newspaper *Western Morning News*, hands in pockets, head down and strolling purposefully, with pipe-smoking Home Office analyst, Dr Roche Lynch, the prosecution's medical expert. The publicity, of which there was much more to come, did his career no harm. The accused was committed for trial.

The trial was a dramatic event, with Du Parcq fainting just prior his giving his final address.[42] The trial judge Mr Justice Alexander Roche (no relation to the Crown's expert), adjourned for a short time. But he warned Patrick that he would have to take over if Du Parcq did not make a speedy recovery. For a short time, Patrick anxiously prepared to deliver the final address. Happily, Du Parcq made an equally dramatic recovery and continued with the trial. Norman Birkett KC gave a final address for the accused which Patrick describes, as always generously, as a 'masterpiece of attractive irrelevance'.[43] However, the jury acquitted Hearn notwithstanding a summing up for the Crown by the trial judge.

[37] Ibid, p 122.
[38] Ibid, p 121.
[39] Ibid, p 121.
[40] Ibid, p 121.
[41] Ibid, p 127.
[42] Ibid, p 130.
[43] Ibid, p 131.

Patrick was urgently required back in London. Jowitt wanted him to assist in yet another high-profile criminal case at the Old Bailey.[44] This was the rather sensational trial of Lord Kylsant, a Welsh businessman, otherwise known as Owen Phillips, (who had held seat in the Commons for the Liberals between 1906 and 1910 and for the Conservatives between 1916 and 1922) and his accountant Harold Morland, a partner of Price Waterhouse. They were charged with publishing a false balance sheet and a false prospectus of the Royal Mail Steam Packet Company of which Lord Kylsant was chairman.

Jowitt led for the Crown. A bevy of talent appeared for the defence, including Sir John Simon KC and Sir Patrick Hastings for Morland. Patrick did not formally appear but assisted Jowitt and others from the sidelines. Kylsant was convicted on the prospectus charge and sentenced to 12 months' imprisonment. He was acquitted on the balance sheet charge, whereas Morland escaped liability entirely. Kylsant appealed to the Court of Criminal Appeal. Patrick did in November 1931 get a spot at the Bar table alongside Jowitt and an interesting man Patrick was to spend time with professionally, Denis Pritt KC. Pritt, a colleague of Jowitt's, was a member of the Labour party who was expelled from the party for his overzealous defence of the Soviets and who George Orwell once described as the 'most effective pro-Soviet publicist in the country'.[45] He was also an accomplished linguist but more importantly a very competent barrister. The appeal was dismissed and Kylsant spent 10 months in Wormwood Scrubs prison.

Patrick's relationship with Madeleine was to say the least blossoming. In August 1931, he and Madeleine spent a romantic holiday in Cologne, Nuremberg, Heidelberg, Munich, Verona, Zurich and parts of France in a chauffeur-driven vehicle supplied by Madeleine's mother. Prior to the trip, Madeleine's mother, who had been widowed in 1921, received a visit from one of Patrick's aunts, the rather meddlesome and spiteful Aunt Lottie. She seems to have been at pains to inform Madeleine's mother that Patrick had no money and was entirely dependent upon Uncle George. Was this a case of a woman wanting to tell the widow Oppenheimer that her prospective son in law would bring no dowry or was it a blatant act of anti-semitism? The latter is more plausible given the staunch anti-semitic Catholic stance in those days. In any event, Madeleine's mother fully appreciated the couple's love and commitment and courteously but firmly rejected Aunt Lottie's venomous approach.[46]

Patrick and Madeleine were married upon their return on Friday, 12 February 1932.[47] Patrick's friend and mentor, Father Bede Jarrett, officiated at the Church of St James, Spanish Place, one of the most beautiful Roman Catholic churches

---

[44] TATF, p 135.

[45] Arthur Ward, *A Guide to War Publications of the First and Second World War: From Training Guides to Propaganda Posters* (Barnsley, Pen and Sword, 2015), p 197.

[46] Email from Timothy Devlin to the Author, 26 April 2016.

[47] The Church of St James, Spanish Place, Marriage Register, 12 February 1932.

in England. The church had played a crucial role in the Catholic life of central London for more than three centuries. As the name might suggest, the history of the church is intimately linked to the Spanish Embassy. The foundation stone for the current church was laid in 1887 and it opened in 1890.[48]

However, as much as Patrick wanted to please his parents by marrying in a Catholic church, Madeleine was Jewish and they would require special dispensation. Patrick's father had to supply the usual assurances that his son, to the best of his knowledge, had not previously been married. He did so on 3 February 1932, in handwriting which unlike his son's, was entirely legible.[49] Earlier, on 16 January, the local priest in Chiselhurst had certified that Patrick was baptised on 1 December 1905 at St Mary's Chiselhurst. The formalities were then attended to in more detail. The following letter passed between the Reverend John Waterkeyn, from the Church of Our Lady of the Assumption, to the Right Reverend Joseph Butt in the following terms:[50]

> My Lord,
>
> A few days ago Mr Patrick Devlin came to see me with his fiancée and told me he had seen your Lordship regarding his marriage, which required a dispensation for disparity of cult. Mr Devlin told me also that he would like to be married in your parish, this of course has my full approval. I am enclosing herewith this dispensation granted for this marriage together with two baptismal certificates.

The formalities out of the way, Patrick and Madeleine were married to the side of the main altar which was the custom in 'mixed' marriages.

An article appeared in one of the London newspapers with a photograph of Patrick and Madeleine under the caption 'Barrister's Wedding': Patrick in a double breasted overcoat and his fedora; Madeleine in a fur-collared coat with corsage, clutching their marriage certificate. The article read:

> Bride and bridegroom leaving St James's Church, Spanish-place, after yesterday's wedding of Mr. Patrick Devlin and Miss Madeleine Hilda Oppenheimer, sister of Sir Michael Oppenheimer. Mr Devlin was a barrister of only eighteen months standing when he was called upon at short notice to conduct the preliminary case for the Crown against Mrs. Annie Hearn, who was subsequently acquitted of the charge of poisoning her sister and a neighbour at Launceston, Cornwall.

After the 1929 Stock Market Crash matters became impossible for Ramsay MacDonald's second Labour government. MacDonald attempted unsuccessfully to find solutions to the insoluble. Achieving a balanced budget to maintain the Pound on the Gold Standard while tax revenues continued to fall proved beyond his capacity. On 24 August MacDonald submitted his resignation. He was, however, prevailed upon by King George V to form a National Government

---

[48] Nicholas Schofield, *The Church of St James Spanish Place: A History and Guide* (Suffolk, The Bidnall Press Limited, 2005).

[49] Letter from William Devlin to the Rt Rev J Butt, 3 February 1932.

[50] Letter from Rev J Waterkeyn to the Rt Rev J Butt, 27 January 1932.

with the Conservatives and Liberals. MacDonald was expelled from the Labour Party. A general election followed in 1931. Of the National Government's 554 seats, MacDonald and his splinter group, National Labour, won only 13 seats, 'Old Labour' secured 52 seats and Lloyd George's splinter group won four seats. Labour was split in two, but MacDonald was still Prime Minister with the largest mandate ever won by a British Prime Minister, despite intense bitterness from his former party.

Patrick was able to weather these harrowing times with considerable equanimity for at least two reasons. First, he had Madeleine at his side. Secondly, Jowitt had also secured him as counsel to the Ministry for Labour. Indeed, Jowitt was one of the few persons willing to continue to serve with MacDonald. Like MacDonald, Jowitt was seen at best as a chameleon, a self-preservationist *par excellence* or at worst, a traitor for having left the Liberals. Although he was Attorney-General for a time, the absence of a safe seat saw him return to the Bar. He would, however, re-enter Parliament in 1939 in a safe Labour seat. Although for a time Patrick lost a little momentum, Jowitt's connections and patronage would prove invaluable. In addition, Patrick began to emerge from the post of devil with some impressive highly publicised solo outings.

Patrick's great leap forward was to be asked to join Jowitt in the chambers he formed in 1921, No. 1 Brick Court. Better still, it was in a spacious room overlooking the entrance to Middle Temple Hall and beyond to the Temple Gardens and the River.[51] By now Patrick and Jowitt had forged a warm and mutually respectful bond. Patrick described his time with Jowitt as an 'immense pleasure'.[52] Patrick got his first private clients when at No. 1. Madeleine also received about £500–600 a year and on top earned a small salary assisting professor of social biology, Lancelot Hogben, in his fascination with identical twins.[53] Patrick soon and somewhat by accident made an entry into the commercial Bar. A solicitor who briefed Patrick in a family court matter retained him in a commercial case because the two had got on so well. A major advance came when he was briefed for a subsidiary of Shell. Already briefed was Australian-born Augustus Andrewes Uthwatt (later created Baron Uthwatt in 1946 on his becoming a Law Lord). Although an excellent lawyer and Vinerian Scholar, Uthwatt was a hopeless advocate. The solicitor wanted an advocate as opposed to just a good lawyer and Patrick was the man. In the end, however, Patrick was led by then Raymond Evershed KC (in due course Master of the Rolls and a Law Lord). Although Shell was unsuccessful, Patrick had given some sound and canny advice which was vindicated by later events. The instructing solicitor never forgot his astute observations and advice. As a result when Uthwatt was elevated, Patrick assumed the retainer for Shell.

---

[51] TATF, pp 153–60.
[52] Ibid, pp 153.
[53] Obituary of Madeleine Devlin, *The Times*, 13 April 2012.

Patrick did not by accident happen to find himself in the company of lawyers who would like him to go on to do great things. To an extent there is an element of luck in starting at the Bar, but ultimately the market – now as it was then – is highly critical and elitist. Given the fees the top practitioners charge, a meritocracy is healthily and thankfully still at work. It is also unsurprisingly unforgiving when mistakes are made. Patrick was obviously assessed not just as a safe pair of hands, but as an innovative, intelligent and highly competent barrister. He needed, as does any fledgling, one opportunity to shine and with a patron like Jowitt his prospects were going to be enhanced immeasurably.

Patrick's father died in 1932, a year which was otherwise filled with joy.[54] How much sorrow his death caused was probably only appreciated by Patrick later with the benefit of reflection and hindsight. One of the obvious consequences of the English boarding school system is that some parents become inanimate objects deferred to merely as matters of fact, who are otherwise irrelevant. The Jesuits in particular could be task masters at perfecting that outcome. Indeed it was unashamedly a stated objective.

Newly married Patrick and Madeleine decided to buy a house in Westminster, at 65 Romney Street, an excellent location for a budding barrister. The couple would stay at that address until the outbreak of war in 1939, when they moved to Farley Green in Surrey.[55]

It is not easy to trace Patrick's career as a barrister accurately; one must assume that the reported cases in which he appeared compose only a fraction of what he did, but they are significant. First, it is clear he established a serious and lucrative practice somewhat rapidly years before the outbreak of the war. Although there was a smattering of crime, by and large his cases were commercial with a healthy mix of trial and appellate work.

However, before the professional year 1934 got very far underway Patrick had another personal tragedy to deal with. His close friend and mentor Father Bede Jarrett died suddenly on St Patrick's Day. This was clearly a blow to both Patrick and Madeleine. It was only two years since he had married the couple. It was moreover a blow to the Dominican and the Catholic community at large. He had been much admired and much loved.

Soon after in July 1934 was Patrick's first reported case.[56] It was before the Court of Criminal Appeal in the matter of Carmen Tomasso, who had been convicted of possession of counterfeit coins with the intent of using them. The accused had been convicted at the Central Criminal Court in June 1934 and sentenced to two years' imprisonment. The sole ground of appeal was what was said to be the inappropriate cross-examination of the accused on his previous conviction of possession of counterfeit coins despite having not put his

[54] Email, Timothy Devlin to the Author, 26 April 2016.
[55] Ibid; TATF p 79.
[56] *R v Carmen Tomasso* (1934) 25 Cr. App. 14.

character in issue in his trial. The appeal was conducted before the Lord Chief Justice, Lord Hewart, and Justices Avory and Swift. Horace Avory was one of the most noted criminal lawyers of his time. He was humourless and acquired the nickname 'The Acid Drop' due to his caustic wit in court. Rigby Swift was from Liverpool and had a large and prosperous practice when he accepted his appointment as a judge in 1920 at the age of 46, the youngest High Court judge at that time. Avory enjoyed the distinction of being featured as the frontispiece of *Country Life* on 5 September 1931 to celebrate his eightieth birthday, 'avec' full regalia but decidedly 'sans' pearls. Hewart is now only remembered as having coined the aphorism that 'justice must not only be done but manifestly and obviously be seen to be done.' He had been Solicitor-General and Attorney-General in the years 1916 to 1922, appointed by Lloyd George. He had considerable ability, but developed a bad judicial reputation. Many years later Patrick would say of Hewart:[57]

> Hewart … has been called the worst Chief Justice since Scroggs and Jeffries in the 17th century. I do not think that is quite fair. When one considers the enormous improvement in judicial standards between the 17th and 20th centuries, I should say that comparatively speaking, he was the worst Chief Justice ever.

Professor Robert Heuston held similar views but more specifically described him as arbitrary and unjudicial. According to Heuston, the author of the famous dictum was incapable of securing its observance in his own court.[58]

Patrick lost. Hewart, perhaps characteristically, stopped Patrick's opponent before he had completed his argument and ruled the question should not have been asked and the conviction was quashed.

In 1935, Patrick appeared in his first House of Lords appeal.[59] It was an important contract case which also concerned the proper function of a jury in civil trials. It involved a question of whether two contracts existed, and if so, the appropriate damages for the breach of each. This was an appeal from the Court of Appeal. The Court of Appeal had set aside the jury verdict. It found that only one contract existed and decided only nominal damages were appropriate for the breach.

This clearly would have been a fascinating exercise for Patrick. The old running mates, Sir Stafford Cripps and Sir William Jowitt were pitted against each other. Both of course were now at the private Bar. Cripps appeared for the Appellants (the Plaintiffs at trial) and Jowitt, leading Patrick, for the Respondents (the Defendants at trial). Jowitt clearly would have played a role in getting Patrick briefed. Presiding was Viscount Sankey, the Lord Chancellor.

---

[57] Patrick Devlin, *Easing the Passing: The Trial of Dr John Bodkin Adams* (London, Faber & Faber, 1985) ('ETP') p 92.

[58] RFV Heuston, *Lives of the Lord Chancellors, 1885–1940* (Oxford, Clarendon Press, 1964), pp 603–4.

[59] *Mechanical and General Inventions Company, Limited v Austin and Austin Motor Company* [1935] AC 346.

The appeal was heard over two days on 24 January and 5 February. Judgment was given on 14 March. Sitting with Sankey were their Lordships Blanesburgh, Atkin, Macmillan and Wright. Although the Lords upheld the Court of Appeal on the existence of only one contract, they restored the jury's verdict on the damages award for the breach found.

Again in 1935, Patrick appeared before a Divisional Court presided over by Justice Clauson (who had specialised in company law at the Bar and had been a judge since 1926) and Justice Luxmoore (a Chancery judge who had played international rugby for England). Both were subsequently elevated to the Court of Appeal in 1938. The case concerned very technical questions of bankruptcy law. Patrick appeared unled.[60] He was unsuccessful. In this case Patrick was briefed by Clifford Turner, a leading London law firm of the day (now Clifford Chance, a global practice).

Nevertheless, Patrick obviously impressed his instructing solicitor because the firm briefed him again early the following year in the Court of Appeal. This time Patrick was successful on an important point of jurisdiction, namely whether an appeal lay to the Court of Appeal from a decision of the Mayor's and City of London Court. Later in 1936 the firm briefed him again in a commercial case for one of their biggest clients the Dunlop Rubber Company concerning the effect of an assignment of debt. The case came before Justice Macnaghten (son of the famous Lord Macnaghten). Although Patrick lost, the trial judge nonetheless remarked on the principle in issue:[61] 'In spite of the excellent argument of Mr Devlin this contention is not I think well founded.'

To have attracted the attention and devotion of a firm like Clifford Turner was an important milestone in Patrick's career. That connection was undoubtedly strengthened over the next few years. In addition, in 1937 Patrick published an article in the *Law Quarterly Review*.[62] Arthur Goodhart was still editor, as he continued to be until 1975. The article dealt with a recent Court of Appeal decision concerning fraudulent misrepresentation and the respective liability of principal and agent. The tenor of the article was to the effect that the Court of Appeal was wrong in principle and had erroneously analysed earlier decisions to arrive at their result. It was a bold theory but argued in an intensely lucid and persuasive style characteristic of much to come. This was also a very important step professionally.

1938 on the other hand brought something more important again into Patrick and Madeleine's life – the birth of their first child, a son, Gilpatrick, on Boxing Day that year.

---

[60] *In re a debtor* [1936] 1 Ch 165.

[61] *MV Bowater & Sons v Davidson's Paper Sales Limited* [1936] 1 KB 146. See also *Dunlop Rubber Company Limited v WB Haigh & Son* [1936] 1 KB 347.

[62] Patrick Devlin, 'Fraudulent Misrepresentation: Division of Responsibility between Principle and Agent' (1937) 53 *Law Quarterly Review* 344–63.

In March 1939, Patrick appeared in the Court of Appeal in an appeal from a decision of Justice Goddard as he then was.[63] Goddard would in due course become Lord Chief Justice and a friend and mentor to Patrick. In any event on this occasion Patrick was led by Sir Stafford Cripps. The case involved a charterparty and the construction of the phrase 'if war breaks out involving Japan'. Their opponents persuaded the court that Justice Goddard was correct in his interpretation of the charterparty. The law firms involved were, unsurprisingly, two specialist marine insurance practices of some standing. Patrick and Cripps had been retained by Thomas Cooper & Co, whose beginnings in the city were in 1825. This was further confirmation that Patrick was held in high standing.

With war declared in 1939 Patrick and Madeleine had some momentous decisions to make. Patrick was ineligible for war service: the rickets he had contracted while at Stonyhurst had left him with a permanent stoop. He joined the Home Guard instead.[64] He also joined the Ministry of Supply. It was also decided that London was no place for the family. So it was decided to relocate to Surrey. Patrick would remain for much of the time in London and would rent flats from time to time in central London at 81 Tufton Street and 296 St James Court, Buckingham Gate. Madeleine was then pregnant with twins.

In February 1939, Jowitt was adopted as the Labour candidate at a by-election in Ashton-under-Lyne and was elected unopposed. Shortly thereafter Churchill appointed him Solicitor-General in his Coalition Government. Over the war years he held many Cabinet positions but he was back, perhaps, where he wanted to be. He and Patrick would in due course cross paths on many occasions.

For three days in February 1940 Patrick did a commercial case involving yet another charterparty.[65] This time he was led by Sir Robert Aske KC. After several failed attempts Aske KC had been successful in winning a seat for the Liberals in 1929 and held it until 1945. He ultimately joined the Conservatives in 1948. He was more a politician than a barrister and only moderately competent in the former occupation. This was a case where prior to the war the brief had been held by Alan Mocatta (later Sir Alan Mocatta and a High Court judge in the Queen's Bench Division). The report of the case makes clear that, as was the practice, Mocatta was on war service. In October 1939 the Bar Council had passed a resolution requiring a barrister who took over a brief for someone on war service to acknowledge that fact and to share the fees with the barrister either as agreed, or if there was no agreement, on a 50-50 basis.[66] Judgment in the case was given on 1 March 1940 and Patrick's client won. That might not

---

[63] *Kawasaki Kisen Kabushiki Kaisha of Kobe v Bantham Steamship Company Limited* [1939] 2 KB 544.

[64] Email from Timothy Devlin to the Author, 26 April 2016.

[65] *Imperial Smelting Corporation Ltd v Joseph Constantine Steamship Line Ltd* [1940] 1 KB 812.

[66] 'Barristers on War Service', *The Law Journal*, Saturday 14 October 1939, p 227.

have had its full impact however, as Madeleine gave birth to twin girls Clare and Virginia on 2 March.

The case went on appeal in June of that year to the Court of Appeal and Patrick's client lost. He was again led by Aske KC. In early 1941 it went to the House of Lords. This time Aske KC and Patrick were successful.[67]

During the balance of 1940 Patrick had a number of appearances before the Court of Appeal (in July and September). In both cases he appeared without a leader. Patrick was successful in both. The July case was a tenancy dispute.[68] In his September case the Court included Goddard LJ and his old leader du Parq LJ.[69] The latter concerned a policy of marine insurance and it would no doubt have pleased Patrick, given the constitution of the bench, that he was successful. He plainly admired both.

1941 saw an increasing number of appearances at all levels in the courts, more often than not without a leader.[70] In 1942 and perhaps not for the first time, he worked with Sir Walter Monckton KC.[71] In addition to this more work with Aske KC ensued, especially in marine insurance.[72]

However, for entirely personal reasons 1941 and 1942 were extraordinarily eventful years. In March 1941, Patrick's youngest sister Frances died in Edinburgh at the age of 32. She, like his older sister Joan, had joined the Society of the Sacred Heart. Although Patrick did not see much of his sisters, he was devastated at her death. They had been very close, although he would not have seen much of either her or his other sister because of their vocation. However, in early December of that year a son, Dominick, was born.

His first case in the Privy Council occurred in January 1943.[73] It was an appeal from the Supreme Court of Gibraltar. Patrick appeared without a leader. The case involved a contract for the payment of a mortgage in a foreign currency. The question was whether the law of Gibraltar was the law governing the contract. Patrick came second but it was a clear sign that he had well and truly acquired stature.

This was confirmed again in the March of that year when he was briefed to appear in a shipping case in the Court of Appeal, again without a leader, but against one of the undoubted leaders of the Bar at that time, Mr 'Tom' Denning KC (later Lord Denning).[74] Denning had been appointed a King's Counsel in 1938 and would be appointed a judge in 1944. He and Patrick would become

---

[67] *Imperial Smelting Corporation v Joseph Constantine Steamship Line Ltd* [1940] 2 KB 430 (Court of Appeal); *Joseph Constantine Steamship Line Ltd v Imperial Steamship Line Ltd* [1942] AC 154 (House of Lords).

[68] *Metropolitan Estates Company Ltd v Wilde* [1940] 2 KB 536.

[69] *J Wharton (Shipping) Ltd v Mortleman & others* [1941] 1 KB 340.

[70] See, eg *Lorentzen v Lydden and Company Ltd* [1942] 2 KB 202.

[71] *Progressive Supply Company Ltd v Dalton* [1943] 1 Ch. 54.

[72] *Polpen Shipping Company Ltd v Commercial Union Assurance Company Ltd* [1943] 1 KB 161.

[73] *Marrache v Ashton* [1943] AC 311.

[74] *Halcyon Steamship Company Ltd v Continental Grain Company* [1943] 1 KB 355.

firm friends. Denning was successful on this occasion. For Patrick to be briefed against high-profile counsel such as Denning was a significant vote of professional confidence in him and a testament to his standing.

A few weeks later he was again briefed unled, this time against the leading libel junior of the day, Valentine Holmes.[75] It was an important case about the construction of an Act of parliament concerning the powers of the Minister of Supply. A month or so later in July he was back in the Privy Council in an appeal from the Supreme Court of Ontario.[76] At the end of the same month he was again in the Privy Council in an appeal from the Supreme Court of Canada.[77] In the first case he was against Sir Walter Monckton KC and in the second he appeared with him. By now the two had also become firm friends.

In October, Patrick appeared, again on his own, in the Court of Appeal in a contract case.[78] In the November he appeared in the Privy Council in another appeal from Gibraltar in a shipping case.[79] By 1943 the tempo and quality of his practice had increased exponentially. His personal life had also become hectic. He and Madeleine decided to buy a 450 acre farm near Pewsey in Wiltshire. On it, West Wick House was situated. Built in 1770, it would for many years to come be a source of adventure and unimaginable joy for them and their growing family. It would not only provide the perfect location for relaxation but for Madeleine an opportunity to use her undoubted management and entrepreneurial skills. In due course for example, she would busy herself along with their farm managers in sending their Jersey cream to the likes of Fortnum and Mason in London. It would also be a haven for Patrick to work in during court vacation both on judgments and his extra curial writings. They would also entertain guests there with wonderful dinner parties. The move to the country, however, was largely left to Madeleine, as Patrick's mother died at the end of the year and he dashed to Scotland for the funeral.

Later in 1943, Arthur Goodhart would be appointed a King's Counsel. Although unusual, it was not the first time an academic was appointed silk. Nonetheless the process which was to be followed since 1866, was for a handwritten application to be made to the Lord Chancellor including personal and professional details. It was then also necessary to inform all practitioners senior to the applicant 'on the circuit' of the application.[80] In Goodhart's case, by this stage he had been Professor of Jurisprudence at Oxford since 1931, he had been called to the Bar by the Inner Temple in 1919 and he had been editor of the *Law Quarterly Review* since 1926. Many practitioners and judges had worn a path to his door seeking to have their articles published. Among the throng

---

[75] *Minister of Supply v British Thomson-Houston Company Ltd* [1943] 1 KB 478.
[76] *Abitibi Power and Paper Company Ltd v Montreal Trust Company & others* [1943] AC 536.
[77] *Atlantic Smoke Shops Ltd v Conlon & others* [1943] AC 550.
[78] *Bishop & Baxter, Ltd v Anglo-Eastern Trading & Industrial Company* [1944] 1 KB 12.
[79] *Conservas Cerquiria Limitada v HM Procurator General* [1944] AC 6.
[80] Sir Harold Morris KC, *The Barrister* (London, Geoffrey Bles, 1930), pp 149–53.

were Goddard, Denning, Maxwell Fyfe and of course Patrick himself. Goodhart was rightly revered and influential and hence powerful within the profession.

Patrick wrote to him from Farley Green Farm, Surrey, on 14 June 1943:[81]

> I am so delighted to see your name adding lending distinction to the new list of silks. It's inclusion in a war time list carries a special tribute to your eminence. Please do not dream of answering this. You will be deluged with letters. Madeleine too sends her congratulations and hopes that the Lord Chancellor will have taken some steps to provide the necessary quantity of silk.

In addition on 7 March 1944, Denning was appointed a judge of the Probate, Divorce and Admiralty Division at the age of 45. Patrick wrote to him:[82] 'Of course a seat on the bench was your inevitable destiny, but it is nice that you should have got there so young.' In just a few years Patrick would surpass that milestone, but in the meantime it did Patrick's career no harm to have a major competitor leave the Bar, leaving room for others to progress. In the meantime, another son, Timothy, was born on 28 July.

In 1944 and early 1945 Patrick was regularly appearing on his own in all manner of cases at trial and on appeal and in a variety of jurisdictions. His prominence in the profession was clearly established. However, just as important for Patrick's career was the appointment of Jowitt as Lord Chancellor by Attlee on 26 July 1945.

In 1945 Patrick also applied for silk. Successful on his first attempt, his appointment was announced on 29 June 1945.[83] He was then only 40. Amongst his brethren were two others who would in due course also like Patrick be elevated to the House of Lords, Terence Donovan and Edward Holroyd Pearce.

Arthur Goodhart reciprocated good wishes of the year before. Patrick responded on 7 July 1945:[84]

> Thank you for your charming letter and the nice things you say. But neither you nor anybody else would have been able to say them at all, if it had not been for the start you gave me.
>
> Do let us dine together. It is aeons since I have seen you for more than a fleeting minute. Will you say when you are going to be in London.
>
> Madeleine sends her love.

Patrick is first reported as having appeared as silk in the Court of Appeal in November 1945 being led by Aske KC.[85] This would not be unusual if a barrister

---

[81] Letter from Devlin to Goodhart, 14 June 1943, papers of Arthur Lehman Goodhart, Bodleian Library University of Oxford, folio 69.

[82] Letter from Devlin to Denning, 7 March 1944, Hampshire Record Office 55, as quoted in Edmund Heward, *Lord Denning a Biography* (Chichester, Barry Rose Law Publishers, 1997), p 34.

[83] 'New King's Counsel', *The Times*, 29 June 1945, p 2.

[84] Letter from Devlin to Goodhart, 7 July 1945, papers of Arthur Lehman Goodhart, Bodleian Library Archives, University of Oxford, folio 70.

[85] *Athel Line, Ltd v Liverpool & London War Risks Insurance Association, Ltd* [1945] 1 KB 117 (CA).

had previously been briefed as a junior and took silk in the meantime. In any event it was yet another case on marine insurance. The first reported case in which he appeared on his own as a silk was in February of 1946, again in the Court of Appeal and again in a shipping case.[86] In May, another marine insurance case in the Court of Appeal occupied him for several days.[87]

But in 1946 another event occurred which would turn out very much to Patrick's advantage. In January, Rayner Goddard, as he was known all his life, was appointed Lord Chief Justice by the Attlee government. He had been promoted several times in his career and in 1944 had been appointed a Lord of Appeal in Ordinary on the death of Lord Atkin. His predecessor Viscount Caldecote had suffered a stroke the year before.

Sadly, Uncle George, Patrick's de facto father and long-time patron died aged 70 in May 1946. Uncle George left Patrick and his brother William £15,000 each.[88] It was a considerable sum in those days by any standards. Notwithstanding Patrick's success and prosperity at the Bar, this would have had a profound effect on the life of himself, Madeleine and their ever expanding family. Indeed on 8 June that year, another addition was made to the family with the birth of another son, Matthew on 8 June. Financially, they were very secure.

Measured by the quality and quantity of his work, Patrick's career accelerated further, if that were humanly possible. He was rightly in demand in many places.

On 16 June 1947 he was appointed the Attorney-General of the Duchy of Cornwall, an ancient but largely ceremonial office.[89] The Duchy was created in 1337 by Edward III for his son and heir Prince Edward. then aged six. Patrick was appointed by George VI, undoubtedly on the advice and recommendation of Walter Monckton who had in 1945 been Solicitor-General in Churchill's caretaker government. Prior to that, through his connections Monckton had been appointed advisor to the Nizam of Hyderabad.

On 17 June Patrick wrote to Goodhart:[90]

I have been told I am to be elected a Bencher of Grays' Inn and have been invited – provisionally – to attend the Guest Night on Thursday next 24 July and to bring a guest. As it will be my first appearance as a Bencher, de facto if not de jure, I should like you above all people to be my guest for that occasion, and it would be a great honour if you could come. Besides as an experienced Bencher yourself, you would be able to see that I committed no grave error of deportment! I do hope you are able.

---

[86] *The Tolten* [1946] P 135 (CA).

[87] *Ocean Steamship Co., Ltd v Liverpool and London War Risks Insurance Association Ltd* [1946] 1 KB 561 (CA).

[88] TATE, p 37.

[89] *London Gazette*, 20 June 1947, p 2798.

[90] Letter from Devlin to Goodhart, 17 June 1947, papers of Arthur Lehman Goodhart, Bodleian Library Archives, Oxford University, folio 71.

In the meantime, Monckton KC telegrammed Patrick on 24 June 1947 from Lake View House, Hyderabad, addressed to 'Patrick Devlin KC, Attorney-General, Duchy of Cornwall Office'. It read:[91] 'Congratulations Mr Attorney on getting the best appointment at the Bar. Could not have wished for better successor. Wish you all happiness ahead.'

A few days later on 27 June, Patrick responded:[92]

> It was sweet of you send a cable from your fortress in Hyderabad. I am very proud to be your successor. But it is sad that you should have to have a successor at all. It seems hard and miserable that you cannot arrange your private life as you want without all the repercussions. I hope that when the fuss is over you will be able to make your own life in the tranquillity and happiness that you want. You have my very best wishes for that. When are you coming back to London? I have a lot of things that I want to ask you. Will you let me know?

Monckton KC, who no doubt at first benefited enormously from his Royal connections, was now paying the price. He had become close friends with the Prince of Wales and had been his guiding hand during the Abdication. Through these connections he had been introduced to the Nizam of Hyderabad and in 1947 was still filling the role of the Nizam's advisor. But after nearly a decade of crisis after crisis, Monckton KC was exhausted. He wanted to return to some sort of normality – perhaps the Bar or a judicial appointment. Sadly, much of Monckton KC's genius as a negotiator and mediator would be hidden from public gaze and would not be fully appreciated for many years to come. He was tired. Patrick as a good friend did what he could to provide such support as he could.

In early 1948 Patrick appeared in a Court of Appeal case which went for many days.[93] It was another shipping case involving allegations of breach of warranty and negligence. On this occasion he led one of his old pupils, Charles Fletcher-Cooke. Like Patrick, Fletcher-Cooke had been President of the Cambridge Union in 1936. In due course he would win a seat for the Conservative Party in the 1951 General Election.

Goodhart received an honorary knighthood in early 1948. This was cause for much celebration, especially in the Devlin household. Patrick was one of the first to congratulate him. However, later in the year reciprocation was again due. On 4 October Patrick wrote to Goodhart:[94]

> This is to let you know very confidentially that I expect shortly – I don't know the exact date – to be appointed to the Bench. You will know that I am always conscious

---

[91] Telegram from Monckton to Devlin, 24 June 1947, archives of Balliol College, Oxford, papers of Sir Walter Monckton, folio 18.

[92] Letter from Devlin to Monckton, 27 June 1947, archives of Balliol College, Oxford, papers of Sir Walter Monckton, folio 20.

[93] *The Owners of the Steamship Towerfield v Workington Harbour and Dock Board* [1949] P 10.

[94] Letter from Devlin to Goodhart, 4 October 1948, papers of Arthur Lehman Goodhart, Bodleian Library Archives, Oxford University, folio 74.

how much that is due to your kindness and help to me in the early days. I expect to go out on circuit next term and am wondering whether Phillip[95] has reached the age when he would like to go marshalling.

P.S. I hope you will use your influence to see that I am dealt with leniently in the L.Q.R.!

Patrick was appointed to the King's Bench Division on 12 October.[96] Jowitt, as Lord Chancellor, was clearly responsible. He would have needed no endorsement but no doubt Goddard's views were sought. He would clearly have endorsed Patrick as well. Goddard's wife had died in 1928 after a surgical procedure. Goddard brought up his three daughters aged 20, 18 and 15 at the time, with the aid of a loyal governess. He led a lonely existence as a barrister and again as a judge and was always up for a dinner invitation. Patrick and Madeleine entertained Goddard at home frequently and the two became friends. Although they were divided in outlook, they were not in friendship. Patrick found him to be a 'truly loveable man'.[97]

Patrick would have been approached confidentially, either by Jowitt himself or someone from his department, about the possibility of appointment. Madeleine and Patrick would no doubt have also discussed it at length before he accepted. Patrick would turn 43 in the November of that year and by then, he and Madeleine had six children under 10, with the youngest only two years old. But this was a remarkable opportunity he would not want to refuse.

His appointment was effective from 12 October and with it came the customary knighthood. He was one of the youngest judges ever appointed to high office. Along with his appointment in *The Times* on 13 October were articles regarding the elevation of others including Denning as a Lord Justice of Appeal. Denning was only 49. Goddard held a dinner to congratulate Patrick on his elevation.

---

[95] Goodhart's eldest son.
[96] 'New Lords Justices', *The Times*, 13 October 1948, *The London Gazette*, 15 October 1948. Patrick's customary knighthood was announced in *The London Gazette*, 2 November 1948.
[97] ETP, p 34.

4

A Relentless Workload

THE CELEBRATIONS OVER, the bench wig, red robes, white leather gloves and other regalia were ordered at Ede and Ravenscroft in Chancery Lane, and the staff appointed. Patrick started the demanding work of a judge in the King's Bench Division. Judges in that Division of the High Court, then, as now, do a range of work, both civil and criminal. Patrick would excel at both. Although he had done some criminal work as a junior, his main area of practice prior to elevation was commercial law and in particular insurance and admiralty work. He would sit as a trial judge (although not exclusively so) for almost 12 years. He later described this as his happiest time. The work as a trial judge is often rightly described as relentless. It is less demanding than the work of a leading barrister, but it can pose cruel tests for those who lack the necessary talent, tenacity and judgement. Most judges find little time for anything but their judicial duties – but not Patrick. However, without Madeleine none of it would have been possible. Yes, he could live in Gray's Inn and work the long hours required and he could recuperate at West Wick House on weekends and long vacation. But six children do not bring themselves up all alone. But together and both with boundless energy, Patrick and Madeleine more than managed.

On the Bench Patrick was an impressive figure. The judicial robes concealed a stoop which became very pronounced in later life. The wig concealed a thick head of hair which in youth had been distinctly red, but it also emphasised the high cheek bones, firm chin and full mouth. Professor Heuston asserts 'his voice and diction were admirable – clear and resonant, if a trifle metallic in tone'.[1]

Patrick described the role in his work entitled *The Judge*:[2]

A judge's time for extra-judicial activities, that is outside office hours, is limited. Such activities have to compete with the need for a reasonable amount of leisure in a mentally exacting job. Indeed the wise use of leisure is a part of the job. A research scientist for example, could work every evening and all weekends without, if he preserved his health, making his research any less accurate. A judge who did likewise would truly be living in an ivory tower which his critics would always suppose to be his chosen habitation. A knowledge of what is going on in politics and what

---

[1] RVF Heuston, 'Patrick Arthur Devlin 1905–1992' (1993) 84 *Proceedings of the British Academy* 247–62 at 250.
[2] Patrick Devlin, *The Judge* (Oxford, Oxford University Press, 1979), p 49.

is interesting people generally is the stuff of social talk; a judge needs it, as also he needs to read outside the law.

Patrick practised what he preached not only in the wide choice of friends which he and Madeleine made but also in his professional life. He was ready for a challenge. Indeed, sometimes to the disdain of his judicial colleagues, on occasions he accepted unconventional assignments whilst a sitting judge. He fully appreciated (although in his case it was not relevant) that ability was not the most important thing. Indeed, he told Anthony Sampson, writer, journalist and biographer of Mandela:[3]

> In most cases the facts aren't very difficult to get at: no, the most important thing for a judge is – curiously enough – judgment. It's not so very different from qualities of the successful businessman or civil servant. I'm always struck by how alike men in high positions seem to be. It's rather like seeing a lot of different parts of the stage, and finding that they're all Gerald du Maurier in the end.

A survey of the reported cases in which Patrick sat as a trial judge discloses the number of commercial cases he sat in, an area he was very familiar with. As was the practice in the King's Bench Division, he sat frequently in the Court of Criminal Appeal, often with Goddard presiding. More often than not Goddard would give judgment ex tempore. Patrick would usually agree. But over time Patrick would give the judgment with Goddard, not infrequently deferring to him. Whether sitting in civil or criminal law Patrick would himself give prompt judgment, rarely exceeding a short number of weeks, more usually the next day or at least within days after the hearing. His first reported case in early 1949 involved a claim for personal injuries.[4] He heard the case on 20 January, and gave his judgment the next day.

Juries and criminal law were of course only two of Patrick's jurisprudential interests. In the early 1950s Patrick's innovative mind turned to the topic of contract law. Along with others of his brethren, he was sometimes affronted by a merchant being able to rely on an exemption clause to the great disadvantage of a hapless consumer. An effective judicial method of railing against such an outcome was to give a narrow or strict construction to the particular clause. But Patrick, relying on some old cases, began attempting to formulate circumstances where some sort of principle could be articulated which went beyond the particular clause and its construction. He was prepared to grant relief to a litigant in the face of an exemption clause, having found a breach of 'some fundamental or basic condition of the contract' and where there was a 'fundamental breach going to the root of the contract'. In a number of subsequent cases he purported further to explain how his approach might work. Some other judges followed suit. Unfortunately for Patrick, the House of Lords

---

[3] Anthony Sampson, *Anatomy of Britain* (London, Hodder and Stoughton, 1962), p 156 – Interview with Lord Devlin.
[4] *Finch v Telegraph Construction and Maintenance Co Ltd* [1949] 1 All ER 542.

would ultimately reject his whole idea of fundamental breach and a breach of a fundamental term at least as having determinative significance.[5] Unsurprisingly, the modern approach is to construe the particular provision in the context of the contract as a whole.

A figure who at all times loomed large in Patrick's life as well as that of other legal luminaries of the day was Arthur Goodhart. As editor of a prestigious law journal of the day, Goodhart was in a quite a powerful situation. Each of Patrick, Denning and Goddard and many others vied for space for their articles or commentaries on their latest judgments in its pages. It must not be forgotten that Goodhart was an extremely wealthy, philanthropic anglophile. He clearly discerned the anxiety which gripped many who wanted recognition in the journal. Goodhart fully appreciated his influence. He was appointed to the prestigious office of Master of 'Univ' (University College, Oxford) in June 1951 which led to much celebration and further enhanced his position of influence. It is a little difficult now to appreciate quite the position Goodhart occupied at the time and his potency. His appointment as silk in 1943 and his knighthood in 1948 are ample examples of it. In late 1943 when a prominent member of the legal profession was sought out by the Home Office for a Parliamentary Committee, Goodhart was the favourite. However, Sir Claud Schuster, the long time and entirely autocratic permanent secretary to the Lord Chancellor's Office for some 30 years (of whom it was said that he ruled, whilst the Lord Chancellor of the day merely reigned) thought that notwithstanding Goodhart's ability and character, 'his talk and manner are so strongly Jewish' that he could not be counted upon 'to control such a Committee'.[6] Goodhart would never have known or perhaps even cared about Schuster's anti-semitism. There was not much room in his cap for many more feathers anyway. Patrick, for obvious reasons, would have been appalled at Schuster's views.[7]

As a judge, Patrick regularly saw counsel of varying qualities and abilities. However, on more than one occasion distinguished friends such as Sir Walter Monckton KC would appear before him, in obviously important cases.

In 1951 Sir Reginald Manningham-Buller was Solicitor-General. He was born in the same year as Patrick and had held a seat in the House of Commons for the Conservatives off and on since 1943. He was appointed King's Counsel in 1947 and Solicitor-General by Churchill in 1951, and accordingly knighted. He was

---

[5] See: *Chandris v Isbrandtsen-Moller Co. Inc.* [1951] 1 KB 240 at 248, 251 (Devlin J); *Alexander v Railway Executive* [1951] 2 KB 882 at 888–90 (Devlin J); *Smeaton Hanscomb and Co. Ltd. v Sassoon Setty Son & Co (No. 1)* [1953] 1 WLR 1468 at 1470 (Devlin J). See: *Swan Hunter and Wigham Richardson Ltd v France Fenwick Tyre & Wear Company (The Albion)* [1953] 1 WLR 1026 at 1030–32 (the Court of Appeal gave qualified support to Devlin's thesis). See also: *Swiss Atlantique Societé d'Armament SA v NV Rotterdamsche Kolen Centrale* [1967] 1 AC 361 (where the House of Lords rejected the notion of breach of a fundamental term). See also: Lord Devlin, 'The Treatment of Breach of Contract' (1966) 24(2) *Cambridge Law Journal* 192.

[6] Robert Stevens, *The Independence of the Judiciary, A View from the Lord Chancellor's Office* (Oxford, Oxford University Press, 1993), p 44.

[7] Ibid, 43–44.

known to friends and enemies alike as 'Reggie'. He was not without ability and industry. But both qualities were often disguised by a brusque manner or downright rudeness. Hence Bernard Levin's sobriquet for him: 'Bullying-Manner'. But in August 1952 as Solicitor-General he appeared before Patrick and two of his colleagues, Slade and Gorman JJ, constituting the Court of Criminal Appeal. It was a death penalty case involving the conviction of the appellant at the Winchester Assizes for the murder of a young girl. The trial judge, it was said, had erred in admitting evidence of two other murders and of statements allegedly made by the accused to police officers without the usual caution being administered. Although Justice Slade wrote the judgment Patrick and Justice Gorman concurred. This was perhaps the first time Manningham-Buller appeared before Patrick.[8] But the two would have their lives intertwined in a way neither could possibly then ever have imagined.

In further good news for the family, the energetic and vivacious Madeleine was appointed a lay magistrate. She would later become Chairman of her local branch. In May the same year, the ever active Patrick published an article in the *Modern Law Review* entitled 'The relation between commercial law and commercial practice'.[9] It explored how the commercial law remained relevant to contemporary business practices. There was unsurprisingly an emphasis on maritime and insurance cases, two areas Patrick had a lifelong interest in. The article showed how quickly Patrick's stature as a judge had grown in the first three years on the bench. Soon afterwards, Patrick was asked to deliver a paper on 'The Principles of Construction of Charterparties, Bills of Lading and Marine Policies' to the Norwegian Maritime Law Association in Oslo.[10]

From the outset, Patrick settled into a judicial style that would set him apart from others. He would habitually commence his judgments with a concise but entirely captivating and descriptive paragraph or two setting the scene and then more often than not, announce the result. This approach was a boon to the professional reader and student alike. And it showcased his erudition and sound judgement. He was always exceedingly thorough. Louis Blom-Cooper QC (who was called to Middle Temple in 1952) remembered as a very junior junior, not long after Patrick was appointed, assisting the legendary IH Jacob before Patrick on the construction of an arbitration agreement. There was no appearance for the defendant. Notwithstanding that, Patrick required full argument on 5 October 1953. He reserved and delivered a detailed judgment on 7 October.[11]

---

[8] *R v Straffen* [1952] 2 All ER 657.
[9] A lecture given at the London School of Economics and Political Science on 1 May 1951. Patrick Devlin, 'The Relation between Commercial Law and Commercial Practice' (1951) 14(3) *Modern Law Review* 249.
[10] Lecture given before the Norwegian Maritime Law Association on 4 June 1952, and printed in (1953) 1 *Arkiv for Sjørett* 281 (Oslo, University Press).
[11] Interview between Sir Louis Blom-Cooper QC and the Author, London, 16 January 2018. See also: *Christopher Brown Ltd v Genossenschaft Österreichischer Waldbesitzer Holzwirtschaftsbetriebe GmbH* [1953] 2 All ER 1039, [1954] 1 QB 8.

Whilst the public might rightly expect this conduct to be standard, there are many judges who are never capable of attaining it. Blom-Cooper's surprise on the other hand, is best explained by a lack of experience. Counsel, when appearing without opposition, must be entirely candid and a judge will rightly need to give reasons, especially if the result is against the absent litigant.

Patrick in a sense made the point himself in correspondence with Arthur Goodhart in discussing the difference, as he saw it, between perception and evaluation and fact-finding in general. He said:[12]

> In a case of importance or difficulty I always try to find the facts (perceived) in detail so as to let the Court of Appeal have all the scope it wants for evaluation. But I do not think this is practicable in every case. Take the ordinary running down case. If it is simply a question of saying yes or no did the defendant put his hand out, that is one thing. But the picture is rarely drawn in black and white. The defendant swears he did put his hand out for at least half a minute, the plaintiff says that is quite impossible as he never saw it. The truth certainly lies somewhere between the two ... It would be unnecessarily laborious if in this type of case, of which he tries two or three a day on circuit, he had to go through the facts and state exactly what he finds about the way in which the accident had happened in order that the Court of Appeal might evaluate them. To have to come down on one side or the other on each point of disputed fact would not only be laborious but would give in the end an untrue picture because it would force the judge into drawing it precisely in black and white when in truth what emerges from the evidence is rather blurred and there is what President Wilson called 'a penumbra about the edges of each statement of fact'.

The passage is interesting for a number of reasons. First the obvious – Patrick's 'perception' of his role as a judge, but secondly very few people knew he was then starting a 20-year project – a biography of Woodrow Wilson.

The year 1953 was an unusual one in Patrick's diary. It was the year he would for a short time relinquish his role as judge and take up a role as litigant. Judges for obvious reasons should be wary of venturing into the courts. It is clearly best avoided. Clearly if a person is sued in their private capacity and they happen to be a judge not much can be done about it. But becoming a plaintiff is a very different situation.

Patrick and Madeleine had a particularly difficult neighbour on the adjoining farm in Wiltshire – a Mr Drewry. Patrick claimed a right of way for agricultural purposes over part of it. As any reasonable person would, Patrick tried to settle the case by having the neighbour agree to appoint counsel to investigate the matter, and abide by the result of the opinion, the loser paying the other's costs. Drewry would have no part of it, so Patrick was left with little choice. The matter was appropriately brought in the Chancery Division and came on

---

[12] Letter from Devlin to Goodhart, 18 June 1954, papers Arthur Lehman Goodhart, Bodleian Library Archives, University of Oxford, folios 87–92.

for hearing before Mr Justice Upjohn between 8 and 10 July 1953. The line-up was stellar.

Mr Justice Upjohn had been appointed two years earlier to the Chancery Division. In time he would join Patrick in the Court of Appeal and the House of Lords. Both parties retained Queen's Counsel. Patrick had Charles Russell QC, part of the Russell legal dynasty. He would be appointed to the Chancery Division in 1960, the Court of Appeal in 1962 and ultimately the House of Lords in 1975. Drewry had retained Reginald Goff QC, who also became a judge of appeal. In Patrick's case he had instructed his old firm Withers.

Patrick's case was that a trackway led from the northern part of his farm across Drewry's farm and that since the common vendor of his farm and Drewry's farm had used the trackway in connection with Patrick's farm there was on the sale to Patrick an implied grant of a right of way. Alternatively, he relied on the Prescription Act 1832. Drewry, as part of defending the case, had padlocked a gate preventing Patrick access. He accepted that the public used the trackway from time to time but denied Patrick's right to use of the trackway for heavy vehicles, which he asserted had or would damage the trackway.

Anthony Hurd, a local Conservative MP, had been a tenant of Drewry's farm for many years between 1926 and 1947. He had used the trackway for transporting some farming equipment without complaint and never asked permission to do so from the then owner. The managing director of a lime company which delivered lime said he was quite satisfied the trackway would accommodate a lorry of size without causing any damage. Finally, Patrick gave evidence of his purchase of his farm in 1943 and his use of the trackway for agricultural purposes without asking permission until 1952, when the gate was locked.

In cross-examination, Goff QC challenged Patrick on precisely what he was claiming as a right, to which he somewhat cheekily responded that if counsel went to the site he could see the track for himself and that how it differs from the surrounding land. This was a first for Patrick both in giving evidence as well as in being cross-examined and in due course judged publicly by one of his colleagues. In any event Patrick said he did not think the trackway had been damaged by lorries delivering and spreading lime but accepted that lorries should not perhaps deliver in bad weather. Drewry gave evidence saying he had used the trackway to drive sheep and walking and riding. He asserted the trackway had become a shambles. When asked by Russell QC whether any witness other than himself had described the trackway as a shambles, he said that Patrick's actions amounted to 'sheer vandalism'.

The judge in ruling in Patrick's favour did so largely on Goff QC's proper concession that the trackway had long been used for agricultural purposes since at least 1889, not only for pedestrians and riders, but also for vehicles. Goff QC, however, argued Patrick could not use the trackway for heavy vehicles, especially in wet weather. The judge said Patrick's use of the trackway had to be reasonable and that he knew there would be a consequence if he used heavy vehicles in wet weather, however there was no evidence he would do that. Patrick got the relief he had sought without restriction and was also awarded costs.[13]

Parochial a case though it was, it is always a high-risk strategy for a sitting judge to pursue actively a remedy before the very court of which the judge is a member. This is especially so when issues of credit are likely to arise. Litigation is a burdensome and expensive distraction for anyone, let alone a judge. Given the obvious state of the evidence however, which was all one way on long user, Drewry clearly must have rejected advice to give in. On the available evidence there was really only one outcome available. But court lists are overflowing with litigants who simply want their day in court. For Drewry no doubt it was inevitably a very expensive three days.

Domestic distractions over 1954 brought some very flattering news for Patrick. Excitedly he told Goodhart on 18 March that he had been invited to deliver the prestigious Hamlyn Lectures in 1956. In due course they would be published over again and for decades would be regarded as salutary reading for aspiring trial judges. He presumed, probably accurately, that Goodhart had recommended him. He would join good company. Denning had delivered the first series in 1949 and Goodhart had followed a few years later in 1952. Patrick chose the jury as his topic. In writing his lectures he was to coin one of the most frequently quoted remarks ever made about the institution when he said in his concluding lecture and in the context of its declining use:[14]

> Each jury is a little parliament. The jury sense is the parliamentary sense. I cannot see one dying and the other surviving. The first object of any tyrant in Whitehall would be to make Parliament utterly subservient to his will; and the next to overthrow or diminish trial by jury, for no tyrant could afford to leave a subject's freedom in the hands of twelve of his countrymen. So that trial by jury is more than an instrument of justice and more than one wheel of the constitution: it is the lamp that shows freedom lives.

For most trial judges, appointment is followed by some period of service. Promotion to a higher court or diversity of function is something many never have the opportunity of experiencing. Patrick got both.

In July 1955 Patrick was invited by Sir Walter Monckton QC to chair a committee to inquire into the operation of the Dock Workers Scheme.[15] He was joined by four others comprising of academics and civil servants. The task was to review the scheme and suggest any amendments thought necessary. The Scheme covered some 81,000 relevant employees and some 1248 registered employers. The essence of the Scheme as it existed provided for dual control of the docks by the National Dock Labour Board, on which both sides of industry were equally represented. It also regulated the terms and conditions of

---

[13] *Devlin v Drewry*, *Times Law Reports*, 8, 9 and 10 July 1953.

[14] The eighth in a series of lectures delivered at London University in November 1956.

[15] Report of a Committee appointed on 27 July 1955, to Inquire into the Operation of the Dock Workers (Regulation of Employment) Scheme 1947 (Cmd. 9813, 1955–56).

employment of employees registered under the Scheme. Notwithstanding the dual management of the docks, but rather because of it, they had become an unhappy place. Major strikes, alleged conflicts of interest, inter-union rivalry and indiscipline were just some of the issues which had made the employers discontent. They wanted substantial change.

Patrick and his fellow committee members gave a comprehensive report in which they recommended the employers' requests be denied, although not without an element of sarcasm from Patrick. In praising the uncomplaining and sincere adherence on the part of the employers to the Scheme the report in part reads:[16]

> We are satisfied that the Employers are, as they say, suffering from a feeling of frustration. For eight years they have fulfilled the letter of the Scheme. They have not haggled about their obligation under; it does not appear that they have ever quarrelled about the size of the levy or about the expenditure on welfare or about the big reserves which the Board has been allowed to build up. This to our mind disposes of any charge of insincerity. They have scrupulously kept their side of all the bargains made in the National Joint Council. A substantial proportion of the men have not; and the repudiation has been not once but again and again. Consequently the Employers have had to face a continual disturbance of the essential conditions of their trade. Even if they had been prepared – and there is no reason why they should – to forego their rights under agreements freely negotiated by the men's representatives, they still would have been subjected to serious injury arising from Trade Union rivalries and other causes which are no concern of theirs. They say, we think with justification, that the Trade Union leaders look on all this far too complacently. The latter do not propose any means of dealing with the general problem of unrest; and they have given us, as well as the Employers, the impression that they have not sufficiently considered whether there are any such means. They appear to look upon these troubles rather as our forefathers regarded the plague; there is nothing to do about it except to expect a visitation from time to time, wait till it was over and bury the dead.

From about 1948 when he first proposed it, Sir David Maxwell-Fyfe KC (knighted in 1942 upon being appointed Solicitor-General, later Viscount Kilmuir) had agitated for a 'Restrictive Practices Commission' with specific responsibility for handling claims against companies alleged to be benefiting from monopolies and other restrictive trade arrangements. Numerous debates, legislation and various government reports later, the Lord Chancellor, Viscount Kilmuir thought that a body similar to a court of law ought to be created to apply legal criteria to determine trade disputes including issues concerning alleged monopolistic behaviour. The real debate concerned the appropriateness of giving to judges power to make decisions about industry matters hitherto made by the state. Intense feelings were provoked by the issue, not least among the judges themselves. Lord Kilmuir stood firm on his proposal. The new Court

---

[16] Ibid, p 46.

would be seised with deciding whether a trade agreement was in the public interest. Appeals to traditional courts on points of law would ensure certainty and predictability. Kilmuir was at least politically astute enough to appreciate that a judge might not be seen to provide an impartial outcome in what otherwise could so easily be characterised as a political issue about competition by descending into the arena of public affairs. The majority of Chancery judges told the Lord Chancellor's office (relevantly Sir George Coldstream, Permanent Secretary of the Lord Chancellor's Office) that they did not want the job or thought it inappropriate for a sitting judge. The judges of the Queen's Bench Division were also opposed. Lord Goddard called a special meeting of judges to discuss the issue. Coldstream himself thought the notion 'thoroughly unsound' and tried to mobilise views amongst other senior civil servants in the true style of Sir Humphrey Appleby.[17] The Labour party also opposed it. But the Federation of British Industry insisted on a court. Patrick emphatically and conspicuously put his hand up in support of the idea.

Patrick wrote unsolicited to Kilmuir on 7 March 1956 in what was tantamount to a job application:[18]

> I do not see why the working of the judicial part of it should lead to any exceptional difficulty and I welcome a decision that issues of great importance between Government and individuals should be determined by the High Court.

Kilmuir cooed on 8 March: 'You put exactly my view on a subject which has worried me a great deal.'[19]

Patrick with encouragement and a good deal of familiarity, responded on 12 March:[20]

> I feel that the idea you are using in the bill, – the combination of the judiciary with those experienced in other sorts of administration, – might with the aid of a new and flexible procedure develop into the right way of dealing with the whole problem of the Government's legal relation to the citizen. What will then be needed is the creation of new jurisprudence and a Hardwicke or a Mansfield or a Marshall to do it. Tom Denning would do it superbly. I should like to see the Exchequer Division revived with him at the head of it ...

> If it (the High Court) is going to play its full part in the future life of the nation, it must not barricade itself within its existing functions, even though an adaptation may contain an element of risk. At least that is what I believe, but clearly it is not at all the general view of the judges. If this experiment failed, – not necessarily a breakdown but a failure to produce convincing results, – the stand-patters will be

---

[17] Robert Stevens, *Independence of the Judiciary, a View from the Lord Chancellor's Office* (Oxford, Clarendon Press, 1993), p 103. Sir Humphrey Appleby was a fictional character in the BBC TV series *Yes Minister* (1980–84) and *Yes Prime Minister* (1986–88). The Permanent Secretary in the 'Department of Administrative Affairs', he was a master of obfuscation and manipulation.
[18] Ibid, p 107.
[19] Ibid, p 107.
[20] Ibid, p 107.

confirmed and it will be very difficult again to use the High Court for the solution for any new problems.

To complete the flattery Patrick referred to a speech delivered by Kilmuir on the dynamic nature of the common law on 19 March:[21] 'I am very glad you will be (barring some Socialist intermissions!) Lord Chancellor for the next twenty years or more and that you think as I do.'

Perhaps there was no surprise that Patrick was appointed the first President of the Court, which began hearing cases in April 1958. Clearly whatever view Coldstream had of his appointment, it would have been necessary for Goddard to have agreed. Whilst Patrick set about emphasising the judicial nature of his role, he was adamant that the basic policy of decision-making was the promotion of competition. He sought carefully to nurture competition on the basis that it would benefit the public unless the contrary was proved to encourage greater efficiency within an industry. Patrick's somewhat doctrinaire approach was not always favoured by successive judicial Presidents but the tone was well and truly set.[22]

Leading counsel of the day took little time in producing treatises on the operation of the legislation, including Charles Fletcher-Cooke, a barrister who had been one of Patrick's pupils and would ultimately write Patrick's obituary in *The Times* in 1992.[23]

To cap off 1956 Patrick felt honoured to be invited to deliver the Sherrill Lectures at Yale University Law School.[24] Again, Patrick chose a criminal theme: the prosecution of crime from the time of arrest until the time of arraignment, and the rights and duties of the Crown and of the accused while the case for prosecution was being prepared for trial. Like the Hamlyn Lectures, they would be published over again. Apart from Glanville Williams (an academic of repute), no judge had previously provided insight into these issues.[25]

1956 also saw Patrick become the President of the Bentham Club. It was formed in 1949 in order to maintain and strengthen relationships between alumni and friends of University College London. The first President was Lord du Parq, followed by the likes of Lord Justice Denning (1952), and Lord Evershed (1953). Patrick was the its eighth President. Each year the President is obliged to give an occasional address. In his year Patrick chose 'The Common Law, Public Policy and the Executive' as his topic, which exposed what Patrick saw as the receding

---

[21] Ibid, p 107.

[22] RB Stevens and BS Yamey, *The Restrictive Practices Court* (London, Weidenfeld & Nicholson, 1965), pp 119–21.

[23] Michael Albery QC and CF Fletcher-Cooke, *Monopolies and Restrictive Trade Practices* (London, Stevens & Sons, 1956).

[24] The Sherrill Lectures were delivered in September 1957 at the Yale University Law School. They were published the following year: Sir Patrick Devlin, *The Criminal Prosecution in England* (New Haven CT, Yale University Press, 1958).

[25] See, for example Glanville Williams, *The Proof of Guilt: A Study of the English Criminal Trial*. The Hamlyn Lectures Seventh Series (London, Steven & Sons Limited, 1955).

ability of the common law to protect citizens from the state, largely due to the increase in the amount of statutory law.[26] Common law, he said, had grown by the formation of precedents which in turn controlled its development. But precedent he asserted, when finally established became as rigid as the branch of a tree. With all its faults, he concluded that judge-made law was better than statute law. The Parliament, he concluded was now the ultimate keeper of the public interest:[27]

> I have not, it is true paid all the usual tributes to Our Lady of the Common Law. I have ventured instead to say that she is not as young as she once was and that she cannot any longer indulge in the activities which in her youth she would have taken in her stride.

While a little on the dour side, it was a considered and important analysis.

But something much more momentous was occurring in the Devlin family. Indeed, a quiet revolution was afoot. Patrick's brother Christopher, a Jesuit priest, was conducting missionary work in Africa. He and Patrick, and in time Madeleine, were very close. Christopher has a special bond with each of Patrick's children. Christopher was a scholar and intellectual of note, though he was only appreciated in a very narrow context. He was himself a published author. In 1956 his *Life of Robert Southwell* about the Elizabethan poet and martyr was published to rightful acclaim.[28] He dedicated the book to Patrick and Madeleine. Patrick's relationship with the church was frayed and remained so until shortly before his death. He told his children he was agnostic. Although a number of them had been baptised, none attended Catholic schools and none had, at least until 1956, been brought up in the Catholic faith. As Patrick was both titular and intellectual head of the family, Christopher was its spiritual leader. The impact of Christopher's sacrifice and selflessness in his priestly activities profoundly affected Madeleine and the children with whom he individually corresponded.

The revolution took the form of Madeleine's decision to become a Catholic, followed by that of a number of the children.[29] The decisions were actively encouraged by Christopher. Patrick did not interfere and indeed to some extent was supportive. Christopher's work as a missionary not only provided amusing as well as accurate and moving portraits of Africa. It provided for all concerned an example of priestly work at its best. But despite Christopher's example, Patrick remained unmoved. When the family attended Mass on Sunday, Patrick

---

[26] Address by Devlin as President of the Bentham Club given in 1956 and published in (1956) 9(1) *Current Legal Problems* 1.

[27] Ibid, p 15.

[28] Christopher Devlin, *The Life of Robert Southwell, poet and martyr* (dedicated to 'Patrick and Madeleine') (London, Longmans, Green & Co Ltd, 1956).

[29] See: Madeleine Devlin, *Christopher Devlin, A Biography* (London, McMillan, 1970), pp 136–39. See also: email from Timothy Devlin to the Author, 24 April 2016.

would not venture inside the church but would often walk to meet them as they returned.[30]

Christmas 1956 brought a case that could have come straight out of a law student's examination. The case concerned the liability (if any) for the keeping of dangerous animals and the application of the scienter rule. It involved a circus, a fun-fair, a married couple (the plaintiffs), six Burmese elephants (who ran amok) and a very naughty but small dog named Simba, whose barking caused the problem.[31] The issue was whether the defendant circus owners were liable for the damage the elephants caused when the barking of the dog (owned by the plaintiffs' manager) caused the elephants to stampede. A roaring fire at West Wick and a decent glass of Bordeaux produced a judgment and an award of damages in January 1957 for the husband and wife in the sums of £480 and £2,930 respectively.

---

[30] Email from Timothy Devlin to the Author, 24 July 2015.
[31] *Behrens and Another v Bertram Mills Circus Ltd* [1957] 1 All ER 583.

5

The Celebrity

B Y 1957 PATRICK had been a trial judge for the best part of nine years. He had by then gathered considerable judicial experience across a wide range of legal matters, especially in the area of crime. Partly as a result of his Hamlyn Lectures delivered at the end of 1956, he had become a minor celebrity in legal circles. Arthur Goodhart along with many others sent their congratulations to Patrick. On 7 January Patrick responded to Goodhart's applause with his customary generosity, if a little sycophancy:[1]

> It will be a long time – if ever, before I again get such a nice letter from you: for I cannot foresee an equal trinity of reasons ever recurring! I am particularly pleased that you liked the Hamlyn lectures: your approval of my work always gives me great pride.
>
> I think the R.P. Court work will be very interesting but I'm glad to have your estimate that it is not likely to last more than two or three years. I do not want to be shunted off the common law for too long. With your experience on the Commission and your knowledge of anti-trust law, you must know a very great deal about the subject, and I should very much like to have a talk with you before the work begins – that is not likely to be for some time I gather.

In the year before, and long before Patrick became involved, a general medical practitioner in the beautiful seaside resort town of Eastbourne was to encounter a few difficulties. Dr John Bodkin Adams had practised there since 1922. He brought with him from Ireland a good deal of that country's usual charm, but not much by way of real technical ability. Nonetheless, he had prospered over the years and was now the senior partner in a lucrative practice. He purported to be a deeply religious and self-righteous man. He was in fact stupid, obstinate and dishonest.

Sybille Bedford, who wrote an excellent account of his ultimate trial for murder, *The Best We Can Do*, described him as follows:[2]

> And now the prisoner, the accused himself is here – how had he come, how had one missed the instant of that other clockwork entry? – standing in the front of the dock,

---

[1] Letter from Devlin to Goodhart, 7 January 1957, papers of Arthur Lehman Goodhart, Bodleian Library Archives, Oxford University, folio 96.

[2] Sybille Bedford, *The Best We Can Do: An Account of the Trial of John Bodkin Adams* (London, Collins, 1958), p 17.

spherical, adipose, upholstered in blue serge, red-faced, bald, facing the Judge, facing this day.

Somewhat inconveniently, he had become involved in an inquest into the death of one of his patients, a Mrs Hullett, in July 1956. But that was not to turn out to be the only problem the doctor was to face. The police, who had become suspicious and begun investigations, also became interested in at least two other deaths – her husband, Mr Hullett, and a female patient who had died some years earlier.

As a result of their investigation the police had clearly formed the view that he had systematically been killing off his patients to get money they had left him in their wills. And he had form. In 1935 he had been involved a court case in which an elderly female patient had left him £3,000 under her will and had made him executor. The family was less than impressed, but unsuccessfully contested the will. This was not the only estate from which he had benefited. Rumours had been circulating for years that he had procured gifts of various kinds from grateful patients whilst heavily sedating them and 'easing their passing'. There was another estate in 1954 worth £7,000 of which Dr Adams got £5,200.

Another elderly patient, a Mrs Morrell, was the wealthy widow of a Liverpool businessman. On 25 June 1948 at the age of about 79, she suffered a serious stroke which left her paralysed on the left side. She had been visiting her son in Cheshire and was admitted to a local hospital there. In early July she went to a nursing home in Eastbourne and soon thereafter became one of the doctor's patients. She moved eventually to a house in Eastbourne but remained bedridden until her death in the middle of November 1950. In July the doctor prescribed doses of both morphia (morphine) and heroin in the ensuing months in very large quantities. She survived ten and a half months in his care. Sometimes the drugs were administered by the doctors but on a number of occasions they were administered by nurses.

There was, however, a series of suspicious circumstances. For example, in April 1949 Dr Adams telephoned the patient's solicitor telling him that Mrs Morrell was extremely anxious about her will and requested that he call on Mrs Morrell urgently that day. Thereafter she made a new will in which she bequeathed Dr Adams an oak chest containing silver. He continued to treat Mrs Morrell with the same heavy-handed regime of drugs.

On 8 March 1950 Adams called on Mrs Morrell's solicitor unannounced and told him Mrs Morrell had told Adams that she had forgotten to make provision in her will for him to get a Rolls-Royce motor car and the contents of a strong-box held at her bank which contained jewellery. He insisted that the solicitor make a codicil immediately, even though he told the solicitor she was extremely unwell, but nonetheless clear headed. The solicitor, unsurprisingly troubled by this, suggested he would wait until Mrs Morrell's son visited on the weekend. Not to be deterred, Adams suggested the codicil be prepared and executed and later destroyed if it did not meet her wishes. On 19 July 1950 she executed a codicil leaving all of her estate (which included her house, Rolls-Royce and other possessions) to Adams if her son predeceased her. On 5 August she made a fresh will leaving Adams the above mentioned oak chest containing silver and if her son predeceased her, her Rolls-Royce and an Elizabethan cupboard. However, on or about 15 September when Adams went on holiday, she revoked her gifts to him by a further codicil. She was angry at his going away and made no secret about it. However, by 25 September Adams was back in her favour and the latest codicil torn up. Mrs Morrell died on 13 November 1950. There were irregularities in her death certificate, no mention was made of his inheritance and Adams made some strange statements to Detective Superintendent Hannam when subsequently interviewed.

Some years later, a Mrs Tomlinson became Dr Adams' patient after the death of her first husband in 1950. She was then in her forties and he had been the headmaster of a school in Eastbourne. She was reportedly in poor health both physically and psychologically and from time to time was speaking of suicide. Dr Adams claimed he assisted her regain her health and make new friends. One such friend was a Mr Hullett, a recently widowed man in his sixties. Mr Hullett was also a patient of Adams who would visit him every Sunday morning. The Hulletts married in due course and by all accounts the marriage was a great success.

In November 1955, Mr Hullett had major abdominal surgery and was convalescing at home when he took ill. Dr Adams attended some time later but he died later that evening. Adams certified that the cause of death was cerebral haemorrhage accompanied by coronary thrombosis. He left a large estate substantially to his wife and a £500 legacy to Adams. The doctor continued to treat Mrs Hullett who was quite nervous and began again to speak of suicide. He visited her regularly and prescribed sedatives for her. On 19 July she went to bed complaining of headache, took a massive dose of barbiturates, fell into a coma and died a few days later. She had left letters which spoke of her despair. She left her estate mainly to family, but Dr Adams inherited her Rolls-Royce. Just prior to her death she had given Dr Adams a cheque for £1,000 which apparently related to a promise made by her husband at some stage to buy Dr Adams a car. The doctor had asked for a special clearance of the cheque, which was cleared on the day Mrs Hullett fell into a coma. After she took ill, a Dr Harris from Adams' practice attended upon her prior to death. Adams diagnosed her as having suffered a cerebral vascular event. In due course an inquest was ordered. The post-mortem report found an inordinate amount of barbiturates in her blood. Adams was closely questioned on his treatment regime which had included on one occasion leaving Mrs Hullett with a number of days' supply of sedatives when he went on holiday.

A police investigation got underway almost immediately. An inquest was formally opened in July but the hearing did not resume until August.

At the hearing the coroner instructed the jury that there a number of possible alternatives open, including accident and/or suicide as but two. The coroner was critical of Adams for failing to properly care for Mrs Hullett but appeared to rule out criminal negligence. The jury returned a verdict of suicide: she had died after swallowing the tablets of her own free will.[3]

By now the media had become interested in the case and began reporting rumours about Adams and the allegation that he had been despatching many of his elderly patients for personal gain.

Detective Superintendent Hannam was already on the case but the inquest provoked a major police investigation. Most newspapers portrayed Adams as a mass murderer. However, Percy Hoskins from the *Express* was part of a small minority who thought him innocent and was quite vocal in condemning his fourth estate colleagues. Hannam interviewed Adams in October about drugs and legacies.

Hannam was also known as 'the Count' because of his elegant if not mildly ostentatious dress code and for his taste in expensive cigars. The Count and a colleague called Hewett harboured no doubts about Adams' guilt: too many deaths, too many wills, too many gifts and legacies, and all concerning the same doctor. Hannam discovered exactly what he hoped he would. A search at Somerset House disclosed 132 wills in which Adams was a legatee. Patient files were examined, along with prescription records. Bodies were exhumed and the extent and timing of gifts analysed. But that was the easy part. Proving him guilty of murder was quite another thing. Then again, Adams had said and done some very suspicious things. His behaviour when questioned was odd. He mused about 'easing the passing' of his patients when questioned by Hannam.[4] He had falsely filled out death certificates and taken a course of action on more than one occasion designed to avoid an inquest. In short, he was his own worst enemy. The question was and would forever remain whether he was a knave or only a fool.

But to build a prosecution case required a good deal more evidence. Somewhat extraordinarily, the Attorney-General decided to play politics. He decided he would show Hannam's report to a Dr Macrae, the Honorary Secretary of the British Medical Association, ostensibly so that he could persuade the President that certain Eastbourne doctors should co-operate with police. It may also be that the Attorney-General was trying to get the message across that the prosecution case was overwhelming.

The Attorney-General attracted both questioning and criticism in due course over this strategy.[5] But as always, he adhered to his course. Hannam had also been criticised for allegedly leaking his own report.[6]

---

[3] See: ETP, for a general chronology of 'Principal Dates' and 'The Last Prescriptions' listed at the front of the book, prior to the commencement of the narrative. For a description of the proceedings before the coroner and his findings, see: ETP, pp 14–17.

[4] ETP, 7.

[5] Ibid, p 183.

[6] Pamela Cullen, *A Stranger in Blood, The casefiles on Dr John Bodkin Adams* (London, Elliott and Thompson, 2006), p 656.

There followed interviews with nurses, doctors, solicitors and others, and of course the retaining of expert witnesses on the doctor's drug regime. Consideration was also given to whether or not to proceed with Mrs Morrell's case alone, or to have a second indictment ready for Mrs Hullett's murder as well. This would avoid complex arguments about Dr Adams' system. On 24 November 1956, police searched Adams' home. On 26 November he was arrested on minor charges, involving drugs, cremation certificates, and alleged forgery of NHS documents. Adams told Hannam he had been 'easing the passing' of Mrs Morrell. On 27 November Adams was committed for trial at Lewes Assizes on the minor related charges and granted bail.[7]

On 19 December Adams was charged with the murder of Mrs Morrell and remanded in custody. On 14 January 1957 committal proceedings commenced at Eastbourne on the Morrell murder charge. The Crown alleged he had also murdered Mr and Mrs Hullett. A doctor standing trial for the murder of his patient was both unusual and highly newsworthy. Indeed, it would be an understatement to suggest that such a story could remain of purely local interest. The committal proceedings attracted national publicity.

At committal the Crown was represented by Melford Stevenson QC (who was later to become a judge), with him Malcolm Morris. The defence was led by Geoffrey Lawrence QC (who also later became a judge) and with him Edward Clarke. Defence counsel were retained courtesy of the Medical Defence Union, as were no doubt medical consultants at no cost to Adams, not only to assist counsel to understand the medicine but also to provide Adams with his own expert witnesses.

Neither Stevenson QC nor Lawrence QC were criminal lawyers of any real experience, although both were highly successful barristers. Both had general practices. In Stevenson QC's case, it was predominately commercial. In Lawrence QC's it was planning. However, Stevenson QC had in 1955 unsuccessfully defended a woman charged with murdering her lover. She was found guilty and was hanged. In Lawrence QC's case this was his first criminal trial.

The Crown strategy was to proceed with the charge of alleged murder of one elderly patient whilst seeking to tender the evidence of his treatment of another younger woman in order to suggest some form of system. Each case would have to be advanced as a separate count of murder, in two separate indictments. However, theoretically at least, the facts in one case could be advanced in the other case in order to prove the system. But such evidence could only (at that time) be admitted if each case on its own facts gave rise to a strong suspicion of guilt and if the other case or cases were 'strikingly similar' to the first.

The problem for the Crown was that whoever was the architect of its case had arguably designed a faulty structure. It was not as if there was little to go on. The police had an abundance of material, perhaps too much. They had

---

[7] ETP, chapter 4, in particular pp 32–33.

investigated dozens of cases and interviewed many witnesses including doctors and nurses. Of all the cases, the two which the Crown chose for this prosecution did have decided similarities but perhaps many significant differences.

True, the victims were both patients. They were rich. Each had left the doctor legacies or made gifts to him. Each had been treated and/or heavily medicated for periods by Adams. The Crown called expert evidence from a Doctor Douthwaite, an expert on morphine and heroin, who said unequivocally that the drug regime was excessive, extremely dangerous, unnecessary and ultimately lethal. And so the trial of the century was gathering momentum. For all the investigation undertaken by Hannam and Hewett, there were to be exposed some fundamental flaws in the Crown's case theory. What was remarkable is that vital information was simply not pursued or fully appreciated. The prosecution theory had to be, first, that Adams for financial gain had expedited the death of Mrs Morrell, and secondly, that the drug regime was excessive and not a reasonable or necessary response to her clinical state.

There is little doubt that Rayner Goddard hand-picked Patrick for the trial. The Lord Chief Justice would himself normally have heard such a case. Although he was almost 80, he was extremely fit and well up to the task. It is reasonable to assume that as an admirer of Patrick's, he had Patrick's future in mind – almost certainly as his possible successor. By early 1957 he would have known that he would be retiring the following year and his replacement as Lord Chief Justice had already been the subject of speculation. He also held Sir Hartley Shawcross (who had been Attorney-General between 1945 and 1951 in the Attlee Labour Government) in high regard. According to Shawcross, Goddard broached the possibility of the position with him.[8] However, Shawcross at that stage was still a devout Labour man and correctly regarded himself as having little prospect of being appointed by a Conservative government. He was nonetheless contemplating defecting to the Conservative Party and acquired the nickname 'Shortly Floorcross'. In the end he simply threw his hands in the air and left politics completely.

Although Patrick was not known to Harold Macmillan, Prime Minister since 10 January 1957, his deputy Rab Butler was one of Patrick's closest friends and Lord Kilmuir, then Lord Chancellor, thought very highly of Patrick. Goddard would have fully appreciated, however, that the Attorney-General of the day would have had an historical lien on the job of Lord Chief Justice. For what it is worth it seems Patrick was Goddard's choice, but in the end neither Patrick nor Manningham-Buller would prevail. There were other contenders. Kilmuir would in due course be offered it, but would reject it. Monckton QC would have liked it but was unaware that Goddard was dead against him and said so, ostensibly because Monckton QC had been the guilty party in divorce proceedings.

[8] Lord Birkenhead, *Walter Monckton, The Life of Viscount Monckton of Brenchley* (London, Weidenfeld & Nicolson, 1969), p 304. See also: Hartley Shawcross, *Life Sentence: The Memoirs of Hartley Shawcross* (London, Constable, 1995), pp 73, 168.

Indeed, Goddard said he would continue to serve so long as Monckton QC was a possibility. However it became public knowledge that Monckton QC would leave politics in early 1957. Patrick congratulated him on his move but would have been pleased that another contender was out of the way. He wrote on 6 February:[9]

> I suppose that the notice in Saturday's Times means that you have taken the plunge out of the law and that in due course you will be elected Chairman of the Bank. (If it is necessary to secure your election, I authorise you to assure your fellow directors that I for one shall be quite content to leave my overdraft where it is under the new regime). It is a wonderful post, but no more than you deserve, and I am delighted to think that you will no longer have to make the immense financial sacrifice that you have been for the last six years.
>
> But your leaving the law is a tragedy, – especially just at this moment. However, I suppose that Justice will get the Chief it deserves!

Monckton QC instantly replied:[10]

> Thank you for your letter of today. You are quite right. I have taken the plunge out of the law and I expect in due course, i.e., by 2nd July, to be appointed Chairman of the Midland Bank; though this is not yet public property it seems pretty generally known. It is good of you to say what you do about my leaving the law. I am sad about it but Rayner had told me that he intended to stay until next October. By that time I will be nearer 67 than 66 and may be, particularly if there is a likelihood of a fairly early General Election, he might postpone departure again. In all the circumstances I thought it was unseemly to wait on for him either to shuffle off this mortal coil or off the bench. I further thought I ought to get down at once to whatever further job of work I can still do. The Midland Bank seems a great opportunity and I will do my best with it. Do not let us lose touch. We maintained it somehow during the six years I have been away – it ought to be easier now I will be less overworked.

Goddard always knew the Adams trial would attract an enormous amount of publicity. In picking Patrick for the role, Goddard gave him a showcase in which to expose his wares. He also well appreciated that Manningham-Buller would lead for the prosecution, but that Patrick would hold the upper hand as the trial judge. The two rivals would have to square it off as it were under the arc lights.

Manningham-Buller, a political survivor, *par excellence*, was at all times busy on all manner of responsibilities, political and legal. Although hard-working and in many ways astute, he was not as forensically experienced as Patrick. If Melford Stevenson QC could have put his passion and prejudices to one side he would have been of greater assistance in the preparation of the Prosecution's case. But by the late fifties Bernard Levin had already popularised the soubriquet

[9] Letter from Devlin to Monckton, 6 February 1957, the Balliol College Archives, Oxford University, folio 33.
[10] Letter from Monckton to Devlin, 6 February 1957, the Balliol College Archives, Oxford University, folio 34.

'Bullying-Manner'. Melford Stevenson QC would probably have had difficulty in changing Manningham-Buller's views on anything unless he took him head on, which does not seem to have happened.

Very soon after he was assigned the case Patrick busied himself with a number of important procedural issues. He had discussed aspects of the trial with Goddard and was most concerned about the publicity the committal proceedings had received. He thought of segregating the jury. On the 19 February he wrote to a number of people including the Attorney-General and the Under-Sheriff about arrangements for the trial. Rather oddly, he did not write to Lawrence QC for Adams. Patrick sent Manningham-Buller a typed letter:[11]

> I do not know if you have heard that I am going to try this case which I believe is now to be taken in the March sessions. There are one or two points in connection with the arrangements for it that I would like to have a word with you about some time. There is no hurry, – just when you can make it convenient.

On 20 February Manningham-Buller replied in handwriting:[12] 'Thank you for your letter. Yes, I had heard that you were going to try the case. I would be delighted to come to see you. Perhaps our clerks could arrange a mutually convenient time.'

A note which Patrick later prepared as an agenda for his discussions with Manningham-Buller identified the topics for discussion as follows:[13]

- Segregation of the jury
- Possible sitting a little longer each day if they are segregated, so that do not keep them longer than have to.
- Whether a transcript of evidence taken.

As a result of his Hamlyn Lectures in 1956, Patrick had thought more deeply more recently than almost anyone in the country about juries and jury trials. He was greatly concerned about the way the matter had proceeded to date with all the attendant publicity. As a realist he understood only too well he would be in control of a cause célèbre of mammoth proportions. He understood that his prime obligation above all else was to ensure a fair trial. Segregation was his instinctive response to the challenge. Equally he was a devotee of the jury system – a true believer – and realised every step he would take would be scrutinised by devotee and critic alike. Fundamental to his beliefs was to ensure that the lamp of freedom stayed alight, not just as a flicker but as brightly as possible as a symbol of democracy.

These issues themselves rest on straightforward matters of procedure. But it was quite unacceptable for Patrick to have seen the Attorney-General in

---

[11] Letter from Devlin to Manningham-Buller, 19 February 1957, Devlin-Adams Correspondence file.

[12] Letter from Manningham-Buller to Devlin, 20 February 1957, Devlin-Adams Correspondence File.

[13] Undated note, Patrick Devlin, Devlin-Adams Correspondence file.

Lawrence QC's absence. Quite obviously Lawrence QC may have had a different view from that of the Attorney-General. And seeing the Attorney in Lawrence's absence could have given rise to a claim of apprehended bias. It reflected a serious error of judgement in what was going to be a difficult enough case even without this problem. The Attorney-General obviously did not see the difficulty either. But Lawrence QC was quite rightly upset when he was later told about the meeting.

In any event Patrick saw the Attorney-General late on 21 February, alone. Worse, the Attorney-General told Patrick something quite significant, which on any view should have been said in open court and of course with a representative of the accused present. The Attorney-General advised Patrick that he was not going to use the evidence in the Hullett case (as evidence of system) in the Morrell case and he intended to tell Lawrence QC later in the week. The Attorney-General specifically said it was to save Patrick from reading all the papers.[14] He also told Patrick that if there was a not-guilty verdict on the Morrell case, he would wish immediately to proceed with the second indictment. In the event of a guilty finding on the Morell case he had not made up his mind whether to leave the Hullett case on file or proceed – he would certainly not take the course of offering no evidence on it.

That was a gross oversight on the Attorney-General's part as well. It reflected a complete lack of professional courtesy. Further, it is breathtaking for prosecution counsel in a criminal trial to disclose privately to the trial judge a significant strategic decision taken for the latter's apparent convenience without having previously informed defence counsel. As a beneficiary of the news Patrick ought to have required the Attorney-General immediately to disclose the decision to defence counsel. His inaction was disappointing to say the least. Patrick made a detailed diary note of his meeting with Manningham-Buller on 21 February.[15]

Patrick did write to Lawrence QC after the event, telling him he had had some discussions with Manningham-Buller about the trial and inviting Lawrence QC to come and see him.[16]

However, the extensive publicity given to the committal proceedings made Patrick deeply concerned to ensure that the jury was protected from any possible interference as much as possible. One way to achieve that was to place the jury in isolation in some hotel in the centre of London, to which they could be taken each day after Court and so avoid contact with the outside world as far as possible. Patrick wrote a short document on the question[17] with the intention of showing it to Sir George Coldstream, Permanent Secretary to the Lord Chancellor's Department. Privately, Coldstream disliked the plan; so did the

---

[14] Diary note, '10pm, Thursday 21 February', Devlin-Adams Correspondence File.
[15] Ibid.
[16] Letter from Devlin to Lawrence QC, 21 February 1957, Devlin-Adams Correspondence File.
[17] Undated 3-page memorandum prepared by Devlin on the history of juries, etc, Devlin-Adams Correspondence File.

Under Sheriff, whose task it would have been to organise it. Apart from the cost, it would have required the revival of a practice abandoned in 1939 because of the war. The Lord Chancellor saw no merit in the idea either, and told Coldstream he did not wish to speak to Patrick about the matter.[18] By letter on 22 February, Manningham-Buller told Patrick he too was opposed to the idea.[19] Patrick on the other hand was determined to press on with the idea and wanted to give Lawrence QC the deciding vote, as it were.

On Sunday 24 February an item appeared in the *Sunday Express* under the 'Cross-Bencher' byline. It read:[20]

Attorney waits.

Here is another Minister for whom I forecast disappointment – Sir Reginald Manningham-Buller, the Attorney-General.

Sir Reginald is dancing on tip-toe.

He quivers with impatience. He can hardly wait another moment.

His expectation: That Lord Goddard, Lord Chief Justice England will retire on his 80th birthday in April.

His hope: That Lord Goddard's successor in this majestic office will be Sir Reginald Manningham-Buller.

But I have wretched news for Sir Reginald.

It is that Lord Goddard now thinks of deferring his retirement till the autumn.

And even then Mr Macmillan may not give the job to a politician but to a High Court judge.

He has his eye on a first rate candidate.

Mr Justice Devlin.

Eventually, on 26 February, Patrick saw Lawrence QC. He made a detailed diary note of the meeting.[21] At the outset Lawrence QC made it plain that he thought it quite wrong of the Attorney-General to have seen the judge without him being present. Patrick said he took full responsibility for the decision. He said that only matters which chiefly concerned matters of machinery for the conduct of the trial were discussed. Patrick further explained he had thought that the procedural matters really only concerned the Attorney-General's convenience. Patrick again said he took full blame for the action. His explanation bordered on the pathetic. He moved on to discuss segregation of the jury. He told Lawrence QC that the Attorney-General was against it. Lawrence QC said he thought his client could not in the circumstances get a fair trial in any event, but would like

[18] Diary note dealing with the discussion between Devlin and Sir George Coldstream, 25 February 1957, Devlin-Adams Correspondence File.

[19] Letter from Manningham-Buller to Devlin, 22 February 1957, Devlin-Adams Correspondence File.

[20] 'Cross-Bencher', *Sunday Express*, 24 February 1957.

[21] Diary entry '10pm, Tuesday 26 February', Devlin-Adams Correspondence File.

to consult his junior before making a decision. Patrick had little choice but to agree.

On 1 March Goddard weighed in on the question of segregation of the jury. He was also against it.[22] On 4 March Patrick sent a detailed report to Goddard setting out the various meetings he had had with the parties.[23] On 5 March Lawrence QC told Patrick he simply wished to reserve his position, as he thought his client could not in any event get a fair trial.[24] The same day Patrick told the Under Sheriff he could be relieved from having to consider the matter further. Patrick again somewhat informally set the trial date for Monday, 18 March and told the relevant court officers accordingly.[25]

Manningham-Buller had for some time been the butt of many jokes in the media. He was one of those larger than life characters who seemingly were placed on the earth for the political cartoonists and satirists. On 5 March Patrick wrote to Manningham-Buller about the article in the *Sunday Express*. The letter no longer exists but Manningham-Buller replied on 6 March in the following terms:[26]

> Thank you for your letter of 5 March and for the information you have given me. With regard to the Sunday Express I was very sorry to see your name dragged into an attack on me. Cross-Bencher feeds on offensiveness. It is curious that a few weeks after I did a contempt case against the Evening Standard, I was subjected to a series of attacks and this recent attack follows my cross-examination of the editor of the Sunday Express before the Committee of Privileges. I expect there will be more of them. I am hardened to them but they do disturb one's family. To be praised on the column is politically the kiss of death!

Whilst the communication between the two is to some extent understandable it was again quite inappropriate, especially as Lawrence QC was not told about it.

In the meantime, momentum was gathering in preparation for the trial. Between Parliamentary commitments, Manningham-Buller was busily conferring with his juniors, no doubt preparing for a crushing cross-examination of Adams. He would also have been conferring with the Crown's two expert witnesses, Dr Douthwaite and Dr Ashby. Lawrence QC on the other hand, with the resources of the Medical Defence Union, was preparing a few surprises of his own.

The Devlin household was also abuzz with activity. Patrick and his clerk were going over arrangements and in Patrick's case making some notes on the papers in preparation for some legal points he may have anticipated arising. At this

---

[22] Letter from Goddard to Devlin, 1 March 1957, Devlin-Adams Correspondence File.

[23] Letter from Devlin to Goddard, 4 March 1957, Devlin-Adams Correspondence File.

[24] Diary entry '10:15, 5 March, Tuesday' of conversation between Lawrence QC and Devlin, Devlin-Adams Correspondence File.

[25] Letter, Devlin to the Under Sheriff, 5 March 1957, Devlin-Adams Correspondence File.

[26] Letter from Manningham-Buller to Devlin, 6 March 1957, Devlin-Adams Correspondence File.

stage he and Madeleine were living at 5 Gray's Inn Square, a brisk walk away from the Old Bailey.

On 12 March Madeleine herself wrote to the Clerk of the Court in order to secure seating in the courtroom for her and potentially others for the trial, but especially the summing up.[27] Indeed, throughout the trial Patrick had to keep a list of those friends and acquaintances who had requested reserved seating. Some merely asked to be there for a short time, whereas others specifically requested the summing up. Patrick's clerk was responsible for allocating seating and liaising with the Sheriff.

On 14 March Patrick told Goddard he had cleared the decks so as not to be reserved in any case prior to the start of the trial.[28]

On the morning of the trial Goddard decided to impart some information to Patrick that he thought would lift his spirits if needed, although by this stage the wonder drug adrenalin would have been available in large quantities and to good effect in the Devlin household. It said:[29]

> While you have enough to think about at the moment I heard a piece of news last night which I think you should know – if you don't already. Simonds rang me up and asked if I would join in giving a dinner for Oaksey who is resigning – whether April 5 or at Easter I don't know. This means Denning is going to the Lords and another vacancy in the C.A. Now restrictive practices are all very important no doubt but when you took [it] on you can hardly anticipated 3 vacancies in six weeks or so and I feel it would be very hard on you if you submit to being passed over twice if not 3 times – I say this because perhaps Sellers might have been put up before you though I don't think this would have happened if you had been so to speak, free. I don't know how you feel about this but if there is anything I can do I will. Why should not Pearce take over restrictive practices – he was the other one of us who was apparently willing to do so. Perhaps the Chancellor has in mind to put you later on straight to the Lords – as they did Sam Porter – but neither Tucker nor Somervell look like retiring. I do feel that something should be said by either you or for you and from the point of view of the law it is a serious thing if the C.A. should not have the best man, and if you do get it eventually you will be junior to those who might be junior to you. I shall I believe be seeing the PM on Ap 4th but if Geoff is going on 5th it would be too late then to do anything. As you know I should like for you to follow me and if that could be arranged I would gladly stay on another year for you to be free to take over – but if Kilmuir means to take it, that's that.
>
> Anyway think it over and let me know if there is anything I can do.

Goddard was right about one thing at least. At the time Patrick received his letter he did have more than enough on his mind. Adams was formally requested to enter a plea on the morning of 18 March. He was told the charge he faced was the murder of Mrs Edith Alice Morrell who died on 13 November 1950.

[27] Letter from Madeleine Devlin to the Clerk of the Court, 12 March 1957, Devlin-Adams Correspondence File.
[28] Letter from Devlin to Goddard, 14 March 1957, Devlin-Adams Correspondence File.
[29] Letter from Goddard to Devlin, 18 March 1957, Devlin-Adams Correspondence File.

Sybille Bedford, who wrote a contemporaneous and hugely entertaining account of the trial describes the opening moments:[30]

> The Judge came on swiftly. Out of the side-door, an ermined puppet progressing weightless along the bench, head held at an angle, an arm swinging, the other crooked under cloth and gloves, trailing a wake of subtlety, of secret powers, age: an Elizabethan shadow gliding across the arras.
>
> The high-backed chair has been pulled, helped forward, the figure seated, has bowed, and the hundred or so people who had gathered themselves at split notice rustle to their feet, rustle and subside into apportioned place. And now the prisoner the accused himself is here – how had he come, how had one missed the instant of that other clockwork entry? – standing in the front of the dock, spherical, adipose, upholstered in blue serge, red faced, bald, facing the Judge, facing this day. And already the clerk, risen from below the Judge's seat, is addressing him by full name.

Apart from responding to the question of whether he was the accused or not the only other words Adams uttered for the whole trial were the words 'I am not guilty, my Lord', when asked.[31]

March 1957 turned out to be one of warmest springs on record, which no doubt led to a certain amount of discomfort in the courtroom given the interest in the trial. Both domestic and international media were represented in vast numbers. The American press in particular took a great interest. By reason of the usual ban on court photography, the artists from the press and otherwise were in force in at the Old Bailey, including Ronald Searle, who had covered the Nuremberg trials.[32]

The trial would bring Patrick to the attention of the world, not just among lawyers throughout the world. He would be profiled, drawn, written about constantly and frequently stopped in the street from time to time to sign the odd autograph. People clambered for seats in the courtroom and with the media occupying every spare spot, scalpers otherwise would have made a fortune. His clerk kept some seats in the courtroom specially reserved for VIP's which included family, friends, many judges' wives and their family members. A running list of guests was kept, with days and times allocated, and passes issued, appropriately described as 'tickets'.[33]

After all formalities, the Attorney opened the case for the Crown.[34] He took only two hours. This was a perfectly appropriate strategy with a jury who are always anxious to hear the witnesses speak rather than what counsel tell them the witnesses are going to say. Although the trial started on 18 March it would

---

[30] Sybille Bedford, *The Best We Can Do: An Account of the Trial of John Bodkin Adams* (London, Collins, 1958), p 17.

[31] Ibid, p 18.

[32] The cover of the book is one such drawing, done in the course of the trial.

[33] Lists of proposed attendees with allocation of 'tickets', Devlin-Adams Correspondence File.

[34] Sybille Bedford, *The Best We Can Do: An Account of the Trial of John Bodkin Adams* (London, Collins, 1958), pp 19–28.

not conclude until 9 April which, at least by the standards of the time, was a very long trial.

Here was a doctor who, it was alleged, had ordered the administration of massive amounts of harmful drugs, namely heroin and morphine, in circumstances where there was no clinical justification for doing so. Ironically, across London at St Thomas's hospital, Dr William Sargant, a contemporary of Patrick's at Cambridge, was with impunity deliberately and blatantly administering a vast cocktail of drugs in his deep-sleep ward. The treatment, later discredited, involved keeping a patient heavily sedated for sometimes up to three months along with other forms of treatment such as electroconvulsive therapy which on some occasions caused death.

The Crown case began with the nurses. They gave evidence of the drugs prescribed, from which it was to be inferred that they were in fact administered. The whole prosecution case theory as assumed by the expert witnesses was entirely dependent upon that core assumption; that the drugs prescribed were in fact all administered. With that simple formula or case theory, Dr Douthwaite, as the principal Crown expert, would say, murder was an inevitable verdict, especially given the wounding admissions made by Adams to Hannam. A thunderous and crushing cross-examination by the Attorney would follow. Obvious result – conviction.

As to the first of these assumptions neither Hannam nor his assistants had obviously thoroughly checked the existence and or whereabouts of any contemporaneous records. Hannam had asked Adams about his records but clearly did not pursue the issue with sufficient curiosity and rigour. For example, he did not ask the nurses before they went into the witness box whether records had been kept. From answers given in their evidence they would clearly have conceded records were kept and that they had, unsurprisingly, made entries in them. Lawrence QC was able to use these records – which he had studied but which the prosecution was unaware of – with considerable effectiveness. Secondly and equally importantly, the Attorney-General simply assumed that Adams would go into the witness box. This betrayed not only a lack of experience but a complete lack of imagination. A case theory that bears some consistency with admissible and provable evidence is always an advantage – some would say a necessity – in pressing whatever case a lawyer wants to advance.

On any view the trial could not have gone worse for the Crown. Lawrence QC used the actual notes of the nurses in his possession to compare what was in the prescriptions with the lesser quantities the notes recorded as having been administered. This tended to unsettle and perhaps destroy the evidence in chief given by the nurses that everything prescribed had been administered. The nurses were also caught by an unidentified person outside the court and again on a train gossiping unhelpfully about the case and what answers might get one or more of them 'into trouble'. Together these events would undoubtedly assisted Adams considerably.

It may be thought that there was a certain unfairness in Lawrence QC's conduct. The truth is that the nurses probably recorded not everything that happened, but everything that they noticed happening, at least to the extent that their other duties with a very difficult patient allowed them at the time. What is more, there were instances in the evidence which called on great disparities between the records and what actually happened. For example, a locum standing in for Adams was able to contradict what the notebooks said about the number of visits made. But the truth of the matter is that the jury would unsurprisingly be very much influenced by contemporaneous records kept at the time, as opposed to the testimony of the nurses taken on its own.

Patrick went to his farm at the end of the first week to read the transcript and prepare for the week ahead, convinced the Crown would simply throw in the towel at the beginning of the new week. He had, however, somewhat underestimated the Attorney-General's doggedness and Melford Stevenson QC's passionate obsession. No such thoughts would likely have entered either head. They and the police saw themselves as confronting an evil serial killer, callously murdering his patients for financial gain. The Attorney-General would have thought he had a strong case, oblivious to its flaws.

One effect of the revelation of the nurses' actual notes was that the principal Crown expert, Dr Douthwaite, felt obliged to change his whole case theory mid-trial because his previous opinion was based entirely on a set of assumptions – which at least on one view were erroneous.

Patrick would only have been too well aware of how this change of stance might affect the jury. It tended to create the impression that the Crown did not know what its case was. Alternatively, it tended to create the impression that the Crown had clearly failed to take into account a highly relevant piece of evidence, namely a contemporaneous record of what had in fact happened as opposed to what it had assumed had happened. Either impression would make it entirely natural for a member of a jury to lose confidence in the Crown to the extent necessary to raise a reasonable doubt. That would be the start of the rot. It would have likely appeared that the Attorney-General, or more likely the police officers or one of the juniors, critically failed to analyse the materials they had and failed to try to work out what records might exist and to cater for their absence in some way, or worse, failed to find them – as it would seem the defence team had – and deal with them in advance.

The pre-trial publicity had all been one way. It damned Adams as a serial killer who preyed on the old and infirm of Eastbourne to his financial benefit. All of a sudden, the prosecution did not seem to have a grasp on what had happened. Patrick simply sat back, watching the prosecution case implode in the hands of no less a person than the most senior member of the Bar, the Attorney-General. But the worst was yet to come. Although the nurses were discredited, Adams had made some most unwise admissions to Hannam – not the least that Mrs Morrell had indeed received the full doses prescribed. As it happened, in his summing up Patrick directed the jury to not consider whether those admissions were made and what effect they might have. The Attorney-General seems to have been bitter about this error of law all of his life – understandably. That is not to say that the Attorney-General failed to pick up the pieces as best he could as the trial progressed. Some of his re-examination of prosecution witnesses supposedly destroyed by Lawrence QC's questioning effectively pointed out the smallness of the impact that the cross-examination had had in relation to key questions. He displayed a singular capacity to smooth over the flaws in the evidence when called upon at short notice. But in the end whilst he took each blow on the chin without flinching, again and again he did so in the confident expectation he would get his hands on Adams in cross-examination and all would be well.

There was damaging evidence from Mrs Morrell's solicitor about the requests and interventions of Adams in her will. That apart, Lawrence QC skilfully made Adams out to be an inept but highly attentive doctor as opposed to a serial killer. Clearly some of the dialogue Adams had with Superintendent Hannam and others could prove either.

Adams had fumbled some of the answers he gave to the police. For example, when he was arrested and charged on 19 December 1956, he asked Hannam whether he could prove murder, as Mrs Morrell had been dying in any event. During another conversation he had with Hannam in the November, he said all he had done was easing the passing of a dying person and that was 'not all that wicked'.[35] The best that Lawrence QC could do with Hannam was to suggest that it simply did not happen the way presented. Hannam stood his ground. It would in the end be a matter for the jury. As already observed, the popularity of police officers is or was not all that high at the best of times.

In addition the make-up of a jury in any case can have an effect on the outcome, at least so some jury observers believe. The make-up of this particular jury is not known except for the fact that one of their number was a senior businessman from a major building company who at one stage of the trial obtained an indulgence from Patrick to be released one lunch hour to attend to some pressing business in London. That incidental act of consideration would have enhanced further, if it were necessary, the position of the trial judge in the minds of the jury.

One further difficulty that emerged for the prosecution is that on occasions, Dr Harris from Adams' practice attended upon Mrs Morrell and confirmed a matter the prosecution had been at pains to deny – that Mrs Morrell was in pain. She had also been admitted to hospital in Cheshire and, remarkably, the Crown did not even obtain a copy of those records. It would have become obvious to all in Court what damage this witness did by advancing such damning testimony. Worse, Melford Stevenson QC became irritated and attempted blatantly to cross-examine his own witness in re-examination. This would likely have gone unnoticed by the jury, but would not have been lost on Lawrence QC.

---

[35] ETP, p 7.

It is all too apparent to the casual observer when a witness does not come up to proof. The effect can be devastating. Here, for another doctor from Adam's practice called by the Crown as a witness to have merely continued the treatment or acquiesced in it is highly significant. It would be assumed that if another doctor who had an independent duty of care to the patient simply followed the treatment regime of the murderer, then either he or she was also a murderer (which was never suggested), or the treatment was not altogether inappropriate for the particular patient.

Dr Douthwaite, the main expert for the Crown, as a result of the new information about the nurses' notebooks had to cobble together a new theory in order to accommodate the facts. His original theory was a straightforward one. The prescriptions alone enabled him confidently to explain that the doses were excessive. However, with the facts about when and how much medication was administered being apparently more accurately exposed, Dr Douthwaite had to have a new theory. Dr Douthwaite had to admit that he had not taken into account treatment she had had in Cheshire when she had her stroke. This was another matter that Hannam presumably had failed to investigate. The hospital notes from Cheshire disclosed not only that Mrs Morrell had complained of severe pain but she was also given morphia, one of the drugs Dr Douthwaite said was inappropriate. Again, a lack of preparation at the least would have been very apparent. But somewhat bizarrely, Dr Douthwaite's new theory was that Dr Adams varied his treatment regime so to create an addiction on the part of Mrs Morrell to justify increased doses. Painstakingly Lawrence QC managed to unpick Dr Douthwaite to the point where the atmosphere is described as moving from 'dogmatic gloom' to 'a sense of doubt and muddle'.[36] Before he sat down Lawrence QC got Dr Douthwaite to accept a possibility that another doctor might find himself forced to utilise the same treatment as Adams.

However, the questions often in any jury trial which have the most devastating effect are those posed by the judge. The reasons are simple. The jury not unnaturally look to the trial judge for impartial guidance and are bound in any event to accept his or her directions on the law. But the judge will not fail generally to make an impression on the jury even on the facts which are the exclusive province of the jury.

Patrick intervened very little but when he did so it would have had significant effect. With a few well-framed questions he managed to expose on one view Dr Douthwaite's irreconcilable views. His first position when he did not know about the nurses' notebooks was simply to say, too much medication, therefore there was an intent to murder. In order to accommodate the fresh evidence, namely the actual dosing which was subject to variation between morphia and heroin, Patrick got Dr Douthwaite to express the view that the change by Adams in reducing the morphia for a time was part of a sinister and sophisticated plan

---

[36] Sybille Bedford, *The Best We Can Do: An Account of the Trial of John Bodkin Adams* (London, Collins, 1958), p 145.

to make Mrs Morrell more vulnerable when next the morphia was re-introduced with intended lethal effect. Although Lawrence cross-examined the doctor again with great effect, there is little doubt that the judge's questions must have had a considerable impact on the jury, especially when Dr Douthwaite eschewed any idea that the changes in dosage could have been the result of ineptitude. And again, Patrick went home thinking that finally the Attorney-General would have seen the writing on the wall.

Sybille Bedford was watching the trial unfold and picked up the obvious – namely that Dr Douthwaite was advancing an entirely new theory.[37] Bedford records Lawrence QC cross-examining him again on Monday, 1 April, day 11 of the trial. Dr Douthwaite was forced by Lawrence QC to agree that his most recent theory did not fully emerge until questioned by the judge. It is clear from Bedford's contemporaneous remarks that Dr Douthwaite had lost significant credibility.

Undeterred, the Attorney-General called the final witness for the Crown – another doctor, Dr Ashby. This doctor, however, is described by Bedford as a 'giving witness'. According to Bedford, he was a patently honest witness for the concessions he made, which included his concession that death could have been by natural causes.[38]

The Attorney-General did well in the circumstances, but control of the trial had passed out of his hands in its early stages. Although always confident of his position, he never really regained rhythm or momentum. He re-examined the Crown witnesses as well as any professional barrister could, in circumstances where he was taken completely unawares by highly relevant material seen by him and his own witnesses for the first time, mid-flight.

On the morning of day 13, Lawrence QC made an application which, some might think, was doomed to fail. He made a submission of no case to answer which would mean, if successful, that the judge would take the case from the jury and direct it to acquit. But a snag! Normally such an application is made in the absence of the jury. Patrick would not permit that to occur. His refusal was contrary to contemporary and modern practice. Patrick gave no justification for this departure. Lawrence QC had to take an extreme forensic risk. He had to outline his case in the presence of the jury. If they were persuaded (not that they were to be involved at this point other than as bystanders), then all was well and good. Lawrence QC probably never assumed Patrick would require the application to be before the jury but once he started it would have been difficult to stop. The thrust of Lawrence QC's submission was that on the medical evidence called by the Crown no jury reasonably instructed could convict. As might have been expected, Patrick gave the argument short shrift. He pointed to the fact as discretely but as firmly as he could that the jury were entitled to accept Dr Douthwaite. Luckily for Lawrence QC, Patrick did not give detailed reasons

[37] Ibid, pp 151–52.
[38] Ibid, pp 164–67.

for rejecting the argument. Thus, in effect Lawrence QC got an additional address to the jury, together with the benefit of the jury having some time to consider the merits of the points made in his submission that there was no case to answer with a view to them all concluding that even if there was a case to answer, it was one that ought to be rejected by a finding of 'not guilty'.

Next came the surprise of the afternoon. Lawrence QC, in announcing his first witness, also informed the court he would not be calling 'the Doctor'. As Bedford observed:[39]

> The first brute reaction to this is the relative disturbance of a dozen and a half report-ers stumbling over benches and each other to run the news to a telephone. Lawrence with firm matter-of-factness drives on the case.

The expert evidence for the Crown being in disarray, the defence played the ultimate card and only called a medical witness, a Dr Harman: he supported Adams' treatment. The great difficulty any person suing or prosecuting an insured doctor then as now faces is the resources the Medical Defence Union is able to supply, which can be overwhelming. The experts who are regularly made available to assist defence lawyers in such circumstances understand only too well the subtleties connected associated with observation, diagnosis and treat-ment and the room for reasonable minds to differ in many clinical situations. Lawrence QC would not only have had conferences with Dr Harman to qualify him to give evidence, but possibly others as well so as to allow Lawrence to ask the hard questions of someone who would not ultimately be in the witness box. Dr Harman does not disappoint. Trenchantly, but urbanely, he said that the treatment was not producing any harm as it had gone on for over a year. The patient then, having had a stroke, progressively would have deteriorated to natural death from old age. He was familiar with the use of morphia, and morphia and heroin together and importantly he saw no reason to link her death to the doses administered. Better still, in relation to Adams' patient he had seen comparable cases. More importantly, he disagreed entirely with Dr Douthwaite.

The Attorney-General started what turned out to be an unexpectedly rather short, but effective cross-examination. Bedford described the process:[40]

> The Attorney-General has turned formidable. His questions rolled up sluggishly like thunder, are delivered with a crushing weight of condemnation, and this stolid exhalation of disapproval is as damaging as the use of detailed cleverness.

But Dr Harman, seemingly unperturbed, continued to render anodyne much of the Crown's attempted disapprobation of Adams' treatment.

Another somewhat unpleasant surprise came whilst the Attorney-General was in full flight and just after lunch on day 14. Over lunch Lawrence QC had told the Attorney-General of a publication in a magazine, *Newsweek*, a foreign

---

[39] Ibid, p 184.
[40] Sybille Bedford, *The Best We Can Do: An Account of the Trial of John Bodkin Adams* (London, Collins, 1958), p 195.

weekly publication circulating in London and on sale in bookstalls. All content was composed offshore but distributed in England by local companies and there was an individual who worked in London as the circulation manager. But the rub was that the magazine contained material prejudicial to Adams. The possibility of a discharge and a new trial is the last thing most participants in a jury trial ever want, especially when (as here) the matter comes to the attention of a court on day 14 and in a matter involving a capital offence. Happily, as it turned out Patrick decided to raise the matter obliquely with the jury and remind them again not to buy or read anything other than the ordinary newspapers. The events would ultimately lead to a contempt prosecution after the trial, heard by Goddard LCJ, Hilbery and Donovan JJ, in the May of that year. All relevantly concerned received a fine and a conviction for contempt.[41]

The cross-examination continued for a while into the afternoon. At this stage the medical evidence stood as follows: Dr Douthwiate was in no doubt, on whichever theory he purported to propound, that Adams was absolutely a murderer. Dr Ashby thought he might be but was not sure. Dr Harman thought he definitely was not.

Formalities concluded, it was time for addresses. Mrs Morrell had had a heart attack so would not be giving evidence. The end was in sight – the next day was day 15, Friday 5 April.

That night Patrick was somewhat unsettled by a phone call he received from Goddard.[42] The ostensible object was to see how the case was going and when Patrick would be back in the Strand. This type of inquiry would normally be made between clerks. Patrick was not surprised when Goddard asked whether he thought there would be an acquittal. Patrick said he thought there would. Goddard then said he had heard the Attorney-General was still determined to proceed with the second indictment. In that event, if an application for bail was made, he would grant it. This intervention surprised Patrick who had never heard of bail being granted in a murder case. The question is what precisely was Goddard up to? Was this just a fatherly call to give gratuitous but helpful guidance? Or was Patrick being manipulated? Patrick saw nothing wrong in principle with an application for bail if an acquittal was the outcome but the idea, it seems, would never have entered his head in the absence of Goddard's call. Some conspiracy theorists have it that, as Goddard knew Sir Roland Gwynne, a former mayor of Eastbourne and a patient of Adams, this call was an attempt to importune Patrick to give Adams some indulgence.

Meanwhile the next day, Friday 5 April, Lawrence addressed the jury for about three and a half hours. Unsurprisingly, he confronted the failure of Adams to go into the witness box. He moved through the facts with obvious emphasis after Mrs Morrell's stroke. He made the bald point that her estate was worth £175,000 and that her chauffeur got £1,000, nurse Randall £300 and that others

---

[41] 'Adams Case Echo: U.S. Writer is Sued', *The New York Times*, 13 April 1957.
[42] ETP, p 178.

received varying amounts as legacies, whereas Dr Adams got some silver in a cupboard worth £275 and a pre-war Rolls-Royce, dependent upon her son dying before his mother. Lawrence implored the jury not to do anything that 'will haunt your conscience ...'

The Attorney-General took up the balance of the afternoon, commencing as Bedford describes with a 'solemn boom'. But the balance of the afternoon was merely a 'faithful echo of the opening speech, with little added or forgotten'. The Attorney-General drifted into yet another theory that the nurses' notes, which neither the police nor those assisting him managed to locate, must have been kept by Adams for a sinister purpose. But the articulation of important contemporaneous and authentic records can hardly be described as such.

However at the end of the day Patrick had proposed a much more entertaining evening ahead. He and a number of others had planned a little surprise party for Goddard who would turn 80 on 10 April.

Goddard wrote to Patrick the following day:[43]

> My dear Pat,
>
> I just could not trust myself to say much to you and the others last night but I felt it deeply. In the time I have left to me it will be one of my happiest memories. Thank you from the bottom of my heart. You know what I wish for you and may all good fortune attend on you.

Patrick stayed at Gray's Inn that weekend. Sometime the following Monday after the Attorney-General finished his address, Patrick would begin his summing up.

As the first thing on Monday morning the Attorney-General reverted to the will of Mrs Morrell and the admissions made to the police. This was safe territory. The more difficult part of his address was that which had to deal with the new Douthwaite theory that Adams deliberately changed the medication to make Mrs Morrell more vulnerable. The more he elaborated the more implausible it sounded but nonetheless the Prosecution maintained that 'proper verdict is one of murder'.

Bedford observed:[44]

> The wigs and the papers in the well have come to rest; in counsel's row the black and white figures sit with arms folded inside their sleeves. The Judge makes his turn, leans slightly forward, and begins. The voice from the robed public form is private, though immensely practised; the words are spoken words, nearly intimate and at the same time quite aloof. The jury never take their eyes off him.

Like any highly-skilled person, he made it all sound so simple and straightforward. Vitally, from Adams' point of view, Patrick directed the jury that there is no evidence that any drugs were administered to Mrs Morrell over and above the

---

[43] Letter from Goddard to Devlin, 11 April 1957, Devlin-Adams Correspondence File.
[44] Sybille Bedford, *The Best We Can Do: An Account of the Trial of John Bodkin Adams* (London, Collins, 1958), p 219.

injections recorded in the nurses' notebooks. This had a significant effect on the Crown's attempts to rely on what Adams was alleged to have said to Hannam about the quantity of drugs actually administered.

Importantly, he addressed them on the right to silence; again, effortless and matter of fact. Patrick explained:[45]

> I want to face this frankly with you because it is something that may be troubling your minds. It is perhaps a natural reaction for laymen and perhaps for lawyers too to say, 'Why hasn't he gone into the witness-box if he is an innocent man? He is the doctor who attended the patient. He can tell us more about this than anyone else can. Why has he not gone into the witness box, unless he fears that questions will be put to him that he cannot satisfactorily answer?' You heard Mr Lawrence address you on this point. You heard him tell the reasons, or some of the reasons at any rate, why on his advice – and a client might well be a foolish man if he did not in such a matter follow his lawyer's advice – the Doctor had not gone into the witness box. You may have found those reasons convincing, or you may have not. I am not going to deal with them. What I am going to tell you is simply this – that it does not matter. You have not got to judge whether the reasons are convincing or not. The Doctor has a right not to go into the witness-box ... I shall elaborate on this at the end because it is so important ... Let me tell you that it would be, in my judgement – indeed as a matter of Law – utterly wrong if you were to regard the Doctor's silence as contributing in any way towards proof of guilt. The prisoner who goes into the witness-box goes there for his own benefit and his own defence. It is perfectly true that they sometimes make matters worse for themselves. But the prosecution has no right to rely on that at all. The duty of the prosecution is to prove their case before the question ever arises as to whether the prisoner should be called or not.

More drama then took place as Adams' solicitor collapsed with a heart attack and was taken off to hospital. Patrick continued with his summing up which went to the end of the day.

Bedford described the beginning of the last day thus: 'The same crowded court; the same held silence; but stretched today, nervous, tense.'[46]

Tediously but essentially, Patrick reminded the jury of more of the evidence. Patrick made the point about the nurses' notebooks and reminded the jury about what the Attorney-General had said but added:[47]

> What does the prosecution say these books prove – innocence or guilt? If guilt why did the doctor preserve them? If they prove innocence, then surely it does not matter where they come from or who has been keeping them?

Patrick finally let them have his real opinion:[48]

> I dare say it is the first time you have sat in the jury-box. It is not the first time that I have sat in this chair. And not infrequently I have heard a case presented by the

---

[45] Ibid, pp 225–26.
[46] Ibid, pp 242–43.
[47] Ibid, p 247.
[48] Ibid, pp 249–50.

prosecution that seemed to me to be manifestly a strong one, and sometimes I have felt it my duty to tell the jury so. I do not think therefore, that I ought to hesitate to tell you that here the case for the defence seems to me to be manifestly a strong one ... But it is the same question in the end, always the same – is the case for the Crown strong though to carry conviction, to your mind? It is your question. You have to answer it. It lies with you, the jury. Always with you. And you will now consider what the answer shall be.

Bedford in her own summing up captured the mood exquisitely:[49]

For what the Doctor is undergoing now, for what he has undergone in the last days, weeks, months, for what he will undergo, for what will mark him, in the years to come, is there (assuming him to be innocent, assuming him about to be acquitted), is there reparation? Is there comfort, consolation, return? Is there rhyme and reason? Reparation, on the immediate and material level, no. A man accused of murder, with whatever aloofness the law may have held him innocent before the verdict, is nearly always presumed not to have been quite after his acquittal. In the Doctor's case the world, to a spectacular and rare degree – nature, finely spurred by newspapers – did not even presume him innocent before his trial. Doubt, reasonable and unreasonable, will hang about him to the end of his days and after. His life will be broken, or, if one chooses to put it another way, changed. Nor is he likely to get official redress – has not a case strong enough to go to a jury been made out? – in terms of wrongful prosecution or imprisonment; he will not even get a soothing form of words. Comforts, then, compensations? Perhaps. By some fortunate workings of the law of diminishing returns, our capacities for suffering are not infinitely extendable. We bear; and may derive strength from having borne, comfort from being still there, comfort from any mercy: the faith of friends, the match struck by a stranger, discovery of reserves. (During the trial, while almost everyone in street and drawing-room was animated by the casual conviction of course he must have done it – a conviction by no means shared by all who were in court – everyone who knew him, his friends and patients, are said to have been matter-of-factly certain of the Doctor's innocence.) There is compensation – always! and short-lived – in sheer relief: it is over; I may go now; the first steps, the taste of air. Yes; but there are mitigations, themselves contingent on disaster, the mountain's mice ... Why did disaster fall? On this man and not another? Can we ever answer, can we ever cease to ask that question? The usual conjunction, then, ill-starred, of circumstance and character? 'A man guilty of folly; but folly and murder are poles apart.' So are, for most of us, folly and the extremes of retribution, folly and utter downfall. Why on this fool and not on that? Why not on me? There but not for the grace of God ... But why did the grace of God choose thus? Life, one might say has a way of throwing up strange twists – who can tell? – without this piece of bad luck, without that loss, that outright catastrophe, I might never have seen, have met, have known; I would not have had that chance; I should not now be here ... It was all for the best. Do we really say that, and how often? Ought we to say it for another? 'Nous avons tous assez de force pour supporter les maux d'autrui.' Always fortitude enough, words enough, to explain

---

[49] Ibid, pp 251–52.

away another man's misfortune … Can we let it go at that, can we turn now from the Doctor's fate with the sense that, somehow, in some way, all is well; or must we accept that his entanglement was another tale told by an idiot?

In the meantime, Patrick thought he would get counsel and the Clerk of the Court to see what was planned in the event of possible outcomes. A general discussion took place as to what would happen in the event of an acquittal as opposed to a conviction. If a conviction, Patrick made it clear that Adams would go into custody. If not, he would entertain an application for bail (Goddard's dulcet tones ringing). The Attorney-General was, according to Patrick, glum and somewhat non-committal. Lawrence QC on the other hand said candidly he was exhausted and would like a break before the next phase. Counsel had only just left and Patrick had settled down to read the papers in the Hullett matter when he was told the jury was ready to return.

After 44 minutes the jury was ready to come back. The media stampeded into the court.[50]

It is convenient at this point to have recourse to Patrick's copy of the transcript, otherwise heavily marked but the following is in a pristine state:[51]

The clerk of the Court: Members of the Jury, are you agreed upon your verdict?

The foreman of the Jury: We are.

The clerk of the Court: Do you find the prisoner John Bodkin Adams guilty or not guilty?

The foreman of the Jury: Not Guilty.

The clerk of the Court: You find him not guilty, and that is the verdict of you all?

The foreman of the Jury: It is.

Mr Justice Devlin: There is another indictment is there not?

The Attorney-General: Yes my Lord. I have most anxiously considered what course the Crown should pursue in relation to the further indictment charging Doctor Adams with the murder of Mrs Hullett. My learned friend has referred more than once to the difficulty owing to reports and rumours that were current of securing a fair trial of the case which has now terminated. As one of my distinguished predecessors said, the Attorney-General, when deciding whether a particular prosecution is to be carried on, has regard to a variety of considerations and all of them lead to the final question, would a prosecution be in the public interest, including in that phrase, in the interests of justice? One of the considerations I have felt it my duty to consider is that the publicity which has attended the trial would make it even more difficult to secure a fair trial of this second indictment. I have also taken into account the length of the trial, the ordeal Doctor Adams has already undergone, the fact that the case for the Prosecution on this further indictment, based on evidence given before the Eastbourne Magistrates, depends in part on the evidence of Doctor Ashby and very greatly upon the inference not supported as in Mrs Morrell's case, of any admissions.

[50] Ibid, p 252.
[51] Transcript of the trial of Dr John Bodkin Adams, Old Bailey, Day 17, Tuesday, 9 April 1957.

Having given the matter the best consideration I can, I have reached the conclusion that in all the circumstances the public interest does not require that Doctor Adams should undergo the ordeal of a further trial on a charge of murder, and I therefore enter a nolle prosequi in relation to that indictment.

Mr. Justice Devlin: Then, Mr Attorney, all further proceedings on the indictment are stayed and no further action is taken in this Court. Accordingly, John Bodkin Adams, you are now discharged.

However, this was not the end for Adams. In some ways it was to begin again, but on a much smaller scale. As Bedford observed:[52]

The Doctor framing the words, toneless, 'Thank you': making his small grave bow, keeping his eyes, intent, unblinking, on the Judge; the Judge staring back at him, blank and earnest; the Doctor half stumbling, half helped, vanishing from sight; Mr Lawrence rising to ask for bail on some offences under the Drugs Act to come to light in this microscopic investigation; bail fusslessly granted; the Judge thanking the jury with ceremony and near emotion 'your labours have been exceptional ... I therefore discharge you from jury service for the rest of your lives ...'; the Judge's swift exit, the pattern broken, the slow dispersal ...

The crowds were, along with the press, waiting outside for a glimpse of Adams, but:[53] 'They will not see him. The Doctor has been helped out of the building and borne to a place of safe concealment by the potent offices of a friendly newspaper.'

The postscript involved the trial and the Attorney-General's conduct of it being the subject of questions posed in the House of Commons by Colonel George Wigg, Labour MP for Dudley.[54] He asked the Attorney-General whether he would institute an independent inquiry into the preparation, organisation and conduct of the prosecution, to which the Attorney-General, tersely and predictably, said 'No'.[55] Wigg made a second attempt some week or two later but the

---

[52] Sybille Bedford, *The Best We Can Do: An Account of the Trial of John Bodkin Adams* (London, Collins, 1958), p 253.

[53] Ibid, p 254.

[54] ETP, pp 183 and following. See also: 'Trial Inquiry Rejected: Move for Study of Dr. Adams' Prosecution is Rebuffed', *The New York Times*, 2 May 1957; LCB Gower, 'The Aftermath of the Adams Case' (1957) 20(4) *Modern Law Review* 387–91; Henry Palmer, 'Dr Adams' Trial for Murder' [1957] *Criminal Law Review* 365–77.

The trial spawned a number of books and articles. One such article which appeared in the *Observer* on 14 April 1957 described Patrick as the 'greatest judge after Lord Goddard'. Apart from Sybille Bedford's book, at least the following have been written about the trial: Rodney Hallworth and Mark Williams, *Where there's a Will ... The Sensational Life of Dr John Bodkin Adams* (Jersey, The Capstan Press, 1983); Percy Hoskins, *Two Men Were Acquitted. The Trial and Acquittal of Doctor John Bodkin Adams* (London, Secker & Warburg, 1984); John Surtees, *The Strange Case of Dr Bodkin Adams* (Seaford, SB Publications, 2000); Pamela Cullen, *A Stranger in Blood. The casefiles on Dr John Bodkin Adams* (London, Elliott and Thompson, 2006); Jane Robins, *A 1950s Murder Mystery: The Curious Habits of Dr Adams* (London, John Murray, 2013).

[55] ETP, p 183. See also, LCB Gower, 'The Aftermath of the Adams Case' (1957) 20(4) *Modern Law Review* 387–91, p 390.

calloused and seasoned Attorney-General was undistracted by a minor sting as he saw it. Colonel Wigg was joined by others, including Sir Lynn Ungoed-Thomas, a former Solicitor-General. But the storm would soon blow over. Some would have it that these events ruined Manningham-Buller's chance of becoming Lord Chief Justice. Manningham-Buller was an easily disliked person. It is highly likely that the Adams case made him more unpopular even with the public who would hardly have known him. Had he got the job, he would have replicated Goddard in a number of respects – arch-conservative and harsh on criminals. But there is another theory that Macmillan liked Manningham-Buller alongside him with his rhinoceros-like exterior. When Macmillan ruthlessly sacked seven of his ministers in 1962, he survived. Indeed, it may be said that Manningham-Buller was one of the principal beneficiaries, for he was then made Lord Chancellor, the most senior law office in the country and arguably more prestigious than the office of Lord Chief Justice.

But the troubles were not over for Adams. He still had to face all the other charges involving the drugs, cremation certificates and so on. On 30 June 1957 he resigned from the National Health Service. He pleaded guilty at Lewes Assizes on 26 July on all the remaining charges and was fined £2,400. Later that year he was struck off the medical register. He remained off it for four years.

For Patrick, the celebrity status continued. Felix Frankfurter, then a judge of the United States Supreme Court, had read about the trial in the *New York Times* and had taken particular interest in Patrick's summing up, especially on the right to silence. He wrote to his old friend Raymond Evershed, now Master of the Rolls. He was effusive in his praise for Patrick. He wanted copies of it so it could be distributed to judges in the United States. Typically, because the public purse was to be accessed, much protocol had to be observed. Evershed wrote to Patrick on 1 May, to get the ball rolling:[56]

> Can you help an old friend Felix F. as requested. It would be most kind if you could.
>
> When I write I will of course explain (with reference to the somewhat fulsome terms of his paragraph 3) that what made your 'summation' so particularly good was the help you got from me – that it was in truth a 'co-summation' relevantly to be wished by any jury who might have to say the prisoner was to be or not to be.

Goddard had approved the supply of the summing up but also wanted a note prepared by him as to why in some high-profile cases it may be appropriate to have evidence taken in private where there are serious arguments about its ultimate admissibility. Not to be outdone, Patrick ensured Frankfurter also got copies of his Hamlyn Lectures. When the summing up finally reached American soil, copies were distributed to all members of the American College of Trial Lawyers.

---

[56] Letter from Evershed to Devlin, 1 May 1957, Devlin-Adams Correspondence File.

Frankfurter, in anticipation of receiving copies of the summing up, decided to write directly to Patrick. He heaped praise on his work. Patrick replied on 25 May:[57]

> I am immensely pleased and honoured to get your letter. I do not suppose you realise how just your reputation is seen here and how much praise from you is valued. I remember being bitterly disappointed some year ago when I learned – too late – that you had been staying with Sylvester Bates, who is our neighbour here and that I had missed meeting you. I hope that I may be luckier when you are next over here.
>
> There has been some inevitable bureaucracy about the summing up in the Adams case … There seem to be rules which prevent the official shorthand writers certifying copies made for certain limited purposes. But there has been circumvention and Raymond Evershed will shortly be sending you a copy. I am very pleased that you want to make use of it.

Shortly thereafter, perhaps with a twinge of guilt, presumably not a moment of sorrow, Patrick wrote to Manningham-Buller who had taken quite a hammering from some MPs and the press, especially those sections – which accounted for almost all – who had convicted Adams before the trial. Manningham-Buller mournfully replied on 10 June:[58]

> Thank you for your note. Coming from you I naturally appreciate it very much.
>
> My only regret is that I failed to satisfy you by my final speech that Adams' admissions to Hannam that he had administered the drugs prescribed amounted to a prima facie case of the administration of those drugs.

It was time for both Manningham-Buller and Patrick to move on. The former had lots to do in Parliament and the Conservative Party. The latter had to return to the relentless activity of a trial judge. Neither could have expected that the Adams case marked the beginning of a high-profile struggle between them.

On top of the world and always exploring a fresh intellectual challenge, Patrick had become interested in writing a biography of President Woodrow Wilson. He had been invited to deliver the Sherrill Lectures in Yale and planned to spend some time in Washington DC researching his quarry. His lectures focused on the criminal prosecution in England. They were published the following year by Yale University Press (to critical acclaim especially in America).[59] He wrote again to Frankfurter on 25 August 1958:[60]

> I am most delighted to have your card, for I had somehow not expected that you would be in Washington in September. I am going to be there from the 16th to the

---

[57] Letter from Devlin to Frankfurter, 25 May 1957, Howard Gotlieb Archival Research Center Collection, Boston University.

[58] Letter from Manningham-Buller to Devlin, 10 June 1957, Devlin-Adams Correspondence File.

[59] Sir Patrick Devlin, *The Criminal Prosecution in England*, The Sherrill Lectures (New Haven CT, Yale University Press, 1958).

[60] Letter from Devlin to Frankfurter, 25 August 1957, Howard Gotlieb Archival Research Center Collection, Boston University.

18th and just possibly a little longer. I expect to stay at the Congressional Hotel which I am told is near the Library of Congress. I am planning to spend my time there looking at some of the Wilson papers. Outside the law I have a side-line of interest in President Wilson and the Treaty of Versailles; and that is one of many subjects I would like to talk to you about.

It is most kind of you to ask me to lunch and of course I would be delighted to come any day. I am planning on rather a short midday break as my time at the Library will be so limited. But perhaps if you are still free I could come back in the afternoon.

I am leaving here by aeroplane on 7th and going first to Chicago. I am not sure where I am staying there, but by the 11th I shall be with Professor Link whose address is 2676 Orrington Ave, Evanston; so a card there, if I should be too late to write here, will you tell me what day you fix on and I shall look forward to it very much.

In September Patrick had dinner with Frankfurter in Washington. Also attending the dinner was Dean Acheson, a famous American lawyer who was a close friend and walking companion of Frankfurter's. Frankfurter had taught Acheson at Harvard. Acheson had had an illustrious career to that point and amongst other things had been Secretary of State under President Truman (1949–53). Thereafter he had retired from public service and was back in private legal practice. Acheson had over the years spent a good deal of time in England and in particular Cambridge. The two men had exchanged some brief correspondence but at this dinner they struck up a friendship that would become endearing and enduring.

At the same time, Manningham-Buller was buzzing around the Commons, the Party room and furiously prosecuting various persons for contempt arising out of the Adams trial.[61]

The year would not end for Patrick without another fascinating case. In *Winchester v Fleming*,[62] Patrick had to decide whether a wife could sue another person in tort for harbouring her husband. Patrick decided that the old tort whereby a man could sue another for harbouring his wife (thought by Patrick to be 'a decaying form of action') should not be extended to a suit by a wife. Frankfurter had heard about the case and wrote to Patrick on 10 December in a somewhat paternal manner:[63]

Now that Marchioness of Winchester v Fleming is no longer sub judice, at least not sub Devlin J, I am tempted to ask you whether in the light of the social ideals that now dominate your country, it isn't more than 'fair shares' for any judge to have two such fabulous cases as that of Dr Adams and the Marchioness in one year!

The other day I came across an additional ray of light on President Wilson's way of doing business. He had chosen as Secretary of War Lindley M Garrison, an esteemed

[61] 'Adams Case Echo: U.S. Writer is Sued', *The New York Times*, 13 April 1957.
[62] *Winchester v Fleming* [1957] 1 QB 259.
[63] Letter from Frankfurter to Devlin, 10 December 1957, Howard Gotlieb Archival Research Center Collection, Boston University.

Vice Chancellor of New Jersey. Mr Wilson did so according to Secretary Garrison because the President conceived the Philippines to be the most important aspect of the then responsibilities of the Secretary of War. Wilson strangely enough thought that it required someone inured in the principles of equity to discharge our trust vis-a-vis the Filipinos. After reaching some definite conclusions Garrison made several futile attempts to see his chief. Finally, on April 24, 1919, he wrote his President a long letter, headed 'Concerning the Philippines', the first paragraph of which may interest you:

> It is difficult for us to get together for a real talk that I think it better for me from time to time as I think of important matters to write you for mutual benefit.

I continue to find pleasure in the memories of your visit.

With cordial greetings of the season.

By the end of 1957 Patrick had a well-established reputation domestically and internationally both as a judge and a jurist.

6

Friends Across the Atlantic

AFTER A NUMBER of high-profile scandals and prosecutions, among them that of the war hero Alan Turing, the Conservative Government on 24 August 1954 set up a committee of inquiry headed by Sir John Wolfenden. The Home Secretary at the time, Sir David Maxwell-Fyfe appointed Wolfenden, who had been a school teacher and Vice Chancellor of the University of Reading. The committee comprised 15 persons: three women and 12 men. The committee represented a cross-section of the community including doctors, lawyers, clergy and others. One of Patrick's colleagues, Sir Kenneth Diplock, a High Court judge, was also on the committee. It sat for 62 days, of which 32 were devoted to the oral testimony of witnesses. The committee was to consider the law and practice relating to homosexual offences, the treatment of persons convicted of such offences by the court, and the law and practice relating to offences against the criminal law in connection with prostitution and solicitation for immoral purposes; and to recommend what, if any, changes were desirable.

Although the committee's report dealt with the persons who gave oral testimony rather demurely and almost generically to preserve their anonymity, it almost unanimously recommended that homosexual behaviour between consenting adults in private be no longer a criminal offence and that certain reforms also be introduced into the law dealing with prostitution. The committee saw that the function of the criminal law was to:[1]

> preserve public order and decency, to protect the citizen from what is offensive or injurious and to provide sufficient safeguards against exploitation and corruption of others ... [it was] not to intervene in the private lives of citizens, or seek to enforce any particular pattern of behaviour, further than is necessary to carry out the purposes [already outlined].

One member of the committee was a Scottish solicitor and Elder of the Church of Scotland, James Adair. Other members called for some clarification or qualification of the law. But he expressed his implacable opposition to any change to the law relating to homosexuals.[2] His argument was that such behaviour was

---

[1] Report of the Committee on Homosexual Offences and Prosecution, September 1957 (Cmnd 247, 1957) at [9]–[10], [14]–[15]. See also [62], [71]–[72] and [123].
[2] Ibid, reservation by Mr Adair, pp 117–123 at [1]–[14].

contrary to the best interests of the community and 'one which can have very serious effects on the whole moral fabric of social life'. He thought if the recommendation were adopted 'the moral force of the law would be weakened'.

At least two judges volunteered to give written and oral evidence to the committee: Lord Goddard and Patrick. Some sources suggest that Goddard insisted on being the first witness called by the committee. Lord Goddard said that in his opinion, private acts of indecency between adult males ought not to be the concern of the criminal law. Further, he thought such acts have none of the attributes generally considered to be the constituents of a crime except that they may excite disgust and repulsion. He made reference to buggery as having been regarded historically as a crime, which he accepted, perhaps illogically, should be maintained. On the other hand, Patrick said:[3]

> I think that gross indecency by adults in private should not be treated as a crime; and by 'in private' I mean that which does not amount to a public nuisance. I think that where the element of corruption of the young comes in, it should remain a serious crime.

The Committee report was published in September 1957. It immediately attracted Patrick's attention. The Government dithered. But Cabinet was opposed to the implementation of the recommendations. Indeed it would be many, many months before it would be seriously debated.

In the meantime, in the early part of 1958 Patrick and Dean Acheson made arrangements to see each other in England later in the year.

On 2 June 1958 Patrick was invited to deliver the 1959 Maccabaean Lecture in Jurisprudence (delivered every three years) at the British Academy.[4] He knew exactly what he wanted to speak about. The lecture series was endowed by the Maccabaean Society to mark the tercentenary of the Jewish resettlement in England under Cromwell. The lecture was first given in 1956 by Lord Evershed. Patrick was to receive a fee of 50 guineas for his lecture. Patrick rapidly and enthusiastically accepted the invitation on 10 June and immediately nominated 'The Enforcement of Morals' as his subject.[5]

The rest of 1958 saw a busy return to more orthodox judicial activity. But during the latter part of 1957 Patrick had sat on a Court of Criminal Appeal comprising five judges in an important matter involving the newly enacted Homicide Act 1957. Goddard presided and wrote the judgment, the others concurred.[6]

The case called for consideration of whether the Act had in fact achieved its purpose. It was widely thought the point of the reform was to make clear

---

[3] Brian Lewis, *Wolfenden's Witnesses: Homosexuality in Postwar Britain* (Basingstoke/New York, Palgrave Macmillan, 2016), p 69.

[4] Letter from Sir Mortimer Wheeler, on behalf of the Council of the British Academy, to Devlin, 2 June 1958, the British Academy Archives.

[5] Letter from Devlin to Sir Mortimer Wheeler, 10 June 1958, the British Academy Archives.

[6] *R v Vickers* [1957] 2 All ER 741.

that constructive malice in a murder case was insufficient to sustain a finding of murder. The court's judgment was criticised in an article in the *Criminal Law Review* by JW Cecil Turner, a noted criminal law scholar and then one of the editors of *Russell on Crime*.[7] Turner indicated that the substance of the article would be included in the forthcoming 11th edition of *Russell on Crime*.

Turner made clear his opinion that section 1 of the Act purported to remove from the category of murder certain conduct in contexts where malice had to be implied – and yet the section used words to describe murder where the malice aforethought was said to be express or implied. This gave rise to confusion on what the legislation actually meant. The article was a perfectly courteous and reasoned argument intended to do no more than contribute to the reasoned debate about the stance of the Court. As Goddard wrote the only judgment, he was obviously to be seen as the target for a perfectly appropriate analysis, given that the accused's life was at stake if the conviction were upheld. The article sought in effect to portray the judgment as denying the legislation and its apparent intended effect. It portrayed the judgment as confused, and worse, as engaging in a series of non sequiturs and as a backward step in legal reasoning. The problem is that although the criticism was directed at Goddard it also appeared to be directed at the rest of the Bench, which included Patrick. In the end the accused stood convicted of a capital offence with the usual consequences.

Perhaps because he was his mentor or because 1958 saw the end of Goddard as Chief Justice, Patrick felt moved to jump anonymously to the Court's defence in a subsequent edition of the *Review*. This was an extraordinary step. At best it showed misplaced loyalty and gross oversensitivity. At worst it might be thought somewhat unjudicial.

The article could be aptly described in terms of the law of libel as a reply to an attack. It commenced with the following:[8] 'The judgment of the Court of Criminal Appeal in the case of *R v Vickers* was severely criticised by Mr J W Cecil Turner in an article published in the January issue of this review.' But much more intriguingly the asterisk adjacent to the title indicates the following: 'The author of this article regrets he is compelled to remain anonymous. J W C Turner has however, been informed of the views expressed in this article.'

Why 'compelled' one may ask, unless it would otherwise be seen as inappropriate for the actual person to be writing such a riposte? A practitioner or fellow academic would not be permitted such an indulgence. The asterisk points the finger at a judge as the author.

The article is in true Stonyhurst form. It purports to dismantle and then demolish Turner's criticism. It concludes triumphantly with the proposition that none of his criticisms has any validity. It asserts that Turner had significantly and

---

[7] JW Cecil Turner, 'Malice Implied and Constructive', [1958] *Criminal Law Review* 15.

[8] Anonymous, 'With Malice Aforethought: *R v Vickers* reconsidered' [1958] *Criminal Law Review* 714.

crucially misunderstood the judgment of the Court. It contends that his analysis was untenable and that the decision of the Court could not be impugned. The profession did not take too long to conclude that this anonymous correspondent was none other than Patrick himself. There was and is no proof. But it is reasonable to draw that conclusion, as does Professor Robert Heuston who wrote Patrick's obituary for the British Academy.[9] The *Review* were unable to throw light on the matter, but it is a little hard to imagine who else could have written it.[10] It is unlikely to be the apparent author of the judgment, Goddard. As promised, the substance of the criticism found its way into the 11th edition of *Russell on Crime* and also into the 17th edition of *Kenny's Outlines of Criminal Law* (also edited by Mr Turner). No doubt the proliferation of these heretical views was regarded by Patrick as too much to bear.

Goddard was to retire in September 1958. His replacement was in the gift of Prime Minister Macmillan. The choice of Hubert Parker as Goddard's replacement signalled a veritable sea change in judicial attitude and temperament. Parker was described as quiet and unassuming, an admirable leader, and a calm person with a keen sense of inclusiveness. This was the complete antithesis of Goddard and for that matter Manningham-Buller. Parker was five years older than Patrick. Although he had been appointed two years after Patrick in 1950 and had never taken silk, he was a highly regarded commercial lawyer who had sat as an appeal judge since 1954. This made him technically senior to Patrick. Patrick both admired and very much liked Parker and was in no way resentful of his promotion. Strangely, although Patrick was a very different person from Goddard, he was seen as a very close friend and confidant of his, with Goddard as his patron. Because of this, the role may well have been the kiss of death for Patrick.

In any event, Patrick started sitting in the Restrictive Practices Court and continued his extra curial writing. Apart from his proposed Maccabaean Lecture, he would, whenever time permitted, return to his proposed study of Woodrow Wilson. Frankfurter, by now not only a fan but also a friend and regular correspondent, kept as up to date as he could on Patrick's work. Indeed, they would often swap comments on each other's judgments and possible procedural reforms – something that had not only attracted Patrick's attention but became of ongoing concern.

On 18 July 1958, Frankfurter wrote to Patrick:[11]

Assuming as I do that the litigation due to become before the Restrictive Practices Court will, because of the nature of the issues and the mass of materials that will become relevant, raise problems, at least quantitatively different from the ordinary

---

[9] RFV Heuston, 'Patrick Arthur Devlin 1905–1992' (1994) 84 *Proceedings of the British Academy* 247–62 p 251.

[10] Email from Joseph Mosby (House Editor, *Criminal Law Review*) to the Author, 10 February 2015.

[11] Letter from Frankfurter to Devlin, 18 July 1958, Howard Gotlieb Archival Research Center Collection, Boston University.

line of cases before the High Court, I have read with great interest in The Times of the proceedings before you In re <u>Chemists Federation Agreement.</u>[12] I derive from it the high promise that you will avoid the procedural bog in which so much of our antitrust litigation gets stuck. I have no doubt that you have read a rather valuable report on what was journalistically called 'the big case' made by a committee headed by Judge E. Barrett Prettyman of the Court of Appeals for the District of Columbia Circuit, to our Judicial Conference, and also the book by Professor Keysen who was, as it were, the economic assessor of Judge Wyzanski in <u>United Shoe Machinery</u> case. The latter was interestingly reviewed in The Economist some time ago.

I hope I avoid commenting on a case <u>sub judice</u> if I express astonishment at reading the other day that Beyfus addressed the Court of the Appeals for the fifth day in Mrs. Fleming's appeal.[13] I once heard Justice Holmes say that he deemed the author of any three-decker novel a genius, no matter how poor the novel. I take for granted Mr Beyfus' great forensic talents, but that makes me wonder how he could have employed five days, and maybe more, in presenting the appeal. The Lord knows, for even I know, the extensive and deep inefficiencies in the conduct of our judicial business. But it is merely ignorance that makes me ask you to enlighten me as to why it should take that long to argue an appeal in such a case?

Let me turn to a larger issue, not less than Woodrow Wilson's role in the conduct of the war and in peace-making after World War I. You have I assume, read Herbert Hoover's 'The Ordeal of Woodrow Wilson'. While I have no doubt Mr Hoover was moved to write the book out of devotion to the memory of President Wilson, it would not portray one as a cynic to suggest that Mr Hoover was not unwilling to emerge in the book as a much wiser man than the President. The main thesis of the book is the familiar thesis of Wilson's apologists that the story of Paris is, in essence, that of a pure and noble man overcome by the designing and worldly wise. Surely it isn't as simple as all that. Hoover's point of view is essentially that conveyed by Ray Stannard Baker, published shortly after the Versailles treaty and if I can lay my hand, on it I shall – greatly daring – enclose a copy of a review that I wrote at the time of Baker's story.

My wife insists that once she gets on her feet again – a distant but not precluded consummation – we shall go to England.

Long before then you will be seeing Dean Acheson.

Patrick replied on 24 July:[14]

Thank you so much for your letter. It arrived about the same time as my copy of the latest 'Law Quarterly', so I enjoyed with it the amusing correspondence on the M'N------Rules.

I hope that in the Restrictive Practices Court we shall avoid getting things bogged up. That is what I am most ardently trying to do. I should like to introduce some of your appellant methods, so far as they can be made to work, at a trial.

[12] *Re Chemists Federation Agreement (No 2)* [1958] 1 WLR 1192, [1958] 3 All ER 448.
[13] *Winchester v Fleming* [1957] 1 QB 259.
[14] Letter from Devlin to Frankfurter, 24 July 1958, Howard Gotlieb Archival Research Center Collection, Boston University.

Your comment on the Fleming case is well justified. I think it shows off our appellate procedures at their very worst. A dissatisfied party is entitled to ask the court to re-hear the whole case and to disbelieve all the witnesses that the judge has believed and vice-versa. It is rarely successful, because unless the judge has done something idiotic, the Court of Appeal always ends up saying that the judge saw the witnesses and they did not. Nevertheless, the argument cannot be stopped and it enables counsel to intone his way through the whole transcript of the evidence, interspersing objurgations. Beyfus' objurgations are exceptionally turgid. Since none of the Lords Justices is expected to read a single word of the papers beforehand, the intonation can and does last for days. Somewhere about the 8th day, I think, they arrived at the only arguable point in the case and disposed of it in half a day or so.

Of course none of this would have been possible if there had been a trial by jury. When we put forward our claims for the saving of time effected by trials before a judge, alone you have to consider on the other side the vastly increased length of time taken up by appeals. I cannot understand why we do not study your appellate procedure, which I believe is followed in most of the Dominions, and model our own on it. But the Evershed Committee advised against it.

I wish you could find the review you wrote on Baker. If you do, will you send it, and I will undertake to return it if it is your only copy. It would be very interesting to read a contemporary criticism of Baker done as acutely as you would do it. I have got a copy of Hoover on Wilson, but am keeping it for the long vacation to read then. I will also try to get hold of Keysen's book which I did see reviewed in the Economist. But I have not heard of Judge Barrett Prettyman's report. Could you tell me who published it, so that I could write for a copy? I wish I could have thought of you and your wife coming over this Summer. But perhaps it will be next. My wife and I have been invited to go to Jerusalem for an International Lawyers Convention which is being held there in connection with the 10 year celebrations. So we are setting off on August the 14th. A minor attraction is that we have a son doing his National Service in Cyprus and hope to look in there for a week on our way back. But we shall be more than a fortnight away and then I shall begin reading papers for our first Restrictive Practices case. We are sitting in a Court of seven for the first two cases, but after that will split into two divisions and reduce each operating unit to more manageable numbers.

Talking of our appellate procedure, how would you manage in the Supreme Court with a court of nine, if you had to have a full oral hearing, as they do over here, I cannot imagine. The House of Lords with five is bad enough; and I once appeared before a Privy Council of seven and had much difficulty in interrupting their Lordships conversation.

Following Goddard's retirement, Patrick occasionally presided in the Court of Criminal Appeal as a senior puisne judge. Try as he might, he could not even in a modest way effect any procedural reforms. It remained a lifelong frustration.[15]

---

[15] 'Lord Devlin at 80: Lord Devlin interview with Joshua Rozenberg', *BBC Radio 4*, 25 November 1985.

Much of 1958 saw Patrick involved on an increasing basis with the work of the Restrictive Practices Court. In September, in anticipation of Acheson's visit to England, Patrick invited him to stay at West Wick, Patrick's farm. By now the two were regularly corresponding and happily Patrick's appalling handwriting had at last been superseded. In a postscript to a letter to Acheson dated 9 September he said:[16] 'I should be writing this myself if my hand were as good as yours. But it is not. So like Mr. Wilson I use a portable typewriter.'

Acheson replied loquaciously (typed) on 10 November:[17]

I had arrived at this point last Friday when your book, the Yale lectures, came just as I was leaving for Yale. So, most appropriately, I took it along and read most of it on the plane. The rest tonight. I found it absorbing, in part because what you wrote was largely new to me; partly because you, and Maitland, accomplish the miracle of writing about legal matters with style and charm; and partly because what you said about how English judges go about getting standards of conduct accepted is so in accord with my two weeks' observation of how at Cambridge the Masters and the senior members of colleges do the same thing.

I am full of this experience and bore everyone to death, about it. Also about your court and your approach to restrictive practices as against ours. A few years ago I lunched with the twenty odd law clerks at the Supreme Court. There I announced Acheson's law (which is really a development of Devlin's theory) of the simplification of issues. This is that, aside from a few Nobel prize winners, the capacity of the human mind to retain, classify and appraise data in quantity is not great. It is capable of very complicated ideas; but for dealing with great quantities of material the electronic machine is infinitely superior.

In the law this leads to the necessity of reducing the infinite data which together makes up what we call reality – what actually happened – to some sort of pantomime or charade which results in a legal judgement that conduct should or should not continue along certain lines. In England this is brought about by laws which, with whatever imperfection, attempt to spell out legislative command (whereas Congress likes to blur it to get agreement, leaving the courts to provide meaning). But, more than this, simplification is brought about by a system the individual character of which precludes highly organised mass production. No barrister and his junior could master and present – and I doubt any firm of solicitors could prepare – the hundreds of thousands of documents and the whole year of testimony which perhaps twenty lawyers and possibly forty assistants took four years to prepare and present in the DuPont-General Motors case. Apart from the question of whether it is or is not desirable – and I think is not – Acheson's law finds its British agency of simplification in the system itself and all that goes with it – the attitude of the courts, of clients, and so.

In the United States simplification is achieved by the judicial use of fraud, or, more politely, fiction. The law is that the trial judge's findings of fact are upheld unless

[16] Letter from Devlin to Acheson, 9 September 1958, Manuscripts and Archives, Yale University Library, Dean Acheson Papers, folder 96.

[17] Letter from Acheson to Devlin, 10 November 1958, Manuscripts and Archives, Yale University Library, Dean Acheson Papers, folder 96.

they are 'clearly' erroneous. Both sides submit requested findings. The judge usually follows, and always has, those put forward by the winning side, with such changes as he thinks needed.

Simplification occurs on appeal. First counsel undermines the findings by showing how slavishly they follow the request. No independent judgement, etc. Justices who 'take a strong line' against monopoly, or vice-versa, are impressed occasionally though God knows why. Then the 'case' is stated in the briefs – with all kinds of references to the interminable record which are never easily conclusive. A plausible statement which seems to record with 'what every practical man knows' or 'human nature' – e.g., that a capability to control will in fact always be exercised – or 'what stands to reason' supersedes the findings of fact which when they conflict too patently, can be called either 'conclusions' or 'clearly' in conflict with a lot of testimony adduced by the other side. Since no Justice does or could read the record, the process of simplification means that the vast and costly effort which produced it has been rendered useless so far as the judicial process is concerned. It remains the justification of the management to the stockholders and the public opinion, as made by the press. It also affects treble damage suits since the findings as such are more often ignored rather than reversed.

It would be boastful of me to claim that Acheson's law produces this whole result. The teleological tendency in some members of the Court, sometimes called by their uneducated clearks 'result mindedness' plays its full part. But it all adds up, as I said on my way down for the week-end to make the regime of the giant corporations in America, like the rule of Czars, tyranny tempered by assassination. The anti-trust laws furnish the bombs. But no one has been badly hurt – yet.

I am an idle fellow and so write long letters which do not require long answers from busy men. Also each of us may use without discourtesy his preferred mode of writing.

One thing admits of no judicial discretion. You must give my warmest greetings to Lady Devlin, to Virginia, and to Claire (have I spelt the name properly). My wife, who is very jealous of me, wants her included, too. I hope all is well with your boy in Cyprus.

On 26 November an important debate took place in the Commons.[18] While there had been a number of brief skirmishes with the topic, the House had simply managed not to get around to debating it. The then Secretary of State for the Home Department and Lord Privy Seal, Rab Butler, a close personal friend of Patrick's, opened the debate for the Government by thanking Sir John Wolfenden and the Committee for spending so much time 'studying these problems'. After much handwringing he announced:[19]

> The subjects considered by the Committee, as I think it fully realised in its Report, raise in the most acute form one of the perennial dilemmas of organised society. That is how far the law and the compulsion of the law should seek to regulate the behaviour of individuals. I think we all agree that there is a sphere of conduct in which

---

[18] Hansard, House of Commons Debate, 26 November 1958, volume 596 cols 365–508, commencing at 3:32pm.
[19] Ibid, at 3:32 pm.

the behaviour of individuals must be controlled by the sanctions of the law, in their own interests, in the interests of others, and in the interest of society at large. I think it would be agreed that there is a sphere in which it is proper to leave to the dictates of the individual conscience; I mean the individual and the individual conscience as fortified by the teachings of religion and the generally accepted standards of the society in which we live.

Where dispute arises is in defining the limits of those two spheres.

The debate raged for some hours into the late evening. Both sides of politics took a roughly similar view, which involved handwringing and fence-sitting. Only one politician was unequivocal in his support for the decriminalisation of homosexuality. That was barrister, author and biographer Montgomery Hyde, an Ulster Unionist MP for Belfast North.[20] His passionate support for the proposition resulted in his deselection by his party in 1959.

Patrick clearly watched the whole affair no doubt with great interest. But with several letters from Acheson mounting up on his desk, he set about a lengthy reply on 4 December:[21]

> I have a delightful trio of letters from you full of nice things. I'm so glad that you enjoyed the book but you turn my head with references to Maitland.
>
> Madeleine, Clare and Virginia all send their love and many remembrances. Last month we had a great surprise. Gil, our eldest boy who is in Cyprus arrived in the flat at Grays' Inn one evening after dinner. There were three places in a Bristol freighter going back to England and they offered a place to each of the Companies in the Battalion at two hours notice. The conditions were that the successful applicant had to have this passport in order and be prepared to pay his own fare back. Gil was the only person who satisfied both so he got the place and ten days leave. Two of them went in the journey out which was an old-fashioned affair with many stops and not flying above 6000 feet but we had a full week in England and for the Sunday we got all the other three boys home from school and were all reunited which is becoming rare nowadays. I enclose the photograph I took to mark the occasion. If you think I look a little harassed it is because I had to set the automatic timer going and was not sure that I had got to the group in time.
>
> The Regiment comes back for good in the middle of February and I shall be very glad when Gil is out of it. It is no longer at all a pleasant place. I much admire Macmillan and have both admiration and friendship for the Governor Hugh Foot. I know that the British plan was the joint work and I am sure that it was honestly and sincerely meant. But the English can never understand why other people will not accept a practical solution. It is just like Ireland in 1920 and I do not believe there is any more hope for a compromise between two aeroplanes flying at different levels.
>
> With the aid of your stage directions I have read the Bethlehem-Youngstown case and made it all out. This was a great relief because an unkind friend sends me the most enormous quantities of Antitrust literature of a highly esoteric kind. The latest

---

[20] Ibid, at 4:44 pm.

[21] Letter from Devlin to Acheson, 4 December 1958, Manuscripts and Archives, Yale University Library, Dean Acheson Papers, folder 96.

one I have got is headed 'Recent Antitrust Developments' and opens with the state-ment that the past term – 'saw a retreat from the "Times-Picayne philosophy with a concomitant exaltation of the per se approach'. It will take the Restrictive Practices Court another 10 years to reach this sort of standard.

Meanwhile we labour on. But not with the intense devotion of Judge Weidenfeld who according to the New York Times gets up every morning at 5:45 works until midnight, two nights in every week and spends Sunday 'poring over the papers.' I can see that there is a great deal of poring over because the B-Y case produced 3000 pages of testimony. This raises an interesting point. The paper says that the Court hearing occupied 19 days. Seeing that four days of that was devoted to speeches and 15 days to evidence (I admit that I'm a bit influenced in these estimates by the fact that I want to divide 3000 by the number of days and 15 makes an easy division) and that means there was 200 pages of testimony for each day. We think it is very good going if we can produce 60 pages of testimony in day. With that parsimony in public affairs which F.F. has noted and finds not unattractive the English like to make the most of every sheet of paper so it is single line spacing on foolscapsheets. How does this compare with the American practice? The importance of this question you will already have grasped. Acheson's law which is destined to be one of the great legal-scientific discoveries of the age cannot be operated successfully in practice unless there is agreed unit of what must be an International Convention on the principles of pagination. It would never do if it were to be bandied about that the Americans were acquiring a supremacy simply by means of the greater wealth and willingness to squander paper. That would undo all the great work that Mr Nixon has recently been accomplishing. At least I suppose he has been accomplishing it because the papers say-so. So far I've only met one man who met him and he was a Palace official who said he met so many people at the Palace that he had become almost incapable of liking or disliking any of them. But he took a dislike to Mr Nixon.

I was fascinated by your comments on the election. It is sad that Rockefeller is as dislikable as Nixon; I thought he might perhaps provide an acceptable alternative. Still, it really does not look as if either of them would get very much further, – at least for a number of years. I realise the importance of what you were saying at West Wick the advantage of having a candidate to build up. But even with that advantage can the Republicans hope to beat the Democrats now?

Anyway I have the feeling that Nixon will never be President and should not put my ignorant money on him. It seems to me an extraordinary thing that the American system of electing a President with the party conventions to start it off, you cannot say it always, or even generally, produces great Presidents; that would be asking too much of any democracy – but it does seem to me to be surprising how rarely the Nixons get through. My knowledge of American history is scanty and does not go back very far, but I cannot think of any really bad President in the last 80 or 90 years except Harding.

But to return to Acheson's law. There are in England at present two notions about the right judicial method. One is to make it a piece of scientific research. All the data is to be patiently collected and assembled, – with the additional disadvantage that most of it in England has to be done orally during the hearing rather than by prepared documents, – and when you've got the data, you begin to think about the point. And you say, 'the capacity of the human mind to retain, classify and appraise data in quantity is not great'; and accordingly in a complicated case the fog has come down before the search begins. The other notion is that it is the business of the judge to state what he thinks the points are as soon as he is reasonably certain that he has got them right and then to see that the inquiry is directed to them and to nothing else. I am a practitioner in the second class; but I must admit that my conviction that it is the right one maybe influenced by the fact but I am mentally quite incapable of acquiring any knowledge unless I can put it to some immediate use; for that reason I was never any good in examinations. If they had told me the questions beforehand I might have done something with them. This way is getting rather old-fashioned. It is argued that you ought to hold all judgement in suspense until you have heard all the facts. The result of that is that since counsel have not got the slightest idea what you think important and what you think insignificant they go on piling fact upon fact the ripples spread and there is no margin to contain them.

This is what has been happening in the Cotton case which we have just finished. My brethren took the view that we ought to allow everybody to say anything they liked. Perhaps they were right in this case; they argued that it was the first big case in the Court and that it involved semi-political considerations; the cotton industry is one which gives rise to feelings in the part of Lancashire in which it's concentrated; and therefore that it was best to hear the thing out in immense detail. So I assented, entering merely a caveat that it was not to form a precedent for the trial of all future cases. So it lasted 27 days. There were 6 days of argument and 21 days of so-called evidence which consisted of a lot of witnesses arguing with counsel about the way in which all the various points which they thought were relevant ought to be decided. We sat in silence, – more or less, – which undoubtedly gave a fine appearance of impartiality. Many people think that is the right thing to do. They point out, if a judge gets the relevant points wrong and so cuts out a lot of material and argument that ought in fact to been developed, the whole trial is irretrievably messed up; while in this way all the material which anyone can conceivably consider to be relevant gets on to the record. I think however that a judge ought to have sufficient confidence in his powers to feel reasonably sure that he is getting the thing right; and if from time to time he does make a mess of it, there is no point in having a Court of Appeal unless they are prepared to step in and put things right. The occasional new trial that has to be ordered seems to me to be better than having every trial two or three times its proper length.

I adapted myself to the method we employed by spending the first 60 to 90 minutes of each day reading the transcript of the proceedings of the day before. This could be done quite quickly as many pages could be skipped altogether and I made about half a page of notes on anything that seemed at all significant. The rest of the day I spent composing a lecture that I have to deliver at the British Academy in March. By this means I gave a finer appearance of impartial industry than anybody else because I always seemed to be making notes. I think in the end the judgment will be quite short, – probably not very much longer than the Chemists case: I was greatly touched by the fact that you have bothered to read that judgment and encouraged by your comments.

My lecture has to do with the moral law and the criminal law and the relationship between them, – a subject that is arousing some interest here because of the recent recommendations of the Wolfenden Committee on homosexuality and prostitution.

My brother who is in Rhodesia has just sent me a note of a judgment in a Bantu tribal case which seems to put the point very neatly. It runs as follows

'We have power to make you divide your crops, for this is our law, and we shall see that it is done. But we have you behave like an upright man'.

The Edens seem to be settling down happily. He is charming to all and sundry and the socialist population in the neighbourhood is steadily diminishing. We went over there a fortnight or so ago and I found them quite delightful. They are off to Mexico for winter next week. The winter here has been foul so far, – perpetual fog. I am too going off after Christmas but only for a fortnight. There is a legal congress in Delhi and I shall combine learning with a little sun, I hope; and I hope to break the journey at Beirut for a day or two and perhaps see my son if he is lucky enough to get leave from Cyprus.

I am as you see taking you entirely at your word about the method of writing, and I should not have done so unless I had your permission. But the fact is that I hate the physical labour of writing; my hand does not keep pace with my thoughts and every sentence trails away into illegibility while I am thinking of the next one. I have as almost my inseparable companion a small dictating machine with a battery and I like nothing better than to do, as I am doing now, – sit in an armchair and talk away. I expect you will have to treat it, as I treat the transcript and skip most of it.

A happy Christmas and to your wife, whom we all hope to meet before too long, for we like so much of the glimpses of her that we got through your talk. And my warmest regards to Mr. Justice Frankfurter when you next see him; I had no idea he was 76; I thought he was in his late 60s, which he looks.

At the end of 1958 Sybille Bedford's book on the Adams trial came out in the UK. Due to obvious demand a slightly modified version was released in the US a short time later. She sent a copy to Patrick as a gift for Christmas that year. In thanks he wrote to her:[22]

It was extraordinarily kind of you to send me a copy of your book on the Adams trial. I have read it with unexpected enjoyment – unexpected because I thought that I would be bound to find the subject rather stale. But you have made it sound so exciting and have produced something so readable (which I should have thought so impossible out of seventeen days of transcript) and so much of the writing is so good that it leaves me full of admiration.

Christmas at West Wick was a glass or two of decent Bordeaux, the odd cigar, placing finishing touches to any outstanding judgments and of course the Maccabaean lecture. Then off to a meeting of the International Commission of Jurists in Delhi between 5 and 10 January. But in between on December 9, Acheson informed Patrick that Frankfurter had taken seriously ill. The friendship between the two meant that Patrick was deeply concerned.

---

[22] Letter from Devlin to Bedford, 13 November 1958, Archives of the Harry Ransom Center, University of Texas at Austin.

A young Patrick walking with a medical expert in the Hearn case.

Patrick as a trial judge during the Bodkin Adams trial in 1957.

West Wick House, the 18th century farm purchased by Patrick and Madeleine in 1943.

Patrick and Madeleine on their wedding day in February 1932.

Promotional card for *Duc de Montebello*, the champagne Patrick served his guests at his 21st birthday party at Cambridge. The Champagne no longer exits.

Photograph of the town centre of Chiselhurst, Kent, 1914. Patrick was much the same age as the children shown.

Arthur Goodhart, in 1962 as Master of University College Oxford.

Patrick in early 1959 about to board a plane on his way to Rhodesia to conduct his commission of inquiry into Nyasaland.

Double portrait of Patrick and Sir Reginald Manningham-Buller QC during the Bodkin Adams trial.

Sir Walter Monckton, then Minister of Labour leaving No 10 Downing Street in December 1953.

Viscount Radcliffe entering his car outside his home in Duchess of Bedford walk on 16 November 1962 during his inquiry into the Vassall spy case.

Francis L Sullivan playing a barrister in a scene for the film 'Take My Life' screened in 1947.

Patrick at the time of his retirement from the House of Lords in 1964.

Patrick in September 1969.

Patrick at 80.

Lord Goddard speaking at a judicial conference in the United States in November 1959 after he had retired as Lord Chief Justice.

The Earl Jowitt, taken by the Thames in 1953, when he was Leader of the Opposition in the House of Lords.

Patrick and Archbishop Ramsey, Archbishop of Canterbury, at a Foyles Literary lunch at the Dorchester chaired by Patrick in November 1965 to launch Ramsey's book, 'Sacred and Secular'.

7

Up a Notch

1959 would be a demanding and in many ways a very stressful year, with Patrick entering the worlds of both politics and philosophy and regularly lurching from one to the other whilst discharging the relentless demands of the trial judge.

Acheson wrote to Patrick again on 30 January 1959:[1]

Since our legal pilgrims to Delhi are now home it seems probable that you must be either back again or nearing home. I can well believe that the views of some of our representatives whom I know must have given you some entertainment. I should have thought that they would have oscillated from the glib to the pompous. Discussion of the rule of law seems to squeeze the most extraordinary statements out of otherwise fairly earthy creatures. They seem to sprout wings and begin to orbit around the subject with great velocity.

I am tempted myself to get into a phase of this matter and wonder if you have any suggestion as to where I should look or from whom I should seek guidance about it. I have been asked to speak in Williamsburg at an annual meeting they have in spring the title of which is Prelude to Independence which is usually taken up with discussions on Colonial America. I'm rather intrigued with the idea that the prelude to independence is summed up in Jefferson's remarkable document. It seems to me unique among revolutionary documents. It is not concerned with nationalism nor with economic or social ideology but solely with the matter of restraints on power. This led me to wonder when man first began thinking about such an unusual idea because it is unusual. As Holmes said, 'if one has no doubts about one's premises or one's power one exercises it and sweeps away opposition.' British and European experiences one knows a good deal about. Back on this one finds in Judaic literature the conception pretty well-established particularly the interplay with religious and secular authority, the prophets against the kings. Off the bat I can't recall if the Greeks or Romans contributed much but Jewish thinking of course came before theirs. Probably somewhere out of India or China one might begin to see the origins of the idea. I imagine that I shall have to get some of my faculty friends at Yale and Harvard to give me a lead. What do you think?

Felix has been back at work for three weeks. The current week the court is in recess, but for the two preceding ones he sat on the bench for four full days each week. His doctor kept careful check on him and finds not only no strain but steady improvement.

[1] Letter from Acheson to Devlin, 30 January 1959, Manuscripts and Archives, Yale University Library, Dean Acheson Papers, folder 96.

His greatest difficulty is the medical admonition that he must not get into sustained controversy. Since this is rather like telling a fish that it must get out of water, Felix finds it difficult. However he claims that a sort of serene calm in the face of perverse ignorance is gaining possession of him. Yesterday I went to lunch with him, if it can be called lunch since it lasted for four hours and was more like a review of the state of man on this globe.

I had hoped in this letter to be able to give you another chapter in the development of Acheson's law. I cannot give the one I had hoped to, which would've been a specific account of the expenses of the General Motors and Dupont anti-trust proceedings. But the reason that they are not available furnishes a chapter in itself. The stockholder suits had begun following up the decision of the Supreme Court. They are based on the assertion that General Motors profited illegally from its control of General Motors and must make restitution. This produces a litigation of rather unique confusion. You will recall the District Court reviewed the record of transactions over forty years and found that in fact charges of this kind made by the Government were not true. The Supreme Court did not specifically reverse these findings but generally disregarded them and said that control must have been illegal anyway. The District Court's findings would of course not be binding upon the new litigants. Therefore they will probably have to be tried all over again. One can readily understand why in the situation the defendants in the Government's suit are somewhat reluctant to opening files. It would be interesting to see how Acheson's Law operates. It may be that the courts will find a way to escape the tedious nonsense of a retrial or the whole dreary thing may have to be repeated, but on appeal may again be disregarded. I shall keep you informed.

I hope the voyage to India, and return, as well as the time spent there, gave you rest, sun and pleasure. Did you get a chance to see Gil in Cyprus? Did Lady Devlin go with you? I am eager to know about it all. You are a much more adventurous traveller than I am. India rather appals me. At present Alice and I are hoping to get off to Antigua in two weeks for a two week visit with Archie MacLeish in a superb sun and in and out of the superb water part of the British West Indies. Aside from this our other travel ambitions are to go back to Northern Italy as soon as we can. In this connection I spoke vaguely sometime ago of learning Italian. Of this my school teaching daughter in law has given me Italian lessons on phonograph records and it's put me to work. Breakfast conversation now is limited to polite inquiries about the state of one another's health and the route to the railroad – a lovely word 'ferrovioria' – station. I believe that if we could only spend a few months in Italy we would go further and have great fun in finding the way. I have written a story laid at Como which I shall send you when Harpers publishes it in March.

Two weeks ago the New York Times in its Sunday magazine section did the only flattering piece about me that I can remember. You can see therefore why I am eager my friends read it. I thought that it might amuse you and I'm sending a copy along herewith.

Patrick would not get around to responding to Acheson for some weeks, given other commitments, but he did swap some letters with Frankfurter.

From time to time and in a most fatherly fashion, Frankfurter would send Patrick any materials he came across concerning Wilson, despite having been politically opposed to his election. He had been bitterly disappointed when Wilson was elected President over Frankfurter's choice, as it were, Theodore Roosevelt. He would have much greater success with Theodore's distant cousin Franklin. In so many ways Patrick and Frankfurter were strange bedfellows. Almost certainly political opposites, their friendship was one of intellectual affection and admiration entirely transcending partisan politics. However, both were in their own ways deeply conservative. Frankfurter was a deft talent scout. He had successfully recruited many talented young lawyers into Government service. They were called 'Felix's Happy Hot Dogs'.[2] Dean Acheson was one of the 'Dogs'. Patrick, on the other hand, was arguably the British sausage equivalent.

On 3 February 1959, Frankfurter wrote:[3]

Before I had a chance send you a triune appreciation, I had what the doctors have called a mild coronary 'episode' of which you took such encouraging note. You were very kind to write to me. The six weeks in the hospital turned out to be an enjoyable rest-cure and I was sent back to work with the assurance that I was in fitter condition than I was before the episode, provided I would live as sensibly as a man of my years should. To the surprise of all the doubting Thomases among my affectionate friends, I am finding that I can moderate my tempo – one of my friends suggested that I try to strike a balance between Theodore Roosevelt and Buddha – and carry on work as of old if I can only moderate my Gargantuan reading appetite.

And now for my triune appreciation. Your 'Criminal Prosecution' gives fitting employment to that much abused cliché 'It fills a long-felt want.' At last I can turn inquirers to a book that authoritatively and felicitously deals with the English system of criminal prosecution. I know there have been bits here and there, like the book of that old friend of mine Maurice Amos (did you know him in Cambridge?), but I insist that yours is the first adequate treatment.

Secondly I thought you talked well to the young lawyers at Gray's. Most talks by older lawyers to the young are rather pretentious and highfalutin. You talked colloquially about things that are important in the daily life of a barrister. Evidently you suffer much from the mumbling talk of lawyers, for I notice you again referred to that failing in your introduction to Henry Cecil's book.[4] (I confess that I have played with notion that the pseudonym concealed your identity.)

Finally you must let me say that your judgment in the <u>Chemist's case</u> was first-rate. I must even charge you with my partial responsibility for influencing a judicial action of mine. The other day I sent you the opinions of our court in the <u>International Boxing case</u>. My own unwillingness to join in sustaining the harsh terms of the decree was influenced by your refusal to grant the Registrar's request for an injunction against the Chemists.

---

[2] Sujit Raman, 'Felix Frankfurter and his Protégés: Re-examining the "Happy Hot Dogs"' (2014) 39(1) *Journal of Supreme Court History* 79–106.

[3] Letter from Frankfurter to Devlin, 3 February 1959, Howard Gotlieb Archival Research Center Collection, Boston University.

[4] Henry Cecil, *Tipping the Scales* (London, Hutchinson, 1964), Foreword by Lord Devlin.

And now having read your judgment in the <u>Yarn Spinners Case</u> I must add a fourth appreciation. I am not entitled to an opinion on the merits. But even an outsider who has to deal with kindred matters is free to say that the construction you have given to your statute and the balancing of conflicting considerations required under it appear very persuasive. I can think of judges who would have been derailed from stout reasoning by the unemployment which your result confessedly will entail. Your statute makes necessary, or am I wrong, closer analysis than does our own Sherman law, or even the Clayton Act. But as I watch the way you keep your hand on the tiller of litigation under the Act, I find new evidence for my confidence in the resources of judicial administration.

I used to think that British judges, and even one's colleagues in Canada and Australia whose Constitutions have no due process clause are to be envied for not having to adjudicate under that elusive command. Am I to change that feeling on the basis of some items I have seen regarding the Delhi Conference and to infer that the undefined and undefinable scope of due process is now to become part of the common law, as it were the common law of the world? If so I am tempted to say 'They know not what they do'. I should like to recommend to some of the ardent spirits amongst you the reading of the debate, was it in 1912 or 1913, in which the leading legal lights of the Asquith government expanded at length the reasons for the refusal of that Government to accept the due process amendment to their own Home Rule Bill. Indeed I am tempted to say a seasoned experience on this Court might lead them not to fly to evils they know not of.

How is your book on Wilson coming along? I hope there are no restrictive practices hampering its progress.

Patrick replied on 16 February:[5]

I was delighted to get your letter of February 3rd and I can put my delight into a triune too. First because it is a letter from you and as delightful as your letters always are. Secondly it satisfies me that you are really completely recovered and back where you were before, if not better. I'd hardly believed that that could be so and had thought that inevitably you would have to cut out some little extras, such as correspondence with your lesser friends. I share the well-founded surprise of your other friends at the suggestion that you are moderating your reading. Apparently you can still find time for 'Graya', a light work like Henry Cecil and the judgments of the Restrictive Practices Court. A list of current publications you are no longer reading ought to be of interest to posterity.

Thirdly and most of all, I am delighted with your triune appreciation. Praise from you is hard currency and goes into a ledger in which no ordinary compliments are entered up. It is not merely that they come from you, though that counts for a lot but you have a way of putting them so convincingly and firmly that even the most modest man, – and I can lay no claim to being that, – might feel that he safely raise his estimate of himself a little higher.

I am so glad you approve of what we have done so far in the new Court. I gather in your law any sort of price fixing scheme is ipso facto doomed, nothing can save it.

[5] Letter from Devlin to Frankfurter, 19 February 1959, Howard Gotlieb Archival Research Center Collection, Boston University.

Our new statute, as you suspect, requires a balancing operation to be done. I am very hopeful in this sort of operation the experiment of mixing legal and commercial minds will work out satisfactorily. The Commercial men were obviously very much at sea at first. But they are beginning to get a bit of confidence now and are making a sound contribution.

I hope that you are beginning to think again of your trip to England. Is there any chance this summer? I should like to renew the pleasures of our meeting which is now one and a half years old and hear you talk again. In particular I should like to hear much more of your views on 'due process', of which you give a tantalising glimpse in your letter. What has gone wrong with it? I shall try to identify the debate you mention and look it up in Hansard.

The book on Wilson has been practically moribund since I saw you. What with restrictive practices and the setting up of that Court, and the two lots of lectures the Hamlyn, the Sherrill and a third one, – single only, I am glad to say, – that I am delivering next month and shall send you a copy of it, if I may; and generally this and that, including the affairs of six children and a farm, I have not added to it so much as a paragraph. But I am going to get down to it from now on. I am going to spend a quiet summer in Wiltshire – no more legal jaunts and jollities – and I will really hope to get a bit done.

And Patrick finally replied to Acheson's January letter on 2 March:[6]

I am so glad that you sent me the piece from the New York Times. It gives me a great deal of information about you which I do not suppose you would ever have given me yourself. I think that in many ways it does you less than justice, but I dare say that you prefer the butter to be skimped rather than laid on too thick. It certainly makes very clear the part that you are still playing in foreign policy. When you read the other day that you were working on foreign policy statement with the Democratic National Committee, I must say I thought that inevitably you would be wasting your powers and your time, albeit in a good cause. To get any statement of policy out of any committee is difficult, and out of committee politicians I should have said it impossible. But the two 'Democratic programmes for action' which you sent me are admirable. They are clearly your inspiration and I should guess that much if not all of the writing is yours; certainly they are very well-written. They really say something.

On the large question – whether it is right to be firm or forthcoming with Russia, and if both, in what mixture, – I am baffled I have about come to think that there is no question of principle in it and that the correct answer depends upon the correct assessment of the Russian mind. I should very much like to know what do you think should be the attitude of the sane non-student of these problems.

Delhi was interesting and enjoyable. It has reduced the rule of law to a meaningless slogan and has also succeeded in proving that if it did mean anything it would not interest anybody very much nowadays. I dare say it was the Americans who started the rot a year or so ago. You know the common criticism of the Victorian teaching about liberty – that it was concerned only with political freedom and not with

<hr/>

[6]Letter from Devlin to Acheson, 2 March 1959, Manuscripts and Archives, Yale University Library, Dean Acheson Papers, folder 96.

economic freedom; that it was no use giving the man the vote if you did not also give him enough to live on. So it is said that Dicey's conception of the rule of law is similarly outmoded; the rule of law must not only secure a man's freedom from arrest and imprisonment, it must provide him with his food, his health, his education, opportunity to develop himself as a man etc etc; habeas corpus is no use without calories and false teeth to eat them with. There is a fallacy here somewhere but I have not yet worked it out. Isaiah Berlin has recently published a lecture you gave called 'Two concepts of liberty'. I have not yet got a copy owing to the maddening habit of publishers of sending out their things for review before they are available in the bookshops; the consequence is when you try to buy them you can't and then you forget about them until by chance you remember, – as I have done just at this moment, – that you have not got it. But going by the review this thesis was there were two sorts of liberty, – positive and negative; the negative is the old-fashioned and positive this is the new fashioned; his thesis was, I think that in order to give a man the new fashioned economic freedom you had to do it by so many regulations that inevitably you curtailed his political freedom and ended up with a minus quantity.

Anyway whatever its theoretical merits or demerits, the practical effect of the new doctrine is that the rule of law has been expanded to contain everybody's panacea for the social revolution. Instead of prescribing the minimum for the free state it becomes the ideal for the welfare state. Tom Denning, one of our Law Lords who was in Delhi announced his conversion to the new theory which is now all the rage. Even on the Dicey basis, I found it difficult enough to gain any converts for the notion that the rule of law was concerned with the minimum and not the maximum; and with general principles and not with minutiae. On the independence of judges, for example, there were many who thought that the Delhi Congress should lay down what judges ought to be paid in relation to the executive, what precedence they should have as compared with ministers and the length of the vacations!

So the Delhi Congress produced a great deal of rubbish. At the same time it did a lot of remarkably good work in the field of political propaganda. Many of the delegates came from the 'uncommitted' countries and there is no doubt that among them the Anglo-American legal system is a very good selling-point; for this purpose the maximum is more saleable than the minimum.

Delhi itself made a very enjoyable fortnight of sunshine in the middle of a dismal winter we have been having here. Before the Congress began I spent a couple of nights with Malcolm McDonald our High Commissioner there. I had not met him before; he is very agreeable and interesting man. He told me that they are all very concerned about what is going to happen when Nehru dies; there seems to be no successor in sight at all. He said that Nehru is now very aloof; he no longer has any real friends. The old Congress guard that he used to associate with have mostly died off. His only intimate friends are Lord and Lady Mountbatten, whom he writes to, – each of them, – regularly every week.

I was surprised at how friendly they all are to the British. That is true especially of the lawyers. The pleasantest thing that you can say to them is that in the courts that you would not notice the difference. The judges are all very nice, but none of them have any real distinction. They seem to have inherited all of the characteristics of the Englishmen we sent out there, who were mostly very stupid but of course quite incorruptible and with no subservience to the executive. The main trouble in that respect is that they still have a very low retiring age, – 60. The result is that since they all want something to do after they retire, and indeed have to earn some sort of a living; and they are dependent on the executive for getting jobs after retirement.

I did not meet many of the Americans there. There was one Beth Webster, from New York whom I liked very much. The Brownells were there, he seems a smooth man but she is the most predatory woman; if I were dead, I should not care to have her pick my bones.

How did you enjoy your sunshine in Antigua? It sounds more distinguished a place to go to than most of the West Indies. Though I cannot say I really know any more about it than that Sir Thomas Bertram of 'Mansfield Park' had estates there from which if you remember he returned so disastrously in the middle of 'Lovers Vows'. But when do you plan your North Italian trip? I do hope that you will take in England on the way. We have made similar attempts to yours to learn enough Italian to get about but never really persisted. Our books said the railway connection was a 'coincidenza'.

We plan to spend our long vacation firmly in this country. There is a project going on organised by a Judge Zavatt, who is a Federal District Judge in New York, and who has become very enthusiastic about our system of delegating interlocutory judicial work to Masters. He wants to introduce it into the States. The project is that a 'team' should go over to the States to expound the benefits of the system; and the original idea was that I was to lead the crusade. But quite apart from the fact that it is time that I spent a holiday at home, – and I have a feeling in my bones that 1959 ought to be a really good English summer, – I cannot think that I should enjoy a week in New York in the middle of August at a seminar organised by the Institute of Judicial Administration, followed by another week sometime later at Miami where the American Bar Association is meeting.

I was fascinated by what you wrote about restraint on power. It is an idea that I have never considered and I shall be very interested to see how you develop it. I suppose that the American Revolution was the first thing of that sort since the creation of the Roman Republic. Or did the Swiss do anything like it with their Constitution?

I had a very cheerful letter from Frankfurter J. One of the things that I particularly liked in the New York Times was the picture of you and he walking to work.

On 3 March the Governor of Nyasaland declared a state of emergency.[7] After much discussion and soul searching the cabinet decided on 17 March to hold an inquiry presided over by a judge.[8] Lord Morton, a senior judge about to retire, was approached by Alan Lennox-Boyd, the Colonial Secretary but refused, despite repeated attempts to have him change his mind.[9] Patrick was entirely oblivious to these machinations. This would soon change.

---

[7] Nyasaland State of Emergency, presented to Parliament by the Secretary of State to the Colonies, March 1959 (Cmnd 707, 1959). Nyasaland was a British Protectorate established in 1907. Between 1953 and 1963 it formed part of the Federation of Rhodesia and Nyasaland, and in 1964 became independent Malawi.

[8] Colin Baker, *State of Emergency: Crisis in Central Africa, Nyasaland, 1959–1960* (London, IB Tauris, 1997), p 79.

[9] Ibid, p 80.

Much happened on 18 March. In the morning Patrick received an unexpected phone call from the Lord Chancellor, Kilmuir. The newspapers had been reporting on the state of unrest which had reached serious proportions in Nyasaland. Kilmuir told Patrick he wanted him to chair an important public inquiry into the circumstances leading to the declaration of a state of emergency. Kilmuir was at pains to impress upon Patrick the importance of the inquiry and Cabinet's decision that it be chaired by a judge.[10] He wanted Patrick to know that in his view it was a matter of public duty that he accept it. He also told Patrick that it might involve finding to what extent federation was a cause of the disturbances. He was perfectly candid about what the Government's policy was, namely that it believed in federation but it was open to Patrick to find that the ordinary African did not accept that. Kilmuir emphasised that he hoped Patrick would not make that finding, but then if he did the Government would have to accept that outcome. In one sense the request could not have come at a worse time. Apart from other judicial business, which included a busy schedule in the Restrictive Practices Court, Patrick was about to deliver his Maccabaean Lecture that evening. He would think it over and get back to Kilmuir.[11]

Thankfully the same day brought some light relief in the form of another entertaining letter from Acheson.[12]

> I was delighted with your account of your visit to Delhi and the conceptions of the Rule of Law which you heard expounded there. The newer and expansive doctrines are, after all not so very new. It must have been over thirty years ago or even more that Justice Holmes described that philosophy as 'free women and a piano for everyone.' It has gathered some fancy trimmings in the meantime that is essentially the same sort of thing.
>
> Beth Webster I know and like. I have the lowest opinion of both the Brownells.
>
> One of my other prejudices is Indians. I know I ought to like them and indeed have liked some. But by and large they and the country give me the creeps. I remember when Owen Dixon went out as the United Nations Commissioner to try to do something about the Kashmir crisis, he came to see me after his struggles with Nehru, and said 'Dean if you ever allow that man to influence any action of yours in any respect whatsoever you want to go to an institution where they can examine your head.' I have felt that way about him and about Menon.[13] I suppose I ought to feel about them as Mr Choate said he did about the Supreme Judicial Court of Massachusetts: 'I approach this court', he said, 'as a heathen does his idol. I know that it is ugly but I feel that it is great.'
>
> Yesterday Washington was taken over by the Irish. On St Patrick's Day the President met President O'Kelly at the airport and they paraded all over a green bedecked city.

[10] Ibid, pp 80–81.

[11] Ibid, 81.

[12] Letter from Acheson to Devlin, 18 March 1959, Manuscripts and Archives, Yale University Library, Dean Acheson Papers, folder 96.

[13] VK Krishna Menon (1896–1974). Indian diplomat, nationalist and politician and ally of Jawaharlal Nehru, India's first Prime Minister.

In the evening so the newspaper tells me, green was the prevalent note of the dinner – green soup, green desert, green mints, green flowers. Only President O'Kelly disdained green. He's quoted as saying that with a name like his, green would overdo it.

Tomorrow or the next day or the day after that comes Harold MacMillan. I'm not sure that he will do us or the situation much good, because I have a suspicion that he believes or acts upon the belief that all things are negotiable – whereas some are not – and because he seems to believe that any kind of disengagement in Europe is a step toward, instead of the result of, a solution of some of the conflicts with the Soviet Union. However, since there is precious little leadership anywhere else, perhaps his is better than none. My own ideas were given to the world in an article in the Saturday Evening Post, a copy of which I am enclosing. It seems to have stimulated the President into taking exactly the opposite point of view. Perhaps in the future I would do well to make this discount for the reception of my views and myself say the opposite of what I believe.

You asked me about our vacation in Antigua. It was delightful. Archie and Ada MacLeish, friends of almost fifty years are a joy to be with. The days speed by. Everything is a delight, and it is against a background of the most gorgeous sun, water, and West Indian rum you can imagine. Occasionally we expanded our circle to be with other charming friends, usually in an afternoon game of English croquet with some slight American touches to add confusion.

Felix Frankfurter continues his recuperation and tells me that he is now practically well again. We are planning to start walking as soon as the weather becomes a bit warmer. He tells me the cold weather is supposed to put more of a strain on the heart than the more balmy variety.

I am starting an outline of my speech on restraints on power. When it gets a little further along, I shall send you a copy. Perhaps I shall also have before very long another political pamphlet for you.

The Maccabaean Lecture was an examination of the collision between the moral law and the criminal law, with the Wolfenden Report as backdrop. After all, Patrick had given evidence before it two years earlier and still held some firm views on the issue. He had confirmed the topic with his hosts on 23 February. *The Times* would send a representative and the guest list, which Patrick had a hand in, was impressive. Patrick had given oral and written evidence before the Committee, as had Goddard. Both, at least in their written testimony, did not oppose the basic recommendation of Wolfenden to decriminalise homosexual behaviour in private. However, in 1959 Patrick would take an ostensibly different stance.

On 18 March at 5pm sharp Patrick delivered his lecture. It took about an hour and was chaired by the then President of the British Academy, Sir Maurice Bowra. Apart from the applause from the attendant admirers it is highly likely that Bowra, given his sexual proclivities and mischievous sense of humour, would have found the whole affair highly amusing to say the least. However robust Bowra was in the practice of his own homosexuality, he never did, nor would he ever, openly support Wolfenden, which makes the whole evening something of an irony.

Patrick's lecture was distinctly sermonesque in tone and a touch condescending. It started unsurprisingly with a number of quotations from key sections of Wolfenden. He commended the committee for their excellent study. He said that it was 'admirable'. He said that the committee had begun its articulation of principle from a 'modern starting point'; that unlike Patrick, the committee had not set out to compose a paper on the 'jurisprudence of morality'.[14]

Patrick purported to make a disclosure (of sorts) when he said that he had an interest in the whole subject matter as a jurisprudent.[15] But he also had another interest. Patrick had given evidence to the committee. He did not disclose that at the lecture; nor did he reveal the viewpoint he gave in that evidence. He did ultimately disclose the fact in a subsequent publication.[16] In fairness, if anyone had obtained a copy of the report, they would (had they been keen to do so) have discovered his involvement on the very last page of the report which had the list of witnesses. The fact is that Patrick was not coming to the topic for the first time.

There have been numerous attempts over the years to distil the rhetorical questions posed by Patrick for himself to answer. But it is always salutary, as Patrick would have said, to return to the *fons et origo*. He asked three questions:[17]

1. Has society the right to pass judgement at all on matters of morals? Ought there, in other words, to be a public morality, or are morals always a matter of private judgement?
2. If society has a right to pass judgement, has it also the right to use the weapon of the law to enforce it?
3. If so, ought it to use that weapon in all cases or only in some; and if only some, on what principles should it distinguish?

The point of these questions was to take issue with the Wolfenden Report's underlying premise about the proper scope and functions of the criminal law.

Patrick's principal theme repeated many times in the lecture,[18] namely that the basis of the criminal law was:[19]

> that there are certain standards of behaviour or moral principles which society requires to be observed; and the breach of them is an offence not merely against the person who is injured but against society as a whole ... that the criminal law as we know it is based upon moral principle ... There is a case for a collective judgement ... If men and women try to create a society in which there is no fundamental agreement about good and evil they will fail; if having based it on common agreement, the agreement goes, the society will disintegrate. For society is not something that

---

[14] Patrick Devlin, *The Enforcement of Morals*, Maccabaean Lecture in Jurisprudence of the British Academy 1959 (Oxford, Oxford University Press, 1965), p 4.
[15] Ibid, p 6.
[16] Ibid, preface, p 1.
[17] Ibid, p 9.
[18] Ibid.
[19] Ibid, pp 8, 9, 10, 12, 14 and 16.

is kept together physically; it is held by the invisible bonds of common thought ... A common morality is part of the bondage ... it is not possible to set theoretical limits to the power of the State to legislate against immorality ... Immorality then, for the purposes of the law, is what every right-minded person is presumed to consider to be immoral.

Patrick expanded that for something to be punishable by law:[20]

there must be a real feeling of reprobation. Those who are dissatisfied with the present law on homosexuality often say that the opponents of reform are swayed simply by disgust. If that were so it would be wrong, but I do not think one can ignore disgust if it is deeply felt and not manufactured. Its presence is a good indication that the bounds of tolerance are being reached. Not everything is to be tolerated. No society can do without intolerance, indignation, and disgust; that are the forces behind the moral law ...

And finally and in particular:[21]

The fact that adultery, fornication, and lesbianism are untouched by the criminal law does not prove that homosexuality ought not to be touched. The error of jurisprudence in the Wolfenden Report is caused by the search for some single principle to explain the division between crime and sin. The Report finds it in the principle that the criminal law exists for the protection of individuals; on this principle, fornication in private between consenting adults is outside the law and thus it becomes logically indefensible to bring homosexuality between consenting adults in private within it. But the true principle is that the law exists for the protection of society. It does not discharge its function by protecting the individual from injury, annoyance, corruption and exploitation; the law must protect also the institutions and the community of ideas, political and moral, without which people cannot live together. Society cannot ignore the morality of the individual any more than it can his loyalty; it flourishes on both and without either it dies.

In conclusion Patrick thought that:[22]

the morals which underlay the law must be derived from the sense of right and wrong which resides in the community as a whole; it does not matter whence the community of thought comes, whether from one body of doctrine or another or from the knowledge of good and evil which no man is without. If the reasonable man believes that a practice is immoral and believes also – no matter whether that belief is right or wrong, so be it that it is honest and dispassionate – that no right-minded member of his society could think otherwise, then for the purpose of the law it is immoral.

In other words, the criminal law should rightly protect society as a whole, not just individuals. Encore: 'Society cannot live without morals. Its morals are those standards of conduct which the reasonable man approves'.[23]

[20] Ibid, p 17.
[21] Ibid, pp 22–23.
[22] Ibid, p 23.
[23] Ibid, p 25.

Whilst neither overtly homophobic nor even necessarily anti-reform, some interpreted what Patrick said as just that. One of many letters to the editor of *The Times* was from on 24 March from 'HA Williams, Trinity College, Cambridge', which read:[24]

> Sir – In your leading article 'Crime and Sin' on March 19 you say: 'There is a moving and welcome humility in the conceptions that society should not be asked to give its reasons for refusing to tolerate what in its heart it feels intolerable.'
>
> I am afraid we are less humble than we used to be. We once burnt old women because without giving reasons we felt in our heart that witchcraft was intolerable.

Williams was a Church of England priest and academic who later became a monk. He was a homosexual and one of the first Anglican priests to come out.

As a professional judge and not a professional philosopher, this was a bold move by Patrick. But his criticism of Wolfenden's apparent pragmatism was not without some merit. He had clearly thought about the subject matter for some time; after all, years before he, along with others, had given a statement and evidence before it. That said, Professor John Finnis rightly describes the lecture as the ruminations of an English judge of no philosophic formation.[25] Indeed, the question effectively posed by Patrick was the 'legal enforcement of positive morality' which, again, Professor Finnis describes as an 'artless' question. But what it did was to provide a conservative intellectual structure by which persons could be homophobic without overtly embracing the notion.

With the applause still ringing in his ears on 20 March, Patrick joined his close friend and confidant Rab Butler for lunch.[26] At the time Butler was Home Secretary. He and Patrick had a good deal to talk about. Apart from the Maccabaean Lecture and the Wolfenden Report, Patrick confirmed he had accepted Kilmuir's invitation to chair the inquiry into Nyasaland.

Neither he nor Patrick could have envisaged what lay ahead. 1959 would be in many respects another stressful and challenging year for Patrick. It would be his first and possibly only significant incursion into the world of politics. His lecture would in due course provoke a philosophical maelstrom.

[24] Letter to the editor from HA Williams, Trinity College, Cambridge, *The Times*, 24 March 1959.
[25] John Finnis, 'Hart as a Political Philosopher' in *Philosophy of Law, Collected Essays: Volume IV* (Oxford, Oxford University Press, 2011), p 270.
[26] State of Emergency: Crisis in Central Africa, Nyasaland, 1959–1960, p 80.

8

Darkest Africa

THE DEVLIN COMMISSION, as it came to be called, was announced by the British Government on 24 March.[1] It comprised Patrick, ET ('Bill') Williams (son of a clergyman and Warden of Rhodes House who had been Montgomery's chief of intelligence during the war), Sir Percy Wyn-Harris (a former administrative officer from Kenya and Governor of The Gambia, and Everest mountaineer of considerable distinction) and a late appointee, Sir John Ure Primrose (also the son of a clergyman, former Lord Provost, a former MI5 officer and Justice of the Peace).[2]

Nyasaland (now Malawi) became a British protectorate in 1891. From 1 August 1953, it became one of the three territories comprising the Federation of Rhodesia and Nyasaland. The others were Northern Rhodesia (now Zambia), and Southern Rhodesia (now Zimbabwe). Southern Rhodesia had long been, in practice, self-governing in internal affairs. It had a substantial white settler population which maintained power under an electoral system which excluded all but a handful of Africans from political power. In the declining years of the colonial empire, a number of schemes emerged for establishing federations of small colonies. The idea of establishing a Central African Federation with Dominion status was strongly favoured by white settlers in both the Rhodesias and Nyasaland. These schemes all failed in the end.

In 1944 an African nationalist party, the Nyasaland African Congress was formed. From about 1949, when the scheme for federation began to be discussed, the Congress consistently opposed it. The fear was that under an independent federation, the white settler population would occupy a more dominant role and would develop an apartheid system resembling that of South Africa.

As early as 1953, there were disturbances which turned violent, leading to many deaths. Notwithstanding protests, the Federation went ahead. The Congress was demoralised. For a time the situation was quiet, but the controversy developed again around 1955. Both Conservative and Labour parties saw the prospect of creating an African Dominion in which the races would work together in partnership as a good thing. But after a period of inactivity the future constitutional development of the Federation was once more back on the table.

---

[1] Colin Baker, *State of Emergency: Crisis in Central Africa, Nyasaland, 1959–1960* (London, IB Tauris, 1997), p 83.
[2] Brian Simpson, 'The Devlin Commission (1959): Colonialism, Emergencies, and the Rule of Law' (2002) 22(1) *Oxford Journal of Legal Studies* 17, p 26.

In March 1958 Dr Hastings K Banda, travelled to Nyasaland to become the head of the Congress party.[3] Born in Nyasaland but educated in the United States and Britain, Dr Banda had become an elder of the Church of Scotland. He practised medicine in Britain, where he had been very highly regarded by his patients, and also in Ghana. He had also maintained close contacts with nationalists in Nyasaland. On his return, he became the undisputed leader of the nationalist movement. The Congress remained adamantly opposed to the Federation and campaigned for an independent Nyasaland, with a democratic system based upon universal adult suffrage. The conflict which developed between the Colonial Government and the Congress was centred around the question of whether Nyasaland was capable of functioning as a democracy in the fullest sense; whether the Colonial Government was holding the country back. It was supposed that the Colonial Government was intolerant of any opposition on western and democratic lines on the basis that the Congress would be a rival authority.[4]

Alan Lennox-Boyd was at the time Colonial Secretary and had held the office for four years. His family had persuaded him to retire from politics.[5] He had been offered the job as Managing-Director of Guinness. He had intended not to contest the next election and had already told the Prime Minister, who had tried to persuade him to the contrary. He had proposed to tell members of his constituency, but events overtook the announcement. In quick succession trouble broke out in Kenya and Nyasaland making it impossible for him to leave.

Indeed, on 25 January 1959 the Congress held a meeting in which it decided to embark on a policy of non-cooperation and resistance to authority, including violent resistance.[6] The meeting was not attended by Dr Banda and was dominated by his more radical lieutenants. Thereafter widespread disturbances of one kind or another began. Some were violent and it was arguable that the Congress intimidated Africans to consolidate support. The Nyasaland Governor at the time was Sir Robert Armitage, previously Governor of Cyprus. Armitage had been involved in some turbulence already in Cyprus, in which he had been discouraged from declaring a state of emergency. He then was posted as Governor of Nyasaland in 1956.

In late February 1959, Armitage decided that if government control was to be retained, it was essential for emergency powers to be assumed. He particularly wanted to cripple the Congress by detaining Doctor Banda and his most important supporters, and holding them in custody outside the territory. He also wanted to proscribe the Congress as an illegal organisation. He relied upon information and advice from his officials, particularly provincial and

[3] Ibid, p 19.
[4] Ibid, p 20.
[5] Philip Murphy, *Alan Lennox-Boyd, A biography* (London, I.B. Tauris, 1999), pp 198–99.
[6] Brian Simpson, 'The Devlin Commission (1959): Colonialism, Emergencies, and the Rule of Law' (2002) 22(1) *Oxford Journal of Legal Studies* 17, p 20.

district commissioners, police and his 'special branch' of intelligence. The latter comprised some eight European officers and between 20 and 30 Africans who managed a certain number of undercover informers. Armitage was much influenced by reports that there existed a 'murder plot' to assassinate him and to massacre Europeans and Asians living in Nyasaland.[7]

At the time, these attitudes were affected by the fact that in Kenya the 'Mau Mau' insurgents had recently carried out massacres. It was thought not impossible that the same might happen in Nyasaland. Although the number of white settlers murdered in Kenya was small, families had been murdered with the co-operation of their servants, causing alarm and fury in the settlement community. The murder of the Ruck family – a father, pregnant mother and young child – in January 1953 caused alarm all over Africa.[8]

The state of emergency in Nyasaland was declared on 3 March 1959. The British government was under considerable pressure from those who objected to the action taken. There were suspicions that the Governor had been influenced by the desire of Sir Roy Welensky, the then Prime Minister of the Federation of Rhodesia and Nyasaland, to suppress opposition to the Federation. The British Government therefore published its justification for the declaration of an emergency in the form of a dispatch from the Governor, explaining why he had decided to take drastic action.[9]

The Governor's dispatch purported to be a factual account of events. However it described Dr Banda as a powerful, messianic figure to the Africans who opposed the Federation. The Governor went on to insist that every effort had been taken to have Dr Banda influence change by peaceful and constitutional means. But Banda had indicated he was not prepared to make any compromises. Although Banda indicated in public that he was prepared to pursue his ends by constitutional means, his choice of political colleagues, namely the younger, more volatile and extreme persons, indicated that his statements were utterly hypocritical. Dr Banda, the government asserted openly, threatened police and his African political opponents. He was openly against white settlers and Asians alike.[10]

In his narrative the Governor disclosed that he had received information that at a meeting of the Congress on 25 January, which Dr Banda did not attend but which it was believed he had orchestrated, agreement had been reached amongst delegates present that there would be a general strike, including civil servants and others in the event that certain demands were not met. Until such time as the announcement of impending constitutional changes was made, there would be unlawful public meetings and processions, and if Dr Banda was arrested four persons were nominated to run the Congress in his absence. Violence would

---

[7] Ibid, p 22.

[8] Ibid, pp 22–23.

[9] Declaration of the State of Emergency (Cmnd 707, 1959) pp 8–9.

[10] Brian Simpson, 'The Devlin Commission (1959): Colonialism, Emergencies, and the Rule of Law' (2002) 22(1) *Oxford Journal of Legal Studies* 17, p 26.

begin on the day designated by the letter 'R'. 'R' day would probably be from 10 to 21 days after Banda's arrest. The planned violence would include sabotage of telephone wires, roads, rail, bridges, airfields and other installations. It also included murder of District and Provincial Commissioners, District Police Officers and other Europeans, including missionaries. In the townships, Europeans and Asians were to be killed, including women and children. The Governor and other senior British officers would be assassinated.

The Governor continued by describing violent events which had occurred in February, including stones being thrown at cars, police stations and other government offices. At one point during a riot, security forces had had to open fire and two rioters were killed. Other deaths had occurred later on February. The Governor portrayed himself as having his hands tied. He concluded by stating 'No Governor wishes to be placed in a position of having to declare a state of emergency. But the events I have described speak for themselves.'[11]

Within two days of the declaration of the state of emergency, the British Cabinet, notwithstanding Sir Roy Welensky's bitter opposition, determined to hold an inquiry.

Although Patrick had not been not Cabinet's first choice, he was well known to Rab Butler and Kilmuir, but not to Lennox-Boyd. Lord Perth, the Minister of State for Colonial Affairs, also knew Patrick very well from Cambridge days. All reassured Lennox-Boyd that Patrick was a safe pair of hands and a Conservative whose views, so recently expressed in his Maccabaean Lecture, vouched for a satisfactory outcome.[12] Prime Minister Macmillan was at the time out of the country on a trip to Russia and played no role in Patrick's selection. In any event, he did not know Patrick either. Everyone, it may be said, expected a finding supportive of the Colonial Government, and the Governor's decisions and conduct in particular. In his conversation with Patrick on 18 March, Kilmuir had led him to think it was entirely up to him to decide what in the end he might think was an appropriate outcome.[13] That was far from the real position and was more an indication of Kilmuir's integrity. This was a high-profile appointment for Patrick. It continued his celebrity status. It was, however, a rather perilous activity for a sitting judge, although he would have had to pass it by the Lord Chief Justice, who must have agreed.

The situation was extremely volatile. It was made more dangerous by reason of the fact that troops had been brought in from Southern Rhodesia. They carried out two distinct operations. The first one, known as 'Operation Sunrise', involved the arrest and detention of Dr Banda and the hard-core members of the Congress. Many hundreds of others were detained. Secondly, soldiers rather

---

[11] Declaration of the State of Emergency (Cmnd 707, 1959) pp 23–24.

[12] Brian Simpson, 'The Devlin Commission (1959): Colonialism, Emergencies and the Rule of Law' (2002) 22(1) *Oxford Journal of Legal Studies* 17, p 26.

[13] Colin Baker, *State of Emergency: Crisis in Central Africa, Nyasaland, 1959–1960* (London, IB Tauris, 1997, p 81.

than police were sent to certain areas to fine and arrest suspected members of Congress. As a result of these manoeuvres, many Africans (including women) were killed and or wounded. There were no European deaths, though some people were injured.[14] The Labour opposition harshly criticised the Macmillan Government, suggesting that the so-called murder plot was a fiction and the invention of Sir Roy Welensky for obvious political gain.[15]

At a Cabinet meeting on 11 March, the Colonial Secretary, Lennox-Boyd, vigorously supported the Governor.[16]

By 19 March, the Prime Minister was touring Canada and the USA. Butler, as acting Prime Minister, announced that the inquiry would be of a limited factual type.[17] It did however, have the usual powers to compel witnesses, it allowed counsel to appear, and would hold its proceedings in public. The inquiry was not to adjudicate on any charges of misconduct against any individual.[18] The appointment of such a judicial commission was regarded as a most unusual step. The terms of reference were quite narrow, namely to inquire into the recent disturbances in Nyasaland and the events leading up to them and to report thereon. It was intended that the Commission would only report on the facts. It was never intended that there be any recommendations as to what, if any, policy conclusions should be drawn from them.[19]

In 1959 Patrick had been a judge for 11 years and had tried some important cases in diverse areas of law. He had acquired a reputation of an intellectual judge who had abilities and interests far beyond the courtroom. He was utterly committed to his judicial oath and the thought he would play party politics, for anyone who knew him well, was frankly farcical. Unbeknown to many perhaps, he had a brother who was a missionary in Africa who regularly sent home warm and entirely sympathetic portraits of Africa and Africans.

In addition, Cabinet did not seriously contemplate a report which might be pro-African or anti-settler. Nor did it take into account the potency of the Church of Scotland in Africa through its missions, or Banda's very close connections with it. Armitage was told of Devlin's appointment on 24 March and must have also been given the necessary reassurances. The Commons was informed on the same day.[20] The government must have been very confident of the outcome, as the chosen quartet with Patrick at the helm was so obviously

---

[14] Ibid, pp 40–49.

[15] Philip Murphy (ed), *Central Africa, Part 1: Closer Association 1945–1958*. Series B Vol 9 of *British Documents of the End of Empire*, SR Ashton (ed), Institute of Commonwealth Studies (London, TSO, 2005), pp 23–24.

[16] Baker, p 57.

[17] Brian Simpson, 'The Devlin Commission (1959): Colonialism, Emergencies and the Rule of Law' (2002) 22(1) *Oxford Journal of Legal Studies* 17, p 54.

[18] Colin Baker, *State of Emergency: Crisis in Central Africa, Nyasaland, 1959–1960* (London, IB Tauris, 1997), pp 84, 87.

[19] Ibid, p 87.

[20] Ibid, pp 83–84.

impartial, authoritative and rich in experience and competence. Indeed, with Patrick's powerful personality, the team was formidable.

News of the inquiry and its members quickly spread. Frankfurter wrote to Patrick on 25 March with uncanny prescience:[21]

> It is I trust not impertinent for one who has over the years followed more or less closely African affairs, to find comfort in your appointment as Chairman of the Nyasaland Inquiry and to wish you well in this onerous task. While I note the apparently limited terms of reference, yet knowing your qualities, if I may say so I am justified in believing that your report may have a benign and fruitful influence in the evolutionary solution of the complicated and thorny problems of the multiracial society of Africa into which you are projected.

Nomenclature aside, the British government's clear view was that this was not a judicial commission. Patrick, if he was ever told as much by anyone in government, saw it otherwise. Much discussion took place between Patrick and Lennox-Boyd on 2 April about the terms of reference.[22] The Government had already planned for a much wider inquiry for 1960 into wider constitutional issues, which was another reason why it wanted to constrict the scope of Patrick's. There is little doubt that under cross-examination by Patrick, however, Lennox-Boyd did not seek to lay down any hard and fast rules.

Patrick was anxious to get started. He made it clear he wanted to examine all documentary materials and files referred to in Armitage's dispatch. Much discussion took place as to the procedures to be adopted in taking the evidence from the various categories of witnesses.[23] This was regarded as very important because some of Armitage's sources of information were members of his 'special branch'. Their identities and other operational details were closely guarded. And precisely who would and would not be given access to information, what, if any, transcript would be taken, and how and in what way witnesses would be protected, were all the subject of intense discussion. Patrick also asked to interview Sir Roy Welensky. That request sent shivers down the spines of most in Whitehall. The government wanted an inquiry of narrow focus. To interview Welensky would open it up to other issues.

Around 8 or 9 April Patrick set off to Salisbury, then capital of Southern Rhodesia, *en route* ostensibly to Zomba, the capital of Nyasaland. The trip unexpectedly became a family reunion. Patrick's brother Christopher was in Salisbury to meet Patrick. The then Governor of Southern Rhodesia, Sir Peveril William-Powlett, was married to Patrick's and Christopher's cousin Helen, also

---

[21] Letter from Frankfurter to Devlin, 25 March 1959, Howard Gotlieb Archival Research Center Collection, Boston University.

[22] Brian Simpson, 'The Devlin Commission (1959): Colonialism, Emergencies, and the Rule of Law' (2002) 22(1) *Oxford Journal of Legal Studies* 17, p 27.

[23] Colin Baker, *State of Emergency: Crisis in Central Africa, Nyasaland, 1959–1960* (London, IB Tauris, 1997), pp 88–89.

known as Kitten. She was the daughter of their mother's eldest brother, James. Late in the evening when Patrick finally arrived in Salisbury, he and Christopher met in Patrick's hotel. As Christopher remembered it:[24] '10.30 pm … Long conversation while he was in the bath, then wonderful dinner at "Meikles" (the Salisbury Hotel, – really very good.)' They met again a few days later on 13 April, when Christopher wrote:[25]

> We met again for breakfast on Saturday morning and then parted at 10 at which time a car was due to take them to the airport. I should say P., though very tired was extremely cheerful; he finds his fellow commissioners extremely pleasant and seems quite on top of the job. It struck me with increased force after 3 years – what an extremely Good man he is!

Upon arrival in Zomba, Armitage invited the Commissioners to dine with him at Government House. Not only was this invitation firmly declined on Patrick's advice, but any similar invitation would likewise be treated firmly in the negative – as sensitively as they could be in the circumstances. The same approach was adopted with accommodation and dinner invitations. This had the effect of putting a number of European noses out of joint, but had the unsurprisingly opposite effect on the African population. Patrick had even refused to socialise with the local judiciary.[26] Some were deeply offended. The rest of the team, despite some of them having close historical links with some particular white locals, also observed Patrick's embargo.

The official starting date for the commission was 11 April. The first witness was a Captain Caine, an army officer who had been present during an incident in February when an African had been shot.[27] As would be the approach thereafter, Patrick asked nearly all the questions. His cross-examination skills had not been lost. Indeed, they seemed to be reinvigorated. Later Caine and other army officers said they felt that Patrick's main purpose was to discredit the Nyasaland Government and Armitage in particular.[28] They said the tone of his questions suggested that he and the other Commissioners were unsympathetic to the Government and out of touch with the conditions prevailing at the time. The inquiry had no counsel assisting and so it is entirely unsurprising that Patrick would conduct most of the questioning. But that reality did not stop many, including Armitage, from thinking that Patrick was playing the role of cross-examiner, as well as judge and jury. Indeed, it has been said of Patrick that his questioning gave the impression of 'belligerence, of hectoring, of trying to

---

[24] Madeleine Devlin, *Christopher Devlin, a Biography* (Basingstoke/New York, Macmillan, 1970), p 186.
[25] Ibid, p 186.
[26] Colin Baker, *State of Emergency: Crisis in Central Africa, Nyasaland, 1959–1960* (London, IB Tauris, 1997), pp 101–3.
[27] Ibid, p 111.
[28] Ibid, pp 111–12.

trap the witness, of putting words into their mouth, of tying them up in verbal knots'.[29]

Armitage gave evidence on 15 April.[30] The questions centred around his dealings with Welensky and bringing in reinforcements. Patrick formed the view early on that Armitage had acted quite independently in declaring and conducting the emergency. Armitage tried to argue that the Federation had been beneficial to Africans, that bringing troops in was necessary, that there was a murder plot which had to be taken seriously; that the Church of Scotland's role should be examined and more importantly that the inquiry should be directed to whether the Congress had intimidated people into following it. Lastly, Armitage was quite contemptuous of the evidence the Church of Scotland had provided.

On 25 and 26 April Patrick escaped briefly to Salisbury to spend some more time with Christopher. It was during this short visit that Patrick and Welensky met at the Governor's residence.[31]

While the team worked cohesively, Patrick and Bill Williams in particular became quite close and they tended to spend more time together, as opposed to with Primrose or Wyn-Harris. But each respected and deferred to Patrick, especially on the conduct of the Commission and any procedural matters.

In all, Patrick and his team spent five weeks in the protectorate. They travelled extensively and received evidence in all provinces. They also sat for a week in the High Court in Bulawayo, Southern Rhodesia and ultimately four days in the High Court in London. In total they received evidence from 455 individual witnesses and about 1300 witnesses in groups. They also received 585 memoranda, including a petition bearing 1800 signatures collected by missionaries from a wide area. The workload was extraordinary. Patrick had ambitiously intended to hear evidence from an even larger number, but in the end his goal became impracticable. For example, Banda appeared before the inquiry on Saturday, 16 May. About 500 Africans assembled outside the building where the hearings were conducted to hear his testimony. Happily, there were no incidents. In Banda's lengthy evidence he emphatically denied any knowledge, let alone participation, in a murder plot.[32] Devlin was accused of going lightly on Banda by adopting a very different tone and attitude in questioning.[33] Others from the Congress were treated less deferentially by Patrick.

While the Commissioners were in Bulawayo, the General Assembly of the Church of Scotland debated the Nyasaland Emergency. The Church was then at the height of its influence and had its largest active membership in the twentieth century. A measure of how seriously the British Government took the

[29] Ibid, p 125.
[30] Ibid, p 111.
[31] Madeleine Devlin, *Christopher Devlin, a Biography* (Basingstoke, Macmillan, 1970), p 187.
[32] Colin Baker, *State of Emergency: Crisis in Central Africa, Nyasaland, 1959–1960* (London, IB Tauris, 1997), pp 121–25.
[33] Ibid, pp 119–22.

debate was the presence of three British Cabinet Ministers, Rab Butler, Alec Douglas-Home and Lord Perth, in the Visitors' Gallery throughout the debate. Butler and his colleagues were bitterly disappointed but hardly surprised when the Assembly, having discussed the Devlin Commission, voted overwhelmingly to receive reports from the Assembly's Central Committee from Central Africa. These reports included a four-page statement made by the Blantyre Synod, which was highly critical of the situation in Nyasaland.[34] Banda's connection with the Church of Scotland could not have gone unnoticed by the three. He was after all, the only African member of the Church of Scotland in Nyasaland. The Assembly decided to make recommendations to government which were effectively anti-Federation and opposed to it getting Dominion status.

With the last days of the inquiry sitting in London the formalities concluded on 26 June. The report which would later emerge was largely drafted by Patrick himself. He worked from 9am continuously to midnight each day on the task. He produced most of the text in about a week or a little longer. Some of the material included contributions by his colleagues, but very little. The Commission met on 7 July to consider and approve the report. Page proofs were available on 13 July. After some final changes, the report was signed on 15 July and delivered to the Colonial Secretary on 16 July.[35]

The report was published on 23 July. In summary, the Commission took the view that the Governor, being responsible for law and order, had no alternative but to take emergency action on 3 March and had done so on his own initiative and not under pressure from Sir Roy Welensky. It found that Dr Banda had not attended the meeting on 25 January at which the Congress had adopted a policy of defiance of the government. But, his inaction and failure to condemn the use of violence had enabled the Congress to remain defiant. In effect, it rejected the idea that there had been a 'murder plot', but did not think that belief in it was critical in the decision to declare an emergency. It described the arrests in 'Operation Sunrise' and found that in some cases excessive force had been used. It was also critical of the way in which the actions to restore authority had been implemented, finding there had been extensive beatings, bullying, burnings and confiscation of property, not only directed at supposed offenders, but against the population in disaffected areas generally. Much of this had been either authorised or condoned by the Nyasaland Government.[36]

Although thinly disguised, the criticisms of the Government were unmistakable. Patrick had couched his language as if he was directing a jury and Lennox-Boyd was foreman.[37] It was blunt about the use of aggression as being

[34] Andrew C Ross, *Colonialism to Cabinet Crisis, a Political History of Malawi* (Zomba, Kachere Books, 2009), pp 187–88.
[35] Brian Simpson, 'The Devlin Commission (1959): Colonialism, Emergencies and the Rule of Law' (2002) 22(1) *Oxford Journal of Legal Studies* 17, pp 29–30.
[36] Ibid, pp 31–32.
[37] Ibid, p 30.

disproportionate. It also purported to raise for consideration the wisdom of much of the decision-making. Patrick's choice of language and style in adopting the technique of directing a jury was, by implication, strongly critical of the conduct of the Colonial Government. Such a direction is exemplified by the following extract:[38]

> The Government has not at any time either before us or so far as we are aware to anyone else expressed any regret for or disapproval of what has been done ... We record this as a fact and not as indicating that any expression of regret or disapproval is necessarily appropriate; that is a matter for you ...

The report posed the embarrassing question of whether it was proper to react to problems of law and order in colonies in ways which would be considered quite out of the question at home. There had never before been a report like this one, and it was chaired by a British judge. Even the bare but excruciatingly detailed recital of the facts raised so many questions. What the report did was to spell out in meticulous detail precisely what benevolent despotism meant in Nyasaland, once nationalism was thought to be likely to lead to insurrection.

Patrick wanted to make two points. The first was an obvious one – that Nyasaland, like other colonies, was in the middle of an insurrection over the pace of decolonisation. The second point was the lack of respect as he saw it, on the part of the Colonial Government and officials, for the rule of law. Patrick clearly intended a sting in the tail. The somewhat brief summary of the writing and delivery of the final report obscures the drama behind the scenes.

There is little doubt that the Government expected criticism from the Commission. Patrick had drafted a number of paragraphs which never made it into the final report. Some were deleted after discussion between the members of the Commission. Others, however, were deleted as a result of discussions with Lord Perth.[39] There is no direct evidence that Lord Perth tried to influence Patrick's drafting. For example, the pair met on 23 June to discuss the timing of the delivery of the report and a note prepared by Perth about that meeting expressly recorded that he did not ask Patrick (at least then) what the report might contain.

However, by then Patrick had drafted that 'we have also said that we found indifference to the law at every level.'[40] Further, in a somewhat pointed barb:[41]

> We have recorded all these deviations from standards that we think would be universally accepted as applicable in Britain. But as we have said it is for you and not for us to determine whether they are equally applicable to Colonial Government.

Both of these comments were deleted from the final version. Simpson surmises, perhaps accurately, as a result of Perth's intervention.[42]

---

[38] Ibid, p 30.
[39] Ibid, p 34.
[40] Ibid, pp 35–36.
[41] Ibid, pp 35–36.
[42] Ibid, p 36.

On 7 July a letter from Frankfurter provided timely light relief for Patrick:[43]

I see by the papers that you have finished your coroner's inquest in Nyasaland and you are now hibernating to produce your report. (We have such an oppressive heat at the moment that I suppose it is the compelling law of contract that makes me talk of hibernating.) Not only will you soon be through with this highly important but diversionary job of yours, but I gather from what John Megaw writes me that you will soon have worked yourself out of your job on the Restrictive Practices Court by reason of your bold and lucid judgments. I note with interest but not with surprise, in following your Law Reports that Megaw has won to himself a leading place at your Bar. When he came to the Harvard Law School for a year, our now friendly relations had an inauspicious opening. He had some notes of introduction to me and in the first few minutes of our first encounter I had occasion to say something about 'you Englishmen.' Megaw drew himself up to his overpowering height and said in a stentorian voice, 'I am NOT an Englishman. I am an Ulsterman.' The reprimand was so severe that ever since then I had tried to be careful and speak of the various people who come from the British Isles as 'you Britishers'. I have noticed that even as President of the Restrictive Practices Court you're sat in various matters before the High Court.

Our Court has risen after disposing of 2,062 matters which every member of the Court has passed. I need not tell you that the overwhelming bulk of this business here was what Holmes used to call 'the damn certioraris'. There were only 143 argued cases. There were the usual number of cases entangled in emotional public interest but there were a few cases of interest only to us lawyers. I wish I could think that even these were free from considerations not strictly legal, such as a desire to have a jury at all costs for plaintiffs in personal injury cases though they may be seamen's injuries enforceable in admiralty. And there was one case the outcome of which will shock you, or I miss my guess, when you come to read the opinions which go to you under separate cover. It concerns a disciplinary action for a lawyer's harangue at a public meeting concerning a pending criminal trial while *he* – or rather she – was actively engaged in the defense.

You may be also interested in half-dozen opinions touching the film Lady Chatterley's Lover.

You must have encountered Learned Hand[44] either here or in England. I am vain enough to enclose a few lighthearted remarks I made about him on the occasion of celebrating his service as a federal judge for half a century. The old boy now 87 is still going strong at least with his head. He complains that his legs aren't as good as they used to be. Outrageous nature!

I irritate you, I am afraid by asking you what progress your Wilson is making. He is for me such a tantalising character that I am intensely curious to see how he will appear when seen through your lens.

---

[43] Letter, Frankfurter to Devlin, 7 July 1959, Howard Gotlieb Archival Research Center Collection, Boston University.
[44] Billings Learned Hand (1872–1961). United States Judge and legal philosopher.

Patrick had been contemplating just who, if anyone, should see the report prior to publication or even completion. He correctly came to the view that both the Colonial Office and the Governor should see the draft report before it was signed. This would normally be done. Patrick's instincts on this were impeccable. He was chairing an inquiry where people who had given evidence had been in some cases examined and cross-examined. The inquiry would publish its findings. It could hardly be suggested that it would not libel a number of people who were criticised, especially the Governor who, after all, had declared the emergency and would, on any view, be seen as the person ordering or acquiescing in the conduct which was to be the subject of the scrutiny. Indeed many years later in 1984 the Privy Council determined that a judge in New Zealand acting as a Royal Commissioner had breached the rules of natural justice by not giving certain persons an opportunity to address possible adverse findings in advance of his report being finalised.[45] Patrick made the galley and page proofs available on 10 July. There were meant to be only two copies made for the persons concerned, but the Colonial Office distributed others, including to Sir Roy Welensky. Welensky is reported as having said that the Devlin Report was one of the most controversial State Papers of modern times.[46]

On 13 July the Cabinet Secretary, Sir Norman Brook, prepared a precis and comments for the Prime Minister. He was able to reassure Macmillan that some of the extreme wording in the earlier drafts had been removed. The report, Brook told Macmillan, vindicated the decision to declare a state of emergency but dismissed any notion of a murder plot and made some harsh criticisms of the measures taken.[47] Macmillan convened a meeting at 10 am on 14 July with the Commonwealth and Colonial Secretaries, the Chief Whip, Sir Norman Brook and Lord Perth. It was decided that a report on troubles in Kenya would be simultaneously released with the Devlin Commission's report and that Armitage would be summoned to London so he could prepare a 'robust' reply, also to be issued at the same time. Even expurgated, the terms of the report would, Macmillan thought, cause both the Governor and the Colonial Secretary to resign. Arrangements were made to have the Governor arrive in London on Saturday 18 July, go straight to Chequers and start working on the reply. He would be assisted by Denys Roberts, then Solicitor-General of Nyasaland (who had appeared before Patrick for the Government in some of the hearings in Nyasaland) and the Attorney-General, Manningham-Buller.[48]

---

[45] *Mahon v Air New Zealand* [1984] AC 808.

[46] Robert Stevens, *The Independence of the Judiciary, A View from the Lord Chancellor's Office* (Oxford, Clarendon Press, 1993), p 170.

[47] Colin Baker, *State of Emergency: Crisis in Central Africa, Nyasaland, 1959–1960* (London, IB Tauris, 1997), pp 182–83.

[48] Denys Roberts, *I'll do better next time*, Barry Rose Publishers, 1995, pp 237–39.

Macmillan was furious with Patrick, as was Armitage. Macmillan's reaction was petulant and tasteless. Macmillan recorded in his diary on 13 July:[49]

> Why Devlin? The poor Lord Chancellor – the sweetest and most naive of men – chose him: He was able, a Conservative; runner up or nearly so for Lord Chief Justice. I have since discovered that he is (a) *Irish* – no doubt with the Fenian blood that makes Irishmen anti-Government on principle, (b) a *lapsed* Roman Catholic. His brother is a Jesuit priest; his sister is a nun. He married a Jewess, who was converted and was *received* a Catholic: c) a hunchback; d) *bitterly* disappointed at not being made Lord Chief Justice. I am not at all surprised that this report is dynamite. It may well blow the Government out of office.

Even in a private diary this was childish and pathetic. Macmillan knew he would be facing an election in 1959 and was no doubt angry and frustrated with a report that did not provide him with the endorsement he wanted. At this stage, he undoubtedly regarded the report as an obstacle to his re-election.

On 17 July Patrick responded to Frankfurter:[50]

> I owe you more than a letter and a debt of thanks for all your good wishes in my latest enterprise. We finished our work yesterday and delivered our report duly signed and sealed. I expect it will be printed by next week and I shall send you a copy of it, if I may. It has been a tremendously rushed job and we have no time to dot the i's and cross the t's or even to take a second look at the whole. So I am afraid it will read rather badly. I always like to put a thing like that away for a week or so, and think about something else, and then look at it again. But everyone seems anxious to have a debate on Nyasaland before the House rises; and to get the disturbances out of the way before they start thinking about larger issues. It is a long time since I have done so much work in a short period – certainly I have never had to do it in my judicial days. It took me back to the days at the Bar which I thought I had left far behind, and it was quite satisfactory to find that I could do some hard work if really needed. It was not at all what could be described a judicial enquiry. We never could sit down to any one incident and get all the facts relating to it presented to us at one time. We just picked them up as we went along. And of course instead of sitting back and allowing counsel to present the fruits of their labours, we had to do all the digging ourselves, or most of it. I am not sure it will turn out to be a useful form of enquiry. I think we need something that is equivalent to a Congressional enquiry, though perhaps done in a more restrained way. But if Parliament is to keep some sort of control over the goings on of the executive in Colonial territories, it must be informed somehow about the facts. In Britain control can be kept to some extent by parliamentary questions. But in a Colony there is no sort of parliament and the Governor does as he likes; the British Parliament is presumably expected to do what would be done by an effective local parliament, but it cannot do that unless it has the facts.

---

[49] Brian Simpson, 'The Devlin Commission 1959 – Colonialism, Emergencies and the Rule of Law' (2002) 22(1) *Oxford Journal of Legal Studies* 17, p 46. Simpson provides multiple references for the diary note, which differ in some instances. The version quoted here is the one most commonly quoted.

[50] Letter from Devlin to Frankfurter, 17 July 1959, Howard Gotlieb Archival Research Center Collection, Boston University.

So what we have tried to do is to present the facts as objectively as possible. I never know how objective it is possible to be; but if it is not objective, at least it reflects a common viewpoint by four very different people. I think it is quite clear that it will not be liked by the Government. But I hope that the natural dislike of the executive for having its affairs pried into will not take effect so strongly as to eliminate this sort of enquiry in the future. I am sure that we need every weapon we can lay our hands on to keep the executive everywhere under watch and control.

Well, that job being over I am off to the country to begin a long vacation a fortnight earlier than usual as some reward for my pains. I would have stayed if there was anything to do in the Restrictive Practices Court, but there is not. It has become quite clear that the Court is top-heavy. We have done only 4 cases this year and something like 5 or 6 times that amount have been disposed of by consent orders. If all those cases had been fought, the balance between the staff of the Board of Trade that is getting the stuff up and the personnel of the Court would I dare say have been about right. But the enormous incurable English habit of settled cases at the last moment, and after all the work has been done on them, has defeated all calculations. Before I went away they were trying to work out some new scheme. I have not had much time to talk about it since I got back, but I think that they have abandoned any new approach. The result is that we shall continue to wade through the list of agreements that were made before the Act came into force and were registered under it, at the rate, I suppose, of 30 or 40 a year with about 10 or 20 per cent being actually fought. So I plan to go back to my ordinary work for a bit and see what happens. If they really mean business, they will have to strengthen immensely the Government department so that it can not only get through the existing agreements much more quickly; but can set about following American precedents and seeing how many unwritten understandings there are operating beneath the surface.

Patrick would have been oblivious to the fact that over the weekend (17 July being a Friday) a team was working on a response from Armitage and a robust attack on Patrick. The attack would necessarily involve a good deal of hand wringing and a generous tablespoon of hypocrisy. The exercise was to cherry-pick what the Government liked about the conclusions of the Commission and to somehow reject others, including to justify why parts could not be accepted. Those activities were stage managed and ultimately executed by the Attorney-General.[51]

It is a little hard to imagine that this was an occasion for any humour, but with the passage of years it has been portrayed with some mischievous fun by Sir Denys Roberts in his memoir *I'll do better next time*. First, Roberts was Crown Counsel for the Nyasaland Government in 1959. He not only appeared before Patrick by calling witnesses, but he also made final submissions before the Commission in London on behalf of the Colonial Government. His humorous account of the state of emergency and his appearances before Patrick are illuminating. He records Patrick rather pointedly asking:[52] 'If there were any excesses

[51] Colin Baker, *State of Emergency: Crisis in Central Africa, Nyasaland, 1959–1960* (London, IB Tauris, 1997), pp 154–55.
[52] Denys Roberts, *I'll do better next time* (Southampton, Barry Rose Law Publishers, 1995), p 242.

for which the Governor was responsible, would it be right for him to say he was sorry for them?' Roberts says he responded:[53]

> Certainly it would my Lord. But nobody asked him about that. It was entirely my fault that this was omitted. I am sure that he would want me to say how sorry he was if anything of the kind took place, which of course he does not admit.

This was hardly conciliatory however.

He then gives what appears to be a first-hand account of a meeting with the Attorney-General at Chequers. He describes the scene when he first met the Attorney-General sitting in an armchair beside a small table on which there was a large plate of sandwiches. Roberts says the Attorney-General garbled his introduction as his mouth was full of food. Roberts asserts the following exchange:[54]

> *The Attorney-General*: I've been reading Devlin's report – would you pass me some cakes (taking four) – I never liked the fellow.
>
> *Roberts*: Oh really, sir,? Why is that?
>
> *The Attorney-General*: I warned Macmillan. I told him not to appoint Devlin. I said there would be trouble. Devlin's a closet Socialist, you know. Owns two houses and drives a Bentley.
>
> *Roberts*: I thought he was a good Judge?
>
> *The Attorney-General*: Certainly not. They will have to put him in the House of Lords to get him out of the way. I prosecuted a case in front of him once ... Thanks entirely to Patrick Devlin who told the jury that my evidence was inadequate and that they should acquit.

When Roberts wrote this colourful account, he was purporting to recall events that occurred almost 40 years earlier without, it seems, contemporaneous notes. If the Attorney-General did say he had warned Macmillan, that was false because Macmillan does not seem to have played any role in appointing Patrick. That was the whole point of Macmillan's derisory remarks about Kilmuir in his diary. When Roberts wrote his account, all the relevant players, including Patrick, were dead. A degree of artistic licence together with a serious bout of relevance deprivation may have set in for Roberts. There is little doubt, however, that neither Patrick nor Manningham-Buller thought the very best of each other.

The Devlin Report, as it quickly came to be known, was discussed in the Cabinet on 20 July. By then the heavy-handed response of the Attorney-General and Armitage was also available for discussion. It was decided the Government's riposte need to be shortened and was not to appear too hostile, as this might weaken the report's general exoneration of the Colonial Government over the declaration of an emergency. At the same time the release of the report on Kenya and the 'Mau Mau' uprising was meant to dilute some of the report's criticisms. Macmillan stage-managed the Cabinet meeting by asking if each member continued to support the Colonial Secretary. Unsurprisingly, all present did.

[53] Ibid, p 242.
[54] Ibid, pp 247–48.

On 21 July Patrick wrote to Acheson:[55]

I like 'Prelude to Independence' very much. You have performed a process which I always enjoy especially when it is done as skilfully as you do it – the induction from the problems of the past of their true solving principle followed by its application to the problem of the present. The thing that I had not properly realised was the extent to which the colonials went in asserting their rights as Englishmen. There is something of a parallel to that in Nyasaland in which Sir Roy Welensky is cast in the role of George III. There is no anti-British feeling, as we say in our report. One forcible critic wound up a denunciation of the Governor by saying that he was a disgrace to the British Empire. The Governor and his servants have no conception at all of restraint upon power. They look upon the law as something that the natives have to keep. They are good conscientious men who have never learnt any constitutional history. When I asked the Governor about some of his obligations he said he knew nothing about the law but was satisfied that what he had done was administratively correct – Droit Administratif! It would have been better, I thought, if instead of saying in his public pronouncements that he was determined to stamp out lawlessness, he had proclaimed a Crusade of Administrative Correctitude. A lot of things make us all very angry and we constantly restrain our own power of saying disagreeable things against people who could not effectively answer back. The work is over and due to be published this week. That is why I am vegetating in the country and why you are having to struggle with my handwriting. But I did not like to delay too long an answer to your letter lest you might be piling up engagements for October and we might miss a chance of seeing you. On 5 October I start out on Circuit; but fortunately my first county is Wiltshire. So I should be here the next weekend. Can you spare us all or any of that – this time, – I hope you bring your wife to stay. What a fascinating 'IF' about you and the Solicitor-General. It is quite in the classic line of IF Napoleon had won the Battle of Waterloo. 'If Acheson had become Solicitor-General' will be a prize winning essay in the history school half a century hence. All I can hope for is a much more limited circulation for 'If Devlin J had not delivered his judgment in Bloggs v Blinks'.

As expected, the publication of the Devlin Report on 21 July immediately attracted a good deal of media coverage. As part of the camouflage, the Government also formally announced the Monckton Commission to inquire into the Federation. The Government published its riposte on 23 July. The Government claimed in its missive that, in so far as Patrick and his team had reached conclusions adverse to the Colonial Government, they had got it all wrong. This was presented as coming from Governor Armitage and not from either the Prime Minister or Colonial Secretary. Although Armitage was fuming and no doubt agreed with what was said, Macmillan and Lennox-Boyd appear to have been responsible.

The Times carried an article on 24 July which reported the Commission's findings but especially gave prominence to its rejection of the alleged 'murder plot' and the characterisation of Nyasaland as a police state. It did report

[55] Letter from Devlin to Acheson, 21 July 1959, Manuscripts and Archives, Yale University Library, Dean Acheson Papers, folder 96. The letter to which Patrick is responding to no longer exists.

Armitage's denial of the idea of a police state.[56] The article was repeated the same day in the *The New York Times*. At around the same time, Lord Beaverbrook's *Sunday Express* called for the removal of Lennox-Boyd from his position, because it might not only damage future African policy, but harm the Conservatives in the forthcoming general election.[57] Coming from Beaverbook, a devout Conservative, this had particular potency. Although he did not like Macmillan and would have preferred Butler as Prime Minister, he wanted to be careful not to make life too easy for Labour.

The New York Times ran an article on Patrick on the next day containing what even Patrick might have regarded as far too much saccharin. Adjacent to the article was a recent photograph of Patrick with the caption: 'He is capable of tempering justice with mercy.'[58]

> On his quest for truth in the Dark Continent Sir Patrick Arthur Devlin was armed with the skills acquired in a lifetime of tracking that elusive quarry, justice, through the bramble bush of common law. He worked with the assurance of a Masai hunter tracking a wounded elephant ... Not the slightest doubt was raised as to the fairness of the tall, stooped jurist investigating the controversial charges of a 'massacre plot'. Justice Devlin is the most widely respected judge in England.

After a reminder of the Adams case cause célèbre, the article continued:

> Sir Patrick speaks quietly and courteously in court and never makes a witticism. Yet he is a truly magisterial figure. His large grave features seem made for the frame of the judicial wig. His interventions to question a witness and his summations are delivered with grace and clarity that bespeak a power of understanding untainted by sentimentality or harshness.

So far as the American press was concerned, the Nyasaland Commission was yet another affirmation of Patrick's celebrity status. Not so with Macmillan and his Attorney-General.

Having read the Government's riposte and correctly anticipated what would happen when the report was debated in Parliament, the press in England (at least that which counted), was clearly on Patrick's side. An editorial in *The Times* on 27 July in describing the 'tribunal' as 'formidably manned' warned the Government that it would be unsafe in the extreme to attack Patrick, having set up the Commission in the first place and selected the panel.[59]

On the same day Patrick wrote to Bill Williams:[60]

---

[56] Walter H Waggoner, 'Nyasaland "Plot" Denied by Inquiry: British White Paper Rejects Basis of Arrest of Leaders of Nationalist Party', *The Times*, 24 July 1959.

[57] Cited in Walter H Waggoner, 'Nyasaland "Plot" Denied by Inquiry: British White Paper Rejects Basis of Arrest of Leaders of Nationalist Party', *The Times*, 24 July 1959.

[58] 'An Inquiring Judge, Sir Patrick Arthur Devlin', *The New York Times*, 25 July 1959.

[59] '"In and Out of Parliament" Electoral Stakes in the Nyasaland Debate', *The Times*, 27 July 1959.

[60] Letter from Devlin to Williams, 27 July 1959, Bodleian Library Archives Special Collection, Oxford University, folio 21.

Your letter could not have come at a happier time. It so to speak mentally crossed one of mine to you. For I have been feeling for a long time that I not only failed to show – a thing I am always clumsy about – my appreciation for all you did from start to finish, but that at times I might have appeared positively ungrateful. It was not so. Your wise advice was invaluable at every turn. You have in particular one quality which I very much admire – and that is the art of persuasion. It does not exist in repeating crescendo all the arguments that appeal to the presenter but in finding out what is the trouble in the other man's mind and addressing yourself to curing it. I am very troubled by the present situation. I think it is clear that the Govt. never intended to accept my hostile finding. I don't think they intended a sham inquiry from the beginning. I think that like many litigants they were confident that they would win and just did not contemplate a situation in which they lost. When it came, they found it politically impossible to do otherwise than close their eyes. If they were attempting to make any real assessment of the Report and reasonably come to the conclusion we had made a balls of it we could not complain. They are simply saying in effect 'We always believed the Governor was right and we still do so, while going on doing so no matter what anyone says.' The consequence is that the standing of the report is inevitably made into a political issue, or the Devlin report becomes an electoral counter. That is very damaging, especially to a judge whose value depends on a complete detachment from party politics. It is no use attempting anything in the present hubbub. But when things have calmed down and it is possible to get a detached view of the whole I would very much like to consult you to see if anything can be done to put things right.

But the Attorney-General was innately and predictably aggressive as a leopard. On 28 July he rose to his feet in the Commons. Disingenuously he began:[61]

That this House takes note of the Report the Nyasaland Commission of Inquiry and the Despatch from Governor of Nyasaland thereon and extends its thanks to the Chairman and members of the Commission for their work; endorses their conclusion that a policy of violence was adopted by the Nyasaland African Congress Leadership and that the declaration of the state of emergency was fully justified; deeply regrets the loss of life that occurred but acknowledges the prompt and effective action by the Governor prevented the development of a more serious situation; expresses its gratitude to the Administration and to the Security Forces for their loyal service in circumstances of great difficulty and looks forward to the restoration of normal conditions in Nyasaland and to the continued constitutional and economic progress of its people on the basis for respect for law and order. The Commission was appointed on 6th April. Members of the Commission spent five weeks in Nyasaland, they sat for a week in Southern Rhodesia, they heard evidence from 455 individuals and they say about 1300 witnesses in groups. May I say in passing, Mr Speaker that I am rather intrigued about how that was done. Hearing witnesses in groups strikes me as a somewhat novel procedure. It would certainly save time in the courts, but it sounds rather a noisy business and questioning witnesses in groups must have been rather difficult. Still they did it, and they studied no less than 585 memoranda. I mention these facts which the Commission itself records for they clearly establish that

[61] Hansard, House of Commons, 28 July 1959, volume 610 cols 317–454, at 3:31 pm.

its task was no light one. I should not like it to be thought by anyone in this House or by anyone outside that because the Government do not accept all the Commission's conclusions and all its criticisms we are not grateful to the Commission for voluntarily devoting so much time and effort to its task.

The Attorney-General went on to explain that the Government was not obliged to accept all the Commission had said as a matter of principle. He then proceeded to cherry-pick his way through the report. He went on to make clear that the Government really accepted the findings and indeed judgement of the Governor in effect over the Commission wherever the two diverged. The Attorney-General then reminded the throng that a Court of Appeal 'in my profession' could overturn a trial judge if their decision was against the weight of the evidence and he invited the House to do so. The Attorney-General took about an hour to deliver his coup de grâce.

Other Members of Parliament followed, supporting or criticising the Government, in particular along party lines. Lennox-Boyd spoke last and gave much more measured support for the Attorney-General in particular. He was obviously especially aware of his own vulnerabilities.

The Government, through the Attorney-General as principal mouthpiece, devised a predictable but not very intelligent strategy. Sarcasm, ritual humiliation, scorn and inviting, in effect, disbelief as to the volume and quality of the work performed was clearly intended, by pointing to alleged defects in the methodology, to in turn raise the prospect that the findings on important factual issues should also be regarded as defective and for that reason disregarded. This was a deliberate and serious libel not only of Patrick but each of his colleagues, committed under absolute parliamentary privilege. The Attorney-General, as one of Macmillan's loyal supporters, had, according to Macmillan, performed brilliantly but in fact arguably less than honourably. Labour, predictably for their own purposes, vigorously supported Patrick.

On 28 July, Bill Williams, one of Patrick's fellow Commissioners, wrote to another, Sir John Primrose:[62]

> I've meant to write to you before. What I was going to say whenever I did get around to writing was that if anybody should feel that the Devlin report has a note of humanity running through it (and I do hope people may feel that on reading it) it will be, in my considered and affectionate opinion, due to one John Primrose and the great strength and warmth he gave to his colleagues. I don't know how else to put it, John, and I may not get the words right (one never can in such matters) but I have been wanting to say something of the sort to you so here it is, with my gratitude and affection. I am sorry I talked so much. The judge is very down. He feels that he is being made a political football and he's obviously very hurt. If you found time to send him a friendly wave at this hour it would be well taken, I fancy. I am not so down as he seems to be but rather I alternate between being donnish, philosophical and hopping

[62] Letter from Williams to Primrose, 28 July 1959, Bodleian Library Archives Special Collection, Oxford University, folio 22.

mad. Shortly this is it: You hire four chaps to get you out of a Parliamentary scrape and you play up their integrity and their freedom from politics. Then damn it, they come back and though it's impossible to impugn their integrity without imperilling your own, you have to pretend that though they are upright they are so upright their feet never hit the ground. (P-Wyn[-Harris], for example whose behind almost bumps the ground when he walks). All this one now comes to recognise as Boyd's law of the discarded Kleenex.

The debate continued the next day in the House of Lords. Lord Perth began by name-dropping and in a patronising manner describing Patrick as 'an old Cambridge friend of mine'.[63] But he went on far more elegantly and pleasantly than the Attorney-General nonetheless, to cherry-pick at the report. Not so others. Lord Coleraine (Richard Law) was particularly insulting. He suggested that there were three reasons for rejection of the report: first that it was irresponsible; secondly that it was 'almost unbelievably naive' and innocent; and finally it was remarkably disingenuous. Not content, he continued:

> But what I am sure is that this Report is characterised by that peculiar kind of silliness which you can only find in very clever men and by that peculiar lack of scruple which in my experience, often distinguishes the very high-minded.[64]

When baited he accused the Commission of intellectual dishonesty in terms. Precisely what provoked Coleraine's bile is a little hard to fathom. But his brutal and gratuitous attack did neither him nor the Conservative Party any service. His attack was puerile and cowardly.

Patrick was clearly distressed at the time. Often and especially when asked by one of his children how he was feeling, he regularly invoked the sentiments and verse of the famous WE Henley poem, 'Invictus' – his head was 'bloody, but unbowed'.[65] Patrick would in time stop hurting in most respects, but so far as the Attorney-General was concerned, he would wait another day. Whilst it would be most unfair to dismiss the Attorney-General as a mere battering ram, he was a man who all his life was capable of evoking great dislike from many quarters, political and legal. He could be instinctively rude and abrasive. The author has had personal experience of appearing before him in the Privy Council. He could cross-examine effectively. He was a hard worker but unlike Patrick not so subtle a thinker. Macmillan liked him because he was loyal, predictable and likely to be sycophantic. Butler likened him to a 'clumber spaniel sniffing round the hedgerows'.[66] He was not as stupid as Patrick thought he was, and he was

---

[63] Hansard, House of Lords, 29 July 1959, volume 218 cols 757–802, at 3:00 pm.

[64] Hansard, House of Lords, 29 July 1959, volume 218 cols 825–830, after 5:49 pm.

[65] Email from Timothy Devlin to the Author, 24 July 2015.

[66] DR Thorpe, *Supermac: The Life of Harold Macmillan* (London, Chatto & Windus, 2010), p 569; Alistair Horne, *Macmillan 1957–1986, Volume II of the Official Biography* (London, Macmillan, 1989), p 558.

not as vain as Patrick certainly was. His rudeness was part of his personality but he was not particularly mean. Patrick on the other hand had on occasion a cruel streak which seemed so effortlessly to float to the surface. The two would find themselves – at least from Patrick's point of view – entwined in eternity. In a sense Patrick planned that. The Attorney-General, perhaps as always, was oblivious to it. His somewhat pathetically amateurish theatrics in the House were not of much use in the end.

Many of the principal participants emerged bruised by the encounter; Patrick, certainly, as did Armitage. Armitage maintained his anger at the Nyasaland Commission right until the end. In a BBC television series about Nyasaland entitled 'End of Empire', Armitage was interviewed and did not hold back on his criticism of Patrick. Although Patrick was long retired, he did not participate in the broadcast.[67] Armitage also wrote some lengthy unpublished memoirs, the flavour of which can be gleaned by the following:[68]

> The Commission seems to have concentrated almost exclusively with Government witnesses on actual incidents and events and orders given during the Emergency. They appeared to have cross-examined ceaselessly witnesses as to the need for using fire-arms, the need for firing a number of shots, the need for searching houses and burning them, the need for arresting persons and how this was done and whether they should be handcuffed and so on. I must emphasise that in these circumstances the Commission has been very much like a court of law without the oaths being taken, or evidence led, etc. Government officials have certainly come out from the presence feeling that all the Commission was interested in was trying to establish what they had done was wrong.

And: 'The Report, when published did not give me any feeling that Devlin allowed any member of the Commission to hold views that were contrary to his own.'

Patrick however, need not have worried. He had an excellent reputation as a judge and an intellectual (the two do not necessarily go together). On 31 July *The Spectator* was scathing about Macmillan and the whole idea of cherry-picking sections of the report to suit the Government's needs.[69] The lead article for that day ended with the following:

> An epitaph for Mr Macmillan's colonial record suggests itself: 'his honour rooted in dishonour stood'. He has allowed Britain's good name in Central Africa to be destroyed; and when the evidence is brought home to him, he refuses to allow that it can be correct. For this he will not be forgiven.

[67] Episode 13 'The Rider and the Horse', *End of Empire* BBC television series, produced by Granada Television, broadcast in 1985. See also: Brian Lapping, *End of Empire* (London, Guild Publishing, 1985).

[68] Unpublished memoirs, Sir Robert Armitage, Bodleian Library Archives, University of Oxford, box 2, folder 4, folios 1–109. See in particular, folios 51, 56–70, 75–78, 81–92 and 101–9.

[69] 'Rooted in Dishonour', editorial, *The Spectator*, 31 July 1959.

The Economist on 1 August was even more damning of the Government:[70]

The Devlin report is the Government's own self-made boomerang. And it carries a delayed-action charge ... After the Devlin report can the Government keep the Nyasaland Congress detainees untried and under lock and key? A judge, working with distinguished colleagues, has found that the charges on which the detention of many of these men sustained were not proven.

---

[70] 'Living with Devlin', *The Economist*, 1 August 1959.

9

The Return to Normality?

ERBERT HART WAS two years younger than Patrick and had been Professor of Jurisprudence at Oxford since 1952. While Patrick was fencing with Government officials in Nyasaland and being defamed in the Commons (and to a greater extent in the House of Lords), Hart, seething with considerable contempt for Patrick's Maccabaean Lecture, decided to take Patrick on. He thought Patrick's thesis cock-eyed. In a radio broadcast and then an article in *The Listener* on 30 July 1959,[1] Hart responded to Patrick in what Hart would later describe in an interview with Professor David Sugarman as 'one of my best articles', just two days before the article in *the Economist*.[2] Patrick, on one view, may well have thought the walls were closing in.

Many judges can, if they choose, live a relatively monastic life. Most do. They tend to mix, apart from family or close friends, mostly with judicial colleagues. They rarely venture out except for the odd public occasion, usually involving something to do with the legal profession. The need to remain, and appear to remain, entirely removed from any form of public discourse keeps most judges indoors. Some give lectures. Some write books, usually textbooks of some kind. Some write tedious memoirs of their most famous and usually unmemorable war stories. Some even try their hand at fiction and usually fail miserably.

Not so for Patrick. True, he was thrust into the limelight by the likes of the Bodkin Adams trial, the Maccabaean Lecture and the Nyasaland Commission. But in any event and unlike most of his colleagues, he had long since eschewed the monastic life in more ways than one. He enjoyed the public cut and thrust and had done since schooldays. And he was not averse to giving lectures, especially when the invitation put him on the international stage. Patrick's interest in the law was not just in technical points of principle. He had a deep interest and affection for the philosophy of the law. He had a powerful analytical mind which frequently was put to good use both in and out of court.

But by the middle of 1959 Patrick was both angry and distressed. Whilst he was coming to terms with the Attorney-General's attack and the views of other pro-Armitage supporters, Hart denounced Patrick's thesis and reasoning process.

---

[1] HLA Hart, 'Immorality and Treason', *The Listener*, 30 July 1959 at 162–63.

[2] Hart expressed this view to Professor Sugarman in an interview conducted by Professor Sugarman with Hart at University College, Oxford, 9 November 1988. The interview is available at: https://blog.oup.com/2012/12/h-l-a-hart-in-conversation-with-david-sugarman/.

Hart started with sarcasm. He 'damned with faint praise, assented with civil leer'[3] by describing Patrick's argument as 'original and interesting', designed to show that 'prima facie society has the right to legislate against immorality as such' and that the Wolfenden Committee were mistaken in thinking that there is an area of private immorality which is not the law's business. Hart next asserted that Patrick had sought to make a general case and not come clean as to precisely which conduct he was referring to:[4]

> The publication by Sir Patrick of his lecture is in itself an interesting event. It is many years since a distinguished English lawyer delivered himself of general reasoned views about the relationship of morality to the criminal law. The last to do so with comparable skill and clarity was, I think, the great Victorian judge James Fitzjames Stephen. It is worth observing that Stephen, like Sir Patrick, repudiated the liberal point of view. Indeed his gloomy but impressive book, Liberty, Equality, Fraternity was a direct reply to Mill's essay On Liberty. The most remarkable feature of Sir Patrick's lecture is his view of the nature of morality – the morality which the criminal law may enforce. Most previous thinkers who have repudiated the liberal point of view have done so because they thought that morality consisted either of divine commands or rational principles of human conduct discoverable by human reason. Since morality for them has this elevated divine or rational status as the law of God or reason, it seemed obvious that the state should enforce it, and that the function of human law should not be merely to provide men with the opportunity for leading a good life, but actually to see that they lead it. Sir Patrick does not rest his repudiation of the liberal point of view on these religious or rationalist conceptions. Indeed much that he writes reads like an abjuration of the notion that reasoning or thinking has much to do with morality. English popular morality has no doubt its historical connexion with the Christian religion: 'That', says Sir Patrick, 'is how it got there'. But it does not owe its present status or social significance to religion any more than to reason.

Hart continued:[5]

> But what precisely are the relevant feelings, the feelings which may justify the use of the criminal law? Here the argument becomes a little complex. Widespread dislike of a practice is not enough. There must, says Sir Patrick, be 'a real feeling of reprobation'. Disgust is not enough either. What is crucial is a combination of intolerance, indignation and disgust. These three are the forces behind the moral law, without which it is not 'weighty enough to deprive the individual of freedom of choice'.

Hart accused Patrick of choosing which type of conduct to regulate by whether the disgust etc, could be said to have reached a concert-pitch intensity or not. If so – out. What happens, Hart asked rhetorically, if the concert pitch subsides? Accepting that a consensus of moral opinion on certain matters is essential if society is to be worth living in, Hart asserted that there should be a two-stage process. First whether the practice which offends moral feelings is harmful,

---

[3] Alexander Pope, 'Epistle to Dr Arbuthnot', *Prologue to the Satires*, 1734.
[4] HLA Hart, 'Immorality and Treason', *The Listener*, 30 July 1959, 162.
[5] Ibid, p 162.

independently of its repercussions on the general moral code. Secondly, does the repercussion on the moral code really jeopardise the whole fabric of morality and so society? Patrick did not, according to Hart, clearly identify or separate these two notions.

Hart described Patrick's attempts in effect to draw some comparison between homosexual behaviour and treason as grotesque and the analogy 'absurd'. Hart concluded:[6]

> For him a practice is immoral if the thought of it makes the man on the Clapham omnibus sick. So be it. Still, why should we not summon all the resources of our reason, sympathetic understanding, as well as critical intelligence, and insist that before general moral feeling is turned into criminal law it is submitted to scrutiny of a different kind from Sir Patrick's? Surely, the legislator should ask whether the general morality is based on ignorance, superstition, or misunderstanding; whether there is a false conception that those who practise what it condemns are in other ways danger-ous or hostile to society; and whether the misery to many parties, the blackmail and the other evil consequences of criminal punishment, especially for sexual offences, are well understood.

Given his personal psychological and health struggles, Hart arguably spoke from a conflicted position of interest.[7] Nonetheless he assumed the mask and mantle of Mill, complete with the long, pointed nose and prominent sebaceous cyst on his forehead, and assigned to Patrick the balding, mutton chops frown of Stephen.[8] The battle had begun. Neither could have predicted that by enter-ing into this discussion they were unwittingly exhuming the corpses of the two Victorian protagonists whose debate continues to excite and incite to this day. As may be obvious, the debate is as much about politics as it is about philosophy.

It is no coincidence that both Mill and Stephen, oddly both members of the Liberal Party, had political ambitions. Mill was elected to the seat of Westminster in 1865 with Stephen missing out for the seat of Dundee in 1873. While Stephen had been an early and great admirer of Mill, later writings of Mill changed his mind. In particular Stephen entirely disagreed with Mill on women's rights as provocatively articulated in Mill's essay 'The Subjection of Women' published in 1869.[9] It quickly became the early feminists' bible. Stephen was furious and this was one of the factors that provoked Stephen's response in *Liberty, Equality, Fraternity* in 1873.[10] Stephen thought Mill's views on gender

[6] Ibid, p 163.

[7] Nicola Lacey, *A Life of H.L.A. Hart, the Nightmare and the Noble Dream* (Oxford, Oxford Univeristy Press, 2004), pp 3, 42, 310–11, 339, 342–45 (nervous breakdowns/depression), pp 61–62, 73–79, 110–11, 151, 194 and 203–5 (sexuality).

[8] J Sackar and T Prince (eds), *Heydon: Selected Speeches and Papers* (Sydney, Federation Press, 2018), p 551.

[9] John Stuart Mill, *The Subjection of Women*, 1st ed (London, Longmans, Green, Reader & Dyer, 1869).

[10] James Fitzjames Stephen, *Liberty, Quality, Fraternity* (Smith Elder & Co, 1873).

equality misconceived, especially when it came to education. Hart and Devlin's argument provided the catalyst which reignited the debate.[11]

As an aside, Professor RFV Heuston, in his obituary of Patrick written for the British Academy in 1994, asserts that Patrick resigned his chairmanship of the Council of Bedford College when he developed doubts about the value of higher education for women.[12] No source is identified for the assertion and, perhaps mischievously, Heuston drops it in in the context of the Hart/Devlin debate. It should be stated immediately that Professor Heuston was probably one of the best-informed legal gossips of the twentieth century: his books on the Lord Chancellors vouch for that. That said, upon the author's inquiries of Bedford College the minutes recording Patrick's resignation show it was tendered on 15 October 1959.[13] Whilst his original letter no longer exists, it is recorded that he was resigning due to insufficient time. Given what occurred in 1959, this was an entirely plausible reason. In any event, Bedford College was founded in 1849 specifically to provide higher education for women. Patrick chaired the Council for six years until 1959. He obviously knew the history of the institution, so for Heuston's story to be correct this would have required a change of heart. That is not evident from anything Patrick did or said at the time. The story is likely unreliable and unsourced gossip. It should be noted of course that Madeleine herself had gone to Oxford.

The academic dispute between Patrick and Hart was all about the proper scope of the criminal law. As far as academic disputes went, Hart had form, as shown in his attack on Bodenheimer in 1957[14] and his quarrel with

---

[11] A very small selection of materials which have been produced by various academics over the years are as follows. The list is not intended to be exhaustive, however, the debate is discussed in many textbooks as well. See in particular: 'Lord Devlin and the Enforcement of Morals', Ronald Dworkin, (1966) 75 *Yale Law Journal* 986–1005; Joel Feinberg, 'Some Unswept Debris from the Devlin-Hart Debate' (1987) 72 *Synthese* 249–75; Rolf Sartorius, 'The Enforcement of Morality' (1972) 81(5) *Yale Law Journal* 891–910; Robert George, 'Social Cohesion and the Legal Enforcement of Morals: A Reconsideration of the Hart-Devlin Debate' (1990) 35 *American Journal of Jurisprudence* 15–46; SI Strong, 'Justice Scalia as the Modern Law Devlin: Animus and Civil Burdens in Romer v. Evans' (1997) 71(1) *Southern California Law Review* 1–46; Gerald Dworkin, 'Devlin was Right: Law and Enforcement of Morality' (1999) 40 *William and Mary Law Review* 927–46; Bernard Harcourt, 'The Collapse of the Harm Principle' (1999) 90 *Journal of Criminal Law and Criminology* 109–94; Robert A. Burt, 'Moral Offenses and Same Sex Offenses: Revisiting the Hart-Devlin Debate' (2004) 125(4) *Yale Law Journal*; Robert Moffat, 'The Law's Business; the Politics of Tolerance and the Enforcement of Morality' (2005) 57 *Florida Law Review* 1097–1133; Peter Cane, 'Taking Law Seriously: Starting Points of the Hart/Devlin Debate' (2010) 10 *Journal of Ethics* 21–51; William Miller, 'Conservatism and the Hart/Devlin Debate' (2010) 1 *International Journal of Politics and Good Governance* 156–95; James Allan, 'Revisiting the Hart-Devlin Debate: at the periphery and by the numbers' (2017) 54 *San Diego Law Review* 423–39.

[12] RFV Heuston, 'Patrick Arthur Devlin 1905–1992' (1994) 84 *Proceedings of the British Academy* 261.

[13] Email from Annabel Valentine, College Archivist, Royal Holloway College, to the author, 26 August 2015.

[14] See: Edgar Bodenheimer, 'Modern Analytical Jurisprudence and the Limits of its Usefulness' (1956) 104 *University of Pennsylvania Law Review* 1080–86. Hart's reply was entitled 'Analytical Jurisprudence in Mid-Twentieth Century: a Reply to Professor Bodenheimer' (1957) 105 *University of Pennsylvania Law Review* 953–75.

Lon Fuller[15] in the same year. This was the start of numerous follow up lectures and books where Hart and Patrick tried in turn to get one-up on the other. Academics have over the years joined into a feeding frenzy over the debate, each claiming from time to time that their champion was the victor. The debate had the effect, if at all possible, of giving both men much higher profiles than ever. In a sense the debate brought out the very best in both of them. The themes explored by both remained constant but the level of debate was much more sophisticated. The debate would excite and incite both authors and interested onlookers during the lives and well after the deaths of both protagonists. Patrick and Hart died within a few months of each other in 1992.

By August, Patrick was about to go on circuit and return to the relatively cloistered environment of court. He had sent both his Maccabaean Lecture and the Nyasaland report to Frankfurter and Acheson. The wound was still little raw. Frankfurter wrote perceptively to Patrick on 6 August:[16]

> My warm thanks for your two publications: the Maccabaean Lecture and the Devlin Report. Now I have read both, I deplore the barrier of distance that precludes my talking with you about both. An interchange between us on the exciting and far reaching issues that both raise could easily absorb at least one whole week-end. Sketchy notes across the Atlantic are meager and frustrating substitutes for such talk. Before dealing with their subject matter even as cursorily and wholly inadequately as I shall, you must let me express obvious admiration for the intellectual energy, range and capacity by which you were able to consummate two such very solid pieces of work as side ventures to your exacting judicial tasks.
>
> I am with you wholly on your general thesis and comment on the Wolfenden Report. All such dichotomies as between 'sin' and 'crime' or 'morals' and 'crime' seem to me futile endeavours to isolate interrelated problems and phenomena, or at the most indulgences in private systems of classification. The soft spot in your elucidation, if I may say so, and reading between the lines I seem to detect your own awareness of it, is the mode by which one is to determine what are the binding moralities of a society in the enforcement of which it may look to law. This is a problem that has bothered me almost since I came out of law school, but more particularly during my twenty-odd years here. For at bottom it is not unlike the problem that confronts one in the application of our due process clauses, conceiving the judicial nature of due process as I conceive it to be. I enclose the opinion in a case which it would be surprising indeed if you had seen, which may indicate to you the kind of tortures, they are not less than that, through which I go in dealing with this kind of a problem. I note you tell me the answer is to be found by attributing a judgment to the man on the Clapham bus or

---

[15] These disputes were debates by way of exchange of views between Devlin and Professor Fuller from Harvard, a proponent of the natural law theory, and Hart (a confirmed legal positivist at the time) in the *Harvard Law Review*, volume 71. See, HLA Hart, 'Positivism and the Separation of Law and Morals' (1958) 71 *Harvard Law Review* 593–629 and Fuller's response, 'Positivism and Fidelity to Law, a Reply to Professor Hart' (1958) 71 *Harvard Law Review* 630–72.

[16] Letter from Frankfurter to Devlin, 6 August 1959, Manuscripts and Archives, Yale University Library, Dean Acheson Papers, folder 96.

the twelve 'reasonable' people in the jury box. That's a good enough guide as far as it goes – but how far does it go?

Now for the Devlin Report. I have not only read that but also the speeches in both Houses of Parliament. You should find satisfaction, if that is the feeling to be aroused, in that even such severe critics of your report as Lord Salisbury bowed to your findings on the excessive use of force in the making of arrests and the suppression of disturbances. As I read on and on in the report, my mind again and again turned to the history of 'liberation' of people in British dependencies, beginning with the American Colonies. It is the same old story except that the tides of nationalism are running so strongly that the pace of liberation is evidently steadily outgrowing the capacity of adjustment that the Home Government is wisely able to achieve with what I have no doubt is a conscious regard on their part for what they conceive to be their responsibility toward the population as a whole, let alone that toward the European minorities. What you wrote, and more particularly what you implied, led me to recall that wonderful correspondence between Lord Morley and the Earl of Minto – Morley's Reminiscences regarding the extension of self-government in India. I remember particularly Morley's statement of the dilemma that when things are quiet you do not want to disturb them, and when there are disturbances you do not want to yield to force. I am, of course, raising the larger issues which were outside your terms of reference. But I could not but feel that you were asked to report on an irrationally segregated portion of a larger problem, just as I often feel that the particular legal question on which we are asked to pass involves a mutilation of a larger problem. Am I wrong in having found myself in a good deal of observations of the Primate: that the Government should have stopped in its resolution at the end of its first semi-colon, and that your report was really a report on psychology. Psychology, of course – the deep feelings of the people of Nyasaland – concerns the underlying forces that led to the policy of violence by Chimpembere & Co. The disturbances and the declaration of an emergency and these underlying forces and the appropriate responses to them it was not for you to investigate, but you could not keep them out of your reckoning. I have said enough, I hope not too much, to indicate with that fascinated interest, I might almost say concern, I read your powerful document.

My handwriting having for years been the butt of Dean's persiflage, I learn with pleasure that he is now trying to reform you.

Grateful for the soothing adulation of Frankfurter and the receipt of a token of esteem from Williams, Patrick wrote to Williams the next day:[17]

For the last week I have been oscillating between credulity and caution. Surely, I said to myself it is wildly improbable that even Bill would have sent you so magnificent a present. Did I perhaps order a copy some time ago? So ex abundanti cautela as we say in the law, I waited some day for a bill but none has. So it must be your generosity. Thank you so much indeed. It is a lovely thing to have. Well, on the whole I think the Government has emerged as bloody as we are unbowed. I was much more comforted this morning by a letter from Arnold McNair (who used to be the President of the

[17] Letter from Devlin to Williams, 7 August 1959, Bodleian Library Archives Special Collections, Oxford University folio 27.

Hague Court) because he is one of those people who never offer an opinion until he has mastered all the material. Although he has not, he read the Report, the Governor's reply and the debates in both Houses; and then wrote to say that he deeply resented 'the scurvy and ungrateful treatment' that you and your colleagues have received.

More good news for Patrick and his team: an article in *The Spectator* added to the anti-government chorus.[18] In some detail it crowed in Patrick's favour. It was written by Christopher Hollis, a distinguished teacher, academic and Conservative politician, who had known the two younger Devlin boys, Christopher and William, at Stonyhurst. He had also known Patrick for many years. Having made his disclosure of this conflict of interest he said:

There are two points about Patrick Devlin's career which it is at the moment of public interest to make. The first is that, until a judgeship forbade him expressions of party loyalty, he was always a Conservative. It was as a Conservative at a time when fashion there favoured a vague Liberalism, that he was elected President of the Cambridge Union. It is true that when Ramsay MacDonald appointed Sir William Jowitt, as he then was as, Attorney-General in 1929, Devlin went into the office to assist him, but there was no suggestion that this was a political appointment. Jowitt indeed said, 'Frankly I would prefer a Labour man.' But young Socialist barristers were in those days few and far between. In 1945, when I was adopted as candidate for Devizes, I was delighted to learn that Westwick, just outside Pewsey, where the Devlins lived, was in the constituency: and throughout that election campaign he was the outstanding speaker in my support. I remember an interminable summer evening of Socialist heckling that we had to endure together in the dreary little village of Ludgershall. After 1945 Conservative leaders wished him to come into the House to support them, and he could certainly have had a safe seat had he wanted it. But he preferred the law.

The second point is this. There are two sorts of successful judges – the pragmatic and the philosophical. There are good judges who are content merely to take the law as they find it and to administer it competently. There are those whose minds are always restlessly inquiring into the origins, the philosophy and the justification of law. Devlin is par excellence a judge of the second sort. He published a distinguished little volume on Trial by Jury. His last public appearance other than the bench before his Nyasaland appointment was to deliver last March under the chairmanship of Sir Maurice Bowra, the Maccabaean Lecture in Jurisprudence of the British Academy. The title of the lecture was 'The Enforcement of Morals' and the question which it raised was how far the penal law should concern itself with the suppression of sin. This is not the place either to summarise or to criticise his argument. I merely want to show that he is a man above all concerned with the philosophy of the law, and indeed we are told that one day – it may be not until after his retirement – we shall receive what will no doubt be an important book in full statement of his philosophic opinions. Of his general standing as a judge, his work as President of the Restrictive Practices Court and the frequency with which his name was mentioned when the Lord Chief Justiceship was vacant bear testimony. Indeed, had not the Government

---

[18] Christopher Hollis, 'Sir Patrick Devlin', *The Spectator*, 14 August 1959, p 8.

held a high opinion of his abilities they would not have appointed him to head the Commission.

Whatever criticisms may be made of the Nyasaland Report, it would not be possible to imagine anyone more certain to think out clearly exactly which were the questions which he was called on to answer, or to distinguish carefully between what he certainly knew and what he surmised. If the Attorney-General cannot follow some of the distinctions which he draws, it is by no means certain that the fault lies with Mr. Justice Devlin. 'Sir, I have found you an argument, but I cannot find you an understanding.' Lord Coleraine has himself made valuable contributions to the philosophy of politics, but of all possible descriptions of Mr. Justice Devlin's work I should have thought that 'intellectually dishonest' and 'naive' were the most inapt. Agree or disagree, here is a man intellectually honest to the verge of scrupulosity.

While Patrick would not have preferred all the gush and revelations, he would not have rejected the support.

Acheson provided further support on 17 August:[19]

A flurry of writing of my own has delayed the completion of your Report and Lecture until this week. But all this while I have thought about them a great deal. Upon Felix's urging, I read the debate in the House of Lords right after your Report. This amazed me and completed the illusion, begun by the Report of a rollback in time. It might have been about Warren Hastings or Mutiny. I was flabbergasted by Dick Law's[20] outburst. At one time towards end of the War, I knew him pretty well. None of us thought he was very bright but he seemed level-headed and sensible. In the debate he was adolescent, like the exasperating stuffed shirts who would denounce anyone who pointed out any defect in the school team as lacking 'school spirit'.

What to me stood out above all was that none of the debaters seemed to have had any suspicion of what I thought was the ethos of the Report. The heart of it is Paragraphs 255 and 256, a sober and eloquent statement of what one living under British institutions in the mid-twentieth century was led to expect – and what he got in Nyasaland in March, 1959. 8,500 whites cannot hope to govern 2,700,000 blacks in the latter's country in 1959 under British institutions and political mores. It just won't work. When the Empire was established in the eighteenth and early nineteenth centuries those institutions and ideas did not exist – witness the transportations to Australia, the repression of the labor movement and the Chartist riots. Furthermore, nationalism had not reached Africa and Asia. It wouldn't work in Ireland and India in this century and it won't work in Africa. The British people simply can't employ for very long the methods of the Russians in Hungary; and, while the French can, they are not strong enough to make it work in Algeria.

This no one among the debaters – except possibly the Archbishop – seemed even to suspect. The whole discussion reminded me of the furious debate in New Haven

[19] Letter from Acheson to Devlin, 17 August 1959, Manuscripts and Archives, Yale University Library, Dean Acheson Papers, folder 96.
[20] Richard Law, 1st Baron Coleraine (HL 1954–80.)

last March when the undergraduates snowballed a Saint Patrick's Day parade and were charged by baton swinging Irish policemen who pursued them into the hitherto unviolated sanctity of their college courts. Thereafter the infirmary and the town jail were filled with students – there were no police casualties – several unwise professors who had attempted to restrain the young and had been swept up in the net. Town and gown press were for days full of invective about the hooliganism and police brutality, until the Mayor and the President got together to devise fairly simple ways of preventing these silly clashes.

This was the level of the House of Lords debate. Two of your own delightful phrases furnished clubs for both sides. Labor grabbed 'police state' and charged. The Tories, with Cecil at the head, mowed down the enemy with 'The Government had to choose whether to abdicate or govern. It was a fight in which one longed for a part. I would have been a stalwart for the Report, but would have ruined everything by – if I may combine two clichés – letting the cat out of the bag only to put it among the pigeons.

The Report is a great and illuminating document to one reading with the mind as well as the eyes. What to do next, as you said in your letter is a problem which can happily be left in other hands. About your lecture, I don't feel competent to say anything sensible. To use a stuffy English expression, it isn't my line of country. I am all for the secular state staying as secular as possible. Absolutes bother me. Even 'society cannot tolerate rebellion' bothers me, when I recall that Jefferson thought 'a little revolution now and then is a good thing.' Our society is more disorderly than the older ones, and the denizen of it likes to get the room to stretch. Then we are too volatile in our attitudes to lead me to feel happy about accepting 'as public morality, a proposition which most people would readily accept.' 'We have been cock-sure', as Justice Holmes wrote, 'of a good many things that were not so'. Perhaps it is largely a matter of mood, or of too blunt a mind, which makes me confused by considering whether the desirable result is moral or vice versa, rather than in which may the balance of social interest lies. I know, of course – indeed, you make it explicit – that you are not in favor of legislating or adjudging me, so far as may be, into the kingdom of heaven. But this assurance does not extend to all people who would base action on moral principles.

Even though resistant to your thesis, I salute the power of its thought and the incisive brilliance of its expression. To save myself from suspicion of utter depravity, I am sending separately an attempt last year to deal with the place of moral conceptions in international relations.

In a month or so we should be off on our travels. The sap of excited anticipation begins to rise in us – and of nothing more than being with the Devlins again.

As time progressed, Patrick confided more and more in Acheson and to a lesser extent Frankfurter, than he did anyone in the profession in Britain. That is not to say he did not have both good and close friends at home but he was enamoured of the justice system in the United States and the legal thinking of its leaders. As he saw it, it was not hidebound; nor did it obstruct or oppose procedural reforms by sticking to arcane rules for the sake of it. Politics aside, Acheson had become a very close friend with whom Madeleine would also correspond. On 20 August Patrick wrote to Acheson:[21]

> You have sent me off in shame to my typewriter. Casual abuse of my writing I can stand. But I cannot survive the judgment in solemn form which you have delivered on your behalf and your brother Frankfurter. Your measured language, which I could sense that you employed only with deep reluctance and which you expressed the considered conclusion of two men of learning and integrity reached after an anxious review of all the available evidence, came as a shattering condemnation. So I have fled to my portable and am trying to imagine that I am Mr Wilson tapping out those fat sentences in which he would not have been candid with himself if he had attempted to conceal etc, etc. and likewise the President deems it his solemn duty not to with-hold, etc, etc. I suppose this festooning was all part of the Age of Draperies in which no part of anything could be left unclothed. I wonder if F.F. ever saw Mr Wilson type. I fancy him as no one-finger man but a bit of a virtuoso who uncovered his typewriter with the air of a pianist getting ready to perform. But I should like to know.
>
> I do think you and F.F. are extremely good in the way in which you read and digest anything of mine that I send you. It is not only that your comments are so valuable but I feel it is such a compliment that you should give thought to it. In what you say about the Nyasaland Report you put into words my own chief sense of disappoint-ment about the whole proceedings. We went out there, three of us with no knowledge of all the colonial affairs and with the assumption that the form and substance of government was mutatis mutandis much the same as in Britain, the mutata not being anything very fundamental. We found of course that they were quite fundamental; and in so far as we hoped for anything from the Report, – it being our business to set down what we saw as we saw it and not to indulge ourselves with hopes, – we hoped that it would, first, disabuse the ordinary citizen of the notion that 'colonial law and order' allowed the same amount of room for freedom of word and action as would be demanded in Britain, and secondly, to help him make up his mind whether he was willing to pay for colonies the price which their rule demands in the sacrifice of ideas which normally he cherishes. But the Govt. made the Report into a playground in which children searched for 'I-told-you-so's. We depicted it as a conflict between Old and New. They insist on seeing it as a conflict between Right and Wrong. 'My Country is Right, but Right or Wrong My Country' is now, I think, a little diluted, but only a little. An up-to-date version would be 'My Country is Right, but if she isn't no Gentleman will call attention to it'. So the play will go on. The villains must remain villains, and no hint must be given to the audience that there may be a streak of good in them somewhere until the glorious transformation scene at the end when they are made Privy Councillors and invited to Balmoral.
>
> I think I see exactly what you mean about the lecture and I deeply sympathize with it. The lecture should be treated as strictly ex cathedra. I allowed my private cat one peep out of the bag in a bit where I said, – I haven't got the text here, – that history might be a tale of contraction and expansion, the freedom of the individual press-ing against the bondage of society, the slackening and the dissolution and then the

---

[21] Letter from Devlin to Acheson, 20 August 1959, Manuscripts and Archives, Yale University Library, Dean Acheson Papers, folder 96.

new society with a tighter bondage. Always there is the conflict between man's will to be free and his need to be bound. If he had no need to be bound, there would be no society. In this conflict I am emotionally on the side of freedom; I resist and resent bondage. But intellectually I recognise the need for it. One of the few things I remember out of many wise things that must have been said to me in my youth is when a priest told me that it was very easy to rebel and very difficult to be orthodox. If that had not made an impression on me, I wonder whether I should have gone in for the law. For law is the instrument of society. Indeed judges are its pillars. I should love to see you and Jefferson in your off moments, putting a bit of dynamite under any particularly fat pillar that you disliked. But ex cathedra I could only condemn, though, not I hope unctuously.

I am so glad that all this prompted you to send me your article on Morality and Diplomacy which I have so to speak filed under another head, – that of Woodrow Wilson and his works to which some day I hope I shall come back. But the prospect of reading it again with profit did not detract from the pleasure I got from a first reading. I wonder if you write as effortlessly as you seem to. We shall have much to talk of in October. Madeleine is becoming impatient at my tentative hoverings over this typewriter and fearful lest procrastination might lose the day, has written to Mrs Acheson to clinch it. It will I expect, be mainly a family weekend; when the family is effective in any number, it does not leave much room for anyone else! It will really be lovely to see you again.

Given his other commitments to the interrogatories and commentary, Acheson responded reasonably promptly on 27 August:[22]

No, Felix never saw Mr. Wilson type. But while never present at the sacrament he once saw the chalice. It happened when as young man he stayed over after the Taft administration in which he had been an assistant to Mr Stimson, the Secretary of War to help his successor get started. He lived with a group of bachelors in a house, somewhat pretentiously called The House of Truth, which as you well imagine was the center of a good deal of social gaiety. One of his friends knew Margaret Wilson and one day she offered to give them a personally conducted tour of the White House. They did the state room downstairs and then moved on to the family quarters on the second floor, which on the continent is confusingly called the first floor. They were shown the Oval Room, the Lincoln Room and others in a lighthearted casual way. Finally Miss Wilson opened a door into a small room off the Munroe Room. She pointed to a table, her voice sank to a whisper. 'There' she said 'is Father's typewriter'. They gazed in silence. The door was reverently closed.

You must surely be right that Mr Wilson was no one-finger man. But did he uncover his typewriter with the air of a pianist getting ready to perform, of an organist about to play a Bach mass? We can explore this problem in October.

You delight me with the vision of colonial administrators' feast of Assumption when they are made Privy Councillors and taken up to Balmoral. Here we are far more selective. It happens only to ex-Presidents, and only recently since not until

---

[22] Letter from Acheson to Devlin, 27 August 1959, Manuscripts and Archives, Yale University Library, Dean Acheson Papers, folder 96.

Mr Hoover and Mr Truman have they in this century lived long enough for opinion about them to mellow. What occurs is not so much an antithesis of Shakespeare's aphorism, not, so much that the good they did lives after them, but that they live after themselves. They outlive the circumstances and roles which made them, the centers of controversy. They become 'characters', true types of a period, and regarded affectionately as were the thinning ranks of our Civil War veterans without regard to the color of the uniform they wore ...

By the second half of 1959 the Government was preparing for an election and much to Macmillan's relief Africa was not a major issue, especially after the earlier bloodletting. But there were clearly signs of foreboding nonetheless. Both East and Central Africa were teetering on the brink of bloody, racial catastrophe in which Europeans settlers were being pitted against Africans. The civil war in Algeria was a warning for any colonial power. The French Army was unable to restore control there. A bitter earlier division over the Suez added to Britain's problems.

Lennox-Boyd had long wanted to retire. He did not have to wait any longer. The general election was held on 8 October and saw Macmillan returned with a thumping majority. Manningham-Buller, who held the safe seat of Northamptonshire South, was also returned with an increased majority.

Lennox-Boyd was delighted to be replaced by Iain Macleod. Not only was Macmillan in a very good mood at being returned to government, but happily for Patrick, Macleod thought that Patrick had got it right in his Nyasaland Report. On urging from Macmillan, Macleod tackled both Nyasaland and Kenya in tandem. Macleod immediately contacted Patrick and took him to lunch at White's so they could speak freely.[23] He told Patrick that he thought his report was indeed 'technically true' and that he accepted there had been no murder plot. Macleod also told Patrick that he thought Banda was sincere in his offers of a compromise. He was firmly of the view that a substantial part of the solution was to have Banda released from detention, although in the end that did not occur until April 1960. Macleod was entirely blunt with Macmillan, who seems to have accepted Macleod's assessment. As part of the process, the Monckton Commission on the future of the Federation was about to get underway. All this took some, if not all, of the previous heat and scrutiny from Patrick, much to his relief. With some fanfare the composition of the Monckton Commission was announced, which included members from the United Kingdom, Canada, Australia and Africa.[24]

With a sense of real relief for the first time in months Patrick returned to the work of a trial judge. He went back to sitting in crime which he always enjoyed. The downside, however, was circuit work. Although Patrick normally enjoyed it, in the latter half of 1959 it had started to grate. Madeleine did not

[23] Robert Shepherd, *Iain Macleod, a Biography* (London, Hutchinson, 1994), p 187.
[24] Ibid, pp 188–92.

like Patrick being away either. The Nyasaland Commission and the stress associated with it made him realise the importance of the support of family and friends. Acheson and his wife, Alice, had also played a key role in this regard. Thus Patrick candidly confided in a letter on 4 November:[25]

> Alice and you have been a great delight to us all. Your second visit left us with a great increase of affection for you. I am an ungregarious person (that sounds less offensive than egregious) and I did not expect at my time of life to find again anyone I like as much as you.

The mutual admiration was continued by Madeleine herself in a chatty letter on 10 November, which brought Acheson up to date on the family and Patrick's work.[26] Acheson responded to both in kind on Christmas Eve. Having regaled them with his public and bruising brawl with President Eisenhower and his own Democratic Party, wistfully he concluded:[27]

> We shall be thinking of you all gathered at West Wick for the holidays. We wish that we could be there in that warm and happy atmosphere which you both create about you. We shall have a strenuous time. The children and grandchildren and all ours and their friends come to the house for a gigantic Christmas carol party on Christmas Eve, then family dinner the next day, and then Alice and I will escape to the farm at Sandy Spring to recover the solitude from humanity in the mass.

In late November or early December, Patrick no doubt had a number of conversations with Kilmuir and Butler about whether Nyasaland had put an indelible blot on his copy book. He must have been reassured that it did not. It soon became apparent that there would be two vacancies in the Court of Appeal. John Morris was to be elevated from the Court to the Lords. He had been an appeal judge for almost a decade. Charles Romer, who had been an appeals judge since 1951, had resigned. Kilmuir spoke to Patrick about elevation either to the Court of Appeal or possibly the Lords. Naturally flattered, Patrick nonetheless had to take soundings at West Wick. Madeleine immediately approved and indeed argued strenuously in favour of the move. Patrick was torn. He very enjoyed being a trial judge. He was in control of his court and his calendar to a large extent, and it could not be said he had not had a stimulating number of years.

Some trial judges have firmly resisted attempts to entice them upwards for these very reasons. The work in an appeal court can be equally relentless, but it is very different. When a judge is appointed, possible future promotion should not enter the equation. All appointments will directly or indirectly involve some

---

[25] Letter from Devlin to Acheson, 4 November 1959, Manuscripts and Archives, Yale University Library, Dean Acheson Papers, folder 97.

[26] Letter from Madeleine Devlin to Acheson, 10 November 1959, Manuscripts and Archives, Yale University Library, Dean Acheson Papers, folder 97.

[27] Letter from Acheson to Devlin and Madeleine Devlin, 24 December 1959, Manuscripts and Archives, Yale University Library, Dean Acheson Papers, folder 97.

level of political decision-making. Future promotion can never be guaranteed for that reason alone. In addition, unless they involve the creation of a new court such as the Restrictive Practices Court – which is rare – vacancies generally occur only upon death or resignation.

Another factor may well have played a role. In mid-December came the distressing news that his brother Christopher was seriously ill.[28] How seriously was not immediately known, but on top of everything else this made the year exceptional. Christopher was to be flown home and Patrick knew he and Madeleine would have their hands full in all manner of things. Wrongly, they both perhaps thought appellate work might be less demanding and would give Patrick more time. Christopher arrived just before Christmas and stayed at Patrick and Madeleine's flat at Gray's Inn.[29]

Patrick was, by reason of his intellect and wide experience, an obviously stand-out candidate. No one could seriously question that. Not without a struggle and the odd sleepless night, Patrick told Kilmuir just before Christmas he would accept what was on offer, which by now was the Court of Appeal. He was appointed on 8 January 1960, sworn in on 11 January and made a Privy Councillor.[30] His colleague Gerald Upjohn was sworn in to the Court of Appeal at the same time.

[28] Madeleine Devlin, *Christopher Devlin, A Biography* (London, Macmillan, 1970), p 195.

[29] Ibid, p 208.

[30] Letter from David Stephen, Prime Minister's Department to Devlin, 5 January 1960, Papers from the Lord Chancellor's Office, Crown Office Warrants and Patents, LCO6/3655. See also letter from Sir George Coldstream to Devlin, 7 January 1960, informing him he would begin sitting in the Court of Appeal on Monday 11 January 1960, Papers from the Lord Chancellor's Office, Crown Office Warrants and Patents, LCO6/3655.

10

Appellate Life

Amuch more sedate, inconspicuous and relatively anonymous life lay
ahead. The first consequence would for a time be welcome. The latter
two lost any appeal they may have had reasonably quickly.

One of the first officially to congratulate Patrick was Frankfurter. The message
was only a little garbled in transmission via Western Union:[1] 'Congratulations
to the Court of Appeal and your bar and Happy Years to you.'

Patrick, along with Denning and Radcliffe, were regarded as some of the
most imaginative judges of their generation. Each had soaring intellects. In
Denning's case, no one person who was not a politician could possibly have written as much about himself as he. It is said that he had begun to fall out of favour,
for example, with his book of lectures, *Freedom and the Law*.[2] Many thought,
at least within the Lord Chancellor's Office, that the work showed immense
ignorance of the workings of administrative government. Denning delighted in
being politically incorrect. That was part of his charm and appeal which was
appreciated, especially by law students. In stark contrast, Patrick maintained a
restrained elegance about his thoughts and hence his writings.

Some judges suffer from the delusion that appellate work is not as difficult as
trial work. Both of course are very different endeavours. Many ambitiously seek
promotion to show off and display their superior intellects. Others do it out of a
sense of duty. Some find out to their chagrin that trial work is not to their liking,
but are never given promotion. Some are promoted beyond their real abilities
and experience.

For Patrick appellate work never was to provide him with the stimulation
and satisfaction he hoped for. One factor was the nature of the work. Another
was the nature of his colleagues, or some of them. Running a trial and one's
own courtroom is invigorating and liberating. Appellate contexts rob each judge
procedurally of anything but enforced consensus. Some have argued that the
judicial oath demands that each judge write separately on each occasion. Patrick
did so if and when he had something separate to say. Modern appellate courts

---

[1] Telegram received by telephone from Frankfurter to Devlin, 7 January 1960, Howard Gotlieb
Archival Research Center Collection, Boston University.

[2] Robert Stevens, *The Independence of the Judiciary, A View from the Lord Chancellor's Office*
(Oxford, Clarendon Press, 1993), p 93.

must seek to work as efficiently as possible and it is customary for one of their number to produce the first draft. Quality is as important as the efficiency and capacity of that judge. At all times Patrick was independently driven. He usually had something to say and did.

On more than the odd occasion Patrick wrote the leading judgment. On other occasions he agreed in the result but contributed his own thoughts. He could not complain about the variety in the Court of Appeal. All manner of cases came the Court's way. But it was relentless as usual. It did not take him long to put his stamp on the work of the Court. His power of persuasion in relation to his new judicial colleagues was palpable. Two examples below suffice to make the point.

On top of the workload, Patrick was all too often asked to speak at some event or give some lecture. All too often he said yes. Montgomery Belgion was an author (publishing studies on Edgar Allan Poe and HG Wells), a newspaper editor and an acquaintance of Patrick's from the Saville Club. On 5 March Belgion extended an invitation to Patrick to speak at the Athenaeum Club on the topic of 'Crime and Sin', chaired by the Archbishop of Canterbury.[3] How could he resist? Belgion had been at the Maccabaean Lecture and was thrilled at the prospect of staging a re-run. In addition, as a result of the renewed acquaintance Patrick had found a new correspondent. He happily accepted the invitation on 7 March.[4]

In April 1960 Patrick presided with Lord Justice Ormerod over what appeared on its face to be a somewhat innocuous pleading appeal in *Speidel v Plato Films Ltd*. The case was first heard in chambers by a master. The master had struck out certain portions of the defence. The master's decision had been upheld on appeal by Mr Justice Sachs. The defendants brought an appeal to the Court of Appeal.

The parties and the underlying factual issues made the case somewhat dramatic. The plaintiff had been the Supreme Commander of Allied Land Forces in Central Europe, and brought an action for libel against the defendants in respect of a film they made, depicting him as being privy to the murder of King Alexander of Yugoslavia in 1934 and having betrayed Field-Marshal Rommel to the Nazis in June 1944.[5] The defendants said that was all true. Alternatively, they pleaded in mitigation of damages that the plaintiff was in fact guilty of a whole series of particular acts of misconduct. The defendants submitted they should be permitted to put these factual matters in evidence as going to the plaintiff's bad character. In other words, the question was whether the defendant may offer

---

[3] Letter from Belgion to Devlin, 5 March 1960, Churchill Archives Centre, Churchill College, University of Cambridge.

[4] Letter from Devlin to Belgion, 7 March 1960, Churchill Archives Centre, Churchill College, University of Cambridge.

[5] Rommel was alleged to have participated in a plot to assassinate Hitler.

in mitigation of damages evidence which bears upon the plaintiff's disposition, as distinct from his reputation.

Patrick wrote a lengthy but skilful judgment with which Lord Justice Ormerod agreed.[6] He pointed out that there is always to be drawn a distinction between bad character in the sense of the reputation a person bears, on the one hand, and the person's personal qualities or the disposition he may possess, on the other. Patrick stated clearly and correctly that the inquiry in any libel trial relevantly must be limited to that person's general reputation. However the defendant had under the guise of asserting bad reputation, pleaded matters which comprised specific instances which the defendant alleged arose out of the same libel, and which if true negated any harm the person may have suffered. Patrick thought the pleading should in part be struck out, because the matter the defendant sought to rely upon did not prove bad reputation generally. Although a pleading point, the case was of fundamental importance to the law of libel.

The matter, however, did not end there. It went to the House of Lords. Unanimously, their Lordships upheld Patrick.[7] Each judge wrote a somewhat lengthy endorsement of his reasoning. Their Lordships had been persuaded to give leave on the basis of an argument that in effect the current state of the law operated unjustly in favour of plaintiffs. After three days of argument Viscount Simonds, Lord Radcliffe, Denning, Lord Morris of Borth-y-Gest and Lord Guest declined to reconsider the rule. Denning decided to show off by commencing his analysis with a form of writ which first appeared in the Year Books of 1536.[8] But the decision was a ringing endorsement of Patrick's judgment in every sense of the word.

Towards the middle of the year Patrick sat on a criminal appeal which concerned the important question of when an injunction might be granted to restrain the commission of a criminal offence.[9] For a judge who had little experience in criminal law as a barrister, he had developed not only a fascination for the area but displayed a gift for its understanding and application. Patrick sat with Lord Justices Sellers and Pearce. Although Patrick agreed with both, Sellers relied upon a trial judgment of Patrick's to arrive at the result. The case is notable for one other reason. Rose Heilbron appeared for the unsuccessful respondent. She was the first woman to be made King's Counsel in 1949 at the age of 34, beating even Patrick's record. After she took silk Patrick had warmly welcomed her when sitting at the Liverpool Assizes in 1949. He thereafter became something of a mentor for Heilbron.[10]

---

[6] [1961] AC 1090 at 1098–1105.

[7] *Plato Films v Speidel* [1961] AC 1090–1150.

[8] *Plato Films v Speidel* [1961] AC 1090 at 1133 (Denning LJ).

[9] *Attorney-General v Harris* [1961] 1 QB 74 at 79.

[10] Hilary Heilbron, *Rose Heilbron, The Story of England's First Woman Queen's Counsel and Judge* (Oxford, Hart Publishing, 2012), pp 68 and 137.

Madeleine wrote to Acheson on 22 June in response to a short note from him:[11]

> I think his new job taken as you surmise with misgiving, has taken up a lot of energy – he was tired after Nyasaland and all anyway. But I think it is a success. I am relieved for I was going to be blamed if he hated it, for once in our joint lives I definitely said something on his affairs I mean you will have noticed I am not habitually silent! and said I thought he should go to the Court of Appeal. I am glad you are pleased.

Acheson responded in typically chatty fashion, updating Madeleine on all the American political news including the emergence of potential rivals Kennedy and Nixon.[12]

A few months later on 11 August, Patrick finally wrote to Acheson. Amongst other things he said:[13]

> I am very conscious that I should have been writing to you long ago. I have – by judicial standards been quite overworked and have been slightly below par and told to take a good holiday which I am now doing so do not have to stuff letters in at the tail end of a day's work which never makes for happy writing … I wish I could have seen you both to and from Chicago at Christmas. But in end it boiled down to a five day affair. Madeleine has probably told you that my brother came home at Christmas to have a serious operation and I did want to leave until he was out of danger. (She has been nursing him devotedly and we have just last week returned him to the Jesuits looking as well as ever). The thing was bedevilled by the transfer to the Court of Appeal which I had to decide under some difficulties. There were arguments for and against and it was really Madeleine who cast the die. I like very much work of a trial judge and enjoy circuit as a pleasant variety of it, but circuit is no fun for her. The House of Lords has the advantage in that it sits only four days a week. I don't think it means any less work but the advantage for me it is three days instead of two down here and the light of my life is here and not London. I was told secretly by Rab Butler who knows all that goes on in the governing sphere that I was considered for a 'double remove' but they decided on John Morris on grounds of seniority. Perhaps also this may be an unworthy gloss, the Nyasaland Report had a little to do with it. It might shock the stouter spirits in the Tory party if the mentally dishonest, – even though the recent dealings with Dr Banda might suggest that the dishonesty was not as grave as was first feared, – went forward more than a pace at a time.

> But before I took the step I cleared the prospects with the Lord Chancellor who is a good friend.[14] He told me confidentially that I might expect the next common-law vacancy in the Lords. A hale 79[15] and a rather frailer 72[16] control the reversion; both are thought to be good for a couple of years at least.

---

[11] Letter from Madeleine Devlin to Acheson, 22 June 1960, Manuscripts and Archives, Yale University Library, Dean Acheson Papers, folder 97.

[12] Letter from Acheson to Madeleine Devlin, undated copy of handwritten note, Manuscripts and Archives, Yale University Library, Dean Acheson Papers, folder 97.

[13] Letter from Devlin to Acheson, 11 August 1960, Manuscripts and Archives, Yale University Library, Dean Acheson Papers, folder 97.

[14] Lord Kilmuir.

[15] Viscount Simonds.

[16] Lord Cohen.

But I don't know how long I shall last myself. In three years from now I shall have completed the customary judicial span of fifteen years and can go on half-pay. I shall be 57 and then still young enough, I think to do something else. I should like a quarter-job to add to my half pay – one that might make it possible for me to spend most of my time here and write. I do not find appellate congenial and cannot contemplate another 20 or 25 years of it. Our methods are so tedious compared with yours. We spend hours sitting in Court listening to evidence, documents and law reports being mumbled at a pace that suits the very slowest mind and leaves anybody who is not ritualistically disposed with eternities that decorum forbids him to occupy. And the content of the appellate work is becoming more and more the puzzle of the statute that must be made to fit grammatically with only a limited regard for the good that it is supposed to achieve. That is even more so in H. of L. where access is restricted than in the C. of A. Very different in the Supreme Court. There the art of judicial law making is still one of the humanities, – architecture as compared with engineering. But all this is very nebulous. I have not said a word about it to anybody, not more than a rumble to Madeleine, – and even quite frightened with it when I am confronted with it in print. But all the same I think I shall when the time comes.

Patrick went on to speak about the upcoming Presidential election in the United States and then provide some news about an imminent family wedding.

The letter is insightful and explicable at the same time. First it shows the depth of his friendship with Acheson – although it must be said confession to a third party can often be easier than to a relative. Secondly, Patrick had had a difficult year in 1959. It had been an emotional rollercoaster ending with the deep concern for his brother's health. He was physically and mentally depleted. But what is most interesting is that his distaste for appellate work had confronted him so soon after taking the job.

For Patrick the majority of 1960 was almost entirely consumed in deciding cases in the Court of Appeal, admittedly across a wide range of areas. Although rarely idle, he at least tried for a time to persuade himself he was enjoying the work. The reality was something different.

A little later in the year, however, Patrick accepted an invitation to deliver the Lloyd Roberts Lecture. Dr David Lloyd Roberts was a prominent Manchester physician of the nineteenth century who left a bequest to several institutions. The bequest had been endowed since 1920. Unsurprisingly Patrick chose as the title 'Medicine and the Law'. Somewhat provocatively he commenced:[17]

It is very magnanimous of medical men to honour a lawyer in the way you are honouring me today by inviting me to deliver the Lloyd Roberts lecture. For the law does not treat medicine very well. I do not mean that it has any prejudice against doctors, but it does nothing to help them with the special problems of their calling. Commerce has always been the pet of the English common law. The law merchant as it is called took over the customs of merchants and the rules they made for their

---

[17] The Lloyd Roberts Lecture 1960, delivered before the Medical Society of London, Reproduced in Patrick Devlin, *Samples of Lawmaking* (Oxford, Oxford University Press, 1962), p 83.

markets and made them almost as they stood. Such favouritism is no doubt another proof that the English are but a nation of shopkeepers. But it is fair to remember that in the centuries when the common law was in the making, medical men were of little account in the community. The apothecary and the leech were not socially esteemed and medicine had still to become a learned profession.

In the balance of the paper, prepared largely for a lay audience, he discussed questions of informed consent. But he also discussed the ultimate aim of the administration of treatment, namely the restoration of health. Reverting to the Adams trial he told the audience that a doctor was entitled to do all that was necessary to relieve pain and suffering, even if the measures he takes may incidentally shorten life. Then with a particularly sharp pencil, he jabbed at Manningham-Buller by telling his audience that what he had just said was the direction he had given the jury in the Adams trial, which the 'Attorney-General on behalf of the Crown' did not challenge.[18] Grateful relief and rapturous applause from the audience.

In November and December 1960 Patrick participated in yet another important libel appeal. He sat with Lord Justices Holroyd Pearce and Sellers. The Town Clerk of Manchester brought a libel action against a newspaper, its editor and a journalist in respect of two articles. The articles had been prompted by the passage through Parliament of the Manchester Corporation Act 1958, which had in turn provoked public discussion about Council affairs and allegedly fraudulent activity in connection with the acquisition of a cemetery. The real issue on the appeal was whether damages awarded to a plaintiff for a libel should be reduced if the same accusations had been published previously to or contemporaneously with the libel by another party but in a privileged form.[19] By coincidence, counsel for the plaintiff was Geoffrey Lawrence QC, who had appeared for Bodkin Adams. Each judge wrote somewhat lengthy judgments. Each decided in favour of the plaintiff and indeed increased the damages from £1,100 to £4,000 and rejected the defendant's arguments on mitigation. The House of Lords upheld the Court of Appeal.[20]

As part of his extra-curial interests, Patrick had remained involved with the International Commission of Jurists and was invited to attend a conference in Nigeria on the Rule of Law between 3 and 7 January 1961.[21] He enjoyed very much and indeed encouraged such invitations. He was probably more widely travelled than any other English judge of his generation. Apart from the stimulation, these international conferences had the tendency to make him restless and brought about a feeling that the role of the judge, although important, could be seen as somewhat parochial. But there would always be time for another lecture.

---

[18] Ibid, pp 94–95.
[19] *Dingle v Associated Newspapers* [1961] 2 QB 162.
[20] *Dingle v Associated Newspapers* [1964] AC 371.
[21] The African Congress on the Rule of Law, Lagos, Nigeria, 3–7 January 1961, International Commission of Jurists, p 24.

On 20 January Kennedy was sworn in as the 35th President of the United States of America claiming an extremely narrow victory over Richard Nixon. That was, however, a pleasing outcome for the likes of Acheson, a staunch Democrat. Acheson and Kennedy knew each other well. Although they had differences, they admired each other.

In March 1961, Patrick had managed to become the President of the Holdsworth Club. He gave his Presidential address entitled 'Morals and the Quasi-Criminal Law and the Law of Tort' on 17 March.[22] This was a club formed to stimulate the law students of the University of Birmingham. It had been founded in 1927. Those who had preceded Patrick as President included Jowitt, its first, Goodhart, Radcliffe, Birkett, and Kilmuir.

Patrick had, since his controversy with Hart in 1959, been ruminating and working on a follow up to his Maccabaean Lecture as an extension of his thinking and a riposte to Hart. The Presidential Address provided an opportunity for this.

Hart in the meantime had gazumped Patrick with the publication in the February of that year with his magisterial *The Concept of Law*.[23] Whatever the result in the end of the controversy, Hart's work was described by Brian Simpson as the most successful work on analytical jurisprudence ever to appear in the common law world.[24] It touched much more general philosophical issues and is unlikely to have been provoked by Patrick. It consisted of ideas Hart had been lecturing on since 1952. However, Hart's *Law, Liberty and Morality* published in 1963, was a direct response to Patrick's Maccabaean lecture.[25]

Geoffrey Lawrence QC had appeared before Patrick the year before in the Court of Appeal. Since the Adams case he had unsurprisingly become very much in demand as counsel. He had also been since 1960 Chairman of the Bar Council. Patrick does not seem to have been a particular friend of Lawrence. But for some unexplained reason he invited Lawrence QC to dinner at the Savoy Grill on Wednesday 26 July.[26] It is a little hard to imagine that at that point he was planning the book he wrote more than 20 years later about the trial. But what is even stranger is he took a detailed note of their discussion. It was still with his papers when he died. Two members of the legal profession having a casual dinner, at a smart restaurant, enjoying the odd glass of something pleasant and gossiping for hours is not an unknown phenomenon. As a result of the expert cross-examination by Patrick, Lawrence QC told Patrick some rather extraordinary things. In particular he said that Adams was thoroughly

---

[22] Reproduced in Patrick Devlin, *The Enforcement of Morals, Maccabaean Lecture in Jurisprudence of the British Academy 1959* (Oxford, Oxford University Press, 1965), pp 26–43.

[23] HLA Hart, *The Concept of Law* (Oxford, Oxford University Press, 1961).

[24] AW Brian Simpson, *Reflections on the Concept of Law* (Oxford, Oxford University Press, 2011), p 1.

[25] HLA Hart, *Law, Liberty and Morality* (Oxford, Oxford University Press, 1963), preface.

[26] Handwritten diary note by Devlin, 26 July 1961, prepared at some point presumably after the dinner at the Savoy Grill on that date.

dislikeable, greedy, pigheaded, loquacious and to boot dishonest. Lawrence QC had, however, been totally convinced of his client's innocence and believed in British justice. The reason why Lawrence QC did not call him as a witness was that he thought his dishonesty would be exposed. For example, he had been charging Mrs Morrell for visits he did not make and possibly also charging her for drugs that had not been administered. Lawrence QC was quite confident that there was no evidence an overdose was given. On parting, Lawrence QC told Patrick that Adams had provided not a word, a note or a letter of thanks. What motivated Patrick is intriguing. Was he worried perhaps that a guilty man had gone free? He could not have expected Lawrence QC to open up about the matter as he did, but he would have been comforted that although Lawrence QC thought him to be dishonest in certain respects, he obviously believed his client was innocent. Patrick never spoke about the dinner to anyone as far can be told.

The judicial appellate diet served up to Patrick in 1961 was extremely varied: libel, malicious prosecution, contempt, rating and negligence, to mention but a few areas. Patrick liked the then Chief Justice, Lord Parker, but he did not enjoy the same type of relationship he had shared with Goddard. Parker respected Patrick and would sit him on difficult cases knowing that the judgment that would be produced would be beautifully constructed, with the very first sentence or two pithily setting the scene. The stage set, Patrick would then display a mastery of the law, powerfully persuasive and more often than not plainly correct. It was for this reason that he had such an impact on his judicial colleagues.

But his future was a subject of constant rumination. He had been invited to deliver the Owen J Roberts lecture in Philadelphia in September.[27] Roberts had been the Dean of the Law Faculty at the University of Pennsylvania. The lecture had been delivered each year since 1956. The first one had been given by Frankfurter, the second by Goodhart. In any event the invitation prompted Patrick to write to Acheson on 4 August from West Wick:[28]

> My immediate task, which I postpone from day to day, is the preparation of a suitable lecture for Philadelphia. I have idled away nearly a week since I got down here last Friday, living very pleasantly and wondering whether when I think myself hard at work I am not really wasting time by spending it on insignificant objects. One of the things I want to ask you when we meet is whether you think a man in his fifties can safely abandon the stimulus of regular employment. Looking back on the last eight years, would you have been happier if you had been in office? Well, no: that alters the question, because yours was a great office and what you were doing was not primarily for your own satisfaction. But have you missed the discipline? Do you think a man

---

[27] Patrick Devlin, 'Law, Democracy and Morality', the *Owen J. Roberts Memorial Lecture*, delivered on 28 September 1961, under the auspices of the Pennsylvania Chapter of the Order of the Coif and the University of Pennsylvania Law School, printed in (1961) 110 *University of Pennsylvania Law Review* 635.

[28] Letter from Devlin to Acheson, 4 August 1961, Manuscripts and Archives, Yale University Library, Dean Acheson Papers, folder 97.

who makes himself his own master will find that he has a disgruntled time killer for his servant? Just now the thought of writing no more judgments on piffling technicalities fills me with joy and the long vacation seems all too short. I don't in the least mind writing a lecture. I shan't write it from 10.30 to 4.15 in an insanitary morgue designed by an architect whom even the Victorians thought crazy and I shan't write it after listening to the subject being masticated and gurgitated for nine or ten days at the Bar. A week's holiday is enough but freedom of time could be perpetual ...

Acheson responded with some suggestions, but Patrick remained somewhat despondent and replied on 10 September:[29]

I very much enjoyed your letter from Edgartown and your preliminary observations on the mechanics of successful retirement. I have another two years at least in which to test the ground and shall make good use of them on the lines you suggest. Indeed I suppose I test it every year for a sixth of the year – the long vacation, – quite a good fraction for a sample; and this year as always the time's slithering before I have grasped what is happening and is over before I have begun to feel even a premonition of a yearning for the harness.

Notwithstanding the black clouds, after the letter was posted Patrick got back to lecture writing. It was again on a familiar theme and was entitled 'Democracy and Morality'.[30] Patrick delivered it in Philadelphia on 28 September. This was the first time he had directly and perhaps publicly responded in substance to Hart. First Patrick amplified his theme from the Maccabaean Lecture. He persisted in the arbiter of moral standards being the juror – the reasonable or right-minded man or woman who is a person who has a 'sort of veto upon the enforcement of morals'. However, he explicitly rejected Hart's criticisms as outlined in his article in the *Listener*. In doing so Patrick spent much time defending the majority decision of the House of Lords in *Shaw v Director of Public Prosecutions*,[31] which recognised an offence of conspiracy to corrupt public morals, as a rejection of the teaching of Mill and a ringing endorsement of his theory. The trip to Pennsylvania has a particularly sombre note about it. Before he left, Patrick's brother Christopher had become seriously ill again. This failing health had been obvious since about August. Christopher's new book *Poor Kit Smart* had been published, again to acclaim.[32] By this stage, Madeleine was his full-time carer.[33] West Wick had been rearranged so that he could say mass each day. Patrick had arrived home from the United States just in time to be with his brother before he died around midnight on 5 October. He was 54. The death affected the whole family deeply. Their spiritual leader was gone.

---

[29] Letter from Acheson to Devlin, 10 September 1961, Manuscripts and Archives, Yale University Library, Dean Acheson Papers, folder 97.

[30] Patrick Devlin, 'Democracy and Morality' (1961) 110 *University of Pennsylvania Law Review* 635, 640.

[31] *Shaw v Director of Public Prosecutions* [1962] AC 220.

[32] Christopher Devlin, *Poor Kit Smart* (London, Rupert Hart-Davis Ltd, 1961).

[33] Madeleine Devlin, *Christopher Devlin, a Biography* (London, Macmillan, 1970), pp 208–12.

Sometime well prior to 5 October events were, however, unfolding in the Lord Chancellor's office. Lord Tucker, who had been a member of the House of Lords since 1950, resigned. He had given Kilmuir the customary warning. He had originally sat in the King's Bench Division and had been part of the majority in *Shaw's case*. He was regarded as workmanlike but he had a particular interest in criminal law. Patrick was in the United States in company with Acheson when Kilmuir made contact. Patrick spoke to Madeleine first but he clearly had to accept. Further, the appointment provided the possibility of sorting things out professionally and personally for him. Patrick made contact with Kilmuir from the United States. *The Times* announced the appointment on 29 September.[34]

The article was flattering to say the least, describing Patrick as having shown his intellectual strength since his initial appointment. After describing recent criticism of the House of Lords, the author wrote 'Lord Justice Devlin with his dedication to maintaining a proper relationship between law and morality can now have a deep influence on the development of the law of crime – and other branches of Jurisprudence too.'

Patrick had left the Unites States for London on 3 October. Acheson, his wife Alice and Frankfurter sent a cable on 4 October to Patrick for his arrival:[35] 'We are thinking of you with pride, affection and not a little touch of sympathy.' Christopher's funeral took place on 9 October.[36] On 11 October Patrick was appointed a Lord of Appeal in Ordinary.[37]

Patrick thought very differently from his brethren in many ways. He was creative but highly complex. Although a conservative thinker to a point, he was constantly looking for innovation and elucidation of principle. In a fascinating exercise, Professor Alan Paterson for his book on the House of Lords, *The Law Lords*, interviewed many current and retired judges.[38] Some refused to speak to him. Viscount Dilhorne was one who refused.[39] Patrick, however, did not.[40] What emerged says little about ability and style. Those matters are revealed in the respective judgments. But the book provided a portrait of how each judge saw himself. Patrick indicated for example, that he never read the printed Case. His reason was that all of the material was repeated in oral argument.[41] This became an ongoing problem as it led to enormous inefficiencies. The practice of reading the materials *in extenso* had the obvious effect of blowing out

---

[34] 'Sir Patrick Devlin, a Lord of Appeal in Ordinary', *The Times*, 29 September 1961.

[35] Night cable by phone to Western Union from Acheson to Devlin, 3 October 1961, Manuscripts and Archives, Yale University Library, Dean Acheson Papers, folder 97.

[36] Christopher Devlin was buried in the Cemetery at Heythrop College, London, on 9 October 1961. On 2 December there was a requiem mass on Farm Street celebrated by Father MC D'Arcy, 'at which Lord Devlin and members of the family, a large number of friends and admirers were present'. See his obituary, published in 'Letters and Notices' (1961) 67 *The Month*, pp 59–69.

[37] *All England Law Reports*, 9 January 1962.

[38] Alan Paterson, *The Law Lords* (London, Macmillan Press, 1982), p 5.

[39] Ibid, p 5.

[40] Ibid, p 5.

[41] Ibid, p 36.

the hearing time and increasing costs. But it was the more senior judges like Radcliffe, Reid and Denning who adhered to the practice and were resistant to change. Radcliffe, for example, advanced the rationale of wanting to keep an entirely open mind. As against that group Patrick had no prospect of having the procedure changed. That also meant that very little meaningful dialogue took place between the Law Lords before the case was heard. It certainly excluded any preliminary conclusions being reached.

A conference would take place routinely afterwards where views would be exchanged. Patrick did not try to influence his colleagues but would speak if a colleague was in doubt or perhaps, in his view, wrong. He had no qualms about joint judgments but he did like to write. Patrick told Paterson that he rarely, if ever, changed his mind after hearing the case.[42]

Lord Reid sat on the House of Lords for 26 years and kept all 104 of his judicial notebooks. Amongst other things these notebooks recorded discussions at conferences which took place between the judges. According to Professor Paterson, the notebooks disclose that in a significant number of cases there was a change of vote between the initial conference and the handing down of the judgments. In particular in *Rookes v Barnard* after the initial hearing Patrick was in a minority of one (or possibly two) favouring the appellant. After a second conference and a reconvened hearing Patrick won them all around.[43] Patrick said to Professor Paterson in his interview that Lord Reid told Patrick he did not want to write on the question of exemplary damages and suggested he would consider what Patrick had to say about it and see if he agreed with him. In due course this in fact occurred.

Professor Paterson also observes that in the period 1962–66 there were numerous instances of judicial law-making. Patrick played a significant role in three of the cases Professor Paterson mentions; *Hedley Byrne v Heller*, *Ridge v Baldwin*, and *Rookes v Barnard*.[44] Each of those cases is, on any view, a legal milestone of one sort or another.

On 20 October 1961 Madeleine wrote to Acheson:[45]

> Forgive me my dear Dean for not answering your letter sooner. It gave me the greatest possible pleasure to have you describe Patrick's reactions. I had a second agitated letter from him about the loss of his clerk! It is a very serious matter! And there is a good deal of chaos with all the books and papers moving by degrees from the courts to home – goodness knows where they are going. We need about eighty feet of shelves and I can't imagine where we will find room for that. You know much as I always wanted Patrick to be a Lord of Appeal I hadn't appreciated that it meant joining a rather exclusive club or that he would have a platform on which to speak.

---

[42] Ibid, p 37.

[43] Alan Paterson, *Final Judgment, the Last Law Lords and the Supreme Court* (Oxford, Hart Publishing, 2013), pp 178–79.

[44] Ibid, pp 264–65. *Hedley Byrne & Co Ltd v Heller & Partners Ltd* [1964] AC 465; *Ridge v Baldwin* [1964] AC 40; *Rookes v Barnard* [1964] AC 1129.

[45] Letter from Madeleine Devlin to Acheson, 20 October 1961, Manuscripts and Archives, Yale University Library, Dean Acheson Papers, folder 97.

Though I believe only on non-political matters. P says the excitement and pleasure of the House over Lord Avon's[46] (what a name to choose!) was thrilling and great fun. We had the great introduction ceremony yesterday – quite fantastic but really rather lovely.

Patrick adored his time with you and Alice. I have a great longing to see all as he has described and of course even more to see you both. Are you coming over here soon, I hope sooner than we will be able to leave here. Please visit us even if it is the Hague you are going to really. My lovely task ended gaily and with glory – shortly after Patrick's return – on the 5th, Christopher was wonderful – I am so certain that he is now our advocate in heaven, that I oughtn't to cry at all – still he and Patrick were always very close – and we do miss him horribly. I am glad that you like the little book so much. I haven't touched his papers yet but hope to find something to be published amongst them.

Moving to entirely new premises and clearing out papers is liberating for anyone. In Patrick's case the excitement of the appointment and the challenges ahead came as a welcome distraction, especially given his brother's death. The prospect of more time at West Wick and with Madeleine and the family more generally was a bonus.

Patrick was the youngest of the judges in the House of Lords by some years. He greatly admired most of his new colleagues, particularly Reid. He regarded Reid as an outstanding intellect and said he 'in the last decade has more than any other, shaped the law of Britain'.[47]

Hardly had he moved in to his new chambers when on 30 October, in a relaxed and especially playful mood, he wrote a long and insightful eight-page letter to Acheson.[48] Behind its mocking and self-indulgent tone lay a number of serious matters of substance. He complained rightly about sharing a room with another Law Lord, sharing office equipment, a secretary and the rather detailed protocol expected of members of the House of Lords. He also pointed out the lack of library facilities. Indeed he complained that the whole administrative structure was antiquated. He concluded somewhat scornfully:

> All this is I think, a residue of the notion that decisions in matters of public importance are in the last resort best left to amateurs. Anything in the nature of a special working-place or of professional facilities would tend to corrupt their amateur status.

As might be expected, Patrick had a busy start. His first case would appear to have been on 25 October in an appeal to the Privy Council from the Supreme Court of the Federation of Malaya on 25 October. He sat with Lord Denning and Mr de Silva (a former Solicitor-General from then Ceylon). Patrick wrote the judgment which was delivered on 4 December.[49]

---

[46] Former Prime Minister Anthony Eden. Entered the House of Lords July 1961.

[47] Email from Timothy Devlin to the Author, 4 August 2015.

[48] Letter from Devlin to Acheson, 30 October 1961, Manuscripts and Archives, Yale University Library, Dean Acheson Papers, folder 97.

[49] *A.R.P.L. Palaniappa Chettiar v P.L.A.R. Arunasalam Chettiar* [1962] AC 294 (PC).

In November he sat on two appeals: one to the House of Lords (on patents);[50] and as a member of the Privy Council in an appeal from the Supreme Court of New Zealand (on tax).[51] The next year was equally as busy.

In March 1962 he found the time to continue to explore his theme of law and morals with a lecture at the Queen's University of Belfast, entitled 'Morals and the Law of Contract'.[52] In the lecture he travelled attractively as always through illegality, fiduciary obligations and estoppel. He was, however, resigned to the fact that the

> English law of contract is then a hotch-potch of the common law, equity and statute. Taken as a whole it is biased in favour of commerce rather than morality. It should be easy to devise a workable system that goes further than the English law does in the promotion of good faith and fair dealing.

This was a novel approach. But as time has shown, it has been a difficult area in which to devise a workable formula for everyday use.

In early March Patrick also became the President of the British component association of the Comité Maritime.[53] He had always been interested in maritime work of all kinds and this would continue to provide him with an ongoing interest. In his letter to Acheson dated 30 March he announced his ascension and described his predecessor as an Admiralty judge 'who knew no law and decided everything, frequently correctly, on common sense principles' and who 'really believed Continentals were funny people but quite alright when properly handled'. In the same letter he announced that 'Raymond Evershed and Tom Denning change places', explaining Denning leaving the Lords and becoming Master of the Rolls in place of Evershed, who was elevated to the Lords.[54] Denning much preferred the Court of Appeal where he could constitute courts as he pleased. He would serve twenty years in the role.

When Patrick wrote to Evershed on 26 March congratulating him he could not help returning to his perpetual complaints about the 'straitened circumstances' and the 'insufficient copies' of law reports in the Lords.[55]

On 21 May Patrick wrote a gossipy letter to Frankfurter about the various judicial machinations:[56]

> Alice and Dean spent a very happy week-end with us in the country and they seem also to have spent a very busy time in London. Dean talked with so many people that

[50] *AMP Inc v Hellerman Ltd* [1962] 1 WLR 241 (HL).

[51] *AMP Mutual Providence Society v Commissioner of Inland Review* [1962] AC 135 (PC).

[52] 'Morals and the Law of Contract', a lecture delivered at the Queen's University of Belfast, 2 March 1962, reproduced in Patrick Devlin, *The Enforcement of Morals, Maccabaean Lecture in Jurisprudence of the British Academy 1959* (Oxford, Oxford University Press, 1965), pp 44–61.

[53] Letter from Devlin to Acheson, 30 March 1962, Manuscripts and Archives, Yale University Library, Dean Acheson Papers, folder 97.

[54] Ibid.

[55] Handwritten letter from Devlin to Evershed, 26 March 1962, Devlin Correspondence file.

[56] Letter from Devlin to Frankfurter, 21 May 1962, Howard Gotlieb Archival Research Center Collection, Boston University.

he will return full of information for you on every sort of topic. But he told me before they left for Stockholm that you wanted a satisfactory explanation of the recent judicial changes here. So I shall do my best to supply you with one.

Raymond Evershed, as you know, had really been overworking himself as Master of the Rolls. Apart from the job itself, which is a hard one, he could not resist going everywhere he was asked to go; and of course the invitations were innumerable. The modern solution seems to be for the M.R. to seek repose in the Lords. Wright went from the Lords to become M.R., so providing a precedent for Denning, – and then after his stint went back to the Lords again. Wilfrid Greene went from M.R. to the Lords, but only for a short time for he was then a sick man.

Gavin Simonds always indicated that he would go when he was 80 though I don't think he reached a firm decision until just before. So it was generally expected that Raymond would have to wait for a vacancy until Gavin made one. He could not take the one that I got because that was common law. And I suppose for the same reason they could not do a straight exchange with Tom Denning.

I think that Tom will do the job extremely well and much on the same lines as Raymond. There is no one else who could or would have done that. Fortunately the Attorney-General did not want it: he intends to be Lord Chancellor. Tom himself was not over-enthusiastic about it. Indeed the situation was curious.

Now that the Lord Chancellor has become almost exclusively a political and administrative post, the effective president of the highest court is the senior law lord. In this Scott Reid has now succeeded Gavin. An ex-Lord Chancellor would have the right to precede him when he sat, but the Ex can sit only on the invitation of the ruling Ld. Ch. I am not quite sure about that. But anyway Gavin has no intention of sitting regularly; and if David Kilmuir ever retires, I am sure that he will still busy himself with politics.

Scott Reid is still very good. But he has had two serious operations in the last few years and it is thought that he will not stay on for more than a year or two. The next in succession is Radcliffe. He says firmly that he will go as soon as his fifteen years, the pension qualifying period, is up. That will be in 1964. Tom came next. So that he had the expectation of presiding in the Lords quite soon and for a very long time.

BUT when a peer is appointed a Lord of Appeal he takes his seniority not from the date of his appointment but from the dignity and date of his peerage. (A judicial duke would have no chance of promotion because he would swamp everybody). And if Tom had remained, Raymond would have come in just ahead of him. So bang went Tom's chances, for they are about the same age. And Tom likes presiding very much; and of course he can now preside in the Court of Appeal to his heart's content.

For Tom it is an odd step in an odd career. Most surprisingly he was not an effective advocate, taking all points, good and bad, and cut no figure at the Bar. When in 1944 Simon decided to enlarge the divorce judiciary and knew that he would have to recruit from the common law Bar and could probably not attract the highest, he offered a place to Tom who had impressed him doing a poor person's case in the House of Lords. It at once became apparent that Tom was outstanding as a judge and that he could not be left in divorce; and he was speedily moved to the K.B.

A commission had just reported that the only way of coping with the flood of divorce was to allow it to be done in the county courts. This created great indignation because it was said to belittle the marriage bond. So Tom was made chairman of another commission, which stressed the great importance of trying divorce in the High Court. Confronted with the hard fact that there was no one to try it except the C.C. judges, they found that the solution in divesting the judge pro. tem. of his county court juris- diction and elevating him ad hoc to the High Court as a "Commissioner". So now the county court judge retires and changes his robe and is (I suppose; I've never been there) addressed as My Lord instead of Your Honour and this makes clear to every- one in court the true significance of the marriage vow.

Attlee, who was then Prime Minister, was much impressed with this achievement. It led to the only example I know of in modern times of the P.M. exercising his judicial patronage otherwise than for the purpose of rewarding a politician. The P.M., as you know, has all judicial appointments of the rank of Lord Justice and upwards. In October 1948 there were two vacancies in the Court of Appeal and the Lord Chancellor, Jowitt, sent two recommendations to the P.M. Attlee sent back word that he wanted Denning to have one of the places. Jowitt consulted the M.R. and others, stood firm, would not make the recommendation, said that Denning was too young, inexperienced, etc. For some days there was deadlock, which left me rather in the air as I had been told that I was to have one of the K.B. vacancies.

Then they thought they might anyway offer a place to the Ld. Ch.'s first choice, Lynskey, which they did and he turned it down. It would have been very awkward for Jowitt to produce a third name and dig in his toes about it and he gave in. I dare- say Tom would have remained in the Ct. of App. but for Kilmuir. Simonds would never have promoted him. Of course Tom is very unorthodox and frequently seems to regard legal principles as a means to an end. But a very little of that sort of thing is not bad for the law of England and Tom has great qualities to go with it. It is greatly to Kilmuir's credit, for he after all is a traditionalist, that he should perceive and accept that.

As for the other appointments, Jack Simon should be first class as Pres. of the Divorce Division. He is worth something much better. But I do not think he was very happy as Solicitor-General working with Reggie M.-B. as A-G and I believe he was much pressed to take the job, for which it would be difficult to find anyone of any eminence.

Denning is succeeded in the Lords by Edward Pearce. He and I were appointed to the Bench on the same day, he going to Divorce and I to the K.B. He is a really nice and delightful man of no particular ability, I was surprised when he was made a judge, astonished when he was moved to the K.B., flabbergasted when he was appointed to the C.A. and it never so much as crossed my mind that he would be considered for the Lords. But as I have now been proved wrong at all these four stages you will understand that he must be highly esteemed in quarters that matter and you would do much better to accept their valuation.

Gavin Simonds is one of the most charming and likeable men I have ever met but of iron rigidity. I shall always be proud that I have sat with him in the Lords but it was time that he went. We dined with him last week. He told me that in his 18 years in the Lords, – quite Frankfurterian in length, but not quite, – he has sat with 26 law lords. He said that if he had to pick four of them to make up the ideal team of five to sit with, he would choose Russell of Killowen easily first, then Simon, Normand and Radcliffe.

The survivors of the 26 are giving him a dinner at Brooks' the day after to-morrow. We hoped that old Robert Wright would be there, but he wrote and excused himself, though at 93 he still seems spry.

However, domestic political turmoil arose out of the blue in the middle of 1962, which would have a profound impact not only on Patrick but his judicial colleagues as well. On 13 July, the Prime Minister, for reasons which have arguably never been made entirely clear, sacked one third of his Cabinet.[57] Flagging polls and negative results in by-elections, together with difficult economic times are some of the reasons suggested. To the chagrin no doubt of Patrick and certainly some of his judicial colleagues, Kilmuir was sacked as Lord Chancellor and Manningham-Buller was appointed in his stead. One piece of good news for Patrick was that although Macmillan and Rab Butler were not on good terms, Butler survived. Macmillan was highly suspicious of Butler. Nonetheless he assisted Macmillan in the reshuffle, which helped cement his position. Manningham-Buller on the other hand, received the Great Seal on 16 July and on 17 July was sworn in before the Master of the Rolls. By the afternoon he had become 'Baron Dilhorne of Towcester in our County of Northampton'.

At about the same time Patrick's *Samples of Lawmaking* was published. It was a collection of lectures he had given over the previous 10 years. He sent a copy to historian Veronica Wedgwood (an old friend of Madeleine's and a noted historian and biographer) with an inscription which read:[58]

> This will be of limited interest to you and anyway you will find it trivial. So I am sending it to you only so as to express my admiration for all that I have read of yours, especially your second 'Strafford'[59] which has given more pleasure than anything I have read for a long time.

In the Preface he had stated:[60]

> Publishers, like prisoners before the Evidence Act 1898, cannot give evidence in their own defence. Demarcation in the 'book industry' inexorably ordains as their sole duty the provisions of paper and print; they must not wield the pen. May they and he be sufficiently rewarded – they by making enormous profits out of this book from the pockets of generations yet unborn; and Dr Goodhart by the continuance of that affection, gratitude and admiration which I have had for him always since the days when he first taught me law.

---

[57] Alistair Horne, *Macmillan, 1957–1986, Volume II of the Official Biography* (London, Macmillan, 1989), 'Night of the Long Knives (1962)', pp 159, 339–52, 529 and 620. See also, DR Thorpe, *Supermac, the Life of Harold Macmillan* (London, Chatto & Windus, 2010), 'Searching for a Role 1961–1962', 499 at pp 518, 519–25 and 'Guided Democracy October 1963', 551 at p 564.

[58] Patrick Devlin, *Samples of Lawmaking* (Oxford, Oxford University Press, 1962), author's copy, inscription on first page from Devlin to Wedgewood.

[59] CV Wedgwood, *Thomas Wentworth, First Earl of Strafford, 1593–1641: A Revaluation* (London, Jonathan Cape, 1961).

[60] *Samples of Lawmaking*, preface, p 1.

On 20 July he sent a copy of the book to Goodhart. The two had swapped ideas for the future structure of the Law Reform Committee but along the way Patrick gave Dilhorne a little slap:[61] 'We shall have to see whether the new Lord Chancellor is at all interested in such ideas. On the face of it, it looks unlikely; but I should not rule out that we may be in for a surprise.'

But in August came some distressing news. Acheson informed Patrick that Frankfurter, who had had a stroke earlier in the year, would have to retire. President Kennedy had paid Frankfurter a visit to cheer him up. Acheson told Patrick that retirement was necessary for Frankfurter's wellbeing.[62] By return Patrick told Acheson he and Madeleine would be off to Australia after Christmas for a conference.[63] Frankfurter retired in late August. In the meantime Acheson, however, warned:[64]

> In Australia the great compensation and reward will be Owen Dixon. You must cling to him. He is really your dish of tea. As for the others you must insist on a siesta on the ground that you have become dependent on your hours of rest on the bench. The Australians are cursed with unflagging energy and not much to do with it except to exhaust visitors.

The important case of *Ridge v Baldwin* was argued in the House of Lords in November of 1962.[65] The argument took eight days. It was an appeal by a senior police officer named Charles Ridge from a decision of the Court of Appeal, who had dismissed an appeal of a decision by Justice Streatfield. The judge had in turn dismissed the appellant's claim against a committee of the police authority of the County Borough of Brighton, who had purported to dismiss him as Chief Constable on 7 March 1958. He had been charged with conspiring to obstruct the course of public justice but acquitted after a 19-day trial in the February of that year. On a second charge of accepting a bribe, the prosecution had offered no evidence. On both occasions the trial judge had made statements which reflected on the appellant's leadership ability amongst other things. He was summarily dismissed from service the day following. The principal issue on the appeal was whether the relevant committee (the Brighton Watch Committee) had acted under the correct statutory enactment and if so, whether the committee was nonetheless obliged to apply the rules of natural justice.

The majority determined that in the circumstances the committee was bound to apply the rules of natural justice. This was an important decision because it

---

[61] Letter from Devlin to Goodhart, 23 July 1962, Bodleian Library Archives Special Collection, Oxford University, folio 105.

[62] Letter from Acheson to Devlin, 14 August 1962, Manuscripts and Archives, Yale University Library, Dean Acheson Papers, folder 97.

[63] Letter from Devlin to Acheson, 26 August 1962, Manuscripts and Archives, Yale University Library, Dean Acheson Papers, folder 97.

[64] Letter from Acheson to Devlin, 6 September 1962, Manuscripts and Archives, Yale University Library, Dean Acheson Papers, folder 97.

[65] *Ridge v Baldwin* [1964] AC 40.

purported to extend the rules of natural justice beyond a purely judicial context to an administrative one. The decision had the apparent effect of liberalising the law on the subject. It certainly began a cycle of greater judicial review of administrative action. Whilst the decision is important, Patrick certainly did not have much sympathy for the appellant. To some extent Patrick thought the point was really a technical one, especially where the appellant did not seek reinstatement. He correctly stated that in such a context, the extent to which (if at all) the rules of natural justice applied was essentially one of construction. But if a particular procedure was a precondition for dismissal, it had to be followed. Strict adherence to the prescribed procedure was therefore necessary. However, Patrick correctly asserted that it was always necessary to bear in mind the distinction between a wrong exercise of a jurisdiction that a judge has, and a usurpation of a jurisdiction which he has not. If there is no jurisdiction, the decision is a nullity. If however, there was jurisdiction, but there had been a miscarriage of natural justice, the decision would stand until quashed.[66]

Patrick, despite the excitement displayed by some academics, was taking a position in this case of orthodoxy and common sense. However, he did deplore in the strongest terms the suggestion that the Watch Committee did not hear the appellant because he had had a full opportunity of putting his case before the judge at his criminal trial. Once again he returned to the right to silence that he had so staunchly articulated over many years. He stated in terms that the appellant as an accused had no obligation to put any case before the jury. However the case did break new ground.

In what was a very quick trip Patrick flew to Canada to receive an LLD honours causa. The award was from the University of Toronto. On 23 November, he said amongst other things in his address, although a little sombre but as always poignant, remarks such as 'There is nothing terrible or unique about dying, but it is very sad to die in vain ...' and:[67]

> So many men have lit so many candles. But the age of candlelight is passing and the time is come when men must from out their corporate entity generate a ray of light that shall go round the universe and shall not be put out.

Dying in vain was never on the agenda for Patrick.

On 3 December he commenced hearing another milestone case, in *Lewis v Daily Telegraph*.[68] This was a libel case in which he sat with Lords Reid, Jenkins, Morris of Borth-y-Gest and Hodson. The case took nine days in argument. The case concerned what test should be employed to determine when defamatory meanings arise and the nature of them. The particular newspaper reports referred to Fraud Squad inquiries and investigations into the affairs of

---

[66] *Ridge v Baldwin* [1964] AC 40 at 140–1.
[67] Address delivered at the Fall Convocation at the University of Toronto, 23 November 1962, Manuscripts and Archives, Yale University Library, Dean Acheson Papers, folder 97.
[68] *Rubber Improvement Ltd v Daily Telegraph Ltd* [1964] AC 234.

a company and its chairman. The question was whether the language used in the articles could convey meanings of actual guilt, in addition to suspicion. A question also arose as to the damages awarded by the jury. In a judgment which is clear and compelling, Patrick not only dealt with the appropriate test, but the form of the pleading so as to make clear precisely what the plaintiff's case was. As importantly, he defined the general principles for the ascertainment of the meaning of words in defamation proceedings. On this occasion both Patrick and Lord Reid worked virtually synchronously not only to articulate what the 'ordinary meaning' is in a libel case but the characteristics of the recipient, namely the reasonable reader.[69]

It was Lord Reid on this occasion who used some colourful language in describing the recipient as somewhere between someone who is neither 'unusually suspicious' nor 'unusually naive' and who certainly does not 'live in an ivory tower' but who 'can and does read between the lines'. Patrick explained lucidly the differing forms of imputation, one that arises naturally from the very words or one that only arises in the mind of someone with 'specific information'. Constructively, he dealt with the necessary precision required for a libel pleading and, importantly as a matter of law, why a statement of suspicion does not necessarily itself impute guilt. Partly this was because a reasonable recipient should bear in mind that 'no man is guilty until he is proved so …' He warned, 'a man who wants to talk at large about smoke may have to pick his words very carefully if he wants to exclude the suggestion that there is also a fire; but it can be done'. Patrick had great respect for Reid and clearly the feeling was mutual. When discussing his work at home he would often say that Reid had the finest intellect of any of his colleagues. *Lewis* is a good example of a harmonious collaboration that would shape the law of libel for decades to come.

Patrick took time out from judgment writing to pen a rather dramatic letter to Acheson on 11 December:[70]

> I am letting it be known in a gentle way that I do not think of staying in office much beyond the end of 1963. I bear in mind Henry Nevison's definition of happiness (which I did not know and think is admirable), but believe that I shall fall within it. I doubt if I can at once be entirely master of my time, which is what I should like. But I shall probably have to do something part time to supplement my pension till the children are off my hands. I wish we had things like the Rockefeller and Ford Foundations over here, for I should like to do something semi-academic. But I expect that I shall have to exercise myself in the sort of quasi-public assignments that are considered suitable for the judiciary at large. The great thing is to be quit of London.

During all this time Patrick had been sitting on some important and, one presumes, stimulating cases, but on one view he was simply going through the

---

[69] *Rubber Improvement Ltd v Daily Telegraph Ltd* [1964] AC 234 at 259–60 (Lord Reid), at 277, 279–83 (Lord Devlin).

[70] Letter from Devlin to Acheson, 11 December 1962, Manuscripts and Archives, Yale University Library, Dean Acheson Papers, folder 97.

motions. That he was thoroughly professional there is no doubt. But by this stage his head was very much in resignation mode.

On Friday, 25 January 1963 Patrick delivered his paper at a law conference in Tasmania on restrictive practices and monopolies.[71] He was joined on the podium by then Australian Attorney-General, Sir Garfield Barwick QC, who would within a year become Chief Justice. He was also joined by Justice Schaefer of the Supreme Court of Illinois. He wrote a light-hearted and gossipy letter to Acheson that morning from Government House, Tasmania, where he and Madeleine were staying.[72] At that time he was unaware what his next hearing would be. After they left Australia, he and Madeleine travelled for weeks to various parts of South East Asia, eventually reaching San Francisco. While driving to Carmel, Madeleine, who was driving while Patrick was snoozing, ran off the road and the car they were in overturned. They escaped what might have been the end of one or both of them. Patrick was oblivious to the whole affair until woken up by the overturning of the car.[73] In the previous year Patrick had started to find it more difficult to hear conversations, especially everything said in court. He became concerned, but his way of dealing with it was to teach himself how to lip read.[74]

When he and Madeleine arrived home, there was little time to enjoy West Wick. It was straight back to work. But he did find time to send a chatty letter to Acheson reporting on his travels, particularly his time in Australia:[75]

> You are quite right about Australians and their utter disregard of temperature and their insistence in living in the sub-tropics according to the English model and the need for demanding, if you are to survive, inactivity in the afternoon. We could not do that because our duty was to do twice as much as was demanded of us. That is just possible for about a month, which was our limit. But, although exhausting, it was very enjoyable; and we both came away liking the country and the people much more than we thought we should. Especially I expected to dislike the cities, imagining them as modelled on our industrial cities. And I found them all by comparison most agreeable to look at and to live in. We met hosts of lawyers, of course. We saw quite a lot of Owen Dixon. But there is a general opinion that he is not quite what he was and that the decline recently has been rather rapid. He has become very garrulous. He always had, I'm told, an oblique way of talking and I found him difficult to follow except on one occasion, when he wanted to discuss the work of the Privy Council, and he

---

[71] Patrick Devlin, 'Some Aspects of Australian Proposals for Legislation for the Control of Restrictive Trade Practices and Monopolies', delivered at the 13th Legal Convention of the Law Council of Australia, published by the Law Council of Australia and the Law Book Company of Australasia Pty Ltd.

[72] Letter from Devlin to Acheson on Government House, Tasmania letterhead, 25 January 1963, Manuscripts and Archives, Yale University Library, Dean Acheson Papers, folder 97.

[73] Letter from Devlin to Acheson, 26 February 1963, Manuscripts and Archives, Yale University Library, Dean Acheson Papers, folder 97.

[74] Email from Timothy Devlin to the Author, 6 November 2018.

[75] Letter from Devlin to Acheson, 26 February 1963, Manuscripts and Archives, Yale University Library, Dean Acheson Papers, folder 97.

was obviously concentrating on what he wanted to say. We managed only a weekend in Canberra, and unfortunately Bob Menzies was away.[76] But he was in Sydney just when we were passing through between airflights, just before we left; and we went and had a hour with them both. I thought him well up to his usual form. I admired very much the portrait of him in Parliament House and I want to get the artist to do one in Gray's Inn. Owen Dixon, by the way, had a very good picture of you – a photograph taken I thought but I did not look very closely, from the Illustrated London News ...

He then discovered a change of plan. *Hedley Byrne v Heller* had been due to be heard by Lords Radcliffe, Cohen, MacDermott, Jenkins, and Guest. At the end of the first day's hearing, according to Sir Louis Blom-Cooper who was junior counsel for the respondents, Lord Radcliffe announced to the parties at the end of the first day of hearing that he had been appointed to preside over a public inquiry to investigate the affairs of an Admiralty clerk, John Vassall, said to be a Soviet spy. As Blom-Cooper points out, their Lordships in the original panel had a decided Chancery-slant about them. He further asserts that Gerald Gardiner QC, who appeared for the appellants, was successful in persuading the Lord Chancellor that a panel attuned to the common law would be more appropriate.[77] Viscount Dilhorne agreed and the new bench comprised Lords Reid, Morris of Borth-y-Gest, Hodson, Devlin and Pearce. The argument took eight days.[78] The appellants were advertising agents who had placed substantial forward advertising orders for a company that manufactured electrical goods. The appellants were personally liable for the orders. They asked their bankers to inquire of the respondents, the manufacturer's bankers, as to the manufacturer's financial stability. The respondents gave favourable references but stipulated that these were given without responsibility. In reliance on the references, however, the appellants spent £17,000 on advertising. The manufacturer went into liquidation shortly afterwards. The appellants sued the respondents for negligence. The courts below feeling constrained by the authorities found for the respondents. Previous Court of Appeal authority (*Candler v Crane, Christmas & Co*, in 1951) and the House of Lords (*Derry v Peek* in 1889) were the two problems. *Candler* was a negligence case but *Derry* was a deceit case. Until a Practice Direction in 1966, the House of Lords was not able to depart from its own previous decisions. However, it is now clear that since *Derry v Peek* was not a negligence case, it did not prevent the House from making further development in the law of negligence.

The focus of the case was whether there was a duty of care. The factual ground of the decision in *Hedley Byrne v Heller* was that the bankers successfully excluded any liability they had in negligence by their stipulation of 'no

---

[76] Robert Gordon Menzies, Australian Prime Minister 1939–41 and 1949–66.
[77] L Blom-Cooper, B Dixon and G Drewry (eds), *The Judicial House of Lords, 1876–2009* (Oxford, Oxford University Press, 2009) at 214.
[78] *Hedley Byrne & Co Ltd v Heller & Partners Ltd* [1964] AC 465.

responsibility' for any advice provided. Everything said in the very lengthy and erudite judgments about duty of care was thus strictly speaking only *obiter dicta*, not binding on future courts. But the matter was fully analysed and the judges concluded that but for the exclusion of liability, the bankers would have assumed responsibility for what they said. Lord Reid's notebook on the case makes clear the crucial role played by Patrick in convincing his colleagues about the notion of assumption of responsibility.[79] Patrick, by reason of his respect for precedent, had to be much more creative than Denning had been in *Candler*. The latter had a habit of stating principles about which he harboured seemingly no doubt and which seemed attractive, but which might be contrary to existing authority. Patrick would not overtly disregard precedent. But he was capable of recognising new instances to which existing principles could be applied. This is what he did in *Hedley Byrne* in relation to liability for negligently inflicted pure economic loss. Academics were not at the time always kind and some academics criticised him for innovating in circumstances where the principles he purported to articulate were inconsistent with his extrajudicial pronouncements about judicial creativity. The case opened up a new era of the tort of negligence by embracing liability for negligent misstatements contained in bank and employ-ment references. It was the beginning of the law on professional negligence. It also extended the law of damages by providing a remedy for pure economic loss. The Court held that a duty of care would arise where a defendant assumed responsibility to the claimant for the accuracy of a statement.[80]

In March Patrick gave yet another lecture in his law and morals series at the University of Durham, this time entitled 'Morals and the Law of Marriage'.[81] Evangelically he asserted that the 'institution of marriage is the creation of morality' and that for every detail of matrimony the moral law prescribes a right and wrong. His thesis was that no society had ever left it to the individual to settle for themselves what obligations spouses should undertake towards each other. While he asserted that in this context 'morality is not confounded with religion', he recognised that 'the whole of our moral law is religious in origin'. But he also acknowledged 'it would be absurd to suppose that agnosticism or atheism inevitably produce moral laxity or that either breeds indifference to the marriage bond'. In other words, the secular law must, he thought, be made for unbelievers. Although it is not unusual for judges to speak about matters of law reform, this was an area of some obvious sensitivity which many would have found difficult to tackle.

---

[79] Charles Mitchell and Paul Mitchell (eds), *Landmark Cases in the Law of Tort* (Oxford, Hart Publishing, 2016 Paperback [2010 Hardback]), pp 184–85.

[80] Ibid, pp 171–73, 187–88 and 197. See also Robert Stevens, *Law and Politics, the House of Lords as a Judicial Body 1800–1976* (London, Weidenfeld & Nicolson, 1979), pp 464–68.

[81] The Earl Grey Memorial Lecture, delivered at the University of Durham on 15 March 1963, reproduced in Patrick Devlin, *The Enforcement of Morals, Maccabaean Lecture in Jurisprudence of the British Academy 1959* (Oxford, Oxford University Press, 1965), pp 62–85.

At or about the time Patrick was drafting his lecture on 'Morals and Marriage', the Macmillan government was becoming engulfed in its own scandal of immoral relationships. This concerned former Secretary of State for War John Profumo's infidelities with teenage girls and the involvement of a suspected Soviet operative, Yevgeny Ivanov. Lord Denning was appointed to undertake a most unusual inquiry, sitting alone and in secret, to investigate the circumstances surrounding the whole affair. Denning reported in September 1963.[82] Dilhorne played a role by preparing a preliminary report on Profumo and had discussions with Denning before the latter published his report. The scandal badly and permanently damaged the credibility of the Conservative government, especially when Profumo was forced to admit that he had lied to the House of Commons about the whole affair.

In early March Patrick sat with the Lord Chancellor, Lords Evershed, Morris of Borth-y-Gest and Hodson. It was a criminal case of no specific importance involving a question of statutory construction of the Bankruptcy Act 1914.[83] What is interesting is that there does not appear to be any other case when Patrick was in the Lords and Dilhorne was Lord Chancellor where the two sat together. The Lord Chancellor wrote the only judgment. All their Lordships agreed with him and although Patrick was not there for the delivery of judgment, he requested Lord Hodson to convey his agreement. Patrick and the Lord Chancellor would not sit together again until they sat from time to time on Privy Council appeals.

On 10 May, he again wrote to Acheson:[84]

I am being made quite busy with my year in office as Treasurer at Gray's Inn. Indeed, I am having reluctantly to sacrifice two week-ends to being in London. The pain of that is mitigated by the thought that we shall soon be able to cut adrift from London altogether. I hope for January 1964 and expect April at the latest.

My friends and advisers say I should stay on till after the next election. Being politicians and civil servants, they do not say why directly, but talk mysteriously of the "balance" then being altered and of things being a question of balance. I think what they mean is that I could expect no other public appointments under the present Government, not being persona grata with the Prime Minister. He is said to have been angry about the Nyasaland Report and sadly dismissed all the authors as "unsound". That is a condemnation which in Britain to-day is equivalent to the mediaeval anathema and I must count myself lucky that I have not been excommunicated from the Establishment.

But I doubt if their advice is relevant. It is very difficult to convey to men for whom public life is the breath of the spirit that what I want is private life with a dash of

[82] Lord Denning's Report, presented to Parliament by the Prime Minister, September 1963 (Cmnd. 2152, 1963). See also Chapman Pincher, *Their Trade is Treachery* (London, Sidgwick & Jackson, 1981), pp 78–79.

[83] *Raven v Fisher* [1964] AC 210.

[84] Letter from Devlin to Acheson, 10 May 1963, Manuscripts and Archives, Yale University Library, Dean Acheson Papers, folder 97.

"public" in it as an insurance against insipidity and to put a little more jam on the bread-and-butter. They can think of no happy land between the city and the wilderness.

The newspaper proprietors, as a result of Hartley Shawcross' report on the Press, propose to have a legal chairman for the Press Council, a body which investigates complaints against the Press. I might take that if I am offered it as I probably shall be. But Cyril Radcliffe, whose judgment I greatly respect and who has had much experience of the Press, advises against it. So perhaps I shall do nothing but go in peace.

Further, on 26 June in a letter to Acheson, he got around to expressing his views on the political scene:[85]

What with Profumo and the Pope[86] we have been glued to the newspapers for the last week. I have a semi-proprietary interest in the Profumo affair. We were sworn in to the Privy Council on the same day. I took an immediate dislike to him and cannot imagine how everybody else did not. We are at a terrible disadvantage over here. There are continual mutterings about dreadful revelations still to come, but we do not know what they are, while everybody else does. It is a great disadvantage being the only country with a strict law of libel. The foreign press is said to be full of information; but how do we find out what it is? …

William Haley and Quintin Hailsham[87] have been thundering away, but everybody has told them that they must not hit people when they are down. The Haleys were also at the dinner for Lady Violet and Susan Haley had an amusing story. They were dining at the Swiss Embassy and she went in a car to the Times office to collect William. He kept her waiting some time and then came down and said that she must go on without him. 'The Profumo story has just broken' he said. 'He has admitted that he was lying and I must stay here until the leader is finished. You must go on and explain and I shall come as soon as I can'. So she went on and apologised profusely to her hostess for being late and for the fact that William would be still later. The Ambassadress said that was quite alright because they were still waiting for the Profumos. William and the telephone call from the Profumos eventually arrived at about the same time. It is to me a complete nonsense to blame Mr. Macmillan. But the truth is I suppose, that he is really being blamed for something quite different, for staying on too long. These opinion polls have really upset the British political system. In the old days nobody really knew whether the Government was popular or not. You had to try to work it out from the occasional by-election and that method was not really much more reliable than reading the auguries. Nowadays everybody knows the rating exactly. I suppose that in the States you know that too; but then you also know that there is nothing to be done about it until the due date arrives. The merits of our system are supposed to be that the Government goes when it is no longer supported in the country. That worked alright when there was a decent obscurity

[85] Letter from Devlin to Acheson, 26 June 1963, Manuscripts and Archives, Yale University Library, Dean Acheson Papers, folder 97.

[86] Pope Paul VI began his papacy on 21 June 1963, following the death of Pope John XXIII on 3 June from complications arising from stomach cancer.

[87] Sir William John Haley, former Director General of the BBC (1944–52) and editor of *The Times* newspaper (1952–66). Quintin McGarel Hogg, Viscount Hailsham, Leader of the House of Lords 1960–63.

about whether it was supported or not; but clarity is fatal. Everybody knows that the majority is against the Government; nobody except a few doughty political warriors really believes that the tide will turn. So the Government is being treated with all the exasperation felt towards an unwelcome guest, and everybody in the party is blaming everybody else for the disagreeable state of affairs. The Profumo deceit was very shocking; but if tempers were normal nobody would get angry with Mr. Macmillan about it.

I wonder if he will go. I should to like to see Rab Butler succeed him, for he is one of my oldest friends. But I do not think he will unless they cannot agree on anyone younger. In the Kennedy era youth is all the rage. But who else is there? Quintin would be very good if there were a war, but there is not. The only thing I can see in favour of Maudlin is that there is nothing against him when the music stops. The most extraordinary reason put against Heath in the newspapers is that he is a bachelor. There seems to be no high office these days to which a celibate can safely aspire except the Papacy; and that is a sad change from the good old days. So I expect when you come in September you will find Mr Macmillan still insecurely installed.

Patrick's cat was inevitably going to be let out of the bag. By early July it was widely published that Patrick would become the first independent chairman of Britain's Press Council from 1964. That move signalled two things – his leaving the Lords and his rejection of Radcliffe's advice. On 10 July the *New York Times* announced his appointment to the United States, describing him as 'one of Britain's outstanding judges'.[88] He is quoted as saying that he could not immediately take up the invitation due to judicial commitments.

In early July, Patrick joined Lords Reid, Evershed, Hodson and Pearce in hearing what would become one the most controversial cases he ever sat on, *Rookes v Barnard*.[89] It was heard over a staggering 15 days. After 10 days (on 16 July) the summer vacation interrupted the conclusion of the case. It was adjourned, part heard until November.

The plaintiff was a skilled draughtsman employed by British Overseas Airways Corporation in their design office at London Airport for nine years. He resigned his membership of a trade union. As a result of the refusal on the part of the plaintiff to re-join the union, the other employees threatened to withdraw their labour unless he was removed from office. In fear of the consequences of such conduct the BOAC suspended the plaintiff and later dismissed him. The trial judge found for the plaintiff, who claimed that the union had committed the tort of intimidation, but the Court of Appeal reversed that decision.

At the conclusion of the first round of hearings in July the traditional conference took place. According to Lord Reid's notebooks, Patrick expressed his view firmly in favour of the plaintiff. He was in a minority of one (possibly two). At the end of the year after the second hearing Patrick won them all around. As Professor Paterson points out, Lord Pearce was one of those who switched.

---

[88] 'High British Judge Invited To Be Head of Press Council', *The New York Times*, 10 July 1963.
[89] *Rookes v Barnard* [1964] AC 1129.

His speech indicated the difficulty he experienced in the case and that he was persuaded by Lords Reid and Devlin. Initially he had written in favour of the defendant but found, again according to Professor Paterson, that his reasoning so 'feeble and wrong' that he then rewrote it the other way. Lord Evershed's speech seems to indicate he was the last to switch.[90]

The case involved the question of the measure of damages in the case of the tort of intimidation. It reflected a clear policy decision which again reshaped the legal landscape. Until this case it had been settled law that a defendant's malice increased the appropriate amount of damages for defamation. Mainly through Patrick's judgment, *Rookes v Barnard* recast the law of exemplary damages. Patrick, with whom the other Lords agreed, began his analysis by stating that exemplary damages punished the defendant and this 'confuses the civil and criminal functions of the law'. The civil law's role was only to compensate. However, he continued, that was not to say that the civil law was confined to compensating pecuniary loss. He stated that a court or jury could take the motives of the defendant into account[91] 'where they aggravate the injury done to the plaintiff. There may be malevolence or spite or the manner of committing the wrong may be such as to injure the plaintiff's proper feelings of dignity and pride.'

He also acknowledged that there were cases where the punitive element had been recognised, so for it to be abolished entirely would require a 'complete disregard of precedent'. Therefore he proposed that exemplary damages should be retained but they should be confined to certain categories. *Rookes v Barnard* was a case dealing with the tort of intimidation. His initial point was that in the future exemplary damages should only be available in three categories of case. The first was the oppressive, arbitrary or unconstitutional action by servants of the government. The second category was where the defendant's conduct had been calculated by him to make a profit for himself which may well exceed the compensation payable to the plaintiff. The third category is where exemplary damages are expressly authorised by statute. However the plaintiff must be the victim of punishable behaviour. His second point was that courts would need to keep a supervisory restraint on juries on the award of damages. Thirdly he said that the means of the parties were a relevant consideration. This judgment was greeted with restrained enthusiasm at home but with positive hostility in other common law jurisdictions.[92]

On 26 August Patrick wrote to Acheson:[93]

> The national malaise continues to erupt in all directions. Poor Mr Macmillan is still being blamed for everything. He has not yet been blamed for the Great Train

---

[90] Alan Paterson, *The Final Judgment, the Last Law Lords and the Supreme Court* (Oxford, Hart, 2013), p 179, in particular fn 15.

[91] *Rookes v Barnard* [1964] AC 1129 at 1221.

[92] RFV Heuston, 'Patrick Arthur Devlin 1905–1992' (1994) 84 *Proceedings of the British Academy* 247–62, p 255.

[93] Letter from Devlin to Acheson, 26 August 1963, Manuscripts and Archives, Yale University Library, Dean Acheson Papers, folder 97.

Robbery, but he soon will be. They will be careful to point out of course that he is far too honourable a man to have himself personally directed the robbery; but they will say that is not to the point. The point is that by inciting people to become affluent and substituting materialistic for moral values, his Government has produced the climate in which this sort of thing flourishes. It does not look as if the Denning Report would discover anything unknown; but I think it is quite likely theft will create a sensation which will be more embarrassing to Mr. Macmillan than a revelation. Tom Denning is a very likeable, immensely able and rather erratic lawyer. I use the word 'lawyer' advisedly, because he had neither the capacity nor the experience to be a judge of fact. He was a Trial Judge for only a short period and at the humdrum work was not a success. He has rather a penchant for the startling and sensational and is not at all a safe man to be given the task of reporting on the state of the Augean stables. What Mr. Macmillan wants is a rather dreary Report with some tables of statistics showing that material values have not recently increased but I do not think that is what he will get. For Tom will be full of missionary zeal. The Tories seem fated to choose the wrong Judges to make reports for them. The fact is the British Government are becoming increasingly badly served by their lawyers. The Lord Chancellor is an industrious and competent man but I should not trust his judgment on any point at all. It is not merely that I should not accept it; I should regard it as a pointer in the opposite direction. The Attorney-General is a very nice man but very mediocre; the Solicitor-General is not, I think, from what I have seen of him a particularly nice man and he is certainly a complete nonentity. This is the result of the growing separation between legal and political careers. But the system is based upon the assumption valid a generation ago, that most of the best lawyers were to be found in politics. I think we will come before long to adopting the American and Australian practice and have the Solicitor-General at any rate a non-politician who is chosen on merit alone. Even the judiciary is now under fire. The Court of Criminal Appeal has recently dealt very foolishly with one of the Keeler cases. Two judges have been photographed in their shirt sleeves and mowing the lawn – a thing unheard of in my day. And Cyril Radcliffe has appeared on television to discuss one of his reports, also quite unprecedented ...

1963 had been a tumultuous year in so many ways. Denning had chaired an inquiry into John Profumo and in September announced he found that no secrets had been passed to the Soviets by Profumo. By the middle of the year Macmillan had been diagnosed with what was thought to be terminal prostate cancer and by 18 October sadly, from Patrick's point of view, Macmillan managed to manipulate Alec Douglas-Home into office instead of his close friend Rab Butler. The Lord Chancellor played a role in both events. Dilhorne had also been instrumental in suggesting candidates for Macmillan and reporting back to him so as to assist Macmillan to choose his successor. On 18 October Macmillan resigned as Prime Minister and Douglas-Home was sworn in the next day.[94]

On 22 November, in the middle of writing his controversial draft *Rookes v Barnard* speech, came the news that President Kennedy had been assassinated

---

[94] Alastair Horne, *Macmillan, Volume II of the Official Biography, 1957–1986* (London, Macmillan, 1989), pp 565–66.

in Dallas, Texas. Whilst Britain had had its share of change and tumult that year, Kennedy's murder had a profound effect on the Western world in general.

With an election looming the next year, there were very few guesses as to who might get in. The Tories had been in power for almost 13 years. Macmillan had run out of steam and in the end, Douglas-Home did not fill the void. Dilhorne was still Lord Chancellor, but only for another year. Patrick correctly predicted in a letter to Acheson that Gerald Gardiner QC would in time become the new Lord Chancellor.

Notwithstanding all that had occurred that year, Christmas at West Wick was for once peaceful, happy, restful and most importantly, out of London. The sense of freedom was overpowering. Time for a cigar, another Bordeaux, and Beethoven at full pitch. Patrick had reached the end of his judicial career. He had been a judge for 15 years and was entitled to retire with a full pension. There were a few reserved judgments but no more sitting in the Lords, although he would sit from time to time in the Privy Council. He officially retired on 10 January 1964.

11

Not Quite the Wilderness

W HEN JUDGES RETIRE, they very often are never seen or heard of again. The professional life of any judge is necessarily conducted in full public view. Thereafter relevance deprivation keeps some jumping up and down just to be noticed. Some former judges will comment on everything and anything, often on something they know little about, but the media often like a quotable quote from an ex-someone.

Patrick on the other hand not only began to run the Press Council,[1] but was also in demand for arbitrations in exotic locations. His network, especially in the Unites States, was second to none. Apart from which, for a start, he could settle down to finishing his book on Wilson.

On 25 January he wrote to Acheson from Portugal:[2]

> Life in the last six weeks has been very busy casting off the law and putting on the Press. I have not done either very thoroughly. In spite of arduous work I did not finish all my reserved judgments and had a part heard case that went on the day before we left England. The Press Council has not been very demanding so far but I have had to give a lot of interviews and make portentous pronouncements on subjects I know nothing about ... I have promised to be back by 20 February and it seems a very short time. But then I am beginning to measure things by a new time span now that I am a man of leisure ... President Kennedy's death must have come as a tremendous shock to those of you who were so near. Even in England it felt as if the world had been pushed off course. I remembered that you knew and liked President Johnson and that was a consolation at the time. But I still cannot get the tragedy out of my mind.

Patrick received an invitation when he arrived home. Despite his criticism of Radcliffe, he accepted an invitation to appear on BBC2 in a popular programme called *Encounter* chaired by Robin Day, with Dick Taverne, an MP (Labour at the time) and barrister, and Norman St John-Stevas, another barrister and a member of the Conservative Party. The programme went to air on 7 March. The text was later published in the *Listener*.[3] Both men prodded Patrick on the

---

[1] H Phillip Levy, *The Press Council, History, Procedure and Cases*, with preface by Lord Devlin, (London, Macmillan, 1967).

[2] Letter from Devlin to Acheson, 25 January 1964, Manuscripts and Archives, Yale University Library, Dean Acheson Papers, folder 98.

[3] 'Encounter with Lord Devlin, a discussion on law and morality on BBC-2', *The Listener*, 18 June 1964, vol LXXI, no 1838, pp 979–81.

chosen topic, Law and Morality. The conversation ranged widely from homosexuality, prostitution, abortion to euthanasia. Although clearly slightly out of
his comfort zone, Patrick sounded calm, polished and in control. To some, this
would have appeared a change of tone. Asked directly whether the law should
be used in the case of homosexuality, he stated that he was prepared to accept
the results of the Wolfenden Committee and that no good was done by sending
homosexuals to prison. This again might have appeared a change in attitude.
Patrick also made it abundantly clear that each of these issues must be seen in
a secular setting where religion must be left 'out of it altogether'. Patrick said
that the balance, both with abortion and euthanasia, was all about the sanctity
of life and with abortion one must determine when human life begins and with
euthanasia how it should end.

On March 16 Frankfurter wrote to Patrick:[4]

> I have missed hearing from you, for your letters not only brought me information that
> would not otherwise have reached me, but I gathered stimulus on matters of common
> interest to us. Your letter which has just arrived returns, as I hope, to your old practice
> of writing me from time to time. Fail me not ... I am in the hands of a very wise and
> skilful doctor who has brought me a long way along the road to recovery.

At the end of March Patrick felt compelled to write at length. He began
reiterating a familiar if not monotonous theme which Frankfurter had heard
before but not in its expanded and slightly cheerier form. He knew Frankfurter
was making an application for his company at the very least on paper and would
not disappoint an old friend:[5]

> I was delighted to get your letter and to see from it how well you are. Indeed it
> confirmed what I had heard ... Maurice Bowra was there and gave us recent news of
> you ... I hope very much to be in Washington in the fall and have a chance of seeing
> you again. I am giving the Freund lecture in Chicago this year and I expect it to be
> in the early part of October. I have some other assignments in Canada and I do not
> yet know quite what else ... I have taken very happily to life down here. We went
> away to Portugal for a month or more and enjoyed it very much; and since we came
> back I have been very busy getting things in order and finishing off my judgments
> in the House of Lords. I have just, I hope seen the back of the last one I shall do
> until, I suppose, in the fullness to time I return as we call a member of the 'mothball
> brigade'. We had an exceptional number of interesting cases last term – out of our
> usual rut of income tax and rating. A case on liability for negligent mis-statements in
> which we have made a tentative beginning in following the line that has already been
> marked out in America. Then we have been formally canonising and developing the
> new tort of intimidation, and incidentally creating quite a bother in the Trade Union

---

[4] Letter from Frankfurter to Patrick, 16 March 1964, Howard Gotlieb Archival Research
Center Collection, Boston University.
[5] Letter from Devlin to Frankfurter, 31 March 1964, Howard Gotlieb Archival Research
Center Collection, Boston University.

ranks. We have drastically cut down and systematised the law on exemplary damages. And lastly we have been struggling with double jeopardy and seeing what can be done to stop the Prosecution if it is so minded, from spreading out its case into any number of indictments and different trials. We have taken a look at the doctrine of issue estoppel which is very much the fashion in Australia nowadays. They imported it from you and have put some frills onto it. I cannot say I care for it much in the criminal law. These rather spritely goings on in the House of Lords have been very largely due to Scott Reid. As senior Law Lord he is proving an excellent President. Gavin was getting very tired towards the end: and then he really disliked any development of the law. Scott has a really alert and lively mind and he is ready to accept anything he thinks is sensible without letting new ideas run away with him. I hope that he will be able to continue for some time yet. But the results of his operation have undoubtedly made life difficult for him and he finds the work tiring. There is nothing else he wants to do so I think he will go on for as long as he can. Cyril Radcliffe, I suppose, will stick to his firm plan for going in May. Raymond Evershed has really rather worn himself out. He has this failing of never being able to say 'no' to even the dreariest activity that is proposed for him. He does take things more easily now than he did as Master of the Rolls. But I think if he stopped work for a bit he would get a new lease of life. So if Scott goes I do not quite know what will happen until Tom Denning returns from being Master of the Rolls. Then there will be great rejuvinations.

… I miss the company of my colleagues. But otherwise I have no regrets. I dare say if we had your methods I might still be in harness. But our methods are deadening. After all if a point has been canvassed in two courts and you have three or four judgments on it, you can after reading them form a pretty good idea of the right approach to it and direct your own mind in the way you want it to go. You can read the material and get down the authorities and look through them. You can let counsel argue it, put your own difficulties to him and make sure that you've got the whole of his points. Then you can discuss it thoroughly with your colleagues and reach a final conclusion. I think that would be an enjoyable way of working. I find our practice of going into the case with a blank mind and listening to days and days of argument quite intolerable. If it were all genuine argument, it would be bad enough. For after all, if a man cannot get at the point that really matters much more quickly than the average counsel he ought not to be sitting on the Supreme Appellate Tribunal. But it is not even all irrelevant argument. Days, – literally days, – are occupied with reading out loud the records of evidence and the judgments in the relevant authorities. You cannot even pick up a Law Report and read the parts that you think matter instead of the parts that counsel thinks matter, because there are never enough copies to go round and you have to look over your neighbour and exchange polite glances when the time comes to turn the page. The real vice of the thing is that, while days and days are wasted in this sort of activity no time or facilities are given for what I really think matters, – that is some independent research, through discussion with colleagues and a careful preparation of drafts of the judgment. In the important cases on which I have sat, I have found that at the end of two three weeks argument the point which I think, rightly or wrongly, is the decisive one has hardly been mentioned. Then you have to start work yourself, – without a room, a secretary or even anyone to verify a reference or get down a Law Report from the library shelves. If you are prepared to work six full days a week and a good deal of the vacations, you could give about fifty per cent of your time to supplementing the efforts of counsel and writing a judgment. But a six day week is not really practical unless, like dear John Morris, you cut yourself off from every other activity; and anyway, fifty per cent is not enough. I do not intend to give up the study of the law but I am looking forward to studying it in my own time and in my own way and in reasonable comfort down here. I go to London about one or three days in the month – mostly for the business of the Press Council which is interesting and not very exacting – and so I keep in touch ...

Frankfurter responded on 16 April:[6]

I am delighted that you have accepted the invitation to deliver the Ernst Freund Lecture because it will help to forge one more bond between us since in an extemporaneous talk I initiated the series of lectures in 1953. The picture you give of the handicapping circumstances under which you Lords of Appeal have to labor is difficult to believe. Is there anybody in Treasury who is an ex-lawyer or merely a cultivated man who knows the functions of a legal institution and especially the indispensable conditions of first-rate scholarship for judges? At all events I am grateful you are ready to suffer and unlike a few of the others will not put up with it but go to new fields and pastures green. It is a strange feeling what a deep hold the law has on me because I feel it almost as a personal loss when any man deserts the law ... Thank you very much for news of all my other friends and particularly the news that all is well again with Raymond. I count without compromise on your flight from Chicago to Washington so we can have another of our talks.

In late April Patrick was lecturing again on his familiar theme, this time 'Morals and Contemporary Social Reality' at Cumberland Lodge in Windsor.[7] It was clearly in direct response to HLA Hart's *Law, Liberty and Morality* published in 1963.[8] Again the lecture took a hefty swipe at Hart and John Stuart Mill, Patrick calling in aid and unashamedly aligning himself with James Fitzjames Stephen.

Patrick's mocking response to Hart's criticism that the English judiciary (and Patrick in particular) was unrealistic and out of touch with contemporary society was that the debate was never about the practical considerations of the debate so much as the philosophical. In other words, the debate was 'completely doctrinaire'.[9] Patrick sought to draw a distinction between the theoretical as opposed to the practical. In the case of decriminalising homosexuality, although the overwhelming majority of the Wolfenden Committee had been in favour of

---

[6] Letter from Frankfurter to Devlin, 16 April 1964, Howard Gotlieb Archival Research Center Collection, Boston University.

[7] An address given to a reading party on law and morals at Cumberland Lodge, Windsor, on 20 April 1964. See also, Patrick Devlin, *The Enforcement of Morals, Maccabaean Lecture in Jurisprudence of the British Academy 1959* (Oxford, Oxford University Press, 1965), pp 124–39.

[8] Patrick Devlin, *The Enforcement of Morals, Maccabaean Lecture in Jurisprudence of the British Academy 1959* (Oxford, Oxford University Press, 1965), p 124.

[9] Ibid, p 125.

it being decriminalised, when the matter was before the Commons on a free vote in 1960, it had been turned down by a large majority.[10] He said:[11]

> the pressure of opinion that in the end makes or unmakes laws is not to be found in the mouths of those who talk most about morality and reform but in the hearts of those who continue without much reflection to believe most of what they have learnt from their fathers and to teach their children likewise. What they believe may be quite wrong but it is contemporary and quite real. So in a democracy the existing laws contain the best and most comprehensive statement of contemporary social reality.

Patrick took Hart head on and sought to expose that for some 'wrongs' such as abortion, buggery in the form of bestiality, incest, obscenity (for example sale of pornography or what might be characterised as commercialisation of vice), Hart was silent, picking inconsistently and perhaps hypocritically only homosexuality. Hart clearly thought that homosexuality might be said to fall within the private realm where it was none of the law's business. Patrick then sought to attack Mill, whom Hart had called upon in aid. But this only allowed Patrick to draw blood by saying 'I think if I may say so without impertinence, that Professor Hart's argument might have been clearer if he had left Mill out of it'.[12] And the final coup de grâce, Patrick alleged that since Hart had to modify Mill for his thesis to work, it was[13]

> not, I think, pedantic to insist that if they are to win any degree of acceptance, or even of understanding, they must be stated with a higher degree of exactness. After all Mill's doctrine of liberty, be it right or wrong, was formulated carefully and comprehensively and with exemplary clarity. It deserves the compliment of more precise treatment than it has had at the hands of Professor Hart.

This was now not just a cordial or quiet chat these two were having. It was a full-blown public slanging match. It also excited onlookers, many of whom in due course jumped into the fray on one side or the other, declaring their chosen champion the victor.

The Press Council was not very exciting but Patrick made the best of it and made some good friends along the way, such as Ludovic Kennedy. When time permitted, they would lunch together at one of Patrick's favourite 'watering places' as Kennedy described it, namely the Grillroom at the Connaught Hotel.[14] In particular, he and Patrick shared certain views about police procedures, especially in relation to the obtaining of confessions. Patrick remained at the Press Council until 1969.

---

[10] Ibid, p 126.
[11] Ibid, pp 125–26.
[12] Ibid, p 128.
[13] Ibid, p 133.
[14] See, TATF, Introduction by Ludovic Kennedy; Ludovic Kennedy, *On My Way to the Club, An Autobiography* (London, Collins, 1989).

In the middle of the year it was off to Portugal again and then Turkey. He and Madeleine also very much enjoyed entertaining, and inviting friends to West Wick was a special treat, especially when Patrick could show off his cellar. However, as he playfully told Acheson:[15]

> It is difficult to get disentangled since people go on asking you to things as if you were still in London. We went up to London for a dinner party which Cecil King, – he seems to be the chief press magnate these days, – gave for Harold Wilson. I had a long talk to H.W. and rather liked him. People tend to be more likeable once they have got where they want to be. There seems to be no doubt that they will make Gerald Gardiner Lord Chancellor and start off with a strong dose of law reform ...

> The Wyzanskis came to dine and spent the night last month. Very delightful, but he really is an unbreakable talker. All elision and no punctuation. I do not mind that except at the dinner table. You may be suspended for anguished minutes when you want to ask for the salt or inquire if he would like more claret. Probably you will never get the salt nor the claret. But surely you will say there must be a pause when he puts something into his mouth? That is the extraordinary thing. There does not seem to be. Yet the food disappears some how. It seems like a miracle of the loaves and fishes in reverse. I think the trick is to eat only in midsentence and never to pop anything in at a period. Swallowing without chewing probably helps.

Patrick had another lecture to prepare for in Chicago in October, and in the meantime an invitation to sit on 'from time to time as a judge of some tribunal belonging to the I.L.O.'.[16]

When Patrick got to his feet to deliver his Freund lecture in Chicago, the general election was underway in the United Kingdom. The lecture was entitled 'Mill on Liberty in Morals'.[17] Having attacked the agent in Hart in April, this was an assault on the principal, Mill. This was an emboldened Patrick, letting the world know that Mill's thesis was flawed. He asked rhetorically: 'We have built a society in which a man's religion is his own affair: can we not go a step further and build one in which his morals are his own affair too?'.[18] Mill's view, asserted Patrick, was that a free society was better than a disciplined one, because it was better for a man that he should be free to seek his own good in his own way, and better too for society itself, 'since thereby a way may be found to a greater good for all'.[19] But as Patrick saw it, no good could come from a man doing what he acknowledged was evil. Patrick alleged that Mill demanded

---

[15] Letter from Devlin to Acheson, 2 May 1964, Manuscripts and Archives, Yale University Library, Dean Acheson Papers, folder 98.

[16] Ibid.

[17] Lord Devlin, 'Mill on Liberty in Morals', The Ernst Freund Lecture, delivered at the University of Chicago, 15 October 1964, (1965) 32(2) *University of Chicago Law Review* 215, reproduced in Patrick Devlin, *The Enforcement of Morals, Maccabaean Lecture in Jurisprudence of the British Academy 1959* (Oxford, Oxford University Press, 1965), pp 102–23.

[18] Patrick Devlin, *The Enforcement of Morals, Maccabaean Lecture in Jurisprudence of the British Academy 1959* (Oxford, Oxford University Press, 1965), p 106.

[19] Ibid, p 107–8.

toleration of what was known to be evil and what no one asserted to be good: 'He does not ask that in particular cases we should extend tolerance out of pity: he demands that we should cede it for ever as a right'.[20] He described it as the 'kernel of Mill's freedom'.[21] Because mankind may be mistaken about what is good and what is not, 'Mill demanded almost absolute freedom for the individual to go his own way, the only function of society being to provide him with a framework within which he might experiment in thought and in action secure from physical harm'.[22] As a judge, Patrick thought that a failure to distinguish sufficiently between freedom of thought and freedom of action was the fatal flaw in Mill's thesis.

He concluded:[23]

> But I do not accept it as an ideal. I accept it as an inspiration. What Mill taught about the value of freedom of inquiry and the dangers of intolerance has placed all free men forever in his debt. His admonitions were addressed to a society that was secure and strong and hidebound. Their repetition today is to a society much less solid.

The precise basis for Patrick's last proposition is a little unclear but no doubt it sounded perfectly persuasive to the audience, depending on the demographic.

When Patrick sat down it was either clear or becoming so that the Tories had been voted out, and that Harold Wilson was now the Prime Minister. In early December Wilson made a trip to the United States. A dinner was unsurprisingly held at the White House. Acheson was in attendance and, in advance attended briefings. His letter of 6 December said it all:[24]

> Your new Prime Minister is arriving tomorrow, when Alice and I are in the multitude who dine with him at the White House. I have been called in on the 'briefing' sessions with our own Chief and have tried to move the course toward toughness and realism. The idea of our Government with its great responsibilities and worldwide commitments and unquestioned authority at home contemplating adjustment of its views to care for Mr Wilson's domestic political problems seemed revolting. The United States is not a public convenience.

Anxious for more information, Patrick inquired:[25]

> Did you have any talk with Wilson? I must say I rather like him though I would not trust him very far. But I find him rather engaging. I was bored with the last government and I am disgusted with this one. My disgust with them which is well founded on public grounds is enhanced by the fact that they have given me a dirty job to do which has upset all my plans. This is to enquire into labour

[20] Ibid, p, 110.

[21] Ibid, p 112.

[22] Ibid, p 111.

[23] Ibid, p 123.

[24] Letter from Acheson to Devlin, 6 December 1964, Manuscripts and Archives, Yale University Library, Dean Acheson Papers, folder 98.

[25] Letter from Devlin to Acheson, 22 December 1964, Manuscripts and Archives, Yale University Library, Dean Acheson Papers, folder 98.

troubles at the docks ... That has entirely upset our plans for going to Portugal in January and February ... However I said when I left the Bench that I was willing to help if required ... I have undertaken to write an article on the Warren Report for the Atlantic Monthly. Charles Wyzanski thought it would be a good idea if some appraisal of it were made by a lawyer outside the States. I have some misgivings about criticism by foreigners. But this has now become such an international affair – we now have our own British 'Who Killed Kennedy?' committee, – that perhaps it is permissible. I hope that you think it is. The article is overdue and I just had an uncomplaining cable of inquiry from the Editor. So I must get down to it before Christmas.

Christmas was starting to become a crowded affair at West Wick, but time with children and now grandchildren was a great joy for Patrick and Madeleine. It also gave Patrick time to see his brother William, whom he had become closer to since Christopher's death. His older sister, Joan Mary, was not permitted by her order to have much if any interaction with family. Patrick was to some extent sanguine about respecting that, as he always did her choice and vocation.

Within the month between late January and late February 1965, Winston Churchill died (24 January) as did Frankfurter (22 February). Patrick's letter to Frankfurter of 1 January 1965 was the last he would write. He said for the last time:[26]

> I was really delighted to get your Christmas letter and to see from it that you are as lively as ever. I should love it that we could meet again and wish that I saw some nearer prospect of it than I do. But my retirement so far has been rather a sham. I have been burdened with so many little things, but which in their totality seem to me to be far more formidable than a regular job. I had planned to have a leisurely January and February basking in the sun in Portugal. I was invited to address the New York State Bar Association at the end of January – an invitation I gladly accepted. I thought that it would be a happy break in a leisurely holiday and give me a chance to come down to Washington and see yourself and other old friends. But I have been landed with a miserable job by the Government as Chairman of a committee which is investigating labour relations in the docks ... I have just finished an article on the Warren Report for the Atlantic Monthly ... I followed in your footsteps by delivering the Ernst Freund lecture in Chicago in October ... I was talking about law and morals and the Oxford University Press is bringing out a collection of my lectures on that subject, including Freund in March. I shall send you a copy and follow it up, I hope with a visit in the autumn.

Two days after being told of Frankfurter's death Patrick wrote, perhaps presciently, to Acheson on 24 February:[27]

> I know – because you have told me, – how deeply you will feel Felix's death. Not so deeply as you would have done, if he had died still in his prime. The decline in a man

---

[26] Letter from Devlin to Frankfurter, 1 January 1965, Howard Gotlieb Archival Research Center Collection, Boston University.

[27] Letter from Devlin to Acheson, 24 February 1965, Manuscripts and Archives, Yale University Library, Dean Acheson Papers, folder 98.

of his great faculties which is harder to his friends to bear than it is for himself turns out in the end to be a preparation for and a softening of the grief. But even so you will be very sad now. The thought of what your friendship meant to him and your devotion to him in the end will be your great solace.

Patrick's article in the *Atlantic Monthly* was published as planned.[28] The edition of the magazine was largely devoted to stories about Churchill. A week after Kennedy was assassinated President Johnson had established a commission to investigate the events by Executive Order.[29] The commission was conducted by the then Chief Justice Earl Warren and others. It took almost a year and reported in September 1964. It concluded that the gunman who shot the President had acted alone and in turn the gunman that shot the assassin had also acted alone. More than some scepticism followed the report and it remained a controversial subject. In a lengthy piece in the style of a summing up in a judge alone trial, it exonerated the Chief Justice of the Supreme Court from appealable error. Patrick's article dismissed the commission's critics as persons, in effect, 'avid for scandal'.

Also as planned, in March came the publication of Patrick's lectures on law and morals. The Preface was seen by some to be provocative, and it was clearly intended to be. He explained the background to his delivering the Maccabaean Lecture. He admitted that when he read the Wolfenden Committee's report it was with 'complete approval', including its formulation of the function of the criminal law in matters of morality.[30] For the first time he made public that he had in fact given evidence, along with Lord Chief Justice Goddard, before the Committee. He admitted that he was in favour of reform. He said:[31]

> I agree with everyone who has written or spoken on the subject that homosexuality is usually a miserable way of life and that it is a duty of society, if it can, to save any youth from being led into it. I think that that duty has to be discharged although it may mean much suffering by incurable perverts who seem unable to resist the corruption of boys. But if there is no danger of corruption, I do not think that there is any good the law can do that outweighs the misery that exposure and imprisonment causes addicts who cannot find satisfaction in any other way of life. There is to my mind one really powerful argument against reform and I put it in the form of a question. Can homosexuals be divided into those who corrupt youth and those who do not. If they cannot, is there a danger that the abolition of the offence between consenting adults might lead to an increase in corruption?

---

[28] Lord Devlin, 'The Death of a President; the Established Facts by Lord Devlin', *Atlantic Monthly*, March 1965, pp 112–18. See also: Lord Devlin, 'The Flaw in the Warren Report', *The Observer*, 25 September 1966.

[29] The Report of the Warren Commission on the Assassination of President Kennedy, the New York Times edition (New York, McGraw-Hill, October 1964).

[30] Patrick Devlin, *The Enforcement of Morals, Maccabaean Lecture in Jurisprudence of the British Academy 1959* (Oxford, Oxford University Press, 1965), p V.

[31] Ibid, p V.

Patrick went on to assert that much of the criticism he had received of the Maccabaean Lecture was because some of the terminology he had used in the lecture – words such as 'intolerance, indignation and disgust' – to indicate when society may criminalise or 'stamp out' conduct, was excessive. Somewhat disingenuously, he concluded the Preface with the statement:[32] 'The best justification for printing this collection of lectures is the possibility that it stimulates the professionals to undertake not merely demolition of amateur work but the construction of something better.'

Patrick sent the book to Acheson in April and he diplomatically responded:[33]

> Many thanks for your lectures, 'The Enforcement of Morals', which as I told you at the time they were given leave me a little uneasy if not scared. The test may be the views of the man on the Clapham bus, but over here they are apt to be those of Warren C.J. and Black, Douglas, Brennan and Goldberg JJ. We have had a good deal of their views lately and the beams and planking of the old Ship State groan in the high seas. However you are now my legal mentor and what you say goes. Unguided by Felix and Owen Dixon who is, so Dick Casey says, far from his old self, I am your responsibility.

Charles Wyzanski (a judge since 1941) reviewed Patrick's book of lectures for the *University of Toronto Law Review* in 1965.[34] In a matter perhaps reminiscent of his dinner party style and making no declaration of any conflict of interest, he declared that[35]

> No one of course could hope easily to match his logical clarity, felicity of expression, amplitude of simple illustration, and unmistakeable common-sense judgment. Only an extraordinarily penetrating and robust mind supplemented by the experience of daily life in the High Court makes for such a combination of gifts.

That said, he did not compliantly accept everything Patrick had to say. For example, while he agreed with Patrick that the state could regulate the homosexual or heterosexual conduct of its inhabitants, or prevent them from engaging in any conduct, this required sufficient evidence to persuade it accordingly. It could be done on the basis that the conduct may weaken an individual or tempt others, however futile some may think the attempt to prevent the conduct might be. But unlike Patrick, Wyzanski said that there should be an objection on principle 'to a state prohibiting opinion or its expression or its formulation as a creed, or its presentation by an organised association of its adherents'. And whilst the

---

[32] Ibid, p V.

[33] Letter from Devlin to Acheson, 20 April 1965, Manuscripts and Archives, Yale University Library, Dean Acheson Papers, folder 98.

[34] Charles Wyzanski Jnr, 'Review of Books – *The Enforcement of Morals* by Patrick Devlin' (1966) 16(2) *University of Toronto Law Journal* 455–61.

[35] Ibid, pp 457–58.

state is entitled to regulate the 'satisfaction of physical appetites', the question is whether it should in particular legalise homosexual acts between consenting adults in private.[36,37]

Oddly on one view, Patrick and seven other members of the House of Lords wrote a letter to *The Times* on 11 May 1965 drawing attention to the Wolfenden Committee's recommendation made in 1957, that homosexual behaviour between consenting adults should no longer be a criminal offence, and to the endorsement of the recommendation since that time by numerous august people and bodies.[38] It referred to a motion to be moved the next day in the Lords calling for reforms as a necessary. Some of Patrick's friends were more than a little confused.

Monty Belgion, who Patrick had known since Savile Club days and with whom he had recently corresponded, wrote to Patrick on 28 May:[39]

> I am moved to write to you about your signature to a collective letter in the Times a little while ago about a debate which was then due in the Lords on homosexuality. I was in Paris when the letter appeared, and I did not see it till I was back here. I would not disagree with your endorsement of the letter, for as far back as the time you delivered your lecture on 'The Enforcement of Morals' I felt that you might be underestimating the extent to which feeling or opinion in this country had changed on such subjects. But I was a little surprised to find you reversing an opinion so soon after you had again proclaimed it in your last book. Moreover, if the division in the Commons is any guide, perhaps opinion has not all changed as much as I imagined. I wonder what led you to revise your own view ...

Patrick was adept at a response about a matter, even when he was wrong, which could make the interrogator embarrassed the question had ever been raised. Patrick responded on 29 May:[40]

> No, I have not reversed myself. I have always been in favour of an amendment to the homosexual laws on the simple ground that it was a realm (which albeit the law's business) in which the law was not doing any good. So long as I was a judge, I never said in public that I was in favour of reform, because I think it is wrong for a judge to take sides on questions of that sort. But I did explain my position in the preface to the book. However, no-one reads prefaces, – not even so diligent a reader as yourself! The

[36] Ibid, p 458.

[37] Patrick's book was also reviewed by Eugene Rostow, Professor of Law and Dean of the Law School, Yale University in (1960) 18(2) *Cambridge Law Journal* 174–98; and RE McGarry QC in (1966) 82 *Law Quarterly Review* 115–20.

[38] The other signatories were Lords Leonard Mirmingham, Oliver Bristol, Robert Exon, Robert Londin, Michael St Albans, Brain and Robbins.

[39] Letter from Belgion to Devlin, 28 May 1965, Churchill Archives Centre, Churchill College, University of Cambridge.

[40] Letter from Devlin to Belgion, 29 May 1965, Churchill Archives Centre, Churchill College, University of Cambridge.

only person I know to have read the preface is Arran[41] and as a result of it he rang me and asked if I would support his bill. Thus the letter in the 'Times'.

I have no time for more now. For I have just started a month's intensive work on drafting the report for the docks which we have now promised by early July.

With some justification, Belgion was not satisfied. He replied on 2 June:[42]

Thank you for so gently recalling to me how the preface of your book opens. Yet to me the matter does not seem to be altogether so simple as your letter implies. In the lecture you are very definite in saying (p.22) that the Wolfenden Committee adopts 'a false principle' in order to argue that it is indefensible to retain homosexuality between consenting adults in private among criminal offences. It is reasonable to conclude that therefore in being yourself in favour of reform on this point (page v), you were actuated by another principle, i.e. the principle 'that the law exists for the protection of society'; and hence that the Wolfenden Committee must have neglected to ascertain that public feeling wanted the reform or change. The collective letter in The Times of course fails to refer to this distinction of motive, so that it might seem as though either in the interval you had discovered that public feeling had shifted into favouring the House of Lords bill or else that the difference between the false and the true principle no longer weighed as much as in 1958.

In short, the recommendation of the Committee looked as though it were being supported on a false principle or else that principle did not after all matter.

Just before one hears from Patrick in rebuttal, it is salutary to deal with some history. The Wolfenden Committee heard from many witnesses, one of whom was Patrick. It also heard from Goddard and other judges. Patrick had provided a written statement and gave oral testimony. He is recorded as having said

I think that gross indecency by adults in private should not be treated as a crime; and by 'in private' I mean that which does not amount to a public nuisance. I think where the element of corruption of the young comes in, it should remain a serious crime.[43]

In the final report, the Wolfenden Committee recommended that homosexual behaviour between consenting adults no longer be a criminal offence. But clearly the Maccabaean Lecture stated, or supported the reasonable inference, that he was opposed to reform and that in particular reform was really not safe, because as long as the corruption of youth could not the ruled out as a consequence of decriminalisation, reform should not occur. Outright unqualified support, as may be understood from the group letter to The Times, would clearly appear to be a reversal of view.

[41] Arthur Gore, 8th Earl of Arran (1910-83), who introduced the Sexual Offences Bill 1966 following the death by suicide of his homosexual brother.

[42] Letter from Belgion to Devlin, 2 June 1965, Churchill Archives Centre, Churchill College, University of Cambridge.

[43] Brian Lewis, *Wolfenden's Witnesses, Homosexuality in post-war Britain* (Basingstoke, Palgrave Macmillan, 2016), p 69.

Patrick clearly respected Belgion; hence he favoured him with a comprehensive response on 9 June:[44]

> No, I do not think that your conclusion would be the natural or reasonable one.
>
> Having declared in my lecture that the rigid principle set out in the Wolfenden Report is the wrong one, I proceed at page 16 and thereafter to formulate what I think is the right test, – that is the judgment in each case that balances the public against the private interest in the light of a number of flexible principles. I do not say how I myself would apply that test or what conclusions I should draw from it. But when the reader learns that I am in fact in favour of reform, I think that the reasonable conclusion would be that I had arrived at that by means of the test I advocated and in the light of the flexible principles I set out. One of them (page 20) whether the criminal law is suited to the job of dealing with sexual immorality. I do there drop a hint that I thought on this point the Wolfenden Report was on the right lines.
>
> It is all rather mysterious, of course. It would have been much simpler if I had made any attitude plain but I did not feel it right to do.
>
> It is also true that that is not the way in which the matter is put in the letter in The Times. But I do not think that a joint letter of this sort can contain the reasoning of all the signatories. I thought it a good thing that the Government should be made to sit up and take notice of the question. I think that Arran's bill may need some safeguarding amendments, but I am quite sure that some general reform would be beneficial.

But Belgion had attended the Maccabaean Lecture and taken copious notes. He persisted somewhat, however convolutedly, on 17 June:[45]

> While hesitating, I hope, to bother you with a further letter on the subject, I think it is due to you for me to try to put my point more clearly than I seem to have done so far. I have sought to ascertain what I am really after.
>
> 1. If I go back to the day on which you delivered your lecture on the 'The Enforcement of Morals', I then gathered that you held the Wolfenden Committee to have erred in having made its recommendation about homosexuality without (a) reference to the need of having the law enforce morality, and (b) regardless of the state of English moral opinion, the feelings and views of the 'reasonable man', the average juryman.
> 2. Furthermore, in stating that the source of English morality is the Christian religion, you appeared to imply that current opinion and feeling were too conservative to have approved the committee's recommendation if that opinion and feeling had been consulted.
> 3. Therefore, upon your admitting in the preface to your book that you support the recommendation, you not only imply, it seems to me, that you yourself

---

[44] Letter from Devlin to Belgion, Churchill Archives Centre, Churchill College, University of Cambridge.

[45] Letter from Belgion to Devlin, 17 June 1965, Churchill Archives Centre, Churchill College, University of Cambridge.

have consulted current moral opinion and feeling, but also that the Wolfenden Committee, in omitting to have done this, nonetheless succeeded in interpreting that opinion and feeling.

4.   This can only mean that <u>the committee took the right decision for the wrong reasons</u>. That is quite another topic from that of the force of moral opinion and of the need to reckon with that opinion in modifying the law. The question surely arises: If the right decision can be reached without the right reasons, <u>why bother about these</u>?

5.   Finally, in approving the committee's recommendation (approving for the right reasons), you must be taken as recognising in addition that current moral opinion is no longer conservative, and that the so-called permissive morality of to-day shifted away from its Christian sources.

Patrick was just too busy to respond because he was up to his ears in writing his report on the docks inquiry.

Clearly Belgion, behaving like an inquisitive schoolboy, had raised some complicated questions.

In August Patrick's report on the Port Transport Industry was published.[46] It was an extensive report dealing with issues concerning wages and conditions affecting the industry and had received submissions from associations and unions. This was not the first time he had conducted an inquiry into the docks. In 1955, he had conducted an inquiry into the then Dock Labour Scheme. It was well received. His most recent report drew conclusions on ways both dissension and inefficiencies at the docks could be addressed. It was again well received. *The Spectator*, however, carried an article on 12 August, under the catchy heading of 'Devlin Worship' by Alan Watkins, a senior and respected political journalist.[47] Under the guise of a review of the Devlin docks inquiry, the author ventured much further afield:[48]

> Rarely has any official document become part of the received opinion of the times quite as rapidly as Lord Devlin's report on the docks. It has been praised in the public prints for its lucidity, its thoughtfulness – and a favourite modern word, this – its ruthlessness. It has been welcomed by Ray Gunter and the rest of the Government ... Did it really need Lord Devlin to tell us what to do ... I am a little doubtful about the aptness of a man who has been raised to place and power on the back of the greatest restrictive practice known to mankind – the English legal profession – lecturing those less fortunate than himself on where their duty lies. Lord Devlin is of course one of the strange cabal of committee-sitters ... Lord Devlin in short is wheeled up for the big occasion, and in this he resembles Lord Radcliffe and Lord Denning ... all three possess views that are profoundly authoritarian in their implications ... he (Devlin) has decided to make himself fully available for extra-legal duties. The best source for Lord Devlin's public philosophy – I am sure he would not object to

---

[46] Final Report of the Committee of Inquiry under the Right Hon Lord Devlin into certain matters concerning the Port Transport Industry, August 1965 (Cmnd 2734, 1965).

[47] Alan Watkins, 'Devlin Worship', *The Spectator*, 12 August 1965, pp 7–8.

[48] Ibid, p 7.

the phrase is his somewhat repetitive collection, The Enforcement of Morals, and in particular the essay 'Morals and the Criminal Law'. When this book first appeared, most critics concentrated on those sections which deal with sex and the law. Certainly Lord Devlin's views on this subject are hair-raising enough: on divorce he is particularly repressive. However in this context, as in others it is misleading to become too obsessed with sex. I find Lord Devlin's views on the toleration of political dissent infinitely more disquieting than his views on the Wolfenden Report (which he supports in fact, if not in theory).

After several further scarifying paragraphs pointing out alleged inconsistencies in Patrick's various arguments in the area of law and morals, the author resumed:[49]

> It is not my purpose to show Lord Devlin lacks integrity or independence. He clearly has both qualities as his report on Nyasaland demonstrated. But his opinions on politics and society are wholly obnoxious to me; more important, I would guess that they are thoroughly unsympathetic to the majority of people in this country, who have always had a healthy distrust of lawyers. Lord Devlin is perfectly entitled to propagate his opinions in books and articles. What is disquieting is that he is not content to do this. Elected by no-one, representing nothing, and responsible to nobody, he has let it be known that he is prepared to play an active part in the running of the country. It is bad enough having someone with Lord Devlin's views as a judge ... It is an entirely different matter if after the minimum period as a member of the judiciary he goes out into the rough world of politics and government yet still tries to preserve something of his former judicial status. A final word should perhaps be said of Lord Devlin's chairmanship of the Press Council. This is particularly disquieting. For however much they may guard against it there is bound to be a tendency on the part of newspaper proprietors, editors and journalists to refrain from criticizing him in his public role because he is in a position to do them damage ... There is in fact a case for asking Lord Devlin to give up either the chairmanship of the Press Council or his other public activities. There may even be a case for asking him to give up both. There is certainly a case for treating his pronouncements with less reverence and for ending Devlin worship.

Despite the gratuitous vitriol, Watkins did raise some not unimportant points. Patrick had had a controversial life as a trial judge. Some of the controversy was not his doing but some was self-inflicted. Some take the view that while on the bench, judges should be seen and heard only in their respective courtrooms and in their written or oral judgments. Textbooks and learned articles are permissible, as are lectures on legal topics. But even the last named can raise a potential issue if perchance the judge is to hear a matter about which he or she has expressed a view outside the courtroom, albeit in an academic setting. Sitting or former judges are often the target of politicians who want them to lend their status to enhance the standing of some extra curial task such as an inquiry. But the ability to express views on any matter should not be the sole

---

[49] Ibid, p 8.

domain of the journalist. Judges need to be very careful on what they say, when they say it and, equally important, where they say it. As a general rule, it is best if they confine themselves to the law. However, for Patrick to venture into the Wolfenden Report and topics such as homosexuality was hardly uncontroversial and he clearly must have anticipated the fire he drew. To say that the exercise diminished his reputation or that of the judiciary or that he was not entitled to do so is a stretch, though.

Patrick continued to sit on the Privy Council and the House of Lords, but not on a regular basis. In the years 1966 to 1974 he sat on at least 15 appeals.[50] In 11 of those he sat with Lord Dilhorne. The advantage for the judges was that it was the practice on such appeals that a joint judgment would be written by one of the judges.

Otherwise, he and Madeleine were seemingly constantly travelling. The schedule was punishing. He wrote to Acheson in August:[51]

> The Report was published with a fanfare last Thursday. Anyway propose to sleep until mid-September and contemplate the pleasure of a retirement that hasn't so far turned out entirely as I had hoped. On 14 September we come to New York for four days for a conference of the Comité Maritime ... duty calls us to go to Ottawa ... after that we go to the Azores again. Then Geneva again ...

Patrick lacked neither energy nor tenacity. Why he did not answer Belgion's letter of June 1965 until a year later is a mystery. It is not clear why after that lapse of time, he bothered at all. But he did on 23 March 1966, no doubt because the whole issue troubled him:[52]

> The natural period of gestation has now lapsed since I promised to reflect upon your letter of 17 June 1965 and to answer it in due course. I have finished with the docks, cleared up the arrears as a result of it, been to Ceylon, spent two quiet months in Portugal trying to do some writing; and am now at last trying to make a clean sweep.

---

[50] *Cobb & Co Ltd and others v Norman Eggert Kropp* [1967] 1 AC 141 (PC); *Director of Public Prosecutions v Nasralla* [1967] 2 AC 238 (PC) (with Dilhorne); *Boots the Chemist (New Zealand) Ltd v The Chemists Service Guild of New Zealand Incorporated* [1968] AC 457 (PC); *Alfred Thangarajah Durayabbah of Chundikuly, Mayor of Jaffna v WJ Fernando and others* [1967] 2 AC 337 (PC) (with Dilhorne); *United Engineering Workers' Union v Devanayagam, President Eastern Province Agricultural Cooperative Union Ltd* [1968] AC 356 (PC) (with Dilhorne); *Yorkshire Electricity Board v Naylor* [1968] AC 529 (HL) (with Dilhorne); *Cleary v Inland Review Commissioners* [1968] AC 766 (HL) (with Dilhorne); *Meeruppe Sumanatittsa Terunnanse v Warakapitiye Pangnananda Terunnanse* [1968] AC 1086 (PC) (with Dilhorne); *Ceylon Theatres Limited v Cinemas Limited and others* [1968] AC 792 (PC) (with Dilhorne); *Fox and others v Adamson* [1970] AC 552 (HL) (with Dilhorne); *United Dominions Corporation (Jamaica) Ltd v Michael Mitry Shoucair* [1969] 1 AC 340 (PC) (with Dilhorne); *Shaaban bin Hussien and others v Chong Fook Kam and another* [1970] AC 942 (PC); *Rajapakse Pathurange Don Jayasena v The Queen* [1970] AC 618 (PC) (with Dilhorne); *Dennis Hall v The Queen* [1971] 1 WLR 298 (PC) (with Dilhorne); *Geelong Harbor Trust Commissioners v Gibbs Bright & Co (a firm)* [1974] AC 818 (PC) (with Dilhorne).

[51] Letter from Devlin to Acheson, 8 August 1965, Manuscripts and Archives, Yale University Library, Dean Acheson Papers, folder 98.

[52] Letter from Devlin to Belgion, 23 March 1966, Churchill Archives Centre, Churchill College, University of Cambridge.

No I did not say in the Maccabaean lecture that the Wolfenden Committee head erred in making its recommendation about homosexuality either for the reasons you give or for any reasons. I said at the beginning of the lecture, – it is on page 2 of the book; – that I would not express any opinion about the Committee's conclusions, since that would be outside the scope of the lecture on jurisprudence. What I was concerned to challenge was the general proposition that there could be a realm of private morality and immorality which was not the laws' business. I expressed no public opinion on the recommendations (though I had previously expressed an opinion in private to the Committee) because I think it is wrong for a judge who has to apply the law either to support or oppose contentious proposals for reform. It is one thing to deny that there is a realm of morality which the law cannot enter; and another thing to assert that all morality should be enforced by law. In the lecture I say (pp.16–22) that there are principles which, without circumscribing the operation of the law-making power, should guide those who have to apply it. One of these (p.20) raises the question whether the weapons which the law has at its disposal will really work in the particular case; and I give a fairly broad hint that on this point I thought the Wolfenden Committee was right. This is the main point that weighs with me, as I say in the Preface. I do not think the law does any good and it is on this ground that I would support reform.

Whether Belgion was satisfied or no longer interested, he did not respond on this occasion, but Patrick's cleverness was at work. Whatever he did or did not intend to do he had caused a maelstrom which enveloped academics and judges alike.

Hart, interviewed by David Sugarman in November 1988, said in terms that it was Patrick's Maccabaean Lecture that set him off getting into 'this law and morality':[53]

And then Devlin thought I was perverse in trying to make a case for John Stuart Mill. And I was stimulated to reply … and I mean I think Devlin's arguments are quite bad and misleading and enable reactionary people to claim a philosophical mantle which is quite wrong … It's a tremendous paradox. I got to know him, quite like him. He's a mixture of … he's very clever – a mixture of vanity and cleverness. But the moment when we'd gone through all this he produced his arguments against me … he then wrote a letter to the Times saying he thought the law ought to be altered.

So Belgion was not the only one confused.

In mid-August 1966 Patrick told Acheson the good news as he saw it. On 26 July, the House of Lords issued a Practice Statement which freed the House from following its own precedents.[54] Lord Reid, then the senior Law Lord, had launched a series of attacks on the position historically adopted by the House of Lords in the run up to the announcement. His support was essential to the adoption of the new practice and he provided the new guidelines as to when the Practice Statement should be exercised in a series of deliberate pronouncements

---

[53] Interview between HLA Hart and Professor David Sugarman, 8 November 1988: https://blog. oup.com/2012/12/h-l-a-hart-in-conversation-with-david-sugarman/.

[54] Alan Paterson, *Final Judgment, the Law Lords and the Supreme Court* (Oxford, Hart Publishing, 2013), pp 265–68.

in relevant cases. The announcement was made by Lord Gardiner LC. Patrick explained to Acheson that it 'is very difficult to disentangle the Lords' judicial functions from their legislative functions'. He made his point:[55]

> If what is being debated is a bill, the result of the Lords' approval of the bill will, if it is passed by the Commons and given Royal assent, be a new bit of legislation. If what is being debated is whether an appeal should be allowed, the Lords' decision takes the form of an order 'that the cause be and the same is hereby, remitted back to the High Court of Justice, to do therein as shall be just and consistent with this judgment'. It is then necessary to make a formal application to the High Court for an order to give effect to the judgment. What happens if the High Court refused to make an order I do not know. Much the same as if the Queen refused the Royal assent. But certainly the House of Lords has no direct judicial power.

Patrick for some time had reflected upon the status and structure of the House of Lords. Years later but well before his time, he would suggest the creation of a Supreme Court to replace the House of Lords, ultimately writing an opinion piece in *The Times*.[56] Like most of his ideas, he carried this one from time to time, along with the ever constant and hobby like commitment to conclude his biography of Woodrow Wilson, which travelled with him like a pair of old slippers. Part of the reason Patrick and Madeleine bought a villa in Portugal later that year was to give Patrick extended warm weather in which to write. To top it off Patrick became the High Steward of Cambridge University, following in the footsteps of Rab Butler.[57] He confided in Wyzanski in November 1966:[58]

> I have not yet attained the nirvana that I hope for, but shall some day. At present I am constantly occupied in a succession of small jobs rather than one big one; but as I like variety, that is good as far as it goes. At present I am sitting in the Judicial Committee of the Privy Council where they seem to be perpetually short handed.

At about the same time Patrick discovered that his sister Joan Mary had become seriously ill. She had become a nun in 1924 and was the oldest in the family, having been born a year before Patrick in 1904. She had attained a degree from Oxford in English Literature and over the years had taught at numerous Sacred Heart schools. The protocol for the Order prevented Patrick or any members of the family from making visits to Joan when she was alive. She died on 24 February 1967.[59] This left Patrick and William closer than ever.

---

[55] Letter from Devlin to Acheson, 12 August 1966, Manuscripts and Archives, Yale University Library, Dean Acheson Papers, folder 98.

[56] Lord Devlin, 'The Case for a Supreme Court', *The Times*, 7 October 1987, p 16.

[57] Patrick is listed with Butler among other notable occupants of the office in 'Office of High Steward: Notice', *Cambridge University Reporter*, 26 July 2000. He served from 1966 to 1991.

[58] Letter from Devlin to Wyzanski, 22 November 1966, Wyzanski Papers, 1930–68, Harvard Law School Library, Hard University, Box 2, folder 21.

[59] Letter from Ms Barbara Vesey, archivist, Society of Sacred Heart, Barat House, University of Roehampton, to the Author, 15 June 2018.

Another development was emerging on the legal front. Patrick's judgment in *Rookes v Barnard*[60] had been considered by a number of courts around the Commonwealth and elsewhere. It had not received the acceptance elsewhere that it had for the time being, at least in the United Kingdom. The Australian High Court in *Uren v Australian Consolidated Press*[61] had taken the view that Australian courts need not be limited by the principles enunciated by *Rookes v Barnard*. In a scornful analysis, the High Court rejected Patrick's judgment and reasserted the Australian test of 'conscious wrongdoing in contumelious disregard of another's rights'. The Privy Council heard the case over 8 days in April and May 1967. The Privy Council, comprising Lords Morris of Borth-y-Gest, Pearce, Upjohn, Wilberforce and Sir Alfred North (a New Zealand judge), decided that it was impossible to say that as a matter of Australian law the High Court was wrong.[62] The High Court would continue to apply settled law in Australia. There also appeared to be no faulty reasoning or misconceptions. Hence its decision stood. This was the beginning of a controversy that would rage for some years.

---

[60] *Rookes v Barnard* [1964] AC 1129.

[61] *Uren v Australian Consolidated Press Ltd* (1966) 117 CLR 118; affirmed (1967) 117 CLR 185, [1969] 1 AC 590 (PC). See also: David Rolfe (ed), *Landmark Cases in Defamation Law* (Oxford, Hart Publishing, 2019), chapter 7, pp 151–72.

[62] *Australian Consolidated Press Ltd v Uren* [1969] 1 AC 590, at 628 and following.

12

New Challenges and the Enemy Within

SYDNEY KENTRIDGE SC was in 1969 a leading defence barrister in South Africa. In late November 1968 he began appearing in a trial in Johannesburg for an editor, Laurence Gandar, and a journalist, Benjamin Pogrund. The two had written a series of articles in the *Rand Daily Mail* about conditions in prison for black South Africans and had interviewed prisoners and prison officials. The articles chronicled stories of assaults, sodomy and unhygienic conditions. The Prisons Act 1959 forbade newspapers from discussing conditions in prisons, forbade interviews with prisoners and the like, and also created a criminal offence of negligently publishing incorrect information about prisons. Gandar and Pogrund were charged with various breaches of the Act. The trial lasted 88 days. The two were found guilty of publishing articles in breach of the Act and also of publishing false accounts.[1] Both men were fined and received suspended sentences.[2] It was during the trial that Patrick met Kentridge. Patrick was in Johannesburg on behalf of the International Commission of Jurists to observe the trial. He could only stay for a short time but long enough to glean just what was going on. Kentridge describes the trial judge as one of the worst appointed under the Apartheid regime. He said the judge obviously knew of Patrick and that he was there as an observer. Whenever Patrick was in the courtroom, the judge behaved more or less impeccably. But when Patrick was not present, he shouted a good deal and misbehaved appallingly.

Patrick and Kentridge got on extremely well from the very start. Kentridge invited Patrick home for dinner to meet his family. The two would become close friends for the rest of Patrick's life. Indeed, Kentridge and his family would stay with Patrick and Madeleine at West Wick from time to time. Patrick played some role in introducing Kentridge to members of his old chambers when Kentridge decided to practise in England.[3]

Patrick was kept very busy in 1969 with matters maritime. On 18 March 1967 the SS 'Torrey Canyon', a Suezmax Class oil tanker carrying 120,000 tons

---

[1] 'South Africa, 1984', *The New York Times*, 11 July 1969, p 34.

[2] Benjamin Pogrund, *War of Words: Memoir of a South African Journalist* (New York, 7 Stories Press, 2000). See Review, John Gartley, (2004) 50(4) *Africa Today* 122–24.

[3] Interview between the Author and Sir Sydney Kentridge QC, Lincoln's Inn, 16 January 2016.

of crude oil went aground on the Seven Stones reef between the Scilly Isles and
Land's End. It was at the time one of the largest vessels in the world. The stranding was solely due to the negligence of the master. The stranding, while legally
unresolved, caused many thousands of tons of oil to spill into the ocean. In a
very short time, it began to wash onto Cornish beaches. It was a significant envi-
ronmental disaster. The International Subcommittee of the Comité Maritime
held an inquiry which Patrick chaired.[4] The disaster raised a number of issues,
such as who should be liable and what the level of compensation should be.
Patrick played a leading role in initiating dialogue between the various interests
in order to find solutions. He addressed meetings in Tokyo over a number of
days in late March and early April. As a result, he was instrumental in the introduction of a new international convention dealing with oil pollution and the
various legal consequences that follow.[5]

On 15 February 1970, Patrick wrote to Acheson, this time from Casa Colina
in the Algarve – not that Patrick could sit still for long:[6]

> We are spending the first January and February here in a more modified climate than
> West Wick. The first fortnight was occupied with an arbitration at the Penina Hotel,
> which accounts for my connection there … We return to England at the end of the
> month to start a round of travel, – a tribunal in Geneva, a conference in Tokyo,
> another arbitration in Delhi and perhaps if times fit a visit to South Africa to see what
> is happening at the Gandar trial. All this will last until mid May. After that we shall
> be at peace for the summer at West Wick … I am getting on slowly with my book on
> Woodrow Wilson and shall come to verify my references …

Two days later Patrick wrote again to Acheson to tell him that he had ordered
Acheson's book *Present at the Creation*.[7] 'It has very good reviews has it not,
almost the best yet.'[8]

> In Geneva I am engaged in a very curious occupation,– presiding over a Commission
> which is inquiring into alleged breaches by Greece of various labour conventions.
> Everyone including herself knows that she has, but we are observing the proprie-
> ties. We observe also what I suppose to be Continental legal procedure. I was very
> baffled by it at first. I asked the Scandinavian prosecutor, when he rose to cross-
> examine, how long he expected to be; and he said that he only had five or six
> questions. So I sent a message to Madeleine that I would join her in a quarter of
> an hour. But each question went on for five or ten minutes and the answer, up to

---

[4] The Tokyo Conference, minutes of meeting of the Comité Maritime, 31 March 1969, p 2;
4 April 1969, pp 38–50.

[5] Ibid, 4 April 1969, pp 38–40. International Convention on Civil Liability for Oil Pollution
Damage (Brussels, 29 November 1969).

[6] Letter from Devlin to Acheson, 15 February 1970, Manuscripts and Archives, Yale University
Library, Dean Acheson Papers, folder 98.

[7] Dean Acheson, *Present at the Creation, My Years in the State Department* (New York,
WW Naughton & Company, 1969).

[8] Letter from Devlin to Acheson, 17 February 1970, Manuscripts and Archives, Yale University
Library, Dean Acheson Papers, folder 98.

half an hour. The question consists of observations of the sort that might be made by the chairman of meeting introducing the lecturer and hinting at the topics with which he might be expected to deal, and thus the lecture is launched. These, I am told sternly, forbid any interruption. I have had another strange experience at Brussels in November where I went with the British delegation to a diplomatic conference on oil pollution. We had three weeks in which to produce an international convention, spent two of them on international oratory, and then in the third we went underground into a very small and airless room that reminds me of the House of Lords and did all the work. It was my first experience at 'open covenants openly arrived at' …

But these are diversions. I have given up the Press Council and proceed slowly with my interminable book which is now in its 17th year …

Acheson responded:[9]

Protest is everywhere – by the blacks, by the students, by groups against the war in Vietnam and against the current attempts to withdraw from it, against armaments, against the military, against taxes, against poverty, against discipline. It seems a general rise of mindless anarchy, a retreat from reason before angry emotion – angry, because of the limitations of life and the imperfections of mankind. Those who are not angry, like my grandson Michael, believe 'dedication to service' can conquer all. The idea that competence can help is not widely held. The doctrine of original sin in all over thirty is. I find the outlook depressing.

What hopefully cheered Acheson up was that in 1970 his book *Present at the Creation* won the Pulitzer Prize for 'a distinguished book upon the history of the United States'.[10] Madeleine also published her touching and charming memoir of Patrick's brother Christopher in the same year.[11] She dedicated the book to Patrick. Her style is warm and deeply personal. However, much of it would have been lost on anyone outside the family.

In April 1971 Patrick was to write his last letter to Acheson, to which he received no reply. He told Acheson how much he had enjoyed his book.[12] 'As for my book. I have had to put off, until the fall of 1972, the verifying of my referencing at Princeton, as I have undertaken an inquiry into employees organisations which will keep me busy until then.'

Acheson died of a heart attack at his farm on 12 October 1971. He was found slumped over his desk, no doubt in the midst of answering correspondence.[13]

There were rumblings in the courts. In 1970 a libel case was heard by Mr Justice Lawton and a jury. The plaintiff was a Captain John Broome. He sued the publisher, Cassell & Co Ltd and the author, Mr David Irving, in

[9] Acheson to Devlin, 30 March 1970, Manuscripts and Archives, Yale University Library, Dean Acheson Papers, folder 98.

[10] The 1970 Pulitzer Prize in History, The Pulitzer Prizes: https://www.pulitzer.org/winners/dean-acheson.

[11] Madeleine Devlin, *Christopher Devlin, a Biography* (London, Macmillan, 1970).

[12] Letter from Devlin to Acheson, 23 April 1971, Manuscripts and Archives, Yale University Library, Dean Acheson Papers, folder 98.

[13] 'Dean Acheson Dies on His Farm', *The New York Times*, 13 October 1971.

relation to a book published in 1968 entitled *The Destruction of Convoy PQ17*. The plaintiff alleged the book accused him of being responsible for the loss of merchant ships and the loss of two thirds of the convoy PQ17 in July 1942, due to his carelessness, incompetence and indifference as to its fate by leading it too close to German airfields. In summing up to the jury the trial judge twice read out Patrick's speech in *Rookes v Barnard*. In total the jury awarded £40,000 of which £25,000 comprised punitive or exemplary damages.[14]

The fun, or more accurately the chaos, started in the Court of Appeal. The argument took nine days in February 1971 and judgment was given in less than a month.[15] Lord Denning examined the law before *Rookes v Barnard*. But in language rarely used by an intermediate court, he said of Patrick's judgment that 'Lord Devlin threw over all that we ever knew about exemplary damages. He knocked down the common law as it had existed for centuries ... and all the other Lords agreed with him'.[16] He then commented that the 'new doctrine' had been 'repudiated' in Australia, Canada and New Zealand. He went on to say that the 'wholesale condemnation justifies us, I think, in examining this new doctrine for ourselves ... and I make so bold as to say that it should not be followed any longer in this country.' Bold indeed. He went on to say that the House of Lords had changed the law without having heard argument, excepting an argument from counsel that the precise point decided by Patrick had not been raised in the Lords. Not to be stopped, Denning went on to describe the 'new doctrine' as 'hopelessly illogical and inconsistent'. The final insult was that he thought that future juries should in effect be instructed to abide by the law before *Rookes v Barnard* and therefore ignore it.[17]

Not to be outdone and like some tag team wrestler, Lord Justice Salmon jumped into the ring. Salmon had winkled out of counsel that the matter had not been argued, nor had any of their Lordships so much as mentioned the argument. He went on to assert that none of the categories of cases where exemplary damages could be awarded were supported by any authority and that Patrick's judgment could not be reconciled with either justice or common sense. He agreed with Denning as to how juries should in effect be told to ignore the House of Lords.[18]

Lord Justice Phillimore, in a much more subdued mood, simply said he thought the decision was clearly wrong and was delivered in error.[19]

Lawyers are notorious gossips and the news of the judgment would rapidly have received the attention of the profession, not least other judges. Of those judges who had joined in giving the decision in *Rookes v Barnard*, only Lord Reid was still sitting. Lord Evershed had died in 1966. Lords Hodson and Pearce had

[14] *Broome v Cassell & Co Ltd* [1971] 2 QB 354.
[15] Ibid.
[16] Ibid, at 379–81.
[17] Ibid, at 384.
[18] Ibid, at 386, 387 and 391.
[19] Ibid, at 396.

retired from the Lords in 1971 and 1969 respectively. It is not known what the reaction of all of the others was, but Patrick was furious. Lord Reid discussed the matter with Sir Denis Dobson, the Permanent Secretary of the Lord Chancellor's Department, who was quite calm about the issue and in any event thought Denning might be correct. Lord Reid amplified this view in his speech in the House of Lords in the *Broome v Cassell* appeal.[20]

In the general election in June of 1970, the Tories were returned to power and Lord Hailsham became the Lord Chancellor. Patrick had a sympathetic ear. Patrick was 'much put out' and told Hailsham in an early morning meeting between the two that Denning's publicly expressed views cut across the whole scheme of judicial authority. Although Hailsham told Patrick the matter was going on appeal to the House of Lords, he requested that Hailsham 'give a rebuke to Denning here and now'. Hailsham refused the request, but decided to sit on the appeal. Patrick was not appeased.[21]

The appeal in the House of Lords was heard over 13 days commencing in late November. Judgment was promptly given in early 1972. The bench comprised Lords Hailsham, Reid, Morris of Borth-y-Gest, Viscount Dilhorne, Wilberforce, Diplock and Kilbrandon. The Lords decided that *Rookes v Barnard* was not wrongly decided and that in the hierarchical system of English courts, it was not in any event open to the Court of Appeal to direct judges at first instance to ignore a decision of the House of Lords.

Hailsham said quite expressly that the Court of Appeal was not to give 'gratuitous' advice to trial judges to ignore the Lords.[22] He expressed the view that it would put trial judges in an embarrassing position and lead to chaos. Hailsham also said he thought it should be unnecessary to remind judges of each lower tier that they should loyally accept decisions of the higher tiers. Lord Reid elegantly but tersely said that the Court of Appeal had failed to understand Patrick's speech in *Rookes* and that he would have expected them to know that they had no power to direct judges to disregard a decision of the Lords.[23] Dilhorne's remarks must have made Patrick even angrier. He said that he had some sympathy with the Court of Appeal and that Patrick in effect had not declared what the law was, but what he thought it should be, and that he 'was bowing to the wind of change'. He went on to reiterate his sympathy with the Court of Appeal.[24]

---

[20] Robert Stevens, *The Independence of the Judiciary, a View from the Lord Chancellor's Office* (Oxford, Clarendon Press, 1993), p 95. See also, Robert Stevens, *Law and Politics, The House of Lords as a Judicial Body 1800–1976* (London, Weidenfeld & Nicolson, 1978), pp 474–75; and Louis Blom-Cooper QC, Gavin Drewry and Brice Dickson (eds), *The Judicial House of Lords, 1876–2009* (Oxford, Oxford University Press, 2009), pp 154–55.

[21] Geoffrey Lewis, *Lord Hailsham, A Life* (London, Jonathan Cape, 1997), pp 278–79.

[22] *Cassell & Co Ltd v Broome* [1972] AC 1027 at 1053–54.

[23] At 1084.

[24] At 1156–57.

Hailsham sent a copy of the speeches in the case to Patrick four days after judgment was delivered. Patrick wrote to Hailsham on 27 February 1972:[25]

> How very kind of you to send me the speeches in Broome v Cassell. As you rightly surmise, I was greatly interested and greatly pleased to be able to read the judgments earlier in extenso than otherwise I could. I am heartily glad that you put down with such a firm hand (albeit with 'studied moderation') the antics of the C.A. and that you had unanimous support of the House in so doing. There is enough permissiveness in the world today without its penetration into the doctrine of precedent. I feel that your decision which we discussed in our chat, to deal with the situation in this way has been proved entirely right. I am also of course very glad that our efforts in Rookes v Barnard have not in the end been relegated to the perincurial limbo; and I appreciate in particular the kind things you said about my speech. But what strikes me most of all, if it is not impertinent to say so, is the merit of your own. It is a comprehensive and masterful review of the whole subject, and how you found the time for it I cannot imagine ...

More arbitrations and travel consumed Patrick. It may well be that Acheson's death caused Patrick to get on with his biography of Wilson. The title 'Too Proud to Fight' was a reference to a speech Wilson had delivered in Philadelphia on 10 May 1915 at a naturalisation ceremony.[26] Part of the speech involved Wilson saying:[27]

> The example of America must be a special example. The example of America must be an example not merely of peace because it will not fight, but of peace because peace is the healing and elevating influence of the world and strife is not. There is such a thing as a man being too proud to fight. There is such a thing as a nation being so right it does not need to convince others by force that it is right.

There has been much speculation whether the speech more generally, but this passage in particular, was a reference to the sinking of the RMS 'Lusitania', a Cunard ocean liner, by a German U-boat. It had been carrying just under 2000 passengers, of whom almost 1200 died. 128 of them were Americans. In any event, America entered the war nearly two years later.

The book on any view had had a long gestation period. It was a tome that ran for almost 700 pages. Patrick dedicated it to his cousin, who, aged 20, was killed in action on 26 March 1918 in France. Patrick explained in the dedication:[28]

> When Woodrow Wilson was a young man he was ambitious to 'write something that men might delight to read and which they would not readily let die'. Many would like to do that but not many who have not given their whole life to writing get the chance

---

[25] Letter from Devlin to Hailsham, 27 February 1972, papers of Lord Hailsham, Churchill Archives Centre, Churchill College, University of Cambridge.

[26] Patrick Devlin, *Too Proud to Fight, Woodrow Wilson's Neutrality* (New York/Oxford, Oxford University Press, 1975).

[27] Speech by Woodrow Wilson, 10 May 1915, delivered in Philadelphia.

[28] Patrick Devlin, *Too Proud to Fight, Woodrow Wilson's Neutrality* (New York/Oxford, Oxford University Press, 1975), Dedication.

to try. I get it because I was young enough to miss the Great War of 1914 and so to speed to early attainment through the gaps it blasted out of the classes above me. The chance was bought for me by the dead: my gain is what they lost. I write about life in the office and not on the battlefield, but beneath the text there is the insistent drumming of the fight, of wounds and death. The death of the unripe. All through the writing I have been pricked by that. So I dedicate the book for what is worth to the Unfulfilled, to the memory of John Duncan Abel ...

History is a tale of progress from an uncertain beginning to an uncertain end; and the historian, unable to extract from it more than a moment infinitesimal in the measure of time, searches this moment for a clue which, added to others in a laboratory of all the arts and sciences, may some day make known to man out of what his mind comes and into what it is to go.

The book had in fact almost taken decades to research and write. Patrick had over the years invested heavily in the project. In the last few years he had to go it alone. His close friends such as Frankfurter and Acheson, who had inspired and enthused him, had fallen by the wayside. The journey had for much of the time been lonely and arduous. But Patrick had shown no qualms about taking on the professional philosophers. The professional historians were next on the list. In a sense, that he had finally finished the work and that it was on bookshelves was more than enough satisfaction. The task had been Herculean by any standards. The reviews were by and large pleasing, as no doubt was the launch. But some of the critics were harsh.

Writing in the *Journal of American Studies* Dr John Thompson,[29] a history fellow at St Catharine's College, Cambridge and a published author himself on Wilson said 'With its superbly controlled and precise prose, occasionally rhetorical but more commonly Olympian, this book for all its considerable length, is certainly a pleasure to read'. He said: 'Moreover although the author has directly consulted only a limited range of primary material and has depended greatly on the researches of others ... *Too Proud to Fight* is also a contribution to history'. Thompson continued:

the participants in this long sustained debate will be indebted to him for his lucid analysis of the issues, particularly the legal ones, and his deft and worldly portraits of the personalities involved in the intricate diplomacy of these years.[30]

Professor Accinelli from the Department of History at the University of Toronto responded in a more restrained fashion.[31] Accinelli told the putative reader that although the book in many respects was not novel 'it had much to recommend it'. He said 'Lord Devlin is a shrewd, sensitive, graceful writer, and his account is often insightful and rewarding'. Further, he claimed that 'No recent scholar has

---

[29] John Thompson, 'Book Review: *Too Proud to Fight: Woodrow Wilson's Neutrality*' (1975) 9(2) *Journal of Americans Studies* 246 and following.

[30] Ibid, p 246.

[31] Robert Accinelli, *The New York Times Review of Books*, 1975, pp 261 and following.

better described and analysed the legal dimension of wartime diplomacy'. The review was not entirely uncritical and Accinelli describes Patrick's explanation of why Wilson went to war in the end as 'deficient'.

Professor Lawrence Gelfand, at the University of Iowa's History Department said:[32]

> Some scholarly eyebrows will doubtless be raised on hearing that an interloper has invaded the historical thicket where prudent amateurs might fear to tread ... Devlin's research hardly touched the rich accessible American manuscript sources (it does draw upon British archival material in London) and hence offers little that is factually startling to an understanding of Wilsonian diplomacy. Nevertheless, Devlin's critical eye absorbed an amazing variety of printed evidence. This impressive narrative contains a marvellously rich synthesis, many illuminating insights and often penetrating analyses of individuals as well as the many legal tangles posed for American statesmen by the European war.

After some negatives Gelfand concludes 'By expressing thoughtful criticism Lord Devlin's opus makes an important contribution to the continuous historical dialogue concerning Wilsonian diplomacy'.[33]

By 4 March 1974, the Conservatives under Edward Heath had lost government and Harold Wilson was back in Downing St. Over the years Patrick had been a source of advice for some of his colleagues who had followed his success after leaving office. For example, Hailsham's fortunes had been mixed. He had fared reasonably well politically but had been passed over for leader of the Conservative party when Macmillan retired in 1963. He had, however, been appointed Lord Chancellor under Heath in the years 1970 to 1974. With Harold Wilson back in Downing Street, he was looking around for other opportunities. He asked Patrick what he thought. Indeed, he wrote immediately to Patrick on the day the poll was declared. Patrick responded on 18 March 1974:[34]

> What a bouleversement! I suppose you are used to the ups and downs of political life but all the same this sort of thing must be very disconcerting. Although your time has been cut short – I suppose only temporarily – it has been long enough for you to establish yourself as a judicial figure ... To answer your question I think there is a market in the arbitration field though I have not explored it systematically enough to be sure how it works. I had better give you my experience for what it is worth. I found myself, quite early on, approached by solicitors who represented a German client in a dispute with a British Company over a contract which was governed by English law. Both sides were willing for me to decide the matter. There was a clause in the contract providing for arbitration under the rules of the International Chamber of Commerce. In this way I came into contact with the Chamber; and not very long after they asked

---

[32] Lawrence Gelfand, 'Too Proud to Fight; Woodrow Wilson's Neutrality: Devlin, Patrick, New York: Oxford University Press, 731 pp., Publication Date: January 9, 1975', in (1975) 3(6) *History: Reviews of New Books* 141–42, especially p 141.

[33] Ibid, p 142.

[34] Letter from Devlin to Hailsham, 18 March 1975, papers of Lord Hailsham, Churchill Archives Centre, Churchill College, University of Cambridge.

me to take over an arbitration that had got into difficulties when the Norwegian had to be removed for senility and after one of the earlier arbitrators had a heart attack. Since then I have done several more through the Chamber and one or two casual ones.

Shrewdly and presciently Patrick observed:[35]

> I have not got the least doubt that with your reputation and as an ex-Lord Chancellor you will find yourself approached unless people are deterred by the thought that it may not be long before you are back on the Woolsack again. These arbitrations are long drawn out affairs and take at least three or four years to mature so that unless you are asked to take over someone's place because of death or illness it is not likely to provide work in the short term ... For the longer term have you any thoughts about the Press Council? It adds a reasonable emolument to a pension and is interesting on the benching work?

The problem for Hailsham, which he did not consider, was that Patrick had a high profile as a trial judge, let alone as an appellate one, and that he had achieved considerable prominence outside the law. He was also an extremely commercially minded person, whereas Hailsham had been a career politician. The law was not his natural milieu. In time and as predicted, he would be back on the Woolsack.

It is hard to gauge from his output whether Patrick ever refused any task asked of him by government or otherwise, but if it did happen, it would appear to have happened rarely. As a result of several questionable criminal convictions, on 1 May 1974, the then Home Secretary, Roy Jenkins, a member of the recently elected Wilson Labour government, appointed a small committee with Patrick as chairman to review, in the light of those wrongful convictions, 'all aspects of the law and procedure dealing to the evidence of identification in criminal cases; and to make recommendations'.[36] The committee held its first meeting on 22 May and then on 30 other occasions. It reported to the Government in 1976. The report, which is voluminous, made a number of important findings and recommendations. It had a significant effect on the approach of courts in cases of visual identification. A general rule was recommended under which there could not be a conviction in any case in which the Prosecution relied wholly or mainly on evidence of visual identification, even if that identification was made by more than one witness. However, it was accepted that there should be exceptions to be worked out on a case-by-case basis.[37]

The English Court of Appeal (including the then Chief Justice and four other judges) were not prepared to adopt Patrick's recommendation in full. The judges felt it better to assess the quality of the evidence and not have any notion of exceptional circumstances.

---

[35] Ibid, p 2.
[36] Report to the Secretary of State for the Home Department, of the Departmental Committee on Evidence of Identification in Criminal Cases, Chairman: the Right Hon Lord Devlin, 26 April 1976, pp 5–6.
[37] Ibid.

Relieved at successfully concluding his 'magnum opus' on Wilson, Patrick, for the time being, returned to the more familiar territory of lectures. In the seventies Patrick delivered, as he put it 'half a dozen lectures or addresses in what is for me a short space of time, 1975 to 1978'.[38] The fact is that much to the envy and even chagrin of some of his former colleagues, Patrick was, if possible, busier now than ever before. On top his other commitments, he and Madeleine found that they were not seeing as much of West Wick or Casa Colina as either would have preferred. Patrick appreciated only too well that without Madeleine many of these activities would not have been possible. The lectures and addresses were published ultimately in one volume in 1979.[39] Patrick's book was published at the same time as a book by Lord Denning entitled *The Discipline of the Law*,[40] perhaps a rather odd title given the latter's performance in *Cassell v Broome*.

Justice Wright of the United States Court of Appeals reviewing both works for the *Stanford Law Review*, commented:[41]

> In The Judge, Lord Devlin sounds the contrasting themes of contrasting jurisprudential conservatism. Although he too sat in the Court of Appeal, Devlin has become better known as an author and social critic, and his book aspires to the critic's long-sighted detachment. Warning that judicial reformism grows from the same dangerous root as judicial tyranny, Devlin defends the restraints of jurisprudential formalism ... Devlin characterises his book – reworked from a series of lectures – as an inquiry into the place of the judge in the political life of the country. He draws sharp lines between the political and judicial spheres. And he admonishes judges in crisp terms about their obligations to judicial form and precedent. Devlin's book is a difficult book to review. Ranging over widely disparate matters of judicial concern, it contains no simple or dominant thread about which to weave a discussion. Moreover the book holds several surprises for liberal readers eager for the challenge of intellectual confrontation. In his best known book, The Enforcement of Morals, Devlin spoke as a tough-minded proponent of moral and political reaction. Action undermining the nation's moral sensibilities, he argued, was the logical and moral equivalent of treason, which the law need not hesitate to suppress. His latest expressions are

---

[38] Patrick Devlin, *The Judge* (Oxford, Oxford University Press, 1979), Preface. That statement about his output is to be found in the preface. It is a reference to the fourth Chorley lecture delivered on 25 June 1975 at the London School of Economics entitled 'The Judge as a Lawmaker', an address to the Howard League for Penal Reform entitled 'The Judge as Sentencer' on 30 September 1975, a lecture in a Vacation Course for Foreign Lawyers at the University of Cambridge entitled 'The Judge in the Adversary System' on 21 July 1976, the Cameron-Gifford lecture at the University of Nottingham entitled 'The Judge and the *Aequum et Bonum*' on 20 October 1977, the 'Judge and Jury', the fourth Blackstone lecture (in two parts) at Pembroke College, Oxford on 2 May and 18 November 1978, and finally 'The Judge and Case law' at the University of Cambridge on 18 July 1978.

[39] Patrick Devlin, *The Judge* (Oxford, Oxford University Press, 1979).

[40] Lord Denning, *The Discipline of the Law* (London, Butterworths, 1979).

[41] Patrick Devlin, *The Judge*, reviewed by J Skelly Wright, Chief Judge, United States Court of Appeal for the District of Colombia circuit, 'Law and the Logic of Experience: Reflections on Denning, Devlin and Judicial Innovation in the British Context' (1980) 33(1) *Stanford Law Review* 179–99.

more temperate. Devlin remains a strict constructionist on law and a traditionalist in morals, but he now worries increasingly about the law's capacity to protect the liberties respected by traditional morality. He therefore supports the enactment of a bill of rights – a mildly surprising stance, since such a document would restrict the power of Parliament to translate popular moral prejudices into legislation ... Devlin retains his penchant for clear, provocative and contentious statement – qualities that make this a lively and readable book ...

With the compliments out of the way, Wright then accused Patrick of a lack of analytical consistency and coherence which led to 'collapsed dichotomies and hence thematic confusion'.[42] This criticism is a fair one simply because Patrick tries too hard to reconcile the notion that those democratically elected should make the law, with the recognition that the Parliament is unreliable in some areas to ensure that the law made is good law. He concluded:[43]

Devlin wants on the one hand a sharp dichotomy between adjudication and lawmaking and on the other hand a legal system responsive to changed and changing social conditions. Ironically his book helps to illustrate that he cannot have both.

In fairness to Patrick, book reviews are often used by the reviewer as a platform to display their own mastery of the topic or push their own school of thought. In short, the review often becomes a piece more about the reviewer than the reviewed. This is very much the case with Wright's review, that is, when he was not being patronising to the English judiciary.

In England the book was reviewed by Lord Simon of Glaisdale, a former Conservative MP, Solicitor-General and Law Lord, for the *Cambridge Law Journal*.[44] It is a concise piece, making the point that Patrick is better known for his writings on the law rather his judgments, and: 'The book under review is to my mind Lord Devlin's best – indeed the most important book written on the function of the English in society'. However, it was not all smooth sailing. Simon pointed to inconsistencies also identified by Wright. He concluded:[45]

No summary of this book can really do justice to it. Almost every page has a striking and vigorous and often witty phrase which compels thought. Its pungent and aphoristic style arises not from any search for smartness, but as the natural expression of a powerful, penetrating, balanced, judicious and sometimes sardonic mind reasoning closely to produce order from complicated material.

There is no doubt that in the decade since he had left the Lords, Patrick established himself as a writer, biographer, and lecturer. He had ceased sitting in the Privy Council by around 1973. At the time *The Judge* was published in about 1979, he was 75 and showing no signs of slowing down.

---

[42] Ibid, p 195.
[43] Ibid, p 198.
[44] Books Reviews, Simon of Glaisdale, '*The Judge* by Patrick Devlin' (1980) 39 *Cambridge Law Journal* 371–72.
[45] Ibid, p 372.

13

Revenge

D ILHORNE HAD BEEN created a peer in 1962. He had never enjoyed
Patrick's success as a judge. That is not to say he was not a good lawyer,
but he had the reputation of being gruff and a bully. He was as fiercely
committed to his family as he was to the Conservative Party, both of which had
loyally served. But his junior legal practice was at best nondescript. He could
be rude to his opponents when he was in practice and was positively disliked as
a judge. Although he took silk in 1946, he did not have much of a practice in
that role either. But he was diligent and worked extremely hard. He had been a
member of the House of Commons from 1943 and was made Solicitor-General
in 1951 and, in 1954, Attorney-General. In the middle to the late fifties,
Dilhorne was frequently the subject of derision in a column in *The Spectator*
under the pseudonym Taper.[1] He was regarded by many as 'an arrogant, rather
square-toed individual, not very clever and not very good at his job',[2] which
in some respects was an entirely unjustified view. But he was a loyal Tory who
survived politically, partly because of his robust personality.

In politics, loyalty is often not enough. Kilmuir had been loyal, as had others,
but in 1962 Macmillan had decided that they were expendable. Dilhorne was an
aggressive performer and was a very effective combatant in the Commons. In the
right case, the same was true of his role in the courtroom. On occasion he could
be quite sensitive. In 1978 during a debate on the Scotland Bill in the House of
Lords, Hailsham had expressed a view on the legislation. Referring to a standard
English legal textbook (Halsbury) and poking fun at Hailsham, he referred to
the 'Hailsham edition' in a mocking way.[3] He made other somewhat flippant
remarks which were also critical of Hailsham. When Hailsham got to his feet
remarkably, he unleashed a vitriolic attack on his fellow Tory no doubt to the
delight of many others. He accused Dilhorne of using 'populist and rhetorical
language' and 'rhetorical demagogy', saying that Dilhorne had been 'talking

---

[1] RFV Heuston, *Lives of the Lord Chancellors, 1940–1970* (Oxford, Clarendon Press, 1987),
pp 183–89.

[2] Ibid, p 189.

[3] Hansard, House of Lords Debates, Debate on the Scotland Bill, 12 April 1978, volume 390
cols 728–76 at 8:21 pm.

nonsense' and 'the most arrant nonsense'.[4] Dilhorne then wrote to Hailsham on 13 April 1978:[5]

> I was hurt by your attack, very hurt. It was so unexpected and some of the things you said, were too personal and went too far. I am all in favour of lively debate and having fun. Perhaps I took what you said too seriously. Let's forget all about it. But next time you propose to have fun at my expense give me a little warning so that I can put my armour on and polish up my weapons.

Dilhorne could be extremely rude in court. Indeed the author has witnessed it at first hand. On occasion he had justification. That behaviour was not unique, especially if the presiding Law Lord was of the courteous and silent type, such as Lord Wilberforce.[6] For some he was slightly more affectionately described as a large 'clumber spaniel'.[7] But Patrick never liked him or trusted him. Nyasaland was the most bruising experience he had directly at the hands of Dilhorne, and he never forgave or forgot it.

With the election of Margaret Thatcher as Prime Minister on 4 May 1979, Hailsham was once again Lord Chancellor. Notwithstanding the exchange over the Scotland Bill, he and Dilhorne remained firm friends all of their lives. Towards the middle of 1980 Dilhorne retired. Hailsham wrote to him wishing a happy retirement. Dilhorne replied on 31 July 1980:[8]

> It was kind of you to write as you did, I do appreciate it. I think it is the most flattering letter I have ever received – and I always thought you very truthful. I shall have to buy a new hat. I have been very lucky. I have enjoyed it all. When I was summonsed from Scotland to see Harold when the office of LCJ was vacant, I told Mary that I hoped I would not be offered the post, but if I was, it was one that could not be refused. I was relieved – somewhat to Harold's astonishment – when it did not come my way. I think it is the most arduous office in our profession. Great responsibility and little power – and LCJ's don't seem to last long. I would have liked to have sat on the Woolsack a little longer but that was not to be. I have enjoyed the work of a Lord of Appeal. Now I shall not be so busy though I hope you will call me from time to time. I hope you will go on sitting on the Woolsack for a long time. No retirement please and don't let them work you too hard.

---

[4] Ibid, at 9:37 pm.

[5] Letter from Dilhorne to Hailsham, 13 April 1978, papers of Lord Hailsham, Churchill Archives Centre, Churchill College, University of Cambridge.

[6] Alan Paterson, *The Law Lords* (London, Macmillan Press, 1982), p 70.

[7] DR Thorpe, *Supermac: The Life of Harold Macmillan* (London, Chatto & Windus, 2010), p 569; Alistair Horne, *Macmillan 1957–1986, Volume II of the Official Biography* (London, Macmillan, 1989), p 558.

[8] Letter from Dilhorne to Hailsham, 31 July 1980, papers of Lord Hailsham, Churchill Archives Centre, Churchill College, University of Cambridge.

Hailsham went about his work, as did Patrick. On 7 September Dilhorne was walking in Scotland and rather unexpectedly died. On 9 September Hailsham recorded in his diary:[9]

> Reggie Dilhorne is dead: MCH rang me on the way home in car y'day. Apparently in Scotland. Grand day on the hill. Some fine heads seen. In the night fell ill and sent for daughter and son: 'I think this is the end', and died. Wrote Mary D. Sad for her. Old school friend. Will be sadly missed. But his life's work ended w: retirement last July. Fine character. Sound values. Unflagging industry. Filled each office he held with distinction. End at the top of his powers: no slow decline, no long illness.

Dilhorne was appropriately accorded many tributes from all sides in the House of Lords on 6 October. Lord Soames perhaps captured the joint mood of the House when he said:[10] 'Behind the bluff and perhaps sometimes forbidding exterior there lay a deep sensitivity and a strong sense of humour.' Lord Elwyn-Jones, a former Labour Lord Chancellor who had sat with Dilhorne in the Lords, said:[11]

> Those of us who served with him in another place will remember always his tough robustness in the face of stormy parliamentary onslaughts ... I did not often agree with him politically but this never affected our longstanding friendship which extended over a span of 40 years. Few men were kinder in personal relationships than he was.

These views were certainly not shared by Patrick, or by others who had unhappily borne the brunt of his rudeness and arrogance.

Precisely when Patrick started thinking about his next major project is not entirely clear but it is possible, like Woodrow Wilson, it had been on the drawing board for some little time. Certainly, Dilhorne's death might have started him thinking, but what must have confirmed his view as to timing was the death on 4 July 1983 of Dr Adams.[12] Other key players were also dead, Geoffrey Lawrence QC in 1967, Lord Goddard in 1971 and Dr Douthwaite in 1974. In any event by 1984 Patrick started preparing to write a book on the Adams trial.

He commenced gathering the records, including the transcripts of proceedings, and somehow some of the original exhibits such as the infamous nurses' notebooks. As Patrick reconsidered the meticulously kept, typed nurses' notebooks, he was no doubt reminded of the very substantial forensic advantage

---

[9] Diary of Lord Hailsham, 9 September 1980, papers of Lord Hailsham, Churchill Archives Centre, Churchill College, University of Cambridge.
[10] Hansard, House of Lords Debates, 6 October 1980, volume 413, cols 1–5.
[11] Ibid.
[12] 'Friends say Farewell to Bodkin Adams', *The Times*, 21 July 1983, p 3.

which defence counsel, Lawrence QC enjoyed at the trial, including being able to cross-examine the nurses on the distinction between drugs prescribed and drugs administered. The notebooks were singularly important in allowing Lawrence to dismantle and destroy a fundamental plank of the Prosecution's case.[13]

Many judges and for that matter lawyers over the years have written memoirs. They are usually a collection of war stories and often include their greatest cross-examinations and victories, unashamedly name dropping as they go. But this was a book of an entirely different kind for the genre. No judge had ever written a full-length book about a trial over which he had presided.

Patrick wrote to Dilhorne's son on 19 July 1984:[14]

> I do not know if you have recollection of the Adams case in 1957 in which I was the judge and your father was the Attorney-General led for the Crown. Reggie always held the view that the acquittal was due to a misdirection by me. He made the point in a letter (copy enclosed) soon after verdict. I should like to quote the second paragraph in which he puts the point in his own words. Would you permit this? I should say that the book is very critical of Reggie. We were always friendly and got on well, but we disagreed in almost every conceivable point. I think he intended to write about the case himself and it was sad that he died so suddenly after he retired. We were about the same age but he always looked so robust that I find it strange to have outlived him.

This was an odd letter. Apart from seeking the consent to quote a portion of a letter addressed to Patrick, it is a little hard to fathom the point in the letter. If it was some socially awkward way of forewarning him of a critical piece about his father, it is hardly surprising it does not appear to have been answered. In any event, Patrick just went back to his study and continued sharpening his pencil.

In addition, Patrick prepared a precis or proposal for prospective publishers. He sketched the plot and the twists and turns he intended to deal with. He described Dilhorne as 'the last of the lawyer-political careerists, a man more disliked than liked, uninspired but competent'.[15] It was clear from the outset that whatever other motivation Patrick might have had in writing the book, an important one was to blatantly attack Dilhorne.

In so far as the book could be described as an impartial description and analysis of a public event, namely a major criminal trial, it was justifiable, as the events had, as Professor Heuston describes, crossed the border which divides current affairs from history. And no doubt very much by reason the stature and unique position of the author, the descriptions and insights are fascinating. With his skills, Patrick made readable the cross-examination of the nurses.

---

[13] Original exhibits from the Adams trial, typed nurses' notebooks covering the periods 21 June 1949–13 November 1950, from the papers of Lord Devlin.

[14] Letter from Devlin to Lord Dilhorne, 19 July 1984, Devlin correspondence file.

[15] 'Easing the Passing by Patrick Devlin: A book of about 80,000 words to be written on lines planned as set out below, TS to be delivered not later than 1 March 1984 for publication autumn 1984', Precis.

But intertwined with the factual is a unique consideration of such important notions as the accused's right to silence. He teased the reader with somewhat ambiguous statements about his true view as to Adams' guilt or innocence. His summing up was clearly in favour of acquittal, but that was difficult to reconcile with his description of the accused as 'The mercenary mercy-killer fits best the picture of him that I have in my mind'.[16] But given the way in which he treated Dilhorne in the book, it was equally consistent with the view that a probably guilty man went free due to the incompetence and stupidity of prosecuting counsel, and that the jury by reason of that incompetence were simply, but understandably, unable to convict.

Mixed with his fascinating narrative, Patrick carefully contrived descriptions of Dilhorne which, if not uncalled for, were 'below the belt', hurtful to his family and gratuitous. If poor judgement or lack of experience was Patrick's real view of Dilhorne, and that had an impact on the trial, there is no reason why the point could not be made. His death put an end to any libel and Patrick would have been very well aware of that. But his insults, although they may have caused a titter amongst Dilhorne's detractors, were unworthy of Patrick. Many of Patrick's sentiments when taken in isolation give a distinct impression of fairness, objectivity and the odd dose of generosity. However, the overwhelming impact is one of almost utter contempt for Dilhorne.

In the end the title for the book suggested itself. When interviewed by the police on 26 November 1956 about the death of Mrs Morrell, Adams unprovoked had said:[17] 'Easing the passing of a dying person is not all that wicked. She wanted to die. That cannot be murder. It is impossible to accuse a doctor.' It may well not have the original title, as Patrick's papers are simply catalogued as 'The Adams Case'. But the more preparation he did, the more obvious that he must have thought that the doctor, whatever his motive, undoubtedly 'eased' the passing. Patrick explained his thinking in part when he said:[18]

> A quarter of a century has now passed since the trial of Dr Adams, long enough to allow publication without indecorum and not too long to destroy recollection. What I am writing is not primarily a descriptive account but an analytical narrative of the progress of the trial. For the most part it was what was passing through my mind. It is the sort of talk that would have gone on in the evening if I had been explaining to an interested amateur the significance of what had happened during the day. There was much to explain. Most trials are no more than the acting out of the prosecution's opening speech diversified by the struggle of the defence to infect the mass of material with the reasonable doubt. The trial was quite outside the usual pattern and fascinating in its twists and turns.

> Yet the whole story of Dr Adams was not told at the trial.

[16] ETP, p 199.
[17] Ibid, p 7.
[18] Ibid, p 8.

By page two Patrick had started the scarification process with the following when describing Dilhorne's opening address. As a warm up:[19] 'The Attorney-General continued. He was not an orator, but his manner was earnest and either, as some might say, impressive or, as others, ponderous.' He continued by describing Dilhorne having little 'breadth of view' or 'flexibility'. In a more patronising tone, he continued:[20]

> The Attorney-General was called Reggie by friend and foe alike because he was the sort of person who obviously ought to be called Reggie ... I had had a casual acquaintance with him for some time. He had, I am sure, chosen the Bar as a profession not out of any interest in justice or the law but because it was generally thought to be a good ground for a career to grow in, especially if fertilised by politics ...

> 'The world continues to offer glittering prizes to those who have stout hearts and sharp swords'. Reggie never learnt swordsmanship but he was effective with a blunt instrument and certainly had a stout heart. What was almost unique about him and makes his career so fascinating is that what the ordinary careerist achieves by making himself agreeable, falsely or otherwise, Reggie achieved by making himself disagreeable. Sections of the press, which he permanently antagonised, liked to parody his name by calling him Sir Bullying Manner. This was wrong. He was a bully without a bullying manner. His bludgeoning was quiet. He could be downright rude but he did not shout or bluster. Yet his disagreeableness was so pervasive, his persistence so interminable, the obstructions he manned so far flung, his objectives apparently so insignificant, that sooner or later you would be tempted to ask yourself whether the game was worth the candle: if asked yourself that, you were finished ...

> He was neither a saint nor a villain. But since most of his convictions were wrong-headed, he was ineluctably a do-badder, by which I mean a person whose activities bear the same relation to villainy as those of a do-gooder to sanctity.

> His dislikes, however strong, seemed to me impersonal. They did not exclude many small kindnesses and courtesies. There was no malice in him. At least I do not think there was. Clumsiness? Almost invariably. Stupidity? Yes, from time to time. Amounting to perversity? I think that it must be conceded that sometimes it did. And might there have been on occasions only a dim perception, as Melford might have put it, of the borderline between perversity and malice? Possibly.

What a reader might think all of this character assassination had to do with a trial at the Old Bailey would be a fair question to pose. And the logical answer would be nothing at all, except to use the occasion to get it off the author's chest and to settle an old score. The next topic was Dilhorne's mediocre practice at the Bar again, except for the occasional outing. Patrick suggested that he got silk because of political reasons not associated with the ability of the applicant or the size of his practice.[21] Patrick moved on to Dilhorne's failure to secure the

---

[19] Ibid, p 2.
[20] Ibid, pp 39–40.
[21] Ibid, p 40.

job of Lord Chief Justice,[22] and that many of his critics were eagerly waiting to see how he would perform in 'a spectacular criminal trial'.[23] Patrick explained his vitriolic journey through the man's career as an explanation of the 'dramatis personae'.[24] That is just a little unconvincing.

The book more or less returned to its main theme of the trial but not before extolling the professional ability of Dilhorne's opponent Geoffrey Lawrence QC: 'Reggie was not an artist like Lawrence. He would not even remotely have understood the mental processes of Dr Adams.'[25]

Patrick had the ability to give words the properties of razor blades. He accused the Attorney-General of a lack of imagination and of adopting a simplistic storybook analysis to the case.[26] Not once, apart from accepting that Dilhorne had parliamentary commitments that would have distracted him, did he acknowledge the fact that the case had been the subject of intense police inquiry. Nor did he acknowledge the role of the solicitors involved, along with a bevy of juniors, and that they might or should take some responsibility for the gathering and deployment of the facts or the shape the case took at trial. Further, Patrick alleged that Dilhorne had left the Crown case in some confusion and that he was unprofessional and had 'bungled' a weak case.[27] Notwithstanding the profile of the case, he was incapable of rising to the occasion.

More than once Patrick returned to the theme of Dilhorne not having become Lord Chief Justice. But he hardly addressed his own ambitions or his own failure to achieve that position. Not content with the taunts about all manner of things Patrick decided it was also appropriate to discuss Nyasaland and Dilhorne's role in that issue.[28] Again, it may rhetorically be asked what this might have to do with the Adams trial. Perhaps something more than mere 'dramatis personae'? Even Patrick felt the need for some explanation, saying:[29]

> If I have dwelt on this episode in too great detail, it is partly to offer a small revenge to the reader who may have found curious some of the workings of the law which I too blandly take for granted and who may now enjoy without malice my entanglement in the political process which I found incomprehensible. Having got so far, I ought to disclose that the entanglement was not the end of me. It ought to have been.

The scars were deep and clearly the wounds had not healed. But that, arguably, did not give Patrick licence gratuitously to attack Dilhorne, by then a corpse of five years, with a hatchet. He even had a swipe at Dilhorne's obituary in *The Times* as being 'generous'.[30]

[22] Ibid, p 41.
[23] Ibid, pp 41–42.
[24] Ibid, p 42.
[25] Ibid, p 146.
[26] Ibid, p 49.
[27] Ibid, p 122.
[28] Ibid, p 191.
[29] Ibid, p 191.
[30] Ibid, p 195.

Patrick was correct about Dilhorne in a number of respects. He was straight-forward, a man of simple tastes. He was entirely uncomplicated. He had an all-consuming sense of duty. With Dilhorne you knew where you stood. He could be unapologetically rude but did not carry any grudges. He wrote no great works, no tomes, and he did not think deeply about the law. Indeed, he was everything Patrick wasn't.

It could have come as no surprise that Patrick drew criticism from a number of quarters when the book was published. There were serious critics who thought, with some justification, that to write about Dilhorne in the manner he did was disrespectful of a colleague. Lord Scarman and Lord Bridge of Harwich both criticised Patrick in the *Times Literary Supplement* saying that it may well be Patrick's reputation that might suffer as a result of the book rather than Dilhorne's.[31] In John Baker's memoirs, he recounts a conversation with Hailsham:[32]

> I recall Lord Hailsham once asking if I had read it. I had not. He then declaimed furiously 'He ought never have written it'. He then changed his expression to a mischievous grin and said, 'But it's a jolly good read!' – and burst into loud laughter.

Hailsham also expressed that view to others. Some thought that Hailsham's views were frivolously indulgent to Patrick.[33]

As was expected the book was to be reviewed. First in the *Irish Jurist*,[34] Ronan Keane, having discussed the trial and Patrick's account, said:[35]

> If that were all Easing the Passing might be regarded as no more than an interesting and unusual memoir, perhaps somewhat lightweight judged by the standards of Trial by Jury and The Enforcement of Morals. But unfortunately it is more likely to be remembered for the posthumous attack Lord Devlin has seen fit to launch in its pages on Sir Reginald Manningham-Buller. His strictures on his deceased colleague are not limited to his conduct of the prosecution in the Adams trial: he is mercilessly pilloried as the worst type of careerist, stupid, disagreeable and, it is not too delicately hinted, capable of downright malevolence.

Keane concluded:[36]

> In any event his quarry is beyond him. But it does introduce a sad and sour note: surely these bones could have been left in peace.

---

[31] See Ronan Keane, Justice of High Court of Ireland, 'Review and Notices: Lord Patrick Devlin, Easing the Passing' (1984) 19(2) *Irish Jurist* 362, p 365.

[32] John Baker, *Ballot Box to Jury Box, the Life and Times of an English Crown Court Judge* (Hook, Waterside Press, 2005), p 123.

[33] Ian Thorpe (ed), *Who loses, who wins: the Journals of Kenneth Rose, Volume Two: 1979–2013,* (London, Weidenfeld & Nicholson, 2019), pp 121, 359 and 431.

[34] Ronan Keane, Justice of High Court of Ireland, 'Review and Notices: Lord Patrick Devlin, Easing the Passing' (1984) 19(2) *Irish Jurist* 362–66.

[35] Ibid, p 362.

[36] Ibid, p 366.

Brian Simpson also reviewed the book for the *Michigan Law Review*.[37] Simpson's review is less judgmental. He saw the very serious jurisprudential issues raised and although he repeats many of the pejorative epithets. Although he accepted and explained Patrick's attack on Dilhorne as a mere historical incident of their relationship, he did say:[38]

> Some might object to this book on the grounds of impropriety, but I should think that the lapse of time, the death of Dr Adams (and the other possible villain), the absence of a close family and the fact that most of the information used is in the public domain, operate together as an answer. Indeed, since Victorian times, judicial reminiscences have frequently been published without censure. But so detailed an account of a single trial by the presiding judge is without precedent, so that this is a most unusual book …

> There is a subplot, essentially concerned with Lord Devlin's own biography. It renders the book both more interesting and more amusing and brings the writing occasionally and agreeably near the boundaries of good taste.

However Simpson also observed:[39]

> This story lies close to the surface of this book, and gives the writing a bite which in my view adds to the fascination of this trip behind the scenes of the English legal world. Where law and politics come together it all becomes less than perfectly gentlemanly.

Simpson's analysis of the complex politico-legal goings on behind the scenes involving Patrick and Dilhorne was masterful. Preferring, however, to rise above the obvious, Simpson rightly attributed to Patrick a discussion about the theoretical line between legitimate medical practice and murder, 'a line not easy to draw, particularly in cases where pain-killing drugs, administered in quantities adequate to alleviate distress, will also have the effect of shortening life'.[40]

At the date of publication of the book Patrick had turned 80. He was clearly stung by some of the criticisms. He was interviewed by Joshua Rozenberg on his birthday in 1985. Rozenberg in his customary and elegant manner asked Patrick about a number of topics. He confirmed, for example, that he disliked appellate work and would have very much liked to have been Lord Chief Justice. When asked about Adams he said he was in no doubt that he was innocent and that the Crown case was doomed from the start. When confronted with the book Patrick said he had no regrets about writing it. He regretted any hurt to Dilhorne's family, but said that he gave as good as he got. In particular he said:[41]

> *Joshua Rozenberg*: The prosecution of Dr Adams was handled in court by the then Attorney-General, Sir Reginald Manningham-Buller, who was popularly known as

[37] AW Simpson, 'Euthanasia for sale' (1986) 84 *Michigan Law Review* 807–18.
[38] Ibid, pp 810–11.
[39] Ibid, p 811.
[40] Ibid, p 812.
[41] 'Lord Devlin at 80: Lord Devlin interview with Joshua Rozenberg', *BBC Radio 4*, 25 November 1985.

'Bulling-Manner' and throughout the book you're absolutely scornful of him. You say 'there was no malice in him' but 'stupidity, yes, for time to time'. And you say that 'presenting the true character of Adams would've been far beyond his imagination, he had to settle for storybook simplicity'. I want to ask you; would Adams have been convicted if the prosecution had been handled by anybody else?

Lord Devlin: Not a hope. They had no hope from the very beginning. First of all, he was one of the rare cases of a man who proved his innocence. That is to say, he satisfied me that he was an innocent man. If I'd been asked on the bog standard of the civil proof, 'is he probably innocent or probably guilty?' I would have said probably, if not certainly innocent of the murder of Mrs Morrell, which was the only crime he was accused of.

Joshua Rozenberg: Was this because of the nurses' notebooks which Dr Adams happened to find at home?

Lord Devlin: I think even without the notebooks he would have been acquitted. I think the Prosecution's case was really unfounded from the very beginning. Nobody could've got a verdict on it.

Joshua Rozenberg: Nevertheless you are very critical of Sir Reginald Manningham-Buller, Viscount Dilhorne, as he later became, and Sir Robin Dunn who is a retired Lord Justice of Appeal, says that your picture of him has caused much anguish to his family and Sir Robin says, he praises Viscount Dilhorne's judgments and says 'It's my belief that their clarity and certainty will ensure that many of Lord Dilhorne's judgments will be remembered when the more obscure pronouncements of some who regard themselves as his intellectual superiors are forgotten.' Is he referring to you?

Lord Devlin: Yes, well that's very likely. I mean I think judgments are only remembered for so long as they're useful. Useful to other judges. And I wouldn't like to take a bet on whether any of mine are more likely to be useful than Reggie Manningham-Buller's. He delivered many more. I should think he gets first to the winning post. I naturally very much regret it, if it had caused anguish to his wife and family. But he died five years ago. He was a man who gave and received, I said, hard knocks, which is indeed true. And he was a man, it was one of the things one always liked about him, who said what he thought, and affected other people to say what they thought. He'd say it's entirely wrong, he would have been very angry no doubt, but that he would have been resentful, I doubt.

Joshua Rozenberg: Do you regret having written the book, which is I believe the first time that a judge has written about a case that he presided over?

Lord Devlin: No, I don't regret it at all. I think it's only really on rare occasions on which it's possible for a judge to write. I am greatly in favour of the law being opened up as far as one can to the public. I think that I was in the position to write a judicial account of a trial and write it with the form of a story which the ordinary public would read, because it was an interesting story, not just a legal treatise, and I think it was a good thing to have done. You have to give an accurate account of what you think. You can't say 'well this is being unkind to ...' – people were unkind to Lord Dilhorne in his life and no doubt they will be equally unkind to me. And one must accept that in the interests of getting an accurate account of what somebody thinks.

Clearly Patrick was affected not only by the criticisms, but also by the likes of those who made them. Unwisely, when the second edition of the book emerged, he penned a postscript which was no doubt meant to clarify some things. It actually made things worse.

In his postscript Patrick forwent the right to silence. He addressed his 'objectors' who he identifies as the *Daily Express* and the 'top-most of the top of the judiciary'.[42] As for the latter, he identified Sir Robin Dunn, a former Lord Justice of Appeal and Lords Scarman and Bridge. Patrick's self-defence goes for some seven pages. He set out and dealt with each of the criticisms in turn.

The first criticism was that the account was posthumous. Patrick rejected the complaint and made the point that he should not be reproached for that, as it would have been impossible in effect to defame either Dilhorne or Adams while they were still alive. It would also have been unseemly and would have caused a lot of unpleasantness. There is little doubt Patrick did wait until both Reggie and the doctor were dead, but it is also true that an account of the trial while either was alive would have been regarded by Patrick as dreary and uninteresting. He knew he could not have got away with his book if both were still alive. To that extent it could be said he was being cynical but pragmatic.

The second criticism was that he had attacked a former judicial colleague. He said:[43]

> All Lords of Appeal in Ordinary are formally colleagues of the Lord Chancellor but he rarely sits on judicial business and I never sat with Lord Chancellor Dilhorne. After we had retired we were both on what may be called a supplementary list and in this way we came to sit together in perhaps half a dozen cases during the rest of the 1960's. Such was the extent of our judicial colloguing.

Patrick's self-defence is a painful exercise to read. First, the facts are that Patrick *did* sit with Dilhorne as Lord Chancellor at least once.[44] Thereafter, they sat in more than double the number of cases Patrick recalls.[45] The language used by Patrick in his defence is equivocating and fencing and unworthy of his intellect; as is his treatment of the third criticism, namely that he made the statement about Dilhorne with contempt. Patrick described that charge as 'hardly believable'. He states expressly:[46] 'I have not in this book and never anywhere else expressed contempt for Lord Dilhorne. I have never felt it.'

As Professor Heuston correctly put it, Patrick had held Dilhorne up to public ridicule and contempt when he could no longer defend himself.[47] This so-called defence provided Patrick with a further opportunity to, terrier-like,

---

[42] ETP, Postscript, pp 219–20.
[43] Ibid, p 221.
[44] See Chapter 10 of this book, 'Appellate Life', fn 83.
[45] See Chapter 11 of this book 'Not Quite the Wilderness', fn 50.
[46] ETP, 2nd edn (1986), Postscript, p 222.
[47] RFV Heuston, 'Patrick Arthur Devlin 1905–1992' (1994) 84 *Proceedings of the British Academy* 247–62.

defame Dilhorne. Incapable of accepting any liability for the very hurtful words he himself chose, he employed a few more razor blades with just an ounce of projection: 'Dilhorne was a man who took himself much more seriously than I can take myself or him'.[48] Dilhorne's virtues and vices never changed, but in different lights they looked different. His handicap was that he went through life blinkered. He wished to see only what was in front of him.

In dismissing Scarman and Bridge he said disdainfully:[49]

> If the Scarman-Bridge letter had been content to emphasise the picture I painted was not the whole picture of the man, I should have been glad to agree with the obvious. But its loud deplorings and threats of lowered reputation are worth no more than the lamentations of viewers at an exhibition who, if a portrait has not the likeness with which they are familiar, condemn the painter.

Clever, articulate, overly defensive and indeed offensive, but with a certain brittleness bordering on fragility. This was not Patrick's finest hour. The book, however, was and is an important milestone because of its novelty. It remains an important contribution to the workings of a judge in the trial process.

If anything, the book kept Patrick in the limelight as much as the case. He would hardly complain about that. He continued to be an almost perennial subject for interviews. Marcel Berlins conducted yet another extensive interview for *The Times*, where the (one could think by now) usual chronology and topics were covered as if only recently discovered. Patrick had long since become a cult figure whose life remained of constant and intense interest. He was still innovating on 7 October 1987 when he wrote an article for *The Times* as to why there should be a Supreme Court in the United Kingdom.[50]

He had not yet stopped. Perhaps the last serious piece he wrote was fittingly in the *Law Quarterly Review* in July 1991, a little over a year before he died.[51] It was entitled 'The Conscience of the Jury'. It was a return to a familiar theme in many ways, but in the context of a number of miscarriages of justice in the Guilford Four, the Maguire Seven and the Birmingham Six, which Patrick rightly described as 'the greatest disasters that have shaken British justice in my time'. The article explored the causes in one view without answer, except to reassert that the jury, while not the perfect solution, was still the best mode of obtaining justice. Provocative as always, he posed the following question:[52] 'Were the judges at fault? Or did the police deceive both judge and jury? Or was it just that the system was unable to withstand the stresses imposed upon it by men whose fanaticism blinded them to evil?' This was yet another fascinating excursion into the history of jury trials – this time his ultimate. Realistically Patrick observed:[53]

---

[48] ETP, 2nd edn (1986) postscript, p 222.
[49] Ibid, p 220.
[50] Lord Devlin, 'The Case for a Supreme Court', *The Times*, 7 October 1987.
[51] Patrick Devlin, 'The Conscience of the Jury' (July 1991) 107 *Law Quarterly Review* 398–404.
[52] Ibid, p 398.
[53] Ibid, p 402.

'I think it is true that the postwar generation of judges ... has begun to question the value of the jury.' But loyal to the bitter end Patrick exclaimed:[54]

> It is not our great liberties that are threatened today. If they were, they would be guarded by judges. It is the little liberties which are infringed. Since the infringements are embedded in the statute the judges are powerless; the jury is not. It respects the law but it will not put it above the justice of the case.

> Is this a picture of Lord Denning institutionalised? Perhaps so, but with one very big difference. The power that puts the jury above the law can never safely be entrusted to a single person or to an institution, no matter how great or how good. For it is an absolute power and, given time, absolute power corrupts absolutely. But jurors are anonymous characters who meet upon a random and unexpected summons to a single task (or perhaps a few), whose accomplishment is their dissolution. Power lies beneath their feet but they tread on it so swiftly that they are not burnt.

During the last few years Patrick had been working on a memoir. It was published four years after his death and is entitled *Taken at the Flood*. It is not clear whether he chose the title but it is clear that the work was the subject of editing by Madeleine and other members of his family. It starts with his family history and ends somewhat abruptly around the year 1941. It was, it has been said, to be written for junior lawyers. Alan Watkins, who reviewed it for *The Spectator* describes it fairly in some respects as an 'uncompleted autobiography'.[55] What is telling in some respects is that although Patrick discloses much, there was one secret that went with him to the grave. Whilst it may be accepted that a man's politics and religion are his own to manifestly exercise his right to silence, Patrick did so only in relation to the latter. Why did he choose the church as a vocation and then abandon it? Why did he always in his public discourse, apart from historical references, always put religion to one side?

It may be accepted that he regarded the topic as irrelevant to almost every-thing that he did. The book in one sense, apart from the numerous confessions about his appalling handwriting, tells us very little of the man himself. However, there are two prophetic statements that do provide real insight. The first and perhaps most telling is:[56]

> Between me and the service of the law there was no pledge. When a man has a vocation he has to answer the call and the call commands his life: if he ignores it he will not be happy. I had no vocation and so had a field of choice. It was not constricted by any personal or family obligation. What factors should govern the choice? I reached then a conclusion from which I have not varied that the aim should be to obtain the greatest enjoyment out of life.

But nevertheless, 'there is no pleasure except in a life of occupation.'[57] This clearly explains that Patrick felt under no sense of obligation or duty to remain

---

[54] Ibid, p 404.
[55] A Watkins, 'The judge who retired unhurt', *The Spectator*, 1997, p 173.
[56] TATF, p 73.
[57] Ibid, p 74.

a judge. He found the work and perhaps many of his colleagues dreary. But after he left, he never stopped writing about the law, almost to the exclusion of everything else. It fascinated him and clearly consumed much of his post-judicial life. The truth is that despite having left the bench, he was never far away from it. He did not suddenly discover science or mathematics. Words were his joy and his music – Beethoven was always a close second.

The other prophetic statement in his memoir is:[58] 'Compassion and justice are very compatible, but, if forced to choose, I would rather be just than compassionate.'

Patrick had been ruthlessly true to both ideals.

Patrick died at home after a relatively brief illness on 9 August 1992. His various obituaries told similar stories. His obituary in *The Times*[59] was written by Charles Fletcher-Cooke, who had been one of Patrick's pupils at the Bar and remained a good friend.[60] Professors Tony Honoré[61] and Robert Heuston[62] added to it, along with *Graya*.[63] Other obituaries were published by *The Independent*,[64] Christ's College[65] and Stonyhurst,[66] as expected. A requiem mass was conducted at St James's church, Spanish Place where Patrick and Madeleine had been married almost 60 years earlier. The mass, entirely in Latin, was conducted by special permission according to the old Dominican rites.[67]

Madeleine in a letter to Stonyhurst shortly after, said that she wanted them to know:[68]

> Patrick in his last days went back much of the time to his days at Woodchester … Patrick's faith returned and really the violence of it, as though it had been pent up all these years; I felt he would want it widely known. Christopher as you suggest, may well be smiling. He had offered his sufferings. As it was, when not loving us, Patrick was praying in Latin – and with the Dominicans. No doubt Fr Bede Jarrett had prayed too.

Dying declarations bear a special significance in the law. Patrick, as was his right, ultimately gave up his right to silence.

---

[58] Ibid, p 74.

[59] 'Lord Devlin', *The Times*, 11 August 1992, p 13.

[60] Although the obituary is listed without an author, the Author was informed of Fletcher-Cooke's identity as the author of the obituary by the management of *The Times*.

[61] Tony Honoré, 'Devlin, Patrick Arthur, Baron Devlin (1905–1992)', *Oxford Dictionary of National Biography* (Oxford, Oxford University Press, 2004).

[62] RFV Heuston, 'Patrick Arthur Devlin, 1905–1992' (1994) 84 *Proceedings of the British Academy* 247–62.

[63] John Megaw, 'In Memoriam: Master Lord Devlin' (1992) 96 *Graya* 46–50.

[64] James Morton, 'Obituary: Lord Devlin', *The Independent*, 10 August 1992.

[65] 'Patrick Devlin (1950–1992)', Christ's College, University of Cambridge.

[66] 'Lord Devlin (1914–22)', (Autumn 1993) *The Stonyhurst Magazine* vol XLV, no. 489, pp 238–40.

[67] Undated letter, from Madeleine Devlin to Stonyhurst College, Stonyhurst Archives.

[68] Ibid.

Biographical Details of Some of the Figures Appearing in the Book

Acheson, Dean Goderham (1893–1971), lawyer and diplomat. Initially attending Yale, graduating in 1915, he studied law at Harvard, graduating in 1918. He spent the first two years after graduation as law clerk to Supreme Court Justice, Louis Brandeis. He was also much influenced by Oliver Wendell Holmes. Later he became close friends with Felix Frankfurter. The two agreed on all issues except Israel, which they by mutual consent never discussed. In 1921 he joined a large law firm, now Covington & Burling, from which he practised law for many years when not in government. He was continuously a member of the State Department from 1941 to 1953 which encompassed the final four years of Truman's presidency. He was one of the principal moulders of the American posture in the post-war world. It was said that he was urbanely elegant, sharp-minded and sharp-tongued. That said, he was responsible for numerous hugely important international initiatives including the North Atlantic Treaty Organisation (NATO). He was not always a person free of controversy or criticism. Formal, almost school-teacherish in public, he was colloquial and earthy in private. He was offered a position on the bench of the Court of Appeals of the District of Columbia, but he rejected it. He won a Pulitzer Prize for History for his work, 'Present at the Creation', in the year before he died.

Aitken, William Maxwell, first Baron Beaverbrook (1879–1964), newspaper proprietor and politician. Won a seat in the House of Commons for the Conservative Party in December 1910. He was knighted in 1911. He acquired a peerage during World War I. In February 1918 he became the first Minister of Information. He also became the Chancellor of the Duchy of Lancaster, with a seat in the cabinet. He often backed lost causes such as Edward the VIII's attempt to retain the throne and, in the late 1930s, the policy of appeasement. He became Minister of Aircraft Production during World War II and joined the war cabinet in due course. He had an on and off love affair with the Conservative Party.

Armitage, Sir Robert Perceval (1906–1990), colonial governor and civil servant. Educated at Winchester College and New College, Oxford. He joined the colonial administrative service in Kenya. He was posted to the Nairobi secretariat in 1939 in various administrative posts. He was awarded an MBE in 1944. In 1948 he was transferred to the Gold Coast. He played a major role in ensuring the sound economy of Ghana. He was awarded the CMG in 1951. As Governor of Cyprus in 1954, he was awarded a KCMG. He was replaced in that role and appointed Governor of Nyasaland in 1955. He declared a state of emergency in 1959, leading to the Devlin commission. He left Nyasaland in April 1961 and retired to Wiltshire where he devoted much of his time to the St John Ambulance movement. He remained angry about Nyasaland and the role of the British government in the breakup of the federation of Rhodesia and Nyasaland.

Baldwin, Stanley, first Earl of Bewdley (1867–1947), politician and Prime Minister. From Harrow to Trinity College, Cambridge, he went into the family business, which was sheet metal manufacturing. In 1906 he joined the board of Great Western Railway and Metropolitan Bank. Upon his father's death he stood for his father's seat of Bewdley, Worcestershire, and was elected unopposed for the Conservatives. He entered the Commons on 3 March 1908. Final rejection of Lloyd-George led to Andrew Bonar-Law becoming the leader of the Conservatives and Prime Minister in 1922. He would in turn retire by May 1923. By a stroke of good fortune, the politically inexperienced Baldwin became Prime Minister on 22 May 1923. He successfully contested the 1924 election and the Conservatives returned to power. In 1929 he was, however, in opposition. He was back as Prime Minister in 1935. But the emergence of Hitler and the self-indulgent Edward VIII took their toll on Baldwin. He passed the office of prime minister over to Neville Chamberlain in late May 1937.

Banda, Hastings Kamuzu (1898–1997), doctor and politician. Born in Nyasaland, his education started in Africa and was completed in the United States. He graduated from universities in Indiana and Chicago in 1931 and graduated in medicine from the University of Tennessee in 1937. He did further qualifications in Edinburgh in 1941. In the same year he became an elder of the Church of Scotland. He built a prosperous medical practice, but his real concern was the future of his birthplace, Nyasaland. His interest intensified with the founding of the Nyasaland African Congress. Civil unrest in Nyasaland led to a declaration of a state of emergency and he was arrested. Released in April 1960, he became Prime Minister of Malawi (formerly Nyasaland) in 1963. His regime ultimately crumbled in 1993. In 1995 he was placed under house arrest for the murder of four politicians many years before but was eventually freed due to a lack of evidence.

Belgion, Harold Montgomery (1893–1973), journalist and author. He attended Cambridge after which he went into journalism. He was the editor of the *Westminster Gazette* 1924–25. He fought in both world wars. He published works on Edgar Allan Poe and HG Wells. He also sought a pardon for Nazi collaborator and Vichy General, Marshal Petain, and thought, apparently, that Albert Speer should be treated likewise.

Blom-Cooper, Sir Louis (1926–2018), lawyer and writer. King's College, London, Fitzwilliam College, Cambridge, and Municipal University of Amsterdam. He was called to the bar at Middle Temple in 1952. He took silk in 1970 and was knighted in 1992. He was an academic at the University of London from

1962 to 1984 but he wrote books and practised as a barrister and sometimes as a journalist. He was Chair of the Mental Health Act Commission from 1987 to 1994 and Chairman of the Press Council 1989–90. He was an opponent of the death penalty, a supporter of prisoner's rights and a visionary in the field of administrative law. He had very firm views about most things, including people around him in the profession.

Bodenheimer, Edgar (1908–1991), academic. Born in Berlin, he received his legal qualifications from universities in Geneva, Munich, Heidelberg and Berlin. He emigrated to the United States in 1933. He worked for a New York law firm and also attended NYU, completing his American law degree in 1937. He became a naturalised US citizen in 1939 and was admitted to the bar. As an attorney in Washington he worked for the US Department of Labor and ultimately for the Office of Alien Property Custodian, assisting in the preparation of the prosecution brief for the Nuremberg War Crimes Trials in 1945. As an academic his main area of interest was jurisprudence.

Boyd, Alan Tindall Lennox, first Viscount Boyd of Merton (1904–1983), politician. Elected to parliament in October 1931 for the Conservatives. Appointed Parliamentary Secretary at the Ministry of Labour in 1938. In 1951 he was appointed Minister of State at the Colonial Office. Became Colonial Secretary in 1954. He was elevated to the House of Lords in 1960 and left parliament to become the joint and then the sole managing director of Arthur Guinness & Co Ltd.

Bowra, Sir (Cecil) Maurice (1898–1971), classical scholar and university administrator. He went to New College, Oxford, in 1919 and became a fellow of Wadham College from 1922 to 1938. He was warden from 1938 to 1970. He was mischievous, amusing and an excellent mimic. His scholarly output was prodigious. From 1946 to 1951 he held the chair in poetry at Oxford, a position which gave him particular pleasure. He was Vice Chancellor of Oxford from 1951 to 1954 and president of the British Academy from 1958 to 1962. He bore the nickname Rhino which suited him admirably. He was sexually ambiguous.

Birkett, (William) Norman, first Baron Birkett (1883–1962), barrister and judge. Although he initially decided to go into the clergy he chose law while at Cambridge. He was called to the bar by the Inner Temple in 1913. Twice rejected for military service, he stayed at the bar during the Great War and took silk in 1924. He was a talented barrister and appeared in many cause célèbres. He had first stood for parliament in 1918 for the Liberal party. He was knighted in 1941 for unpaid work he performed for the Home Secretary during World War II. He was appointed to the Queen's Bench in 1941. In 1945 he was appointed the British judge for the Nuremberg War Crime Trials but only as an alternate judge which upset him. He was appointed to the Court of Appeal in 1950 but disliked the work immensely. He retired in 1956. In 1958 he obtained a peerage. He became much sought after as a speechmaker.

Butler, Sir Geoffrey Gilbert (1887–1929), historian and politician. He became a fellow at Corpus Christi College, Cambridge in 1910. He mentored a number of people at Cambridge on behalf of the Cambridge University Conservative Association. In 1925 he joined the Conservative ministry as Parliamentary Private Secretary to Sir Samuel Hoare, the Secretary of State for Air.

Butler, Richard Austen (Rab), Baron Butler of Saffron Walden (1902–1992), politician. Part of an academic dynasty of Cambridge dons (since 1794). Educated at Eton and Pembroke College, Cambridge. Always haunted by bad mental health, he nonetheless managed to marry an heiress which assisted greatly in him being able to choose politics from the start. He entered the political world by becoming Under-Secretary to the India Secretary. Under Neville Chamberlain he became Parliamentary Secretary at the Ministry of Labour. Butler enjoyed a good relationship with Churchill despite his support for Chamberlain's policy of appeasement. In October 1951 he was appointed Chancellor of the Exchequer contrary to his expectation. On more than one occasion he effectively ran the government when Churchill and/or Eden were ill. He was a success as Chancellor but as he was not the most astute political strategist he was ultimately out played by Macmillan for the top job. Macmillan offered Butler the Home Office, which he accepted. In 1959 he became chairman of the Conservative Party. When Macmillan became ill in 1963, Macmillan played a pivotal role in stopping Butler from succeeding him, supporting Douglas-Home instead. Running the Foreign Office was small consolation. Harold Wilson as the new Labour Prime Minister offered him the mastership of Trinity College, Cambridge, which he accepted. A life peerage came in 1965. He wrote what has been said to be a lively, wise, and relatively accurate autobiography. He retired from Trinity in 1977.

Clarke, Sir Edward George (1841–1931), lawyer and politician. His education was mixed and somewhat haphazard. He obtained a scholarship to Lincoln's Inn in 1861 and was called to the bar in 1864. In 1880 he took silk. He was one of the most, if not the most, eminent leaders of the common law bar. He entered parliament in 1880 in the seat of Southwark for the Conservatives, later holding the seat of Plymouth. In 1886 he was appointed Solicitor-General and knighted. He briefly held the position of senior member for the city of London but resigned due to ill health. In retirement he published a book on Disraeli.

Coldstream, Sir George Phillips (1907–2004), lawyer and civil servant. He read law at Oriel College, Oxford and was called to the bar by Lincoln's Inn in 1930. He practised for only four years before becoming a parliamentary counsel. Coldstream was transferred to the Lord Chancellor's office in 1939. In due course he prepared paperwork for the Nuremberg trials. In 1954 he succeeded Sir Albert Napier as Permanent Secretary to the Lord Chancellor. He was knighted in 1955 and appointed a QC in 1960. He served four Lord Chancellors, Simonds, Kilmuir, Dilhorne and Gardiner. He was a kind and avuncular person much liked by all who worked with him, including the senior staff at Buckingham Palace. He retired in 1968.

Denning, Alfred Thompson, Baron Denning (1899–1999), judge. He was called to the bar in 1923 by Lincoln's Inn and took silk in 1938. He was appointed a justice of the High Court in the Probate, Divorce and Admiralty Division in 1944, and to the King's Bench Division in 1945. In 1948 he was appointed to Court of Appeal and in 1957, he was appointed to the House of Lords. In 1962 he returned to the Court of Appeal as Master of the Rolls, from which he retired in 1982. From time to time he was regarded as a maverick and a revolutionary. He wrote numerous books and was a prolific self-promoter.

Devlin, Madeleine (1909–2012), wife, mother, magistrate and author. She was the youngest child of Sir Bernard Oppenheimer elder brother of Sir Earnest Oppenheimer. Between them, the two brothers controlled the market for South African diamonds. She grew up in London, attending Frances Holland School followed by Oxford where she took the then new PPE course. After leaving Oxford she worked for Lancelot Hogben, a professor of zoology (later professor of social biology) from Cape Town, in his research into twins. Madeleine married Patrick in 1932. She successfully ran their farm, near Pewsey in Wiltshire, and in particular their herd of jersey cattle. Fortnum and Mason, for example, purchased jersey cream the farm produced. She was appointed a lay magistrate and was later chairman of the local branch. She converted to Catholicism in 1956. She cared for Patrick's brother Christopher when he became seriously ill and wrote a biography of him, published in 1970, which she dedicated to Patrick. She played an important leading role in the building of the Church of the Holy Family at Broadfields, Pewsey. She had as a lifelong friend historian Veronica Wedgwood. She celebrated her 100th birthday with undiminished delight – her dark expressive eyes still twinkling.

Dixon, Sir Owen (1886–1972), barrister and judge. Educated at the University of Melbourne in arts and law. He was called to the Victorian bar in 1910 and took silk in 1922. In 1926 he sat as an Acting Judge of the Supreme Court of Victoria but declined permanent appointment. In 1929 he was appointed to the High Court of Australia. In 1939 he became the chairman of various government boards. In 1942 he was appointed to Washington as Australia's minister (Ambassador) to the United States and was temporally relieved of his judicial duties. During this time, he made an enduring friendship with Felix Frankfurter. In 1950 he attempted to mediate an agreement between India and Pakistan. In 1952 he was appointed Chief Justice of the High Court. During his leadership the court commanded international respect. Reserved and circumspect in public, he was sometimes irreverent and indiscreet in private. He retired in 1964 and took no further part in public life.

Douglas-Home, Alexander Frederick, fourteenth Earl of Home (disclaimed for life) and Baron Home of Hirsel (1903–1995), Prime Minister. Having initially failed to gain a seat, he was elected to the House of Commons in 1931 as a National Unionist. In 1936 he was appointed Parliamentary Private Secretary to the Chancellor of the Exchequer, Neville Chamberlain. He was Foreign

Secretary from 1960 to 1963 and 1970 to 1974. Eventually Macmillan stepped aside as Prime Minister and advised the Queen to ask Home to form a government, which he did on October 1963, becoming Prime Minister at that time. His premiership has been described as him being an honourable leader, albeit in an unfashionable tradition. He accepted a life peerage in 1974 and re-entered the House of Lords.

Douthwaite, Arthur Henry (1896–1974), consultant physician. He qualified from Guy's Hospital in 1921 and proceeded to an MD in 1924. He was elected FRCP in 1929. He initially practised as a GP and took an early interest in vascular issues. He was an early user of gastroscopy and liver biopsy. He held many senior medical posts such as president of the Medical Society of London and president of the British Society of Gastroenterology. He was a bon vivant and regarded as one of the finest physicians of his day.

Doyle, Sir Arthur Ignatius Conan (1859–1930), writer and medical practitioner. Doyle attended Stonyhurst College from 1870 to 1875. He thereafter attended Edinburgh University Medical School from 1876, graduating in 1881. After a short time as a ship's surgeon he returned to university to complete an MD in 1885. His doctoral thesis was on syphilis. His first major literary success was with the publication of *A Study in Scarlet* which brought together for the first time Sherlock Holmes and Dr Watson.

Drummond, John David, seventeenth Earl of Perth (1907–2002), government minister, banker, art connoisseur and bibliophile. After Cambridge he joined a merchant bank, Schroders, to begin with, and then others. During World War II he assisted Noel Coward in Paris running a propaganda offce. He was sent to the United States as part of his activities for the War Cabinet Offce. In 1951 he was elected a Scottish representative peer. Macmillan appointed him to the post of Minister of State for Colonial Affairs. Much involved with the arts, he was a member of the advisory council of the Victoria and Albert Museum. He helped raise money for the Museum of Scotland and was a trustee of the National Library of Scotland. He was also a director of the Royal Bank of Scotland. He was a prominent Roman Catholic who often wore pink corduroy trousers to mass.

Du Parcq, Herbert, Baron Du Parcq (1880–1949), judge. He attended Jesus College, Oxford in 1904 and obtained a BCL in 1908. He was called to the bar (Middle Temple) in 1906 and practised on the western circuit. He took silk in 1926 and became a recorder of Portsmouth in 1928 and recorder of Bristol and a judge of the Bristol Tolzey court in the following year. He was appointed a judge of the King's Bench Division in 1931, the Court of Appeal in 1938 and a Law Lord in 1946.

Evershed, (Francis) Raymond, Baron Evershed (1899–1966), judge. Oxford followed by service in the Great War. He was called to the bar by Lincoln's

Inn in January 1923. His ability and charm enabled him quickly to establish an extensive Chancery practice. After only 10 years he took silk at the age of 33 in 1933. He was appointed to the Chancery Division of the High Court in April 1944. After three years he was appointed to the Court of Appeal in 1947. In 1949 he was appointed Master of the Rolls in which office he served for 13 years. He was raised to the peerage in 1956. He resigned in 1962 upon his appointment as a Lord of Appeal in Ordinary only to retire finally in 1965. He served on many committees of importance. He was said to be very good company and was much in demand as a speaker, where he regularly displayed his elegant wit and charm.

Frankfurter, Felix (1882–1965), lawyer and judge. Born in Vienna and emigrated to the United States when he was 12. He graduated from the College of the City of New York in 1902 and from Harvard Law School in 1906. He worked for a New York law firm for a year after graduation but within a short time he was appointed Assistant United States Attorney for the Southern District of New York. He accepted an appointment to the faculty of Harvard Law School. In 1917 he returned to Washington to become the assistant to the Secretary of War. He thereafter held other government posts, returning to Harvard Law School after the war. President Franklin D Roosevelt nominated Frankfurter for the Supreme Court of the United States on 5 January 1939 and the Senate confirmed his appointment on 17 January 1939.

Fuller, Lon L (1903–1978), academic. He graduated from Stanford Law School and began his law teaching career at the University of Oregon Law School. Before the Harvard Law Faculty, he taught at Duke University Law School where one of his pupils was President Richard M Nixon. During the 1960 presidential campaign he contributed to several of Nixon's position papers. He held the Carter Chair in Jurisprudence at Harvard from 1948 until his retirement in 1972. He also practised with the Boston law firm of Ropes, Gray, Best, Coolidge & Rugg. He wrote on morals and the law.

Fyfe, David Patrick Maxwell, Earl of Kilmuir (1900–1967), politician and lawyer. At Oxford he unashamedly put his politics first. After Oxford he studied part time and was called to the bar at Gray's Inn in 1922. He entered the Commons in 1927 for the seat of Spen Valley in Yorkshire. He moved to the seat of West Derby in 1935. He took silk in 1934 and became a recorder from 1936 to 1942. In the same year he was appointed Solicitor-General by Churchill. He served briefly as Attorney-General in 1945. He became the day-to-day head of the British legal team at the Nuremberg War Crimes Trials. Through sheer hard work and preparation rather than skill he was credited with having crushed Goering in cross-examination. Returning to the bar he successfully juggled his practice and the Commons. Although rumoured to be a successor to Churchill he became Lord Chancellor in 1954 with the title of Viscount Kilmuir. He spent eight years as Lord Chancellor until sacked by Macmillan in 1962.

Gandar, Laurence (1915–1998), journalist. He was the editor of the *Rand Daily Mail* from 1957 to 1969. He became an implacable opponent of Apartheid. He wrote numerous scathing articles under the pseudonym 'Owen Vine', expressing his anger about the sterility of parliamentary opposition to Apartheid. He gave attention to black politics and black living conditions. He tried to encourage aggressive investigations of Apartheid evils. He was honoured abroad by both British and American press associations. He was prosecuted for publishing an article about prisons in a high-profile criminal trial which lasted many days. He was found guilty and fined. The newspaper dismissed him as a result.

Gardiner, Gerald Austin, Baron Gardiner (1900–1990), lawyer and politician. He was called to the bar at the Inner Temple in 1925. He took silk in 1948. In 1951 he unsuccessfully ran for the seat of West Croydon for the Labour Party, which he had joined in the 1930s. In 1963 Prime Minister Harold Wilson nominated him for a life peerage and chose him as Lord Chancellor. He was very much involved in law reform, in particular in the areas of divorce and criminal law.

Gerard, John (1564–1637), Jesuit priest. Attended Exeter College, Oxford. Was ordained in 1588.

Goddard, Rayner, Baron Goddard (1877–1971), judge. After Trinity College, Oxford, he was called to the bar in 1899 and appointed King's Counsel in 1923. He was appointed to the King's Bench Division in 1932 and the Court of Appeal in 1938. In 1944 he replaced Lord Atkin on the House of Lords but resigned to take up the position of Lord Chief Justice in 1946.

Goodhart, Arthur Lehman (1891–1978), jurist. Born in New York, he was educated at Yale and thereafter, Trinity College, Cambridge. Then became a fellow at Corpus Christi College, Cambridge. He was appointed Professor of Jurisprudence at Oxford in 1931. Previously at Cambridge he had edited the *Cambridge Law Journal* and been appointed editor of the *Law Quarterly Review*, which was a position he held for 35 years. He published a number of books and gave up the chair in jurisprudence in 1951 to become Master of University College, Oxford. He endowed the college with very substantial funds. He was appointed silk in 1943 and was elected FBA in 1952. A noted jaywalker, he was for many years president of the Pedestrians' Association.

Hart, Herbert Lionel Adolphus (1907–1992), academic. After completing his legal studies, he became a member of Middle Temple and practised at the bar from 1932 to 1940. He served with MI5 during the war. After the war he became a fellow at New College, Oxford in jurisprudence. He was elected to the chair of jurisprudence at Oxford in 1952. He lectured on rights and duties. He collaborated with AM Honoré to write the classic, *Causation and the Law*, in 1959. He taught at Harvard in 1956–57. But it was the controversy with Patrick Devlin that made him a public figure in Britain. He declined a knighthood in 1966. He became intensely interested in Jeremy Bentham and spent many years editing

Bentham's works from the latter's diaries. He suffered bad health, both mental and physical, over the years. He was untidy and absent minded, but with a generous mind, impatient with trivia but above all else the outstanding British legal philosopher of the twentieth century.

Hastings, Macdonald (1909–1982), author, broadcaster and journalist. He attended Stonyhurst College. Lord Beaverbrook offered to pay for him to go to Oxford which he refused. Instead he worked as a freelance journalist and became a revered war correspondent during World War II. After the war he founded the magazine, *Country Fair*, covering the English countryside and field sports. He then successfully wrote for a children's magazine. For the BBC programme, 'Tonight', he contributed hugely popular segments about people and animals. He also did a series of documentaries on the rivers and canals of Britain. From the 1960s he wrote more than 30 biographies. He was also regarded as an expert on sporting shooting and wrote a textbook on the subject.

Hastings, Sir Patrick Gardiner (1880–1952), lawyer. He joined Middle Temple and was called to the bar in 1904. He flirted with both the Liberal and Labour parties, being elected in 1922 as the Labour candidate for Wallsend in Northumberland. He became Attorney-General in 1924, having been appointed by Ramsay MacDonald. He was a remarkable barrister and in particular a brilliant cross-examiner, but a hopeless politician. He retired in 1948, exhausted and in bad health. However, in retirement he wrote books and plays.

Heath, Sir Edward Richard George (1916–2005), Prime Minister. Initially attended Balliol College, Oxford, as a commoner without a scholarship but in due course won an organ scholarship at Balliol. He became the president of the Oxford University Conservative Association in 1937–38. He was an MP and Conservative whip from 1950 to 1959 and a cabinet minister and shadow chancellor from 1959 to 1965. He was leader of the opposition between 1965 and 1970 and Prime Minister between 1970 and 1974.

Heilbron, Rose (1914–2005), lawyer and judge. She was the daughter of a Liverpool boarding house keeper. Educated at Belvedere School and Liverpool University. The year following her graduation with first class honours, she was the Lord Justice Holker Scholar at Gray's Inn. She became one of only two women who did LLM and she was called to the bar in 1939. In 1949 she was one of the first two women to take silk. She had spectacular success as a defence lawyer and her precise, persuasive and direct style set her aside. Her razor-sharp mind was critical in murder trials where she displayed extraordinary forensic judgement. She became Britain's first woman recorder at Burnley in 1956. A year later she was the first woman in 1972 to sit as a judge at the Central Criminal Court. In 1974 she was sworn in as a High Court Judge and was assigned to the Family Division in which she served until she retired in 1988. She married Dr Nathanial Burstein, a general practitioner, in 1945. They had a daughter who entered the law and also became a QC.

Hogg, Quintin McGarel, second Viscount Hailsham, and Baron Hailsham of Marylebone (1907–2001), lawyer and politician. He entered parliament in 1938 for the seat of Oxford. He was called to the bar by Lincoln's Inn in 1932. He took silk in 1953. He wanted to become elder of the Conservative party when Macmillan was about to retire but never achieved his ambition. In 1970 he became Lord Chancellor when Edward Heath was Prime Minister. He went out of office in 1974 but in 1979 when Margaret Thatcher became Prime Minister she once again appointed him Lord Chancellor.

Heuston, Robert Francis Vere (1923–1995), jurist and biographer. Heuston read law at Trinity College, Dublin, and was called to the bar by King's Inn in 1947. At the age of 23 he was appointed Pembroke College Oxford's first law fellow. He remained an academic and indeed became editor of *Salmond on Torts*. He wrote *The Lives of the Lord Chancellors, 1885–1940*, which was published in 1964 and his second volume on the same topic (covering the years 1940–1970), in 1987. He was appointed Regis Professor of Laws in 1970 at Trinity College Dublin. He is also visiting Professor of Laws at numerous universities around the world including Cambridge, Oxford, Melbourne and the Australian National University in Canberra.

Hyde, Harford Montgomery (1907–1989), politician and historian. He read jurisprudence at Oxford and soon after graduation started writing biographical works. He also obtained employment as librarian to the Marquess of Londonderry, a Conservative politician. In 1950 he was elected as an Ulster Unionist for North Belfast. He vigorously supported the recommendations of the Wolfenden Committee which in part cost him his seat. He was appointed professor of history and political science at the University of the Punjab, Lahore. He published numerous biographies to acclaim.

Jones, Elwyn, Baron Elwyn-Jones (1909–1989), Lord Chancellor. Educated at the University of Aberystwyth in Wales and Gonville and Caius College, Cambridge. He was called to the bar in 1935 at Gray's Inn. He was elected to parliament in 1945 as a Labour MP. He became Parliamentary Private Secretary (1946–51) to the Attorney-General, Sir Hartley Shawcross. He took silk in 1953 and became a recorder at Swansea in 1953 and Cardiff in 1960. As a result of the Labour victory in 1964, he became Attorney-General and was knighted. In 1974, he became Lord Chancellor.

Jowitt, William Allen, first Earl Jowitt (1885–1957), lawyer and judge. After reading law at New College, Oxford he was admitted to the Middle Temple on 15 November 1906 and was called to the bar in June 1909. He was elected to parliament in 1922 as a Liberal for Hartlepool. He took silk the same year. He switched to the Labour party and was elected for the seat of Preston in 1929. He became Attorney-General and was given a knighthood. He was made a Privy Councillor in 1931. Following a disagreement, he was expelled from the Labour Party in the same year but was later re-admitted and was re-elected in 1939. At all times he had a huge and prosperous practice. He was appointed Solicitor-General by Churchill in 1940 and then Minister of National Insurance in 1944–45. In 1945 he was made Lord Chancellor with a peerage. He became heavily involved in law reform. He left the Lord Chancellor's role in 1951. In retirement he was the leader of the opposition in the House of Lords. He published several books and continued to add to his fine private collection of art which included works by Matisse, Bonnard and others.

Kentridge, Sir Sydney (1922–), barrister. Born in Johannesburg. He is a graduate of the Universities of Witwatersrand and Oxford. He was admitted to the Johannesburg bar in 1949. He was appointed senior counsel in 1965. He represented Nelson Mandela and the late Chief Albert Luthuli. He became a leading defence lawyer in political trials in South Africa, including the Treason Trial in 1958 and the Prisons Trial in 1968–69. In 1978 he appeared at the inquest into the brutal killing of Steve Biko. With his wife he founded the Legal Resources Centre. He refused to accept an appointment as a judge under the Apartheid Government. He did serve as a judge of the Appeal Court in Botswana. However, he decided to go to London in the seventies and established a hugely successful practice there, being appointed Queen's Counsel in 1984. After the collapse of Apartheid, he spent some time as an acting judge of the Constitutional Court in South Africa. He was knighted in 1999.

Law, Richard Kidston, first Baron Coleraine (1901–1980), politician. St John's College Oxford, then a career in journalism. He worked as a journalist on the *Daily Express* and the *Morning Post* in the United States. He entered parliament in 1931. Although his father had briefly been Prime Minister in late 1923 to early 1924, he displayed little political guile or skill. He served as Financial Secretary to the War Office (1940–41), Parliamentary Under-Secretary of State at the Foreign Office (1941–43) and Minister of State at the Foreign Office with cabinet rank. He was sworn in as a member of the Privy Council in 1943. He was given a peerage in 1954 and moved to the Lords. Late in life he became quite an influential conservative thinker, publishing his last work in 1970, entitled 'For Conservatives Only'. He became deeply religious towards the end of his life and was a regular communicant at Thames-side parish church, Battersea.

Lawrence, Sir Geoffrey (1902–1967), judge. Attended New College, Oxford, and then settled on a career in the law. Called to the bar in 1930 (Middle Temple). Soon developed a large junior practice, taking silk in 1950. Became chairman of the General Council of the Bar (1960–62). He was knighted in 1963 for services to the profession. He was appointed to the High Court in 1965.

MacDonald, (James) Ramsay (1866–1937), politician and Prime Minister. He entered parliament in 1906 as the member for Leicester. Thereafter he held numerous seats. He was Secretary of State for Foreign Affairs briefly in 1924.

In due course he became leader of the Labour Party and ultimately Prime Minister for a few months in 1924 and for six years from 1929 to 1935 when he swapped offices with Baldwin. He died during a pleasure cruise on the liner *Reina del Pacifico* after finishing a game of deck quoits.

Macleod, Iain Norman (1913–1970), politician. He read modern history at Gonville and Caius College, Cambridge and was an amateur poet. He financed his university studies largely through gambling, either at nearby Newmarket but more especially at the bridge table. His bridge playing endowed him with formidable powers of memory and concentration. He entered parliament in February 1950. As a member of the Conservative Party he was favoured initially by Sir Anthony Eden who made him Minister for Labour in 1955 but was also very much appreciated by Harold Macmillan. He assisted Macmillan substantially in the 1959 general election and was a key strategist, designing campaign strategy. In October 1961 Macmillan moved him from the Colonial Office and transferred him to a trinity of posts. He became Chancellor of the Duchy of Lancaster, Leader of the House of Commons, and chairman of the Conservative Party Organisation. At the election of June 1970, he was appointed by Edward Heath as Chancellor of the Exchequer. However, in July of that year he became ill and shortly thereafter died.

Macmillan, (Maurice) Harold, first Earl of Stockton (1894–1986), politician and Prime Minister. Eton and Balliol College, Oxford, then the Grenadier Guards during the Great War. First entered parliament in 1924 for the Conservatives, losing his seat in 1929, only to recapture it in 1931. He joined Churchill's war ministry as Parliamentary Secretary to Herbert Morrison, Minister of Supply. In February 1942 he became Under-Secretary at the Colonial Office. He first joined the cabinet in May 1945 as the Secretary of State for Air in Churchill's caretaker government. In October 1951 he became Minister of Local Government and Planning. Upon Churchill's retirement in 1955 and with Eden as Prime Minister he was made Foreign Secretary. In late 1955 he became the Chancellor of the Exchequer. Eden resigned due to ill-health in January 1957. Macmillan, and not, as expected, RA Butler, became Prime Minister. He remained in that role until early 1964 when he resigned, purportedly due to ill-health. He left the Commons in October 1964. In due course he published his voluminous personal diaries.

Mocatta, Alan (1907–1990), lawyer and judge. After New College, Oxford he went to the bar in 1930. He was awarded an OBE for war services in 1944. After the war he developed an extensive commercial practice and became a Queen's Counsel in 1951. In 1961 he was appointed a judge of the Queen's Bench Division and was knighted. He became the President of the Restrictive Practices Court in 1970. He was very active in the Jewish community and president of numerous Jewish charities and organisations. He was a keen cricketer and played for a small village team in Cornwall where he had a house.

Monckton, Walter Turner, first Viscount Monckton of Brenchley (1891–1965), lawyer and politician. Harrow followed by Balliol College, Oxford. President of the Union in 1913. At about that time, he met Edward Prince of Wales and the two became lifelong friends. Starting his legal career at the outset of the Great war he was called to the bar at the Middle Temple in 1919. In 1927 he was appointed legal adviser to the Simon Commission investigating constitutional reform in India. He took silk in 1927. He became adviser to the Nizam of Hyderbad. He had remained a close personal friend of Edward VIII and advised him right through the abdication process and afterwards. He was knighted in the 1937 honours list. During World War II he was Minister of Information. Churchill appointed him Solicitor-General in 1945 but after the 1945 election he returned to legal practice. He also entered the Commons in 1951 for the Conservative Party, becoming Minister of Labour. He left politics in 1957 and became chairman of Midland Bank. His last public service was to chair an advisory committee on the constitution of the Federation of Rhodesia and Nyasaland.

Murray, William, first Earl of Mansfield (1705–1793), judge and politician. Of Jacobite stock, at the age of 14 he travelled alone by pony from Scotland to London never to return. He attended Westminster school and Christ Church, Oxford with financial assistance of a friend's father. He joined Lincoln's Inn and was called to the bar in November 1730. Although he did some crime his practice was largely work in chancery. He became Solicitor-General in 1742 and entered the House of Commons in the same year. In 1754 he became Attorney-General. In 1756 he qualified as a Serjeant-at-Law and appointed Chief Justice of the Court of the King's Bench and created Lord Mansfield, Baron Mansfield. Financially astute and with a nose for property, he purchased Kenwood House on the northern edge of Hampstead Heath. Expanded by the Adams brothers and with its own dairy and a splendid library, the house enabled him to live a genteel life.

Parker, Hubert Lister, Baron Parker of Waddington (1900–1972), judge. He went to Trinity College, Cambridge University where he studied the natural sciences. He decided however to go to the bar and join Lincoln's Inn in 1924, building up a substantial practice in civil cases, primarily in commercial matters. He was appointed a Treasury Devil and, in 1950, was appointed a judge of the High Court. He was appointed to the Court of Appeal in 1954 and, in 1958, was appointed Lord Chief Justice.

Pogrund, Benjamin (1933–), journalist and author. He was deputy editor of the *Rand Daily Mail* in Johannesburg which was closed down because of its stand on apartheid. He was a colleague and friend of Laurence Gandar and was tried alongside him in South Africa. He has lived in Jerusalem since 1997 and was the founder director of the Yakar's Center for Social Concern. His latest book is *Drawing Fire: Investigating the Accusations of Apartheid in Israel* (2014).

Ponsonby, Arthur Augustus William Harry, first Baron Ponsonby of Shulbrede (1871–1946), politician and peace campaigner. He spent two years at Balliol College, Oxford, and then went on to join the diplomatic service. He was appointed Principal Private Secretary to Campbell-Bannerman when Prime Minister. After the declaration of World War I, he founded the Union of Democratic Control. Because of his views on pacifism, he was not popular in the political context. However, in 1924, he was appointed Parliamentary Under-Secretary at the Foreign Office, Labour having won the 1924 election. In 1931 upon the creation of the National Government, Ponsonby became the Labour leader in the House of Lords. At the outbreak of World War II, he withdrew from active politics.

Pritt, Denis Nowell (1887–1972), lawyer and political activist. He joined the Middle Temple in 1906 and was called to the bar in 1909. He had a flourishing junior practice at the bar and was appointed King's Counsel in 1927. Physically ample and attached to life's good things, he was regarded by most as politically lightweight. Although it is said that his point-scoring was ingenious, it is also said that his writings were devoid of any breath of profundity or imagination.

Radcliffe, Cyril John, Viscount Radcliffe (1899–1977), lawyer and public servant. He was called to the bar by the Inner Temple in 1924. He took silk in 1935. During World War II he became Director-General of the Ministry of Information, resuming practice in 1945. He was appointed directly to the House of Lords in 1949. He retired in 1964.

Ramsey, (Arthur) Michael, Baron Ramsey of Canterbury (1904–1988), cleric. He attended King's College, Cambridge in 1923 and became President of the Cambridge Union in 1926. He was courted by the Liberal Party but in the end chose the church. In 1927 he had a mental breakdown when his mother was killed in a motor accident. He recovered and was made a deacon to serve the parish of Our Lady and St Nicholas near Liverpool. He became a priest in 1929 but also started lecturing, at which he was a great success. In 1939 he became Professor of Divinity at Durham and Canon of the Cathedral. He became Bishop of Durham in 1952 and Archbishop of York in 1956. He was appointed Archbishop of Canterbury in 1961. He retired in 1974.

Reid, James Scott Cumberland, Baron Reid (1890–1975), judge. He read law at Jesus College, Cambridge and began practice in 1919. He took silk in 1932, having entered politics for the Conservative Party the year before in 1931. He became Solicitor-General for Scotland in 1936 and Lord Advocate in 1941. He was appointed directly to the House of Lords in 1948 and held office for 26 years.

Roberts, Sir Denys Tudor Emil (1923–2013), colonial official and judge. Read jurisprudence at Wadham College, Oxford. Finished his degree after the war in 1948 and took a BCL in 1949. Called to the bar by Lincoln's Inn in 1950. Crown Counsel in Nyasaland from 1953 to 1959. He became Attorney-General of Gibraltar in 1960. He then became Hong Kong's Solicitor-General in 1962 and was promoted in 1966 to Attorney-General. In 1973 he was promoted to the post of Colonial Secretary in Hong Kong. He became Chief Justice in 1979. Following his retirement in Hong Kong he became Chief Justice in Brunei and President of the Court of Appeal in Brunei and later Bermuda. From 1997 to 2003, he was a non-permanent judge of the Hong Kong Court of Final Appeal.

Russell, Charles Ritchie, Baron Russell of Killowen (1908–1986), judge. Attended Oriel College, Oxford, graduating in 1929. Called to the bar in 1931 by Lincoln's Inn. After the war, Russell returned to the bar and took silk in 1948. In 1960, he was appointed a judge of the Chancery Division and knighted. In 1962, he was appointed to the Court of Appeal and the Privy Council. It was said of him that he enjoyed claret, partridge, and a good cigar, but was not a gourmet. He was appointed a Lord Justice of Appeal in 1975.

Schuster, Claud, Baron Schuster (1869–1956), civil servant. Educated at Winchester and New College, Oxford. His degree was in history. He was called to the bar by the Inner Temple in 1895 and joined the northern circuit. In 1899 he was appointed a civil servant. In 1915 he was appointed clerk of the Crown in Chancery and Permanent Secretary in the Lord Chancellor's Office. Schuster was knighted in 1913, awarded CVO in 1918, KC in 1919, KCB in 1920, and GCB in 1927. He was also a high sheriff of Dorset in 1941 and was raised to the peerage in 1944.

Searle, Ronald William Fordham (1920–2011), cartoonist and illustrator. Briefly working as a solicitor's clerk, he went to art school in the evenings. He started doing illustrations for *Granta* and the *Daily Express*. He joined the Territorial Army in 1939. Shortly after his company arrived in Singapore he was captured by the Japanese. He was interred in Changi and then on the Siam-Burma railway. He published his graphic drawings of the experience. After the war he published cartoons in *Punch* and many other magazines. His St Trinian Girls cartoons were a huge success, as were his cat drawings. He did a great deal as a court artist and drew the key persons at the trial of Adolf Eichmann. He covered many world events as a caricaturist including the 1960 US Presidential election. He also produced animation for film. He held many exhibitions over time and became extremely collectable. He was rightly recognised for his work with many awards. He was the most delightful dinner companion.

Simpson, Brian (1931–2011), legal historian and legal scholar. Read jurisprudence at Queen's College, Oxford, and graduated in 1954. Became a junior research fellow at St Edmund Hall, Oxford, in 1954 and a fellow and tutor in law at Lincoln College, Oxford from 1955 until 1973 with the exception of the year 1968–69.

Smith, Frederick Edwin, first Earl of Birkenhead (1872–1930), lawyer and politician. Former President of the Union at Oxford and Vinerian scholar. A successful barrister who took silk in 1908. He became Solicitor-General in 1915 and, six months later, Attorney-General with a seat in cabinet. Ultimately appointed Lord-Chancellor in 1919. It is said of him that he was loved and loathed in equal measures by those who enjoyed the warmth of his friendship or suffered the sting of his tongue.

Splisbury, Sir Bernard Henry (1877–1947), forensic pathologist. After Oxford and University College School he commenced his medical studies in 1899, qualifying in 1905. He started in the field of forensic pathology and became well known to the Home Office and Metropolitan Police. He made his money out of autopsies. Between 1907 and 1919 he was a lecturer in pathology at St Mary's hospital. He also lectured in forensic medicine and toxicology at the University of London. He was knighted in 1923. He was elected a Fellow of the Royal College of Physicians in 1931. He soon became known as an expert witness, especially in murder trials. His opinion became virtually unquestioned. In the 1930s he was performing up to 1000 autopsies in any one year. He had virtually no output as a scholar. His health declined and he committed suicide in his laboratory in December 1947.

Stevas, Norman Antony Francis St John, Baron St John Fawsley (1929–2012), politician. He won a scholarship to Fitzwilliam College, Cambridge where he read law. He was president of the Union and chairman of the University's Conservative Association. He also did a BCL at Oxford. In 1953 he was called to the bar by the Middle Temple. He lectured at numerous universities, including Oxford, King's College, London and Yale. He entered parliament for the Conservative Party in 1964 and held the seat of Chelmsford for 23 years. He was Under-Secretary for Education in the Heath government and in due course Minister for the Arts. He was also Minister for the Arts under Thatcher who sacked him in 1981 because he had apparently made too many jokes about her. He stood down as an MP in 1987 and took a life peerage. He was fond of institutions, especially the papacy.

Stevenson, Sir (Aubrey) Melford Steed (1902–1987) judge. He read law at London University and was called to the bar by Inner Temple in 1925. He took silk in 1943. He was unsuccessful in attempting to enter parliament in 1945 for the Conservative Party. In 1957 he was appointed to the High Court in the Probate, Divorce and Admiralty Division, transferring to the Queen's Bench Division in 1961. He was appointed a Privy Councillor in 1973 and retired in 1979.

Wedgwood, Dame (Cicely) Veronica (1910–1997) historian. After home schooling she attended Lady Margaret Hall, Oxford, as a senior scholar in 1928. Following graduation she worked for numerous publishers and newspapers and tutored at Somerville College. Her first book, *Strafford, 1593–1641*, gained her immediate recognition. She revised the work to acclaim 25 years later when the Strafford family papers were opened for research. She would consolidate her reputation as an historian over time with other works on the English civil war, *Charles I* and *Oliver Cromwell*, amongst others. She lectured widely in Britain and America. She was awarded a CBE in 1956 and a DBE in 1968.

Welensky, Sir Roland (Roy) (1907–1991), politician. Of Lithuanian Jewish stock, he was a lifelong if not intolerant teetotaller as a result of his father's alcoholism. At 17 he became a locomotive fireman with Rhodesia Railways. He augmented his income by boxing professionally and became the heavy-weight champion of the Rhodesias in 1927. He was then six feet tall and 20 stone. Retired from the ring he became interested in trade unionism and, in turn, politics. He entered politics as a member of the legislative council of Broken Hill in northern Rhodesia. He was intimately involved in negotiations with the British government which lead to the formation of the Federation of Rhodesia and Nyasaland in 1953. On 1 November 1956 he became Prime Minister. He was hoping the Federation would achieve Dominion status, which it never did. He sent federal troops into Nyasaland during the state of emergency which failed to curtail Dr Hastings Banda. In due course his federal ideal was fractured beyond repair. He felt betrayed by the British government by allowing Nyasaland and then Northern Rhodesia to secede. He was forced in 1963 to cooperate in the orderly winding up of the Federation.

Williams, Sir Edgar Trevor (1912–1995), intelligence officer and historian. Attended Merton College, Oxford, to study modern history. Thereafter became senior scholar at Merton College and in due course assistant lecturer at the University of Liverpool in 1936–1937. During World War II he became Montgomery's assistant throughout the campaigns in North Africa and Italy. In due course became a brigadier in charge of intelligence at the twenty-first army group's headquarters in St Paul's School, London. He was awarded a DSO in 1942, CBE in 1944, and CB in 1946 and the US Legion of Merit in 1945. He was a history fellow of Balliol College, Oxford, in 1947.

Wigg, George Edward Cecil, Baron Wigg (1900–1983), politician. His political career began for the Labour Party when he was elected to the seat of Dudley in 1945. Skilfully, he assisted Harold Wilson's election campaign in 1963. In 1964, he became Paymaster-General and was made a member of the Privy Council at the same time.

Withers, Sir John James (1863–1939), solicitor. After Eton and King's College, Cambridge, he was admitted as a solicitor in 1890. He established his own firm close to the law courts and soon established a significant reputation. By the 1920s his firm had become one of the largest and most successful practices in London. The mainstay of the practice was highly remunerative family and trust cases. He also became a senior burgess for Cambridge University. He was appointed CBE in 1918 in recognition for work done during the Great War. He was a mountaineer of some skill.

Wolfenden, John Fredrick (Jack), Baron Wolfenden (1906–1985), educationist and public servant. Queen's College, Oxford then Princeton University, after which he taught for a time, being made headmaster of Uppingham School in 1934 where he stayed for 10 years. He became Vice Chancellor of the University of Reading in 1950, then full time Chairman of the University Grants Committee from 1963 to 1968. In January 1969 he was appointed director and principal librarian of the British Museum. However, the most renowned departmental committee he ever chaired was in the years 1954 to 1957. The committee was charged with investigating the existing laws governing homosexuality and prostitution and its report caused considerable controversy. Its recommendations about prostitution were promptly hurried into law, but it took some 10 further years before the Sexual Offences Act of 1967 decriminalised homosexuality.

Wyn-Harris, Sir Percy (1903–1979), colonial governor and mountaineer. Apart from natural sciences he became obsessed with mountaineering while at Cambridge. He joined the Colonial Service in Kenya in 1926 where he spent the next 20 years in district administration. He was appointed Governor of Gambia in 1949. He retired in 1958 but maintained his lifelong interest in mountaineering. He was awarded the MBE in 1941, CMG in 1949 and KCMG in 1952.

The information for these biographical notes was drawn from the Oxford Dictionary of National Biography and obituaries from sundry newspapers.

Index

CPSIA information can be obtained
at www.ICGtesting.com
Printed in the USA
LVHW012139290722
724710LV00013B/562